Handbook of
MEDICAL
EMERGENCIES

Second Edition

Edited by

JAY H. SANDERS, M.D.
Professor of Medicine
University of Miami School of Medicine
Miami, Florida

and

LAURENCE B. GARDNER, M.D.
Associate Professor of Medicine
University of Miami School of Medicine
Miami, Florida

 Medical Examination Publishing Co., Inc.
an Excerpta Medica company

969 Stewart Avenue • Garden City, New York 11530

Copyright © 1978 by
MEDICAL EXAMINATION
PUBLISHING CO., INC.

Library of Congress Card Number
78-50127

ISBN 0-87488-635-X

July, 1978

Printed in the United States of America

PREFACE

The utility of any publication is based upon its ability to keep the reader abreast of the rapid accumulation of new knowledge in his/her field of interest. The contents of this book first originated as an attempt to provide our Housestaff at the University of Miami with a "bread and butter" review of the most common emergencies with which they would come in contact in the hospital setting. As a result of requests from community hospitals for a similiar post-graduate education program, it was decided to organize a National Conference on Emergencies in Internal Medicine and allow the experts in the field the opportunity to present their views on the newer trends in diagnosis and management. This book represents the results of that conference.

As simple as this undertaking seemed at the start, it became quite clear that without the dedicated and persistent efforts of Ms. Betty Howard, Director of the Division of Continuing Education at the University of Miami, and the patience and long hours put in by our secretaries, Jennifer Shaw, Cindy DeLine and Geri Null, this book would not have materialized.

To them and our understanding and harassed authors, the editors will be continuously grateful.

CONTRIBUTORS

GUEST FACULTY

ROBERT BROWN, M.D., *Chief,* Pulmonary Section, Veterans Administration Hospital, West Roxbury, Massachusetts; *Instructor in Medicine,* Harvard University School of Medicine, Boston, Massachusetts

HAROLD O. CONN, M.D., *Professor of Medicine,* Yale University School of Medicine, New Haven, Connecticut; *Chief,* Liver Disease Unit, Veterans Administration Hospital, West Haven, Connecticut

JOHN A. KASTOR, M.D., *Professor of Medicine,* University of Pennsylvania School of Medicine; *Chief,* Cardiovascular Section, Hospital of the University of Pennsylvania, Philadelphia, Pennsylvania

ROBERT R. KIRBY, M.D., *Professor of Anesthesiology; Chairman,* Department of Anesthesiology, Tulane University School of Medicine, New Orleans, Louisiana

KEVIN M. McINTYRE, M.D., *Assistant Professor of Medicine,* Harvard Medical School; Cardiovascular Section, Veterans Administration Hospital, West Roxbury, Massachusetts

ALFRED F. PARISI, M.D., *Chief,* Cardiovascular Section, Veterans Administration Hospital, West Roxbury, Massachusetts; *Assistant Professor of Medicine,* Harvard Medical School

ARTHUR A. SASAHARA, M.D., *Professor of Medicine,* Harvard University School of Medicine, Boston, Massachusetts; *Chief,* Medical Service, Veterans Administration Hospital, West Roxbury, Massachusetts

G.V.R.K. SHARMA, M.D., *Director,* MICU-CCU, Veterans Administration Hospital, West Roxbury, Massachusetts; *Instructor in Medicine,* Harvard Medical School

DONALD E. TOW, M.D., *Chief,* Nuclear Medicine Service, Veterans Administration Hospital, West Roxbury, Massachusetts; *Assistant Professor of Radiology,* Harvard Medical School

ARNOLD WEINBERG, M.D., *Professor of Medicine,* Harvard University School of Medicine, Boston, Massachusetts; *Assistant Chief of Medicine,* Massachusetts General Hospital, Boston, Massachusetts

HIBBARD E. WILLIAMS, M.D., *Professor and Vice-Chairman,* Department of Medicine, University of California; *Chief,* Medical Service, San Francisco General Hospital, San Francisco, California

UNIVERSITY OF MIAMI SCHOOL OF MEDICINE: FACULTY

HARVEY E. BROWN, JR., M.D., Ph.D., *Professor of Medicine,* Rheumatology

AGUSTIN CASTELLANOS, JR., M.D., *Professor of Medicine; Director,* Clinical Electrophysiology, Division of Cardiology, Department of Medicine

MORGAN DELANEY, M.D., *Assistant Professor of Medicine*

BERNARD I. ELSER, M.D., *Assistant Professor of Medicine; Director,* Medical Emergency Room, Jackson Memorial Hospital

LEON G. FINE, M.D., *Assistant Professor of Medicine,* Renal Medicine

LAURENCE B. GARDNER, M.D., *Associate Professor of Medicine, Chief,* Division of General Medicine, Jackson Memorial Hospital

MICHAEL S. GOLDSTEIN, M.D., *Assistant Professor of Medicine*

DONALD R. HARKNESS, M.D., *Professor of Medicine; Chief,* Hematology Section, Miami Veterans Administration Hospital

THOMAS A. HOFFMAN, M.D., *Associate Professor of Medicine; Chief,* Division of Infectious Diseases

ROBERT J. MYERBURG, M.D., *Professor of Medicine and Physiology; Chief,* Division of Cardiology

ELISEO C. PEREZ-STABLE, M.D., *Professor of Medicine; Chief,* Medical Service, Veterans Administration Hospital

R. JUDITH RATZAN, M.D., *Assistant Professor of Medicine,* Hematology

ARVEY I. ROGERS, M.D., *Professor of Medicine; Chief,* Gastroenterology Section, Veterans Administration Hospital

MARVIN A. SACKNER, M.D., *Professor of Medicine; Director of Medical Services and Chief,* Division of Pulmonary Diseases, Mount Sinai Medical Center, Miami Beach, Florida

JAY H. SANDERS, M.D., *Professor of Medicine*

ROBERT J. SCHWARTZMAN, M.D., *Associate Professor of Neurology*

RUEY J. SUNG, M.D., *Assistant Professor of Medicine,* Division of Cardiology, Department of Medicine

ANDREW L. TAYLOR, M.D, *Assistant Professor of Medicine*

FRANCIS J. TEDESCO, M.D., *Associate Professor of Medicine,* Gastroenterology

ADEL A. YUNIS, M.D., *Professor of Medicine and Biochemistry; Director,* Division of Hematology

With the Assistance of:

NEAL S. BRICKER, M.D., *Professor of Medicine*

NEAL S. PENNEYS, M.D., Ph.D., *Associate Professor of Dermatology*

HANDBOOK OF MEDICAL EMERGENCIES
Second Edition

CONTENTS

DEDICATED TO:

My Family: Margie, Jon, Marc and Larry

J.H.S.

Abbey, Ben and Behna

L.B.G.

CHAPTER 1: CARDIOLOGICAL EMERGENCIES

A: SUDDEN DEATH AND CARDIAC ARREST
by Alvaro Mayorga-Cortes, M.D.

DEFINITION

Sudden death may be defined as death occurring within 1 or 2 hours after the onset of acute, unexpected symptoms in a patient who may or may not be aware of preexisting cardiovascular disease. One should bear in mind that sudden death is a syndrome that may have multiple etiologies. Cardiac arrest is defined as the abrupt cessation of effective cardiac output. It may be produced by ventricular fibrillation, ventricular asystole, slow idioventricular rhythm or by mechanical factors that reduce cardiac output.

INCIDENCE AND ETIOLOGY

It is very difficult to determine the real incidence of sudden death. It is estimated that 700,000 people die suddenly in this country every year, but many other "natural deaths" could belong to this category. There are two peak incidences of sudden death: during the first six months of life and between the 4th and 6th decades.

Data obtained from mobile coronary care units has shown that at least 90% of sudden deaths are secondary to cardiovascular events and that coronary atherosclerosis is the common denominator in at least 80% of this group. There are three basic mechanisms by which coronary artery disease may produce sudden cardiac death:

1. Ventricular Fibrillation (VF): Electrocardiographically, there are no formed ventricular complexes, but there is an irregular zig-zag pattern, totally erratic and of variable amplitude and rate (Fig. 1.1). Depending on the setting in which ventricular fibrillation occurs, the presentation may vary slightly. The patient suddenly collapses, is found pulseless, and after a few seconds he develops agonal respiration, cyanosis, dilating pupils, and sometimes grand mal seizures. The majority of sudden deaths occur outside the hospital environment creating a major problem in identifying the initial pathophysiologic mechanism. The fire rescue units, usually present at the site of the event within 5 to 8 minutes, have shown that ventricular fibrillation is the most common electrical dysrhythmia in this type of patient.   The true incidence of acute myocardial infarction in patients dying suddenly outside the hospital is also unknown. Preliminary data from Jackson Memorial Hospital, have shown that

11

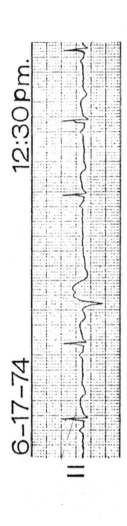

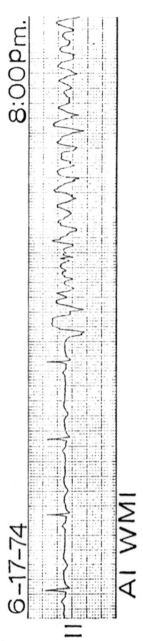

FIG. 1.1

approximately 50% of patients that are resuscitated and admitted to the hospital, fulfill the diagnostic criteria for acute myocardial infarction. In the remaining 50%, coronary atherosclerosis prevails in most of them. In a group of patients with acute myocardial infarction in the coronary care unit, primary ventricular fibrillation develops in approximately 10% of patients. This type of ventricular fibrillation should be differentiated from terminal ventricular fibrillation secondary to end stage cardiac disease. The electrophysiologic mechanism is variable: it may occur secondary to ventricular vulnerability (R on T phenomenon) but may also follow late PVC's. The so called "warning arrhythmias"(frequent PVC's, multiform in configuration, bigeminy and R on T) are present in no more than 50% of the cases of V.F. Based on this data one can conclude that any ventricular ectopic activity can induce ventricular fibrillation during acute ischemia.

2. Ventricular Standstill and Agonal Slow Idioventricular Rhythms: Ventricular standstill is recognized by the complete absence of any sign of ventricular activity in the electrocardiogram. It may develop as the primary electrical event or may follow ventricular fibrillation. Slow idioventricular rhythms frequently are terminal events and are characterized by sporadic, bizarre QRS complexes, usually irregular. Both rhythms are expressions of terminal electrical activity of the heart. The true incidence of these rhythms in the genesis of the sudden death syndrome is also unknown. Ventricular fibrillation frequently degenerates into agonal idioventricular rhythms but the converse is also true. Sudden cessation of cardiac activity like the one produced by paroxysmal heart block, may degenerate after a few seconds into ventricular fibrillation. Severe metabolic acidosis, acute hyperkalemia and massive digitalis intoxication are well known causes of asystole and erratic ventricular rhythms.

3. Mechanical Causes of Sudden Death: A sudden drop in cardiac output, incompatible with life, can also be produced by cardiac tamponade, massive myocardial infarction, cardiac rupture, trauma to the heart and great vessels, and acute cor pulmonale secondary to massive pulmonary embolism.

Perhaps 15-20% of patients with sudden death have normal coronary arteries or insignificant coronary artery disease. Cardiomyopathy, severe aortic stenosis, severe mitral regurgitation, congenital heart disease, and severe IHSS are predisposing factors for sudden cardiac death.

PATHOLOGIC ANATOMY

Atherosclerosis of the coronary arteries is present in the majority of patients. Its severity varies, but is usually significant with double or triple vessel disease. Pathologic studies have been misleading in estimating the incidence of coronary thrombosis and acute myocardial infarction, since the pathologic lesion may not be present when death occurs suddenly. Less common pathologic findings include: cardiomegaly and myocardial fibrosis in cardiomyopathy, severe valvular narrowing and ventricular hypertrophy in valvular stenosis and non atherosclerotic coronary artery disease: i. e. degeneration, embolism or vasculitis of the smaller coronary arteries.

In the differential diagnosis of sudden cardiac death one should also consider non-cardiac causes. The "restaurant death" is characterized by acute asphyxia during a meal produced by tracheal obstruction. Death secondary to severe emotional states is probable secondary to dysrhythmia produced by severe imbalance of the autonomic nervous system. It should also be remembered that a fatal anaphylactic reaction (bee stings drug) can exactly mimic sudden cardiac death.

MANAGEMENT OF CARDIAC ARREST

Adequate cardio-pulmonary resuscitation requires attention to 4 areas:

1. Immediate diagnosis
2. Ventilation
3. Cardiac massage
4. Reestablishing adequate heart rhythm

1. Immediate diagnosis: Sudden collapse of any patient should be considered the result of cardiac arrest until evidence to the contrary is obtained. The absence of femoral pulses will support the diagnosis. Rapid diagnosis is essential because cerebral hypoxic damage occurs after 4 minutes of cardiac arrest.

2. Ventilation: To establish a good airway, one should examine the mouth to be certain that there is no obstruction from vomitus or foreign bodies. The neck should be fully extended so that the base of the tongue does not obstruct the trachea. If respiration is absent, immediate ventilation by the mouth to mouth technique must be begun and continued throughout the resuscitation. In the hospital or with paramedical personnel available, an endotracheal tube can be inserted and ventilation performed with an airbag. Every effort should be made to establish ventilation as rapidly as possible.

3. Cardiac Massage: Closed chest massage is the method of choice. It involves the compression of the heart between the sternum and the spine and requires minimal training. The heel of one hand should make a rhythmic and firm compression with the second hand on top while the patient rests on a hard board. The compression is exerted just above the xyphoid area on the sternum, about 60 to 70 times per minute, and the sternum should be depressed 3 to 5 cms. by a vigorous and quick downward motion, being held in that depressed position for half a second and then rapidly released. Effectiveness can be checked by a palpable arterial pulse. Complications include rib fractures, laceration of the heart and less frequently, pneumo or hemothorax. Direct cardiac massage is used when the chest is open and the heart is directly exposed.

4. Reestablishing Appropriate Heart Rhythm: While ventilation and cardiac massage are proceeding, an intravenous route is established. An immediate injection of 44 mEq of sodium bicarbonate is given and repeated every 10 minutes throughout resuscitation.

A. Ventricular fibrillation: Sometimes mechanical stimulation of the heart by a thump on the chest will defibrillate a patient. Electrical defibrillation is currently performed with direct current (dc). The electrodes are placed one at the base and the other at the apex of the heart and a current of 300-400 watts-seconds is delivered. If the patient continues pulseless, or the ECG monitor shows persistent ventricular fibrillation, multiple attempts to defibrillate can be done, alternating with adequate cardiac massage. In the case of failure to defibrillate, hypo-ventilation and metabolic acidosis have to be corrected.

B. Asystole: If no electrical activity is observed, 5 to 10 ml of Epinephrine (1:10,000) is given intracardiacally after obtaining blood return. A chaotic ventricular rhythm may respond to electrical defibrillation. A current of 200 to 400 watts-seconds with the dc defibrillation may be successful. Patients with end stage pump failure are very difficult to defibrillate. If asystole is present the immediate insertion of a ventricular pacemaker may be lifesaving. Throughout the resuscitation, attention should be paid to the correction of metabolic abnormalities. If ventricular tachycardia is present after successful resuscitation, a Lidocaine bolus of 75 mg followed by a Lidocaine drip of 2-4 mg per minute should be given.

PROGNOSIS

A. Early phase: It is estimated that 15% of patients who arrest in the hospital survive and are discharged. In the hospital, the success depends on the awareness, the expertise, and availability of a cardio-pulmonary resuscitation team. After arrest, the patient should be managed in an intensive care setting. Lidocaine infusion should be used almost routinely in every patient post arrest.

B. Late prognosis: Patients surviving a cardio-pulmonary resuscitation have, in general, a grave prognosis. Hypoxic encephalo-pathy and thoracic and pulmonary complications are common after prolonged resuscitation. If the patient has recovered well, the prognosis will depend on the control of arrhythmias and the management of congestive heart failure if present. Preliminary data from the division of Cardiology at the University of Miami suggests that with a close follow-up and adequate antiarrhythmic therapy, life expectancy may be higher than previously believed. Coronary angiography and cardiac catheterization will be helpful in establishing a prognosis.

The knowledge and insight we currently have of the mechanisms and natural history of sudden cardiac death are in its infancy. The battle against sudden death is the responsibility of the Federal government, the Health Delivery Systems and finally of the community in which one lives. Only a combined and organized effort will enhance the chances of survival of those experiencing sudden death.

REFERENCES

1. Liberthson, R.R., et al: Pathophysiologic observations in pre-hospital ventricular fibrillation and sudden cardiac death. Circulation 49:790, 1974.

2. Myerburg, R.J.: Sudden death in The Heart, 3rd Edition. McGraw-Hill Book Company, New York, 1974, pp. 585-591.

3. Baum, R.S., et al: Survival after resuscitation from out-of-hospital ventricular fibrillation. Circulation 50:1231, 1974.

B: CARDIAC TAMPONADE
by Stephen M. Mallon, M.D. and
Robert J. Myerburg, M.D.

The total spectrum of the group of pathophysiologic abnormalities,
which includes cardiac tamponade, may be referred to as the cardiac
compression states. Cardiac tamponade itself has certain characteristics in common with the other compression states, including
low cardiac output due to inadequate venous return which is due predominantly to extra-cardiac factors. Physiologically, the low venous return to the left ventricle can be mimicked by certain intracardiac lesions such as mitral stenosis, or by abnormal left ventricular function from any cause (e.g.coronary artery disease, aortic or
mitral regurgitation, or any of the volume overload syndromes).
All of these intracardiac abnormalities are separable clinically from
the extra-cardiac compression states. One other category of disease which must be separated from the cardiac compression states
includes the group of diseases primary to muscle or primary to
connective tissue within the myocardium, causing compliance abnormalities. The left or right ventricle, or both, may be unable to dilate in response to an increase in venous return, and in this setting,
the Frank-Starling mechanism is nearly inoperative. Again, in this
setting, exemplified by diseases such as amyloidosis or hemochroma-
tosis, the management of venous return by normal compensatory
mechanisms is inadequate, but not due to extrinsic cardiac factors,
thus separating these diseases from the cardiac compression states.

There are three general categories in which extrinsic factors are
the primary abnormality, these three categories constituting the
group of cardiac compression states. The three categories include
(1) cardiac tamponade, (2) constrictive pericarditis, and (3) the
more recently described effusive-constrictive syndrome. In this
latter group, there is both fluid accumulation, as in the usual cases
of cardiac tamponade, and a degree of constriction due to pericardial
involvement with the disease process.

Cardiac tamponade generally is due to an accumulation of fluid in the
pericardium. The accumulation may be acute or chronic. In the
acute setting, it is most commonly due to trauma to the chest with
either disruption of blood vessels or of a cardiac chamber. In the
case of the latter, atrial disruptions generally result in rapid exsanguination due to the limited amount of muscle supporting the atrial
wall. One rarely sees a survivor from atrial trauma arriving at a
hospital emergency room alive. Those patients with chamber disruption who do survive, therefore,generally have ventricular disruptions which in a limited number of cases, result in survival after
surgery.

Among the infectious causes of acute cardiac tamponade, the most
common is "benign" viral pericarditis. This may be an acute illness

which resolves quickly with appropriate management, or it may be recurrent. It is possible in some cases that it may evolve into a chronic pericarditis. Tuberculosis has to be considered under the infectious causes, but the frequency seems to be decreasing. Acute suppurative infections such as staphylococcal pericarditis generally are dramatic and rapidly progressive problems. They are true medical emergencies and have a high mortality rate.

Neoplasms involving the pericardium, most commonly primary in the lung, are causes of both acute and subacute cardiac tamponade, and also of the effusive-constrictive syndromes (see below). Bleeding has been mentioned in relation to trauma. However, it should also be considered in patients who are on anticoagulants, especially in those with acute myocardial infarction or post-operative valve replacement who present the clinical picture of cardiac tamponade. Hemorrhagic pericarditis, with or without tamponade, must be considered in the uremic patient on chronic dialysis. Finally, iatrogenic causes, which may occur in the emergency room or intensive care unit setting, especially in patients undergoing cardio-pulmonary resuscitation, pericardiocentesis as a diagnostic procedure for pericardial effusion, cardiac catheterization, or pacing or pressure monitoring catheters in coronary care unit patients. Perforation of the right heart chambers is the usual cause in these settings.

From a pathophysiologic point of view, the three hallmarks of cardiac tamponade are (1) a rise in venous pressure, (2) a fall in arterial pressure, and (3) a small quiet heart. None of these signs are completely reliable, but any time the combination of two or more are observed, the diagnosis of cardiac tamponade should be entertained. Decisions are then made regarding the necessity for further diagnostic evaluation. The most unreliable of the three primary signs of cardiac tamponade is the small quiet heart. Cardiac size may range from very small to quite large in a patient with acute cardiac tamponade. The pathophysiology of tamponade, as alluded to earlier, is impairment in diastolic filling of the heart due to an increase in resistance or "stiffness". This results in an inability of the heart to respond to volume changes.

Studies carried out in recent years have led to a better understanding of the cardiovascular responses and adjustments that occur in an individual with cardiac compression due to pericardial effusion, leading toward cardiac tamponade. Increased intrapericardial pressure to an accumulation of fluid may range from very acute to very gradual. In either setting, once the critical level has been reached, it is reflected in an increased intracavitary diastolic pressure. This results in impedance to ventricular filling by preventing the normal volume changes in the ventricle during diastolic filling. Consequently, there is increased venous filling pressure which is translated directly into the ventricles through the open A-V valves. Since atrial pressure during diastole has to exceed ventricular pressure by a small increment in order to maintain forward flow, there has to be a corresponding increase in atrial pressure. The increase in mean atrial pressure triggers the Bainbridge reflex, leading to tachycardia. This increase in heart rate is the first reflex available to increase cardiac output during significant impedance of inflow. At the same time that there is increased atrial pressure and increased ventricular diastolic pressure, there is decreased ventricular filling. This occurs because the increased resistance to ventricular distention imposed by the pressure of the intrapericardial fluid impairs ventricular filling. Consequently, there is a decreased stroke volume because of the decreased end-diastolic ventricular volume. The decreased stroke volume contributes to the reflex tachycardia. As a consequence of a decreased stroke volume, and therefore a decreased cardiac output, peripheral vasoconstriction occurs. The vasoconstriction in this setting involves both the arteriolar and venular system. The generalized vasoconstriction decreases the capacity of the total vascular bed, leading to a fixed circulating blood volume. In this setting, the most dispensable portion of the cardiovascular system is the systemic venous circuit. Thus, there ensues increased systemic venous pressure which helps to maintain right heart filling and cardiac output, working against the inflow resistance offered by the intrapericardial fluid at high pressure. There is a balance between the adjustments that are made and the ability of the heart to respond to these adjustments in the setting of manifest or impending cardiac tamponade.

There is a predictable relationship between the volume of fluid in the pericardium and intrapericardial pressure. This is most dramatic in the hypovolemic setting. Generally, the intrathoracic pressure is transmitted directly to the pericardium so that the intrapericardial pressure is approximately the same as the intrathoracic pressure. This usually ranges from -2 to -4 mmHg in individuals free of pericardial effusion. However, as effusion accumulates in the pericardium, there is a tendency for the pericardial sac to accommodate to the increase in fluid volume with little increase in pressure until a critical level of fluid is achieved. This is generally in the range of 200 cc's, at which point the rate of pressures in response to the rate of changes of volume is very great. A very rapidly developing effusion might increase intrapericardial pressure to tamponade with a lower volume, but generally 150 to 200 cc's of fluid is the threshold for rapid increase in intrapericardial pressure and cardiac tamponade. Once at the tamponade threshold, intrapericardial pressure rises very rapidly in response to any increment in volume. So dramatic are these changes that if one has a patient in tamponade due to acute effusion, taking off as little as 25 cc's of fluid will return this individual from a low output state near death to a normal functioning state. Generally one wishes to take off more fluid than that, but this depends upon the volume of fluid that is present and the ease of removal.

The clinical presentation and cardiac catheterization data observed in the individual with cardiac tamponade can be contrasted to constrictive pericarditis, to the effusive-constrictive syndrome, and to restrictive cardiomyopathies (a form of intracardiac inflow restriction). In all of these states, there is a greater or lesser extent of increased venous pressure and jugular venous pulses are increased and prominent. In tamponade with decompression, the pressure returns rapidly toward normal. In contrast, in the individual with the effusive-constrictive syndrome, it is quite frequent to note neck vein distention persisting after removal of some of the pericardial fluid. This generally occurs in a setting in which there is a component of pericardial thickening due to either tumor or infection, in addition to recurrent effusion in the pericardium. The restrictive myopathies also show jugular venous distention, but to a much less prominent extent. Friedrich's sign, or a rapid Y-descent in the jugular venous pulse, is a very reliable sign in constrictive pericarditis. It is rare in tamponade due to pericardial effusion. In the effusive-constrictive syndrome, and in constrictive cardiomyopathies, a rapid Y-descent to the jugular venous pulse may also occur.

One commonly refers to the "paradoxical pulse" in relationship to the diagnosis of cardiac tamponade. This is generally used in reference to the magnitude of the inspiratory fall in arterial pulse pressure. In this context, the "paradoxical pulse" is not paradoxical but rather an exaggeration of a normal physiologic phenomenon. However, a truly "paradoxical" pulse is Kussmaul's sign. Normally there is a tendency for the neck veins to collapse during inspiration because of the more negative intrathoracic and intrapericardial pressure during this phase of the respiratory cycle. Thus, there is a tendency for the venous return to increase. In Kussmaul's sign, observed usually in constrictive pericarditis or cardiac tamponade due to pericardial effusion, the neck vein response to an inspiratory effort is truly paradoxical. Thus, during inspiration the neck veins engorge rather than collapse. Arterial pulsus paradoxis is a very reliable sign in the setting of acute tamponade, less reliable but still sometimes positive in the individual with constrictive pericarditis, and may also be present in the effusive-constrictive and restrictive disease states. In the setting of acute cardiac tamponade, paradoxical pulse is quantitatively most prominent. Normal levels of "pulsus paradoxis" may range up to 8 to 10 mm, and may be borderline depending on other clinical factors up to 12 mmHg. Beyond 12 mmHg it is clearly abnormal.

Ewart's sign is a dullness to percussion with tubular breath sounds at the tip of the left scapula. This constellation of findings has been considered a good sign of pericardial effusion with tamponade in the past. However, this may also occur in congestive heart failure, chronic lung disease, and several other disease states, and there is a tendency today to disregard this sign. However, if it is observed in the context of the cardinal findings of tamponade (impaired venous return, slowing arterial blood pressure, and a small quiet heart) this sign might be quite valuable. It is generally not observed in the constrictive states, in the effusive-constrictive states, or in the cardiomyopathies unless there is associated cardiomegaly. Finally, ascites may be present in any of the cardiac compression states.

A pericardial friction rub is a valuable sign when it is present, because it usually is present in the setting of tamponade of an acute onset, due to an acute etiology, whether it is uremic, infectious or hemorrhagic; but it is generally not seen in the constrictive states, in the effusive-constrictive states, or in the cardiomyopathies. The problem with relying upon the observation of a pericardial friction rub is the frequency with which this sign is <u>absent</u> in cardiac tamponade.

The hemodynamic characteristics of the cardiac compression states are of interest and of some clinical value. The ventricular pressure curves often demonstrate a very characteristic dip at the end of the systolic left ventricular and right ventricular pressure curves, with a plateau during diastole. This is relatively specific for constrictive pericarditis, rarely seen in tamponade, and only occasionally seen in the effusive-constrictive states or restrictive cardiomyopathies. In addition, in examination of the diastolic pressures across the vascular bed beginning at the right atrial level, progressing through right ventricle, pulmonary artery, left atrium or PA wedge, and left ventricular pressures, one often records both in constrictive pericarditis and cardiac tamponade, a tendency for equalization of the diastolic pressures. In the restrictive cardiomyopathies, the diastolic pressures are much higher on the left side of the circulation than on the right side. The right atrial pressure is of some help in that it tends to be quite high in the constrictive state and in tamponade, but in the restrictive cardiomyopathies it tends to be somewhat lower.

The classical x-ray appearance of water bottle heart, if it is present, is very helpful in identifying tamponade due to effusion when the clinical picture indicates tamponade. The rest of the radiographic examination is generally not a great deal of help because you cannot really differentiate constriction, which may occur with a big heart or a small heart, from effusive constrictive, which is generally associated with a large heart, from restrictive myopathies which also may reveal a big heart or a small heart, and it is important to recognize that the "specific" radiographic signs referred to in the past really aren't specific, except possibly for the "water bottle" heart. Much more sensitive and specific is the use of echocardiography in which we can identify the presence of pericardial effusion very accurately in the individual who has the rest of the clinical picture. In effusive-constrictive patterns, there generally is a much larger degree of pericardial thickening, certainly in excess of 3 to 5 mm, and sometimes over 1 to 2 cm if the degree of infiltration in the pericardium is sufficient. Echocardiography is extremely helpful in pericardial effusion. In an individual with pericardial effusion, there is echo-free space between epicardium and pericardium due to accumulation of fluid.

The best ECG sign of cardiac tamponade due to effusion is the sign of pericardial inflammation which is generalized elevation of the ST segment with upright T waves. In the setting of tamponade and especially in an acute effusive process, one often observes this type of pattern. This may also occur with acute bleeding into the pericardium.

Finally, a brief consideration of the clinical course and response to therapy in the individual with constrictive pericarditis or tamponade is in order. In constriction, there is no clinical response to the removal of any obtainable fluids, and pericardiocentesis is not indicated. Treatment is surgical. Tamponade conversely exhibits very dramatic improvement with removal of small volumes because of the previously discussed pressure-volume relationships. The effusive constrictive state is frequently temporarily relieved by tap, but is also just as frequently recurring and often progressive, and best treated surgically when recognized. The response to drug therapy for an erroneous diagnosis of congestive heart failure in these syndromes is generally unremarkable, and if intravascular volume is depleted, the patient may deteriorate quickly. The patients in the restrictive category and the patients in the effusive category are very sensitive to intravascular volume changes because of the factors that contribute to a fixed intravascular capacity. If one aggressively diureses this category of patient, one can get into a lot of trouble quickly. In tamponade, there may be some improvement with decreased intravascular volume, but more often the situation is aggravated. Generally, pericardiocentesis is very effective and often curative. In the individuals with tamponade due to trauma, which is most often due to bleeding in the pericardium, surgical intervention is the treatment of choice.

REFERENCES

1. Fowler, N.O.: Diseases of the Pericardium. In: The Heart, 3rd Edition. Editors: Hurst, J.W., et al., McGraw-Hill Book Co., New York, Chapter 76, pp. 1387-1405, 1974.

2. Shabetai, R., et al.: The Hemodynamics of Cardiac Tamponade and Constrictive Pericarditis. Am J Cardiol 26: 480, 1970.

3. Beaudry, C., et al.: Uremic Pericarditis and Cardiac Tamponade in Chronic Renal Failure. Ann Intern Med 64: 990, 1966.

C: MYOCARDIAL INFARCTION AND CARDIOGENIC SHOCK
by John A. Kastor, M.D.

Acute myocardial infarction usually kills with ventricular fibrillation
or cardiogenic shock. Prevention and treatment of fatal primary
ventricular arrhythmias can usually be achieved today once the patient enters the hospital and his electrocardiogram is continuously
monitored. Most hospital deaths occur because too much functioning
myocardium has been infarcted for maintenance of adequate perfusion
of the heart itself and the other organs. When cardiogenic shock
from myocardial infarction is established, death can seldom be prevented by ordinary therapeutics. However, before that potentially
fatal condition develops, several important derangements of hemodynamic function may appear which require energetic management.
Finally, even in the presence of cardiogenic shock, the patient may
survive with measures currently considered heroic but which some-
day may be routine.

CLINICAL RECOGNITION OF MYOCARDIAL DYSFUNCTION

The symptoms and physical findings which may suggest the presence
of heart muscle dysfunction during myocardial infarction are produced by three physiological derangements: 1.) inadequate arterial
perfusion of the heart and other organs, 2.) increase of pressure be-
hind the failing ventricles, 3.) hypovolemia and hypervolemia from
drugs, fluids or autonomic tone.

Hypoperfusion of peripheral tissues characteristically produces tired-
ness, weakness and decrease in cerebral function. The findings include: narrow pulse pressure and/or hypotension, cool, sweaty extremities, distal cyanosis, and decreased amplitude of the arterial
pulses. Failure of the infarcted ventricles elevates pressures within
the heart and the pulmonary and systemic venous circulations. Patients complain of shortness of breath and have orthopnea and edema.
Examination may show third and fourth heart sounds (S_3, S_4), systolic murmurs of mitral and/or tricuspid incompetence, rales, pleural effusions, elevated venous pressure, hepatomegaly and peripheral
edema. In addition to these findings suggesting failure, the following
are often present: decrease in the intensity of the first and second
sounds at the apex, an S_4 from decreased ventricular compliance and
a sustained apical impulse. Excess or insufficient effective intravascular volume mimics the symptoms and findings of severe myocardial dysfunction. Anatomical catastrophy during acute myocardial
infarction due to rupture of the ventricular septum or of papillary
muscles is recognized when the hemodynamic profile dramatically
changes and a new systolic murmur appears.

The usual cardiac rhythm during myocardial dysfunction is sinus
tachycardia, the reflex response to reduced cardiac output. Other
cardiac arrhythmias such as atrial fibrillation and atrio-ventricular

block will frequently cause symptoms, findings and hemodynamic measurements which suggest severe myocardial dysfunction. Control or reversion of the arrhythmia may relieve the patient of his distress. (The recognition and management of the rhythm disturbances of myocardial infarction will not be treated in this chapter).

HEMODYNAMIC MEASUREMENTS

In the last eight years, the hemodynamic effects of myocardial infarction have been measured in a wide range of cases with intracardiac flow-directed (Swan-Ganz) catheters which are passed with or without fluoroscopic control into the right atrium (RA), right ventricle (RV) and pulmonary artery (PA). In small pulmonary arteries, the balloons on such catheters can be inflated to occlude antegrade flow. The pressure transmitted from the tip of the catheter accurately records the left atrial events which in turn reflect left ventricular diastolic or filling pressure (pulmonary capillary wedge-PCW-pressure). The cardiac output can also be determined serially by the thermodilution technique with the use of these catheters. Urine output is often measured serially with indwelling urinary catheters to evaluate renal perfusion. The arterial blood pressure can be recorded directly through small catheters in the radial or other systemic arteries and the same source may be used for measurements of arterial pH and oxygen tension. When these data are correlated with clinical evaluation of the patient, an accurate impression of myocardial function and prognosis can usually be determined.

NORMAL FINDINGS: The patient with a first small myocardial infarction whose hemodynamic function has been left relatively intact may have the following findings:

Mentation: Clear
Skin: Dry and Warm
Arterial Pulse: Full
Chest: Clear
Heart: S_4
Brachial artery pressure (BAP): 90-140 mm Hg systolic/60-90 mm Hg diastolic
Central Venous or right atrial mean pressure (RAP): 0-8 mm Hg
Pulmonary Artery Pressure (PAP): 15-30 mm Hg systolic/5-12 mm Hg diastolic
Pulmonary Capillary Wedge Mean Pressure (PCWP): 6-12 mm Hg
Cardiac Index: 2.5-4.2 liters/min/m^2
Arterial pO$_2$: 80-100 mm Hg
Arterial pH: 7.38-7.44
Urine Output: greater than 30 cc/hour

METHODS OF TREATMENT

From a physiological viewpoint, the techniques used in patients with hemodynamic derangements in association with myocardial infarction include: 1.) improvement in myocardial function with digitalis or beta adrenergic catecholamines, 2.) manipulation of preload (intravascular volume), either increasing it with saline or colloids or decreasing it with diuretics, morphine, nitroglycerin or phlebotomy, 3.) manipulation of afterload (systemic blood pressure and coronary perfusion), increasing it with alpha adrenergic catecholamines, or intra-aorta balloon pumping during diastole, or decreasing it with nitroprusside, nitroglycerin, morphine or intra-aortic balloon pumping during systole, 4.) surgical repair of anatomical malfunction such as rupture of ventricular septum or papillary muscle, 5.) surgical revascularization.

ILLUSTRATIVE CASES

Several cases of myocardial infarction with hemodynamic complications will now be presented. Clinical findings, hemodynamic measurements and discussion have been included for each patient.

CARDIOGENIC SHOCK:

History: 52-year-old man with previous inferior myocardial infarction, chest pain and shortness of breath.

Examination: Cyanotic, cool, sweaty, sleepy, decreased pulse amplitude, rales, sustained dilated apex, distant S_1 and S_2, P_2 increased, S_3, S_4, systolic murmur, elevated venous pressure, hepatic tenderness.

ECG: Acute anterior myocardial infarction, old inferior myocardial infarction, sinus tachycardia of 120 beats/min.
BAP: 80/70
PCWP: 28
RAP: 10
Urine: 10

All of the characteristic features of cardiogenic shock are illustrated in this case. Two myocardial infarctions have occurred, much ventricular muscle has been affected, forward flow of blood is subnormal and biventricular congestive heart failure is present. All nonmyocardial causes for the dysfunction have been ruled out. The patient will probably die and if he survives will be severely limited. Treatment in most hospitals will feature administration of catecholamine drugs to sustain blood pressure and myocardial perfusion. Unloading the ventricles with nitroprusside or nitroglycerin may be tried but further decrease in blood pressure and perfusion will result. When available, an intra-aortic balloon may be inserted which will temporarily relieve some of the findings of shock. Most patients

however, will deteriorate further when the balloon is turned off.
Angiographic study of the left ventricle will usually reveal a large
poorly contracting chamber. In those cases, however, where the
LV function is relatively well preserved, revascularization surgery
may be helpful. While trying to improve the hemodynamic condition
the physician must pay particular attention to the symptomatic needs
of the patient. Narcotics may be required for relief of pain and
anxiety and oxygen should be given to decrease hypoxia.

HYPOTENSION AND ATRIAL FIBRILLATION:

History: 60-year-old man with two years of angina pectoris, onset
  of acute myocardial infarction 48 hours ago and recurrent chest
  pain.

Examination: Skin slightly sweaty, rapid irregular pulse with decreased amplitude, basilar rales, increased P_2, S_3, systolic
  murmur, slight elevation of venous pressure.

ECG: Acute anterior myocardial infarction, atrial fibrillation with
  ventricular response at average rate of 150 beats/min.
BAP: 75-50
PCWP: 25
RAP: 10
Urine: 20
pO_2: 65

The previously benign course of this patient with a recent acute myocardial infarction has been interrupted by the development of hypotension, early signs of congestive heart failure and atrial fibrillation.
In this case, the culprit is not myocardial dysfunction primarily, nor
inadequate or excessive preload but rather the arrhythmia itself.
The loss of atrial contraction and the decrease in diastolic ventricular filling time produced by the rapid rate has reduced cardiac output,
already temporarily affected by the acute infarction. Administration
of oxygen, morphine sulfate and diuretics will help to decrease the
signs of failure, but more important is the treatment of the atrial
fibrillation. This is conventionally accomplished with digoxin but
propranolol may also be given for a more rapid effect. The negative
inotropic effect of the drug is not usually deleterious in such cases.
Either drug may produce sinus rhythm in addition to slowing the ventricular response to atrial fibrillation. Only occasionally is cardioversion required, but if the clinical situation deteriorates rapidly,
this approach may be necessary. (Treatment of arrhythmias in myocardial infarction is a topic beyond the scope of this chapter, but one
case has been included in order to emphasize the role which cardiac
arrhythmias may play upon cardiac function during myocardial infarction).

VAGOTONIA ASSOCIATED WITH INFERIOR MYOCARDIAL INFARCTION:

History: 56-year-old man, no previous known cardiac disease, chest pain and nausea.

Examination: Slightly sweaty, warm, slightly decreased pulse amplitude, veins flat at 0^0, S_4.

ECG: Acute inferior myocardial infarction, sinus bradycardia at 50 beats/min
BAP: 70/50
PCWP: 4
RAP: 3
Urine: 20

The inferior myocardial infarction has stimulated the parasympathetic nervous system, and the patient has developed hypotension and bradycardia. Cardiogenic shock may be diagnosed in such a case. However, examination shows that the patient suffers only marginally from decreased perfusion, the lungs are clear and the venous pressure is low. Venous pooling has prevented blood from entering the heart in adequate volume, and the arterial perfusion is consequently reduced. Furthermore, sinus tachycardia, the characteristic response in cardiogenic shock, is absent. The pulse is slow from vagal stimulation.

Treatment in this case consists of administering atropine to release vagal tone. The pulse rate will increase and venous pooling will be released thus permitting more blood to enter the heart. The simple expedient of lowering the head and raising the legs will also increase cardiac input and begin to relieve the findings of "pseudo-shock". If the blood volume has actually been decreased by previous diuretic treatment, for hypertension for example, judicious administration of saline or of colloids may be helpful.

HYPOTENSION DUE TO DRUGS:

History: 60-year-old woman with history of 15 years of hypertension, chest pain.

Examination: Skin slightly cool and sweaty, decreased pulse amplitude, veins flat at 0^0, pupils small, bibasilar rales, S_4, sustained widened apex.

ECG: 75/50
PCWP: 7
RAP: 2
Urine: 5

This hypotensive woman also appears to be in shock. Left ventricular failure is suggested by the bibasilar rales but the venous pressure is low and a third heart sound is not present. The most important clues from the examination are the small pupils, constricted by administration of morphine sulfate for chest pain. The patient has had hypertension, revealed by left ventricular hypertrophy on the electrocardiogram, and she has taken diuretics for several years. Thus the intravascular volume has been depleted and the heart has been further deprived of blood which has pooled in the venous bed by the venodilating effects of morphine which has also decreased arterial tone, dropping the blood pressure more. Vagal tone in this case is not playing as much of a role as it may in such instances since the sinus node has responded to the hypotension by an increase in rate. Preload must be increased by the administration of fluids and colloids. Lowering of the head and raising the feet will temporarily increase the cardiac input. The bibasilar rales have not been produced by left ventricular failure - the left ventricular filling pressures are normal - but rather by hypoventilation from morphine.

PULMONARY EDEMA AND CHEST PAIN AFTER SURGERY:

History: 75-year-old man, two days after prostatectomy, chest pain, confused, dyspnea.

Examination: Skin cool and sweaty, elevated venous pressure, rales, S_3, S_4, systolic murmurs.

ECG: ST segments depressed in leads V_3-V_6, sinus tachycardia at 120 beats/min.
BAP: 110/90
PCWP: 30
RAP: 15
Urine: 15, blood in collection bag.
pO_2: 50

The features of this case are commonly encountered when the internist or cardiologist is called to attend an elderly patient with chest pain which develops after an operation. An acute myocardial infarction must always be considered, but a dynamic imbalance of myocardial perfusion in a patient with coronary disease and no true infarction may actually be present. When hypotension develops, surgeons usually repair the problem by administering blood or fluid but this treatment may sometimes be overzealous in the patient with a previously compromised myocardium. Pulmonary edema ensues, hypoxia increases and myocardial ischemia results. The electrocardiographic finding of depressed ST segments may indicate a temporary myocardial perfusion imbalance rather than the first signs of subendocardial infarction. In such cases quick treatment can relieve the acute symptoms and prevent infarction. Morphine, IV diuretics, tourniquets and oxygen may reverse the dangerous pattern quickly.

LEFT VENTRICULAR FAILURE:

History: 60-year-old man with chest pain, dyspnea and orthopnea, previous subendocardial myocardial infarction.

Examination: Tachypnea, cool sweaty skin, decreased pulse amplitude, elevated venous pressure, summation gallop (S_3 and S_4), systolic murmur, increased P_2, sustained apex with medial paradoxical expansion, rales to the apices of the lungs, tender liver, cyanosis.

ECG: Acute anterior myocardial infarction, sinus tachycardia at 120 beats/min.
BAP: 120/100
PCWP: 30
RAP: 14
Urine: 20
pO_2: 45

A widespread anterior myocardial infarction has destroyed much myocardial tissue. Perfusion drops, the left ventricle fails, and pulmonary edema develops. The systemic response includes an outpouring of autonomic, mostly sympathetic, tone and even though hypotension is absent the peripheral findings suggest shock. The primary myocardial nature of this calamity is supported by the presence of sinus tachycardia. Intracardiac pressures confirm the impression gained from physical examination.

Immediate treatment should include administration of oxygen - which is often forgotten in the midst of this acute emergency - and an intravenous diuretic such as furosemide. This drug rapidly produces venous pooling which helps to decrease preload. Morphine sulfate is also indicated both to relieve pain and anxiety and to decrease preload. Mechanical maneuvers such as rotating tourniquets may be necessary. Phlebotomy is rarely required.

As the pulmonary edema subsides, the signs of congestion may dramatically improve and be replaced by hypotension due to inadequate cardiac input. The assumption that cardiogenic shock has followed left ventricular failure may frequently produce a syndrome mimicking shock. (See previous case)

RIGHT VENTRICULAR FAILURE:

History: 58-year-old woman with three years of angina pectoris, sustained chest pain.

Examination: S_4, elevated venous pressure, no rales.

ECG: Acute inferior myocardial, sinus rhythm at 90 beats/min.
BAP: 95/60
PCWP: 10
RAP: 15
Urine: 50

The surprising feature of this case is that no evidence for left ventricular failure can be found on examination or by measurement,
yet the right ventricle appears to have failed as documented by an
elevated venous pressure on examination and by measurement.
When these findings are observed, the likelihood of an inferior myocardial infarction is high. The coronary distribution is such that in
some patients with inferior infarction the right ventricle will malfunction more than the left ventricle. This variety of myocardial infarction is more common than generally believed and carries a relatively good prognosis. No treatment may be required if the patient
is comfortable. The right ventricle will usually regain function and
the right sided failure will resolve. The administration of diuretics
and/or digitalis may sometimes be necessary.

HYPOTENSION, DYSPNEA AND NEW SYSTOLIC MURMUR:

History: 62-year-old woman with shortness of breath developing
   three days after onset of second acute myocardial infarction.

Examination: Cool, sweaty skin, decreased pulse amplitude,
   elevated venous pressure, rales, S_3, S_4, increased P_2, loud
   systolic murmur.

ECG: Old anterior myocardial infarction, acute inferior myocardial
   infarction, sinus tachycardia at 110 beats/min.
BAP: 80/65
PCWP: 25 with tall systolic waves
RAP: 12
Urine: 20
pO_2: 55

The systolic murmurs produced by acute myocardial infarction
originate from: 1.) papillary muscle dysfunction due to left ventricular myocardial failure, 2.) rupture of the interventricular septum,
3.) rupture of papillary muscles. Papillary muscle dysfunction is
produced by left ventricular infarction without rupture of the mitral
apparatus and cannot be primarily treated with surgery. Rupture
of the interventricular septum or of the papillary muscles, however,
should be recognized because sometimes surgical intervention is
helpful.

In this case the systolic murmur has developed suddenly in association with hypotension and pulmonary edema. Differential diagnosis between rupture of the papillary muscles or of the ventricular
septum may be quite difficult from examination alone. The murmur

of a ventricular septal defect is said to be loudest along the left sternal border and of a papillary muscle at the left ventricular apex. Inferior myocardial infarctions are more commonly associated with papillary muscle rupture and anterior myocardial infarctions with ventricular septal rupture. However, neither of these rules apply consistently, and the picture can be complicated when previous infarction is present. Regardless of the anatomy, the prognosis is always grave.

Medical treatment consists of the usual methods to control severe myocardial failure including digitalis, diuretics and morphine. Decreasing afterload with vasodilating drugs or intra-aortic balloon support has been found effective in some cases. Hopefully the patient can weather the acute episode because operation for repair of either defect during the early days after onset of the infarction carries a very high mortality. If the patient recovers and his cardiac reserve remains limited, surgical repair may be performed later with a more acceptable operative risk.

The diagnosis of papillary muscle rupture versus ventricular systolic rupture can often be made with the Swan-Ganz catheter. With acute mitral regurgitation tall systolic waves are seen in the wedge tracing. With ventricular septal rupture, oxygen saturation in the pulmonary artery is higher than expected and a "step-up" of oxygen saturation within the right ventricle will be observed.

REFERENCES

1. Armstrong, R.W., et al: Vasodilator Therapy in Acute Myocardial Infarction. A comparison of sodium nitroprusside and nitroglycerine. Circulation 52:1118, 1975.

2. Gold, H.K., et al: Intra-aortic Balloon Pumping for Control of Recurrent Myocardial Ischemia. Circulation 47:1197-1203, June, 1973.

3. Mundth, E.D., et al: Symposium: Myocardial Infarction (1972 Part 6), Surgery for Complications of Acute Myocardial Infarction. Circulation 45:1279-1291, June, 1972.

4. Gold, H.K., et al: Intra-aortic Balloon Pumping for Ventricular Septal Defect or Mitral Regurgitation Complicating Acute Myocardial Infarction. Circulation 45:1191-1196, June, 1973.

D: VENTRICULAR ARRHYTHMIAS AND DIGITALIS -
INDUCED ARRHYTHMIAS
by Agustin Castellanos, M.D. and
Ruey J. Sung, M.D.

PART 1: VENTRICULAR ARRHYTHMIAS:

GENERAL APPROACH TO ARRHYTHMIAS: Hurst has emphasized
that cardiac arrhythmias are usually viewed in isolation.[1] This is
manifested in the classical question often asked to the consulting
cardiologist; namely "How do you treat these premature ventricular
contractions (PVC)?" The question should be "Will you discuss
treating this patient with this arrhythmia?"

Most of us learned arrhythmias in abstract without dealing with the
patient as a whole or with the significance of the same arrhythmia
when occurring in different subsettings. Like playing chess, the
analysis of the electrocardiogram of a complex arrhythmia may be
most interesting and time consuming but the effect may not be rewarding to the patient unless the arrhythmia is viewed in the context
of the clinical situation in which it occurs.

Day to day field experience with bright students, house officers and
cardiac fellows shows that they are still not aware that arrhythmias
should be seen in context, because: (a) they are taught electrocardio-
graphy in abstract, generally in the Heart Station; (b) they are taught
electrophysiology in abstract in Weekly conferences and (c) (except
in the Coronary Care Unit) they are taught pharmacology in abstract.

VENTRICULAR ARRHYTHMIAS OCCURRING IN VARIOUS SETTINGS:
If arrhythmias are not viewed in isolation how should they be approached?
"It follows that they should be viewed in context, that is, in the light
of the clinical situation in which they occur".[1] Thus, if a person
has occasional unifocal premature ventricular contractions (PVC's)
and no evidence whatsoever of heart disease these PVCs have no
significance other than the possibility of experiencing "palpitations"
(Fig. 1.2)

On the other extreme, PVCs in patients with severe myocarditis,
i.e. Coxsackie (seen mainly in the pediatric age group) are associated
with cardiomegaly, heart failure, etc. In this setting they have an
ominous prognosis, and require aggressive therapy. (Fig. 1.3)

Arrhythmias occurring in the mitral valve prolapse-click syndrome
are a source of current interest, mainly because this is a relatively
new entity. Although sporadic cases of sudden death have been reported in this syndrome, its probability appears to be low. In an
editorial published in the February (1976) issue of the American
Journal of Cardiology,a leading authority states that "the risk of

sudden death is remote in this syndrome and therefore should not be mentioned to the patient or his family for fear of inducing anxiety and neurosis" (or exaggerating the latter which is almost invariably present we might add).

Chronic PVCs occur frequently in patients with arterio-sclerotic heart disease, hypertensive heart disease, cardiomyopathy and heart failure. In these cases therapy should be oriented initially towards the treatment of heart failure and then towards suppression or reduction of these arrhythmias (which; incidentally, often prove considerably resistant to therapy).

VENTRICULAR ARRHYTHMIAS AND SUDDEN DEATH: In contrast, PVCs occurring in patients surviving an episode of ventricular fibrillation outside the hospital are potentially dangerous. This is one of the areas of medicine where properly applied technology has contributed significantly to the welfare of the citizens in a community. [2] For example, the combination of a highly trained fire rescue squad, capable of interconnecting with a command center via audiovisual telemetry, has provided many cities throughout the world with a medically supervised rescue system which can reach most emergencies within a few minutes after summons (four minutes is the average response time in Miami). [2]

Although our interest has concentrated on acute cardiovascular problems it should be stressed that these squads also respond to psychiatric, pediatric, and traumatic emergencies, as well as other diverse everyday human problems. This is a multi-purpose oriented system which cares for a variety of acute problems. Physicians, public officials, as well as the general public are rapidly becoming aware of the effectiveness of rescue systems.

Newer concepts have been learned since the advent of medical emergency rescue services. [2] For example, patients developing ventricular fibrillation or tachycardia outside the hospital usually have atherosclerotic heart disease. However, contrary to general opinion these patients do not always have an acute myocardial infarction. Transient ischemia, which may involve an area of myocardium too small to increase the serum CPK-MB isoenzyme level, or to produce specific electrocardiographic changes (abnormal Q waves and current of injury) is not infrequent. Those who reach the hospital alive and survive the hospitalization period, almost invariably have premature ventricular contractions and a high incidence of death (28%) within the following year. Thus, a large number appear to maintain the pathological state which predisposes to catastrophic arrhythmias. [2]

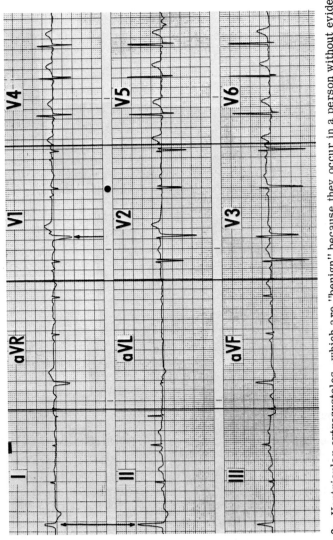

FIG. 1.2: Ventricular extrasystoles, which are "benign" because they occur in a person without evidence of heart disease. Their right ventricular origin is determined by the QS morphology that they display in lead V_1.

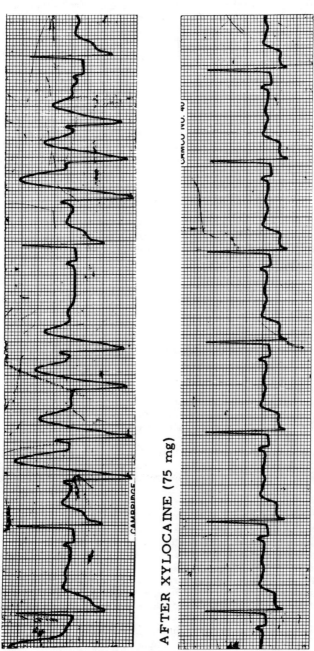

AFTER XYLOCAINE (75 mg)

FIG. 1.3: Short runs of ventricular tachycardia which are malignant because they occur in a patient with acute myocarditis and severe heart failure (monitoring lead II).

Since the outside-hospital mortality from coronary heart disease accounts for about 400,000 deaths per year in the United States and because of the reasons cited above, a joint effort between the facilities of the city of Miami Fire Rescue Squad and the Cardiology Division of the University of Miami School of Medicine was established in order to provide careful follow-up of patients initially seen by the rescue squad.

Preliminary studies appear to indicate that the incidence of sudden death due to non-cardiac conditions, as well as cardiac diseases other than atherosclerotic heart disease is greater than what was previously believed. Attempts are being made to categorize the clinical condition of those patients resuscitated by the Fire Rescue Squad, regardless of their etiology. There are those who believe that in the final analysis, when accidental deaths and the successful management of surgical and infectious disease are excluded, there is very little that can be done to favorably modify the lifespan.

We feel that from the medical point of view, an attitude of cautious optimism is always warranted. Therefore, we can say to the therapeutic nihilist:

1) Not all sudden deaths are inevitable.
2) Further efforts directed towards the prevention of sudden death are warranted.

VENTRICULAR ARRHYTHMIAS IN ACUTE MYOCARDIAL INFARCTION: Acute myocardial infarction poses a special problem. In this setting prompt treatment of any PVC (not necessarily of the "malignant" type) is mandatory. In fact, some authors have recommended that all patients with acute transmural myocardial infarction should be started on a prophylactic intravenous Lidocaine drip, provided that there are no specific contraindications, namely, bradyarrhythmias, age (over 65 years) and advanced liver disease.

If these precautions are taken, little toxicity has been encountered with the administration of prophylactic antiarrhythmic agents in patients with acute myocardial infarctions (MI). In studies on more than 750 MI patients treated with Lidocaine in Melbourne, Stockholm, and Boston, no serious drug toxicity was encountered.[3,4,5] Although involving much smaller numbers of patients, similar studies using oral procainamide, oral quinidine, and intravenous and IM bretylium encountered no significant serious toxicity. However, three of thirty-seven procainamide treated patients and one of twenty-seven quinidine treated patients demonstrated advance degrees of AV and IV block which may have represented drug toxicity. In the procainamide group toxic effects were associated with procainamide blood levels in the known toxic range.

The role of routine antiarrhythmic prophylaxis in acute MI has not been clearly established. One might conclude from the above data that routine prophylaxis should be reserved for situations in which monitoring is less than ideal and premonitory PVC's may be missed. In situations where a Lidocaine drip cannot be adequately regulated, oral therapy with procainamide or quinidine may be preferable.

Despite controversy over the routine use of prophylactic antiarrhythmic agents, most authors agree on certain clearcut indications for antiarrhythmia prophylaxis. These include the so called "malignant" PVCs, namely (Fig. 1.4).

1) PVC's that occur more frequently than 5/minutes
2) PVC's that fall on the previous T wave
3) Multifocal PVC's
4) Two or more PVC's in a row

Patients with acute MI are initially given an IV bolus of Lidocaine (1 mg/kg) followed by a Lidocaine infusion at a rate of 2 mg/minute. Lower doses are unlikely to be effective. If ventricular ectopic beats are not suppressed, a second 1 mg/kg bolus is given and the drip is increased to 3-4 mg/minute (infusion rates in excess of 4 mg/minute frequently lead to signs of central nervous system toxicity). If these measures are effective, Lidocaine is continued 2-3 days. The patient is then switched to an oral regimen using either quinidine, 200-300 mg every six hours, or procainamide, 250 mg every four hours. Lidocaine is continued until adequate blood levels of the second drug would be expected (eight hours for procainamide, twenty-four hours for quinidine). Lidocaine is then stopped and the patient is monitored an additional one-two days to be certain he remains arrhythmia-free on the oral regimen.

Some patients will not respond to Lidocaine, even in moderately large doses. These patients present one of the most challenging management problems encountered in the Coronary Care Unit. As well stated by Margolis and Wagner the goal of therapy here is the obtaining of maximum arrhythmia suppression with the introduction of minimum drug toxicity. [6] It is important to approach this problem as a clinical experiment with a well-defined course of action. Data must be obtained in a uniform manner. A clear-cut therapeutic endpoint must be predetermined. Treatment modalities must be introduced one at a time, given in full therapeutic dosage in a prescribed manner, and allowed time for maximum action. When these rules are ignored, the usual result is a patient receiving multiple drugs, suffering multiple drug interactions and toxicities, who may or may not still have his arrhythmia. The patient's physician is then faced with the problem of which drugs have been effective and which are toxic, which to continue and which to stop.

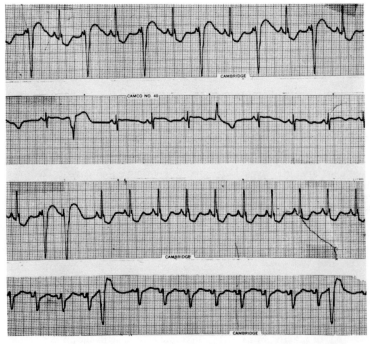

FIG. 1.4: Electrocardiographic features of the ventricular extrasystoles which are considered "malignant" in acute myocardial infarction (so called "warning arrhythmias"):
(a) more than five per minute (lead II); (b) multifocal
(lead II); (c) two (or more) in a row (lead II) and (d) fall-
on the T wave (lead V1). Actually any extrasystole is
"malignant" when occurring in the first seventy-two
hours after a transmural myocardial infarction.

The approach suggested by Margolis and Wagner is to first search for underlying treatable causes such as congestive heart failure, hypovolemia, hypoxia, and hypokalemia.[6] They administer IV potassium even with low-normal serum potassium. Whether or not these patients are whole body potassium depleted, raising serum potassium to above 4 mEq/L will frequently abolish previously refractory ventricular arrhythmias.

Lidocaine is continued on the unproven assumption that the patient is less likely to have sustained ventricular tachycardia or ventricular fibrillation in the presence of adequate blood levels of this drug.

If the arrhythmia persists additional therapy is tried. At this point the most useful are: IV and oral procainamide, oral quinidine, IV diphenylhydantoin (DPH), IV and oral propranolol, digitalis, and overdrive atrial and ventricular pacing. The sequence of introduction of these therapies is not as important as their orderly introduction and a thorough evaluation of their maximum effect in therapeutic dosage.

Intravenous procainamide is usually tried first. This drug is similar to Lidocaine. However, the electrophysiologic actions are somewhat different. Clinically, ventricular arrhythmias refractory to Lidocaine may be abolished with procainamide or a combination of Lidocaine and procainamide. Intravenous infusion of procainamide must be done carefully, under continuous electrocardiographic monitoring, and with frequent measurement of blood pressure. Excessive infusion rates may lead to hypotension and high degrees of AV and IV block. In contrast to Lidocaine, cardiotoxicity can develop before the appearance of extracardiac symptoms.

It has been recommended to administer 100 mg every five minutes until the arrhythmia has been abolished, toxic effects appear, or a total of 0.8-1.0 mgs have been given. We have seen cardiotoxicity develop with this method especially when several medications have been concomitantly used. Hence, it is our custom to administer 100 mg every 10 minutes after the initial 500 mg. If IV procainamide proves effective, usually maintenance therapy is begun with the oral or IM form.

Quinidine sulfate is more useful for chronic than for acute prophylaxis of ventricular arrhythmias. It cannot be safely administered IV. When administered by mouth, some antiarrhythmic effect occurs in two hours. Adequate blood levels are not obtained until 18-24 hours after initiation of therapy using the "popular" dose of 200-300 mg every 4-6 hours.

LONG-ACTING PREPARATIONS SUCH AS QUINIDINE HAVE THE
ADVANTAGE OF ALLOWING ITS ADMINISTRATION Q.I.D.:
Quinidine and procainamide have similar structures, electrophysiologic properties, and clinical effects. Although an individual
arrhythmia may be refractory to one drug and responsive to the
other, it is useful to consider the two drugs as clinical interchange-
able. Effective quinidine blood levels can be maintained with every
six-hour dosage. Procainamide requires more frequent administration. It has been said that it is useful to administer parenteral
procainamide for acute situations, then switch to quinidine for
maintenance therapy.

PART 2: DIGITALIS-INDUCED ARRHYTHMIAS

Although this chapter deals with ventricular arrhythmias, supraventricular rhythm due to digitalis toxicity will be discussed since
they frequently alternate and coexist with ventricular ectopic beats.

Digitalis toxicity may be manifested by gastrointestinal, neurological or cardiovascular signs and symptoms. Cardiac arrhythmias
and conduction disturbance appear in about 80% of patients presenting clinical evidence of digitalis toxicity.

Having been interested in arrhythmias for 27 years it is our impression that the incidence of toxicity has decreased in recent years.
It certainly is so in our institution due to intensive programs oriented
towards producing increasing awareness of these possibilities, the
use (predominantly of Digoxin), adequate potassium supplements and,
most important, changing patterns in digitalis administration.   For
instance, in 1976, Burroughs Wellcome Company the discoverers and
original manufacturers of digoxin stated that "a number of experts
in cardiology" were of the opinion that good therapeutic control of
patients could be obtained with doses of digoxin lower than those
traditionally recommended. Newer lower doses for digoxin were
initially proposed by the FDA in 1974.

PAROXYSMAL ATRIAL TACHYCARDIA (PAT) WITH A-V BLOCK:
In 1959 Von Capeller et al reported the incidence of this arrhythmia
to be 10.1% (15 instances in 148 cases of digitalis intoxication).(7)
Although statistics are not available for 1977, in our institution (1200
bed community hospital) we saw only between 4 to 7 cases last year
(1976). The classical features were: an atrial rate of 150 to 200; a
change in the contour of the P waves; isoelectric baseline between
atrial complexes; and variable degrees of A-V block (Fig. 1.5,
middle strip). If the atrial rate is slowed appreciably by carotid
pressure, the arrhythmia is very unlikely to have been induced by
digitalis. Similarly, atropine will increase the atrial rate in the non-
digitalis atrial tachycardia but will not affect those secondary to digitalis. Carotid sinus massage frequently stops "supraventricular
tachycardia" resulting from A-V reciprocation but will not abolish
PAT with A-V block due to digitalis. Characteristics of the arrhythmia that have not been sufficiently stressed are the variations in

P-P intervals (not due to ventriculophysic arrhythmia) and of the morphology of the P waves. These changes are probably related to an irregular discharge and abnormal propagation from a single center, although the activity of two or more ectopic atrial pacemakers cannot be completely ruled out.[8] This of course does not refer to the so called multifocal atrial tachycardia in which various P wave morphologies are seen.

A-V JUNCTIONAL RHYTHM, TACHYCARDIA AND DISSOCIATION:
A-V junctional premature contractions, junctional rhythm and junctional tachycardia constitute an incidence of 4, 5 and 8 percent, respectively, of digitalis-induced arrhythmias.[8] Second degree and third degree A-V block appear in 13.5 and 6.1 percent, respectively. "A-V junctional" rhythm is a term applied to impulse formation in the upper A-V node, coronary sinus, A-V nodal bypass tracts and His bundle. In A-V junctional tachycardia, the rate varies from 70 to around 150/min (Fig. 1.5, bottom strip; and Fig. 1.6). Junctional rhythm and junctional tachycardia may occur in a paroxysmal or nonparoxysmal fashion and has also been described as passive or active. The term "passive" implies an escape rhythm. An "active" rhythm denotes a relatively rapid arrhythmia resulting from increased automaticity of the junctional tissues, which drives the ventricle because it discharges at a rate faster than that of the S-A node. A-V dissociation which results may be complete or incomplete (see Fig. 1.5, bottom; and see Fig. 1.6). In the presence of atrial fibrillation, the subsequent regularization of the ventricular response (Fig. 1.7, top two strips) may be mistaken for conversion to sinus rhythm unless electrocardiographic documentation is obtained. Two events may take place with increasing digitalis blood levels. (1) block may develop below the ectopic pacemaker with slower regular (see Fig. 1.7, third strip) or irregular (see Fig. 1.7, bottom strip) response. A persistent 3:2 conduction ratio of the nodal impulses may result in ventricular bigeminy. (2) There may be further acceleration of rate leading to higher degrees of block and even ventricular tachycardia (Figs. 1.8, 1.9, and 1.10). In the absence of atrial fibrillation, on the other hand, further digitalization may lead to acceleration of an additional atrial, ventricular or junctional pacemaker, resulting in a double ectopic tachycardia (see below). However, digitalization can also cause an increase of the ventricular rate in atrial fibrillation if it produces ventricular tachycardia (Fig. 1.11).

In 1968 the mortality rate associated with A-V junctional tachycardia as a manifestation of digitalis toxicity was reported as 53 per cent. However, continued administration of digitalis resulted in 81 per cent mortality.[8] It is doubtful that such a high mortality exists today in the United States.

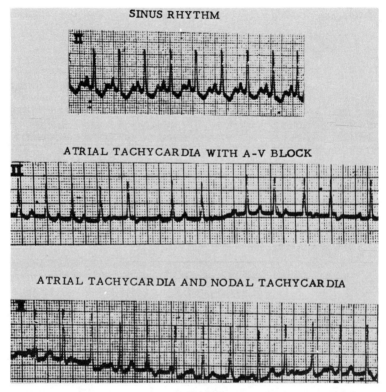

FIG. 1.5: Digitalis induced PAT with A-V block (middle strip) and double atrial and A-V junctional tachycardia (bottom strip). Note that the QRS complexes have the same morphology as during sinus rhythm.

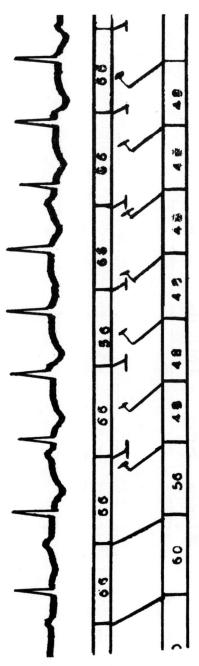

FIG. 1.6: Digitalis induced A-V junctional tachycardia dissociated from an independent sinus rhythm (lead II).

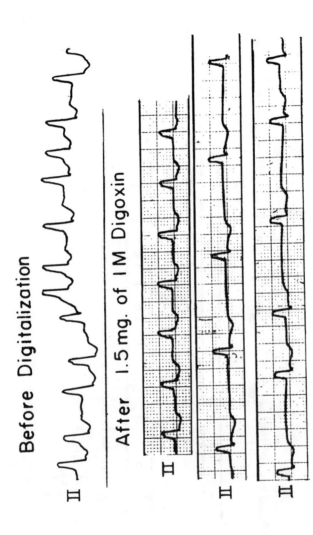

FIG. 1.7: Chronic atrial fibrillation with complete left bundle branch block (upper strip); complete or advanced A–V block with A–V junctional tachycardia with 1:1 A–V conduction (second strip), and 2:1 A–V block (third strip); and complete or advanced A–V block with A–V junctional tachycardia and varying 2:1 and 3:2 A–V block of the Wenckebach type (bottom strip). Note that QRS complexes are wide because of bundle branch block.

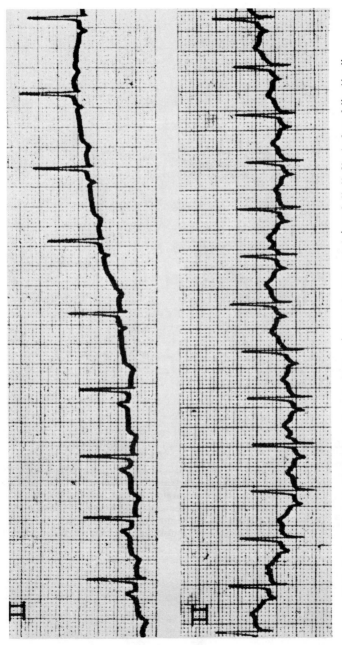

FIG. 1.8: "Passive" A-V junctional rhythm (control, top strip) and digitalis induced "active" (A-V junctional) tachycardia (lower strip).

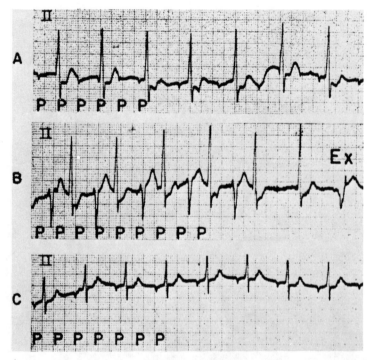

FIG. 1.9: (Same patient as in Fig. 1.8) Digitalis-induced A-V junctional tachycardia with 2:1 A-V block (bottom strip); double A-V junctional and bidirectional (or double) ventricular tachycardia (middle strip) and double A-V junctional and "slow" ventricular tachycardia (top strip). In this patient bidirectional ventricular tachycardia might result from the coexistence of two separate slow ventricular tachycardias (double ventricular tachycardia).

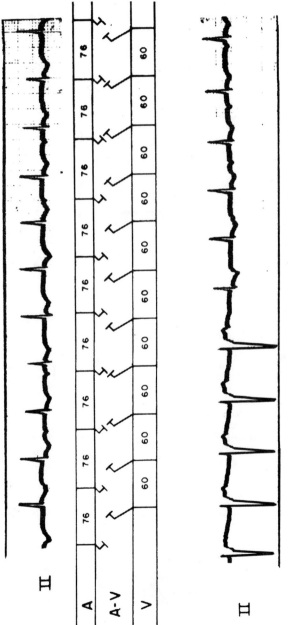

FIG. 1.10: Digitalis-induced double A-V junctional tachycardia (upper strip) and double A-V junctional and "slow" ventricular tachycardia (lower strip). Since this Figure shows three distinct (presumably automatic) arrhythmias, it can be considered as an example of triple tachy-cardia (double A-V junctional and slow ventricular).

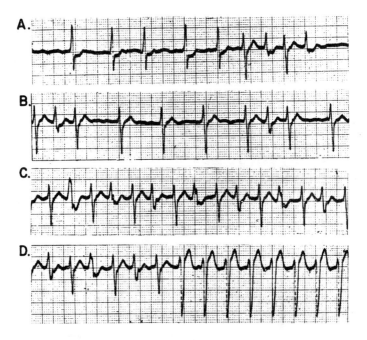

FIG. 1.11: Chronic atrial fibrillation with runs of digitalis induced
"slow" ventricular tachycardia (second strip), and bidirectional tachycardias (all strips). The bottom strip
shows double ventricular tachycardia (bidirectional
tachycardia alternating with unifocal tachycardia from
another center).

A-V BLOCK: Digitalis delays conduction through the A-V node by direct effect on the nodal tissue and indirect effect through the vague nerve, leading to prolongation of the refractory period and varying degrees of A-V block. This property of digitalis is responsible for its therapeutic effect in slowing the ventricular response in atrial flutter and atrial fibrillation.

First degree A-V block (prolongation of the P-R interval) constitutes 12.8 per cent of the arrhythmias induced by digitalis.[8] It is considered by some to be due to digitalis effect and, by others, to be an early sign of digitalis toxicity.[8] In either instance, further digitalization may lead to higher degrees of A-V block and other serious arrhythmias (see Figs. 1.8 and 1.9). We believe, therefore, that if it be progressive, first degree A-V block is an early warning sign of toxicity and warrants termination or reduction of the dose of digitalis.

Second degree A-V block (Wenckebach phenomenon) is a definite manifestation of toxicity. It is characterized by progressive lengthening of the P-R intervals until a beat fails to conduct, and progressively decreasing R-R intervals at the same time. This is due to the fact that although the conduction time through the A-V node is prolonged, the increment from beat to beat becomes progressively smaller.

Further administration of digitalis may lead to third degree A-V block (complete heart block), which occurs in 6.1 per cent of digitalis induced arrhythmias. In most cases the block appears "complete" (but is not "complete"), especially when an accelerated pacemaker coexists with high degree block. True Adams-Stokes seizures are rare. Digitalis can induce syncope through stimulation of the carotid sinus; this mechanism can be abolished by atropine. Seizures are more commonly due to ventricular tachycardia even in the absence of partial or complete heart block (see Fig. 1.11).

VENTRICULAR ARRHYTHMIAS: Ectopic ventricular contractions are the most common and often the earliest expression of digitalis intoxication. The mechanism of the arrhythmia is, either enhanced automaticity of the His-Purkinje system, or some type of reentry mechanism. The dysrhythmia may be unifocal or multifocal; and generally shows a fixed coupling to the preceding conducted beat. However, varying coupling also occurs, with a fully compensatory pause, or there may be interpolation between two beats without a compensatory pause. Although often a manifestation of digitalis toxicity, ectopic ventricular contractions may be a manifestation of myocardial pathology or heart failure which may disappear on using digitalis. The following electrocardiographic features are helpful in establishing the diagnosis of digitalis toxicity: (1) fixed coupling of premature beats of variable bizarre contour, resulting in ventricular bigeminy in atrial fibrillation with a slow ventricular response; (2) their multiplication in short runs; (b) bidirectional type of paroxysmal

tachycardia; and (4) other electrocardiographic changes attributable
to digitalis action, such as ST-T changes and automatic atrial or
A-V junctional tachycardia with block.

When bigeminal rhythm appears during administration of digitalis,
about 75 per cent of the lethal dose has already been administered. [8]
(Further intoxication may lead to multifocal or bidirectional ectopic
beats, ventricular tachycardia, or ventricular fibrillation). The
mortality rate when bigemimy and multifocal ectopic ventricular contractions appear as a manifestation of digitalis intoxication was reported in the older literature to be as high as 10 and 28 per cent. [8]

VENTRICULAR TACHYCARDIA: Paroxysmal ventricular tachycardia constitutes 11.5 per cent of the arrhythmias induced by digitalis
(see Figs. 1.9 - 1.11). The mechanism of this arrhythmia is an
enhanced rate of diastolic depolarization of the His-Purkinje system,
resulting in increased automaticity of the subsidiary pacemakers.
Underlying cardiac disease predisposes to this type of serious arrhythmia. The overall mortality in 20 cases of digitalis-induced ventricular tachycardia was 8 per cent and, in those patients in whom
digitalis was continued, the mortality rate increased to 92 per
cent. [8]

BIDIRECTIONAL TACHYCARDIA: This descriptive term indicates a
tachycardia with alternation in morphology and(or) direction of QRS
complexes. Usually there is alternation of polarity in leads II, III,
and AVF (see Figs. 1.9 and 1.11) and some esophageal leads, while
V1 only shows slight variations in morphology. This arrhythmia has
a multigenetic origin since it can arise in one or two foci located in
the A-V junction, bundle branches, divisions of the left bundle branch
and peripheral Purkinje fibers.

We believe that some paroxysms result from the association of an
automatic "slow" ventricular tachycardia with a slow ventricular
tachycardia arising in another focus as can be seen when comparing
the first with the second strip of Fig. 9 and the second with the third
strip of Fig. 11. Except during a cardiac arrest, bidirectional tachycardias are almost invariably due to severe, life threatening almost
pre-terminal, digitalis intoxication.

VENTRICULAR FIBRILLATION: This occasionally occurs as a
manifestation of digitalis toxicity; however, its frequency might be
greater than what the literature suggests. [8]   To our knowledge,
17 cases of digitalis-induced ventricular fibrillation had been reported
by September, 1968. [8]   It seems that in man, as well as in the
laboratory animal, there are at least two types of digitalis-related
ventricular fibrillation. One appears suddenly and responds to electric countershock; the other is preceded by gradual widening of the
QRS complexes. The latter cannot be abolished electrically. Aggressive antiarrhythmic drug treatment during the pre-fibrillatory tachycardia stage is the treatment of choice.

DOUBLE TACHYCARDIA: Double tachycardia is a term used when tachycardias originate at two dissociated ectopic foci. They include atrial and nodal double tachycardias (see Fig. 1.5), double A-V junctional tachycardia (see Fig. 1.10), atrial and ventricular double tachycardias (see Fig. 1.10) A-V junctional and ventricular double tachycardia (see Figs. 1.9 and 1.10) double ventricular tachycardias (see Figs. 1.9 and 1.11). By far, the most common cause of double tachycardias is digitalis intoxication. It has also been rarely reported following open-heart surgery (especially in operations involving the cardiac septa or their surrounding areas), in acute rheumatic carditis, acute MI, and (spontaneously) in very rare instances.[8]

TRIPLE TACHYCARDIAS: This includes double A-V junctional and ventricular tachycardia (see Fig. 1.10), atrial, A-V junctional and ventricular tachycardia and A-V junctional and double ventricular tachycardias. Calvino from Cuba has seen two patients with quadruple tachycardias due to digitalis toxicity.[9]

DIGITALIS AND THERAPEUTIC ELECTICITY: Digitalis-induced ventricular automaticity can be concealed. Vagal stimulation, a method used to slow the ventricular rate by producing sino-atrial block of A-V block, has been used experimentally in dogs to unmask digitalis-induced ventricular ectopic rhythms. Electric countershock may expose latent digitalis intoxication, when used in terminating supraventricular arrhythmias, even when there has been no previous evidence of digitalis excess. In addition, there have been some instances in which electrical discharges of low intensity (pacemaker range) and of high energies (countershock range) unmasked the toxic effects of cardiac glycosides at a time when they were not apparent in the electrocardiogram (for a review on this subject see reference 10).

In patients with digitalis-induced PAT with block not receiving antiarrhythmic agents, electrical discharges can produce extrasystoles and short runs of ventricular tachycardia. The arrhythmia is usually not abolished, as it is probably unifocal, and some studies have shown this type to be very resistant to countershock. On the other hand, as is well known atrial flutter is easily terminated by low-energy electrical discharges, as this arrhythmia is probably due to some sort of re-entry mechanism.

The appearance of extrasystoles in patients with atrial flutter does not indicate that the atrial arrhythmia was due to digitalis but that he had received pretoxic amounts of the drug, a pretoxicity manifested by concealed ventricular automaticity. Countershock-exposed ventricular ectopic rhythm in atrial flutter is most frequently seen in patients in whom a high degree of A-V conduction disturbance appeared after therapy. (Fig. 1.12)

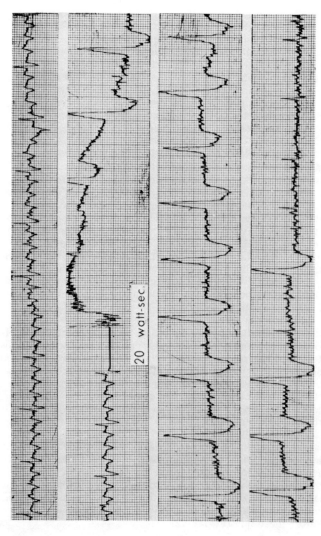

FIG. 1.12: Digitalis-induced ectopic ventricular rhythm appearing after delivering a low energy electrical discharge (cardioversion with 20 watt-sec) to a patient with atrial flutter with (digitalis related) high degree A-V block.

TREATMENT OF DIGITALIS TOXICITY: A specific digitalis antagonist is yet to be found. However, withdrawal of digitalis for a
few days or reduction in dosage and potassium replacement may
suffice for mild cases, i.e., digitalis toxicity manifested by progressively prolonged P-R interval (A-V block) or occasional ectopic ventricular contractions. Withholding of diuretics and restriction
of activity of the patient are other measures to be taken. For more
serious arrhythmias, more aggressive measures may be needed.

POTASSIUM: The value of potassium in treatment of digitalis toxicity is well established. Oral potassium chloride may be given in
divided doses totaling 4 to 6 gm for adults provided that renal function is adequate. When correction of the arrhythmia is urgent and
serum potassium level is low or normal it is administered IV in a
solution of 5% dextrose in water. Intravenously administered potassium is a safe agent when given under continuous electrocardiographic observation (safer indeed than orally administered potassium
chloride) and provides more physiological replacement therapy in
digitalis intoxication secondary to potassium depletion. However,
the use of potassium is dangerous in the presence of renal failure,
hyperkalemia, or high degree of A-V block (except when profound
hypokalemia coexists) and, in these instances, the potassium deficit
should be corrected slowly. The toxic effects of potassium have
been reported to be mitigated and its therapeutic effect to be increased when administered in the form of monopotassium glutamate,
presumably due to improved transport of potassium across the cell
membrane by the glutamate ion, but adequate clinical proof is lacking. Early hopes that potassium could serve as a specific antagonist
to the toxic effects of digitalis have not been realized. We appreciate
now that this salt is a non-specific depressant of myocardial excitability and that it shares several of the major disadvantages of other
depressant drugs. The sine qua non for its administration remains
cellular (myocardial) depletion of potassium. Unfortunately, serum
potassium is not an accurate reflection of intracellular stores and in
the absence of hypokalemia, the clinician must be guided primarily
by the history. Has the patient been eating adequately? Did the patient experience diarrhea, vomiting, or massive diuresis after administration of potent diuretic agents? Toxic dosages of digitalis
interfere with the uptake of extracellular potassium by muscle, and
transient hyperpotassemia is an ever present danger if this drug is
administered too rapidly. As noted, in patients with digitalis-induced heart block (during sinus rhythm) potassium may further depress conduction in atrioventricular tissue.

Intravenous Lidocaine is the treatment of choice of digitalis induced
ventricular tachycardia or in any ventricular arrhythmias coexisting
with depressed renal function. The method of administration of this
drug is similar to that outlined for the treatment of acute MI.

REFERENCES

1. Hurst, J.W., et al: Approach to the problem of cardiac arrhythmias. In: The Heart, 3rd Edition. McGraw-Hill, New York, p. 415, 1974.

2. Sudden coronary death outside the hospital. Circulation (Supplement) Number III 57: No 6, December 1975.

3. Mogensen, L.: Ventricular tachyarrhythmias and lidocaine prophylaxis in acute myocardial infarction. Acta Med Scand, Suppl. 513, pp. 1-80, 1970.

4. Pitt, A., et al: Lidocaine given prophylactically to patients with acute myocardial infarction. Lancet 1: 612-616, 1971.

5. Lown, B., et al: Coronary and precoronary care. Am J Med 46:705-724, 1969.

6. Margolis, J.R. and Wagner, G.S.: Arrhythmias in acute myocardial infarction. Booklet prepared for the Coronary Clinic Committee of the Council on Clinical Cardiology and the Committee on Medical Education, American Heart Association (This booklet can be obtained directly from the AHA).

7. Von Capeller, D., et al: Digitalis intoxication: A clinical report of 148 cases. Ann. Intern. Med. 50:869, 1959.

8. Castellanos, A. Jr., et al: Digitalis-induced arrhythmias: recognition and therapy. Cardiovasc Therapy 1:No. 3, 108, 1970.

9. Calvino, J.M.: Taquicardias quadruples debido a intoxication digitalis. X Congress Interamericana de Cardiologia, Caracas, Venezuela, September 5-11, 1976.

10. Castellanos, A. Jr and Lemberg, L.: Electrophysiology of Pacing and Cardioversion. Appleton-Century-Crofts, New York, 1969.

E: EMERGENCY PACEMAKER INSERTION
TECHNIQUE, INDICATIONS AND COMPLICATIONS
by Alvaro Mayorga-Cortes, M.D.

There are five modes of cardiac pacing: (1) fixed-rate asynchronous
pacemaker, (2) QRS-triggered synchronous pacemaker, (3) ventri-
cular-inhibited pacemaker, (4) atrial triggered or atrial synchronous
pacemaker, and (5) sequential atrio-ventricular pacemaker. The
most frequently used today is the QRS-inhibited demand ventricular
pacemaker. It has stimulating and sensing mechanisms. By the
sensing mechanism, the patient's own beat is recognized and inhibits
the pacemaker spike, firing only after a pre-set interval.

TECHNIQUE

An electrode for temporary cardiac pacing may be inserted by several
different methods. The approaches most commonly used are (a)
through a cutdown of the basilic vein and (b) percutaneous catheterization of a vein: basilic, subclavian, internal jugular, external jugular, or femoral. The subclavian approach is rapid, reliable, and in
expert hands, reasonably safe. The percutaneous technique, as described by Seldinger, requires the insertion of a guide wire through a
number 18 thin-wall needle. This is followed by the insertion of a
Teflon dilator over the wire and a catheter sheath of a size that can
accommodate the pacemaker electrode, usually bipolar. Under emergency circumstances, one can also use a number 14 or 16 needle;
that will fit a 5F catheter. For extreme emergencies, transthoracic
needles are also available with a small wire that can be passed
through the needle for direct ventricular pacing.

The optimal site for pacing is the apex of the right ventricle. Catheterization can be blindly accomplished by electrocardiographic monitoring, connecting the electrode to the V lead of a well-grounded
electrocardiograph. Large, negative P waves indicate the proximity
of the right atrium. When a portable image intensifier is available,
fluoroscopic visualization in the posteroanterior view will show the
typical horizontal direction of the distal end of the pacemaker electrode after crossing the tricuspid valve. Sometimes catheterization
of the coronary sinus will appear in the AP view superimposed on
the right ventricular apex. However, inspection of the cardiac
shadow in the lateral projection suggests the diagnosis as the tip of
the catheter is directed posteriorly and not anteriorly as when located
in the right ventricular apex. Also available is a balloon-tipped pacing electrode. When the latter is advanced to the superior vena cava,
the balloon is inflated and follows the bloodstream to the right side of
the heart. Regardless of the technique used, one should be able to
obtain constant pacing at a low threshold (usually less than 0.7 milli-
amp) and a morphology on the paced beats corresponding to that of the
right ventricular apex.

In the normally positioned heart, the apex of the right ventricle is the most anterior and inferior endocardial site. Depolarization originating in that site will generate a mean QRS axis directed superiorly and posteriorly. Thus, the morphology of the paced beat will have a LBBB pattern, a negative QRS in V_1 and a superior axis (left axis deviation) in the frontal plane, manifested as QS pattern in leads II, III, and aVF (see Fig. 1.2 in Section D). When pacing the right ventricular outflow, the mean QRS axis becomes normal and the QRS remains negative in V_1. Pacing of the left ventricle may be suggested by the presence of a dominant R wave in V_1 (a predominantly positive QRS). The implications, therefore, are that a 12-lead electrocardiogram, the measurement of the threshold pacing potential, and the radiologic visualization in PA and lateral projections are required before accepting a pacing site as optimal.

THERAPEUTIC INDICATIONS FOR PACEMAKER INSERTION

Atrial and ventricular pacing are invaluable in the electrophysiologic evaluation of patients with malignant arrhythmias, sinus dysfunction and pre-excitation with cardiovascular symptoms. However, very seldom is such evaluation considered an emergency. We will now refer to the therapeutic indications of temporary cardiac pacing.

Continuous atrial pacing may be indicated in severe sinus dysfunction, S-A block and to overdrive arrhythmias, as long as A-V conduction is normal. It has the advantage of maintaining the atrial mechanism. In the rare cases where atrial transport is essential for maintaining cardiac output and when A-V conduction is impaired, an atrio-ventricular (bifocal demand) pacemaker may be used.

The following are indications for a temporary demand ventricular pacemaker:

(1) Sick sinus syndrome: bradycardia-tachycardia syndrome, sinus arrest, severe sinus bradycardia.

(2) Atrio-ventricular block: paroxysmal A-V block, chronic bifascicular block with syncope, evidence of chronic conduction system disease with severe cardiac decompensation.

(3) Overdrive suppression for acute tachyarrhythmias: recurrent ventricular tachycardia, refractory PVC's, tachyarrhythmias of W-P-W syndrome, reentry tachyarrhythmias.

(4) Acute myocardial infarction: In ANTERIOR infarction, temporary pacing is indicated for the development of acute right or left bundle branch block, bifascicular block, paroxysmal A-V block and complete heart block. In INFERIOR infarction, cardiac pacing is indicated for the management of symptomatic bradyarrhythmias and symptomatic second and third degree A-V block.

COMPLICATIONS

Bleeding, phlebitis, thrombosis and infection at the site of entrance are well-recognized complications. A sterile technique and periodic replacement of the catheters are mandatory. The use of minidose Heparin to prevent thrombosis has not been evaluated but may be helpful in high-risk patients. The risks of the subclavian approach are puncture of the subclavian artery and pneumothorax; the latter, fortunately, is uncommon. In the setting of acute ischemia, mechanical stimulations of the right ventricle by the pacemaker electrode may induce PVC's, sometimes ventricular tachycardia, and rarely ventricular fibrillation. It is also estimated that in approximately 5 to 10% of cases, transient right bundle branch block may occur secondary to local trauma during pacemaker insertion. As a rule, it is benign and short-lasting.

A. Abnormalities Related to Capture: The most common cause of intermittent failure to capture is displacement of the electrode where repositioning is indicated. Perforation should be suspected when the following is observed: (1) a change from a LBBB to a RBBB; (2) diaphragmatic stimulation; (3) an unusual position of the catheter on x-ray. Withdrawal of the catheter and careful observation are necessary. Sometimes it is not possible to find acceptable pacing thresholds because of ischemia, fibrosis, cardiomyopathy, or an enlarged right ventricle. When pacemaker spikes are not seen on the electrocardiogram, the cause may be power failure of the generator or a broken electrode.

B. Abnormalities Related to Sensing: Lack of sensing can be defined as no recognition by the pacemaker of the electrical signal generated by the heart. In addition to catheter displacement, loss of sensing may be secondary to the development of a new bundle block, electrolyte imbalance particularly hyperkalemia and acidosis, antiarrhythmic drugs and extension of ischemia. Sensing can sometimes be restored by repositioning the catheter, converting from bipolar to unipolar pacing or by increasing the sensitivity of the sensing mechanism. Oversensing can be defined as sensing electrical signals other than the patient's own QRS. An example is the sensing of large P or T waves. This can be avoided by switching to a lead where the QRS has an appropriate signal.

REFERENCES

1. Lown, B., Kosowsky, B.: Artificial cardiac pacemakers. New England Journal of Medicine, 283:907, 1023, 1970.

2. Dorney, E.R.: The use of pacemakers in the treatment of cardiac arrhythmias. In: The Heart, McGraw-Hill, pp. 563-569, 1974.

3. Barold, S.: Clinical problems with temporary ventricular pacing. In: Modern Cardiac Pacing, Charles Press Publishers, pp. 115-134, 1975.

CHAPTER 2: TREATMENT OF ENDOCRINE EMERGENCIES
by Hibbard E. Williams, M.D.

DIABETIC KETOACIDOSIS

The clinical picture of diabetic ketoacidosis is familiar to most physicians and will not be reviewed here. Important clinical and metabolic features which must be monitored carefully during treatment include dehydration and hypovolemia, marked hyperglycemia and sometimes hyperosmolality, acidosis, depletion of total body potassium and a spectrum of neurological features culminating in deep coma. Infection and withdrawal of insulin remain the most common precipitating events with the former accounting for approximately 50% of the cases. With better understanding of the metabolic aberrations of diabetic ketoacidosis, the mortality has been reduced to less than 50% during the past decade.

Treatment of this emergency will be considered under 6 headings: fluids, insulin, potassium, alkali, glucose and other needs.

A. FLUIDS: Patients with diabetic ketoacidosis are markedly depleted of body water, usually in excess of losses of electrolytes. Hyperosmolality of moderate degree is often found. Therefore, large amounts of IV fluids must be administered rapidly to these patients. Since total body water depletion has been estimated at 5-10 liters in these patients, this amount of fluid should be replaced in the first 24 - 48 hours of treatment. Most patients can tolerate rates of fluid administration of at least 1 liter per hour in the first few hours of therapy. If hypotension is present, normal saline should be administered initially to re-establish a normal perfusing pressure. If this fails, whole blood or plasma expanders may be needed. If hypotension is not a problem, hypotonic saline may be given to correct the hyperosmolality. The potential dangers of cerebral edema with rapid transport of water into the central nervous system has led some to recommend normal saline in all patients with diabetic ketoacidosis, although the clinical documentation of this complication is poor. If heart failure is encountered, central venous pressure monitoring is essential to assist in rates of fluid administration.

B. INSULIN: All patients with ketoacidosis need insulin to correct both the hyperglycemia and ketoacidosis. Although insulin resistance has been suspected in patients with ketoacidosis, recent studies have dispelled this concept. Recent schedules of insulin therapy have shown that usually only 50 U of insulin is needed to correct the hyperglycemia and acidosis. A number of methods of insulin administration are now available. In general, a loading dose of 10-15 units of in-sulin is given either I.V. or I.M. Subsequent insulin may then be given either every hour I.M. in a dose of 0.1U/Kg or as a continuous I.V. drip using approximately 5-10U/hour depending on the severity of the condition. An infusion pump gives the most accurate insulin infusion in the latter method and small amounts of albumin added to the I.V. bottle may prevent insulin absorption to glass, although the importance of this is questionable. Both these methods have seemed superior to the more commonly used intermittent I.V. bolus tech-nique using 50-100U/hour, in that they have decreased the incidence of both hypoglycemia and hypokalemia while correcting the hyper-glycemia and acidosis as effectively as the high dose bolus technique. Regardless of the method of insulin administration, careful monitor-ing of blood glucose, potassium and serum acetone is essential.

C. POTASSIUM: Estimates of potassium depletion in diabetic keto-acidosis indicate that as much as 30% of the total body potassium may have been lost during the episode. Not surprisingly, therefore, hy-pokalemia still represents a common cause of death during therapy of these patients. For this reason, large amounts of potassium must be administered during the first 24-48 hours (often between 300 and 600 mEq). Initially, patients with ketoacidosis are hyperkalemic and therefore, potassium cannot be administered until this serum level falls to less than 6.0 mEq./L. Once this occurs, or if the pa-tient is normokalemic at the onset, I.V. potassium should be ad-ministered at rates usually between 20 and 40 mEq./hour. Careful monitoring of the electrocardiogram, serum potassium level, and urine output is mandatory. Decreased urine output is common in early ketoacidosis and this alone should not limit potassium adminis-tration since the total body deficit is so great.

D ALKALI: The acidosis of ketoacidosis may be quite severe and when arterial pH is less than 7.1 treatment of the acidosis with I.V. bicarbonate is required. However, acidosis with an arterial pH greater than 7.1, usually responds promptly to fluid and insulin ad-ministration and does not require additional bicarbonate. In fact, in this setting bicarbonate may be harmful since it may help lower the serum potassium precipitously and, in some cases, worsen the acido-sis, converting ketoacidosis to lactic acidosis. The latter phenomenon may be due to the protective effect of acidosis on the transport of oxygen to tissues. Correction of the acidosis may lead to increased hemoglobin affinity for oxygen (perhaps secondary to low erythrocyte 2, 3-DPG levels) and thereby, decreased tissue oxygenation. For this reason alkali therapy should be reserved for those patients with only severe degrees of acidosis, and when bicarbonate is administered in this setting, it should be done only to raise the arterial pH above 7.1 at which point insulin and fluid therapy would be expected to con-tinue the correction.

E. GLUCOSE: All patients with ketoacidosis have lost large amounts of glucose during the episode and complete correction of the ketoacidosis is dependent upon restoration of normal carbohydrate stores. Therefore, I.V. and oral glucose should be administered to all patients once the blood glucose level has fallen below 300 mg/100 ml. In fact, blood glucose should not be allowed to fall below 250 mg/100 ml in any patient with ketoacidosis since this could precipitate the appearance of cerebral edema. Oral carbohydrate feeding should be given to these patients as soon as they are alert and free of gastrointestinal symptoms.

F. OTHER NEEDS: Hypophosphatemia may be encountered in patients with ketoacidosis and may be very important in determining the response to therapy. For this reason, it should be treated when serum levels of phosphate are less than 1.0 mEq/L. Hypomagnesemia rarely complicates ketoacidosis but this should be investigated in any patient who does not respond to other modes of therapy. Since infection is so common in patients with ketoacidosis broad spectrum antibiotic coverage should be used in the patient who is febrile, even if a specific source of infection cannot be identified initially. Paralytic ileus and gastric dilatation should be treated with nasogastric suction when suspected. If the patient is comatose nasogastric suctioning should be preceded by intubation to prevent possible aspiration.

HYPEROSMOLAR COMA

This syndrome is differentiated from diabetic ketoacidosis by the following features: deep coma with focal seizures common, marked hyperglycemia (usually greater than 1000 mgm/100 ml), absence of significant ketoacidosis, more severe hyperosmolality (greater than 350 mOsm/L) and a much higher mortality. Infection as a precipitating event and marked depletion of total body potassium represent features of similarity with the ketoacidosis syndrome. Patients with the hyperosmolar syndrome tend to be older than patients with ketoacidosis; often have not had a previous history of diabetes; may have been taking drugs such as dilantin, corticosteroids, or diuretics which can precipitate the syndrome; and often have a number of complicating diseases such as congestive heart failure, chronic renal failure, chronic pulmonary disease, etc.

Treatment principles are similar to those described above for diabetic ketoacidosis. Fluid needs are high and generally half-normal saline has been recommended although some physicians prefer normal saline. Insulin requirements are quite low and only the low dose schedule should be used, either I.M. or continuous I.V. infusion. Potassium depletion has often been as severe in this setting as in diabetic ketoacidosis and large amounts of potassium must be administered. Alkali is not needed here because of the absence of acidosis. Glucose replacement will eventually be necessary once the blood glucose falls below 300 mg/100 ml.   Hypophosphatemia, hypomagnesemia and infection should be looked for. As noted above, many of these patients have severe complicating illnesses which also must be treated concomitantly with the hyperosmolar coma.

THYROTOXIC CRISIS

This syndrome representing the most extreme form of hyperthyroidism is characterized by hyperpyrexia, extreme weakness, dehydration, marked tachycardia, and a spectrum of neurological findings ranging from disorientation to frank coma. The syndrome is seen most often following surgery or an acute infection in partially treated patients with hyperthyroidism. The exact mechanism for the acute onset of this syndrome is unknown.

Treatment of thyrotoxic crisis includes a number of important therapeutic considerations. Because of the relatively high mortality of this syndrome (10-20%) admission of the patient to an intensive care unit is mandatory. Initial intravenous fluid replacement should include glucose and vitamins to meet the increased metabolic needs of the patient. In view of the increased insensible fluid losses large fluids loads are usually necessary to maintain adequate hydration. If congestive heart failure is present, careful monitoring of central venous pressure is essential.

Drug therapy is initially directed at reducing thyroid hormone synthesis and blocking its secretion from the gland. Prophylthiouracil (PTU) or methimazol should be used to inhibit hormone synthesis, although the former may be preferable because of its possible action in blocking the conversion of T4 to T3 peripherally. Because of the short half life of these drugs, they should be administered on an every 6 hour basis. Iodide in the form of oral saturated potassium iodide solutions or intravenous sodium iodide should be administered to inhibit the secretion of stored hormone. This should be done after starting PTU or methimazole in order to prevent an accumulation of intrathyroidal iodide and continued new hormone synthesis.

Propranolol has proven quite useful in patients with thyrotoxic crisis particularly for the tachycardia and other cardiac manifestations. Although not all of the cardiovascular complications of thyrotoxic crisis are catecholamine mediated, propranolol will quickly reduce the tachycardia and work of the heart. It can be administered either orally in a dose of 20-40 mg q 6 h or intravenously, 1-2 mg q 4 h.

Corticosteroids have generally been recommended during the initial stages of therapy although no definite proof exists of their need or efficiency. Phenobarbital in small doses (30 mg q 6 h) may increase the metabolism of thyroid hormone although several days are often required to achieve a significant effect. Finally, hyperpyrexia should be treated promptly with cooling blankets or ice water soaks in preference to aspirin since the latter may increase the metabolic rate.

MYXEDEMA COMA

Severe hypothyroidism may occasionally present as the syndrome of myxedema coma. This syndrome is characterized by the following clinical features: hypothermia, profound depression of physiological functions, bradycardia, stupor or frank coma, grand mal seizures, and florid features of classic hypothyroidism. Precipitating events of this syndrome have included infection, trauma, sedative drugs and exposure to a cold environment. Complicating features of this serious and life-threatening illness are alveolar hypoventilation leading to CO_2 retention and respiratory acidosis and hyponatremia secondary to inability of the myxedematous patient to excrete free water normally. Mortality in this syndrome may be as high as 50%, for reasons that are not entirely understood. Because of this high mortality, treatment in an intensive care unit is essential. The treatment of myxedema coma requires two major approaches: correction of the hypothyroid state and treatment of the secondary complicating features. Correction of the hypothyroid state should be instituted intravenously with either T4 or T3. The marked depletion of the extrathyroidal pool of thyroid hormone and the relative undersaturation of plasma binding sites requires that a large dose of T4 be administered (400-500 μ gms) followed by daily replacement therapy. Despite the potential dangers of such a loading dose clinical studies have not reported serious cardiac arrhythmias or precipitation of congestive heart failure. T3 may be used in smaller doses since this is less well bound to proteins and has a smaller pool. The potential advantage of a more rapid onset of action of T3 when compared with T4 is obviated by the fact that T4 can be rapidly converted in vivo to T3 in the hypothyroid patient.

Fluid therapy must be monitored carefully since myxedema coma patients generally have lowered insensible fluid losses.

Treatment of complicating features also requires careful monitoring of electrolytes, blood gases and body temperature. Hypothermia should be treated with central core covering leaving the extremities exposed. Too rapid warming may be dangerous in terms of precipitation of arrhythmias and too rapid an increase in metabolic needs. Hyponatremia can usually be handled with careful fluid administration of normal saline. Hypertonic saline is rarely needed. Hypoventilation may be marked, leading to severe degrees of CO_2 retention in which case assisted ventilation may be needed. Corticosteroids should be administered intravenously as these patients often have relative adrenal insufficiency once the metabolic rate begins to increase following thyroid hormone therapy. Finally, all medications given to patients with myxedema coma should be administered intravenously because of the variable gastrointestinal absorption.

ADRENAL CRISIS

This syndrome represents one of the rarest endocrine emergencies and is probably one of the easiest and most satisfying to treat. Clinical features of adrenal crisis include hypotension secondary to both hypovolemia and diminished cardiac output, marked nausea, vomiting and abdominal pain, hyperpigmentation and desquamation, fever, hypoglycemia and occasionally the clinical manifestations of hyperkalemia. A precipitating event is common and as with the syndromes described above, infection and trauma are common ones. Failure of the patient to take replacement steroids and exposure to excessive heat may also precipitate a crisis.

Treatment of adrenal crisis requires immediate replacement of fluids, electrolytes and corticosteroids. Intravenous saline should be given in quantities sufficient to improve hypotension and increase urine output. Corticosteroids in the form of hydrocortisone should be administered in a dose of 300 mg per 24 hours. This can be administered either by continuous I.V. drip or by every eight hourly bolus injections of 100 mgms. Hypoglycemia should be suspected and treated with appropriate doses of intravenous dextrose. Hyperkalemia will usually be quickly corrected by fluid replacement and corticosteroid therapy, and therefore other measures to lower serum potassium are rarely necessary. Metabolic acidosis similarly disappears rapidly with correction of hypovolemia and should not be treated with sodium bicarbonate unless initial arterial pH values are less than 7.1. Although fever is common in these patients, even in the absence of infection, sepsis should be looked for carefully and antibiotics used if the index of suspicion is high.

REFERENCES

1. Williams, R.H. and Porte, D., Jr.: The Pancreas in Textbook of Endocrinology, 5th Edition edited by R.H. Williams, Saunders, Philadelphia, pp. 502-626, 1974.

2. Williams, H.E. and Becker, C.E.: Endocrine Disorders in Clinical Pharmacology, edited by Melmon, K.D. and Morelli, H.F., Macmillan, pp. 290-353, 1972.

3. Felig, R.: Diabetic Ketoacidosis, New Engl J Med. 290: 1360-1363, 1974.

4. Mackin, J.F., et al: Thyroid storm and its management. New Engl J Med 291: 1396-1398, 1974.

5. Menendez, C.E. and Rivlin, R.S. Thyrotoxic crisis and myxedema coma. Med Clin N Amer 57: 1463-1470, 1973.

CHAPTER 3: GASTROINTESTINAL EMERGENCIES

A: ACUTE GASTROINTESTINAL BLEEDING
by Francis J. Tedesco, M.D.

Massive gastrointestinal bleeding is one of the most difficult clinical situations facing the primary care physician. This clinical problem demands that immediate and life saving therapy be instituted either prior to or while diagnostic endeavors are occurring. The mortality of massive gastrointestinal bleeding has been reported to vary from 5 to 50%. Some factors contributing to this unacceptably high mortality rate are A) delay in instituting therapeutic modalities while diagnostic attempts are performed, B) failure to assess the severity of the situation and C) failure to utilize the team approach; i.e., primary care physician, radiologist, gastroenterologist and surgeon. This may lead to unnecessary delays and, at times, diagnostic errors.

In upper gastrointestinal bleeding, the usual clinical presentation is vomiting of blood or coffee ground material and/or melena. In the case of severe, massive upper gastrointestinal bleeding, with orthostatic changes, the patient may present with bright red or maroon rectal bleeding with or without vomiting blood or coffee ground material.

In the initial evaluation of the massive gastrointestinal bleeder (Table I), a few pointed questions dealing with past history of ulcer disease, abdominal pain, alcohol usage, aspirin usage, and bleeding diathesis should be asked in conjunction with initiating therapeutic efforts to stabilize the hemodynamic status of the patient. In the compensated patient, a more detailed history dealing with the pain character, temporal relationship of the bleeding to vomiting or to pain would be reasonable.

Some of the immediate clinical findings which one needs to help define the severity of the patient's blood loss are blood pressure, pulse, and skin color. If the blood pressure, in a previously normotensive man, is less than 100 mm Hg systolic or the pulse is greater than 100, then one is usually dealing with a 20 percent loss of volume. If on sitting the patient up, the blood pressure drops greater than 10 mm Hg or the pulse increases by 20 beats per minute, then one is usually dealing with an acute blood loss of 100cc. If a patient presents in shock, the physician should not attempt to perform any postural maneuvers. Associated pallor, clammy, cold skin, and thirst are supportive findings. Skin changes such as telangiectasis, brown pigmentation of the lips and buccal mucosa or bluish nevi may give us a clue to the diagnosis of heritable disorders such as Osler-Weber-Rendu disease,

Peutz-Jeghers syndrome or Blue-rubber-bleb nevus syndrome. A rough estimate of the extent of blood loss may also be obtained from the history of the amount of blood vomited, passed per rectum or obtained by nasogastric lavage.

TABLE I
ASSESSMENT OF THE MASSIVE UPPER GASTROINTESTINAL BLEEDING PATIENT

1. HISTORY
 	
   A) previous ulcer disease and/or surgery
   B) alcohol or aspirin abuse
   C) antacid usage
   D) bleeding diathesis
 	
2. PHYSICAL EXAMINATION
 	
   A) general appearance - skin color, skin lesions
   B) blood pressure $\big\}$ orthostatic changes
   C) pulse

In general, the management (Table II) of a patient with a massive GI bleed demands immediate steps to stabilize the patient.

The first step is to insert a large bore intravenous line. At times, more than one catheter (14-16 gauge needles) may be necessary. Blood for immediate laboratory analysis may be obtained at the same time. Laboratory tests should include blood for type and cross match, CBC, BUN, protime, platelets, partial thromboplastin time and liver function tests. The physician should remember that a hematocrit obtained early in the course of bleeding may be misleading. The hematocrit progressively drops as the intravascular space is re-established with extravascular fluid. The immediate therapeutic goal remains volume replacement, initially with normal saline, Ringer's lactate solution, dextran or plasmanate until the blood is available. Packed red blood cells may be necessary in elderly patients or patients with a compromised cardiovascular status.

A large bore nasogastric tube (Ewald tube) should be passed after the intravenous lines have been established. This allows the stomach to be lavaged and large clots of blood to be removed. Also, if the nasogastric aspirate returns blood, this places the site of bleeding proximal to the ligament of Treitz. Remember, one needs to obtain bile stained fluid without blood or coffee ground material prior to concluding that the nasogastric aspirate was negative. Finally, the nasogastric tube may help define the duration and activity of the bleeding.

TABLE II
MANAGEMENT OF THE MASSIVE UPPER GASTROINTESTINAL BLEEDING PATIENT

1. Insert large bore intravenous line.
 	
2. Blood for type and cross match, CBC, BUN, protime, platelets, partial thromboplastin time and liver function test.
 	
3. Volume replacement
 	
4. Diagnostic tests:
  A) Ewald tube
  B) Upper gastrointestinal panendoscopy
  C) Selective angiography
 	
5. Therapeutic:
  A) Endoscopy (on the horizon)
    (1) electrocoagulation
    (2) laser phototherapy
    (3) tissue adhesives
 	
  B) Infusion of vasopressin
    (1) intravenously
    (2) intra-arterially
 	
  C) Sengstaken-Blakemore triple lumen tube
 	
  D) Surgery

If the patient continues to bleed, but not vigorously, or if the patient has either an alcoholic history of known varices, or if surgical intervention is contemplated, emergent upper gastrointestinal panendoscopy should be undertaken. There is no question that endoscopic evaluation has greatly increased the diagnostic accuracy in upper gastrointestinal bleeding. Unfortunately, at this time, emergent endoscopy has not clearly been shown to improve the morbidity or mortality in upper gastrointestinal bleeding. Newer developments may allow the upper gastrointestinal endoscope to become an important therapeutic modality. Some of these therapeutic modalities being tested are electrocoagulation, laser phototherapy and tissue adhesives.

If the patient continues to have uncontrolled active bleeding, at a rate of 2.0 ml/min or greater (p. 5 ml/min in experimental studies), selective angiography can be used as both a diagnostic and therapeutic measure. Arterial infusion of vasopressin has been demonstrated to control both upper GI and lower GI lesions. In most patients, vasopressin is infused at a rate of 0.2 U/min for 24-36 hours. If the patient stops bleeding, the vasopressin infusion is then decreased to .1 U/min for 12 to 24 hours and then dextrose is used to maintain the patency of the catheter for 12 hours. Recently,continuous intravenous infusion of vasopressin has been effective in treating variceal bleeders. Currently a prospective study is being performed to define the role of intravenous vasopressin, as a continuous infusion, in the management of GI bleeders.

If a patient is found to be bleeding from esophageal varices, the use of the Sengstaken-Blakemore triple lumen may be used if the above measures have been either not available or unsuccessful.

Barium contrast upper gastrointestinal x-ray remains one of the most useful diagnostic tests in a stable, non-bleeding patient. The value of barium contrast x-rays in the acute, active bleeder is limited.

In lower gastrointestinal bleeding, the usual clinical presentation is that of bright red rectal bleeding. The initial approach (Table III) to lower gastrointestinal bleeding is similar to upper gastrointestinal bleeding with (A) insertion of an intravenous line, (B) appropriate laboratory tests and (C) volume replacement. Once these measures are instituted the physician should do a proctoscopic examination. This examination may allow the physician to diagnose inflammatory bowel disease or to note that the bleeding is coming from above the area which is being examined by the proctoscope. If the patient is actively and/or massively bleeding, selective angiography may be used both as a diagnostic and as a therapeutic modality.

TABLE III
MANAGEMENT OF MASSIVE LOWER GASTROINTESTINAL BLEEDING
1. Insert intravenous line
2. Appropriate laboratory studies
3. Volume replacement
4. Proctosigmoidoscopy
5. Selective angiography

If the patient is not bleeding, barium enema contrast examination should be undertaken. The role of fiberoptic colonoscopy in lower gastrointestinal bleeding has not been as clearly defined as in upper gastrointestinal bleeding. It appears that fiberoptic colonoscopic examination has limited value in the actively bleeding patient. Colonoscopy seems to be of value in the non-bleeding lower gastrointestinal bleeder and as a complementary diagnostic test to barium enema examination.

Emergent surgical intervention must be considered for uncontrollable massive bleeders. The previously described modalities (endoscopy, angiography, etc.) should greatly facilitate the surgeon in deciding on the best operative approach. The decision of whether or not to proceed with surgical intervention should be made with the combined input of the primary care physician, the gastroenterologist and the surgeon.

REFERENCES

1. Brick, I.B., Jeghers, H.G.: Gastrointestinal hemorrhage. New Engl J Med 253:348, 511, 555, 1955.

2. Chandler, G.N.: Bleeding from the upper gastrointestinal tract. Brit Med J 4:723, 1967.

3. Mailer, C., Goldberg, A., Harder, R., et al: Diagnosis of upper gastrointestinal bleeding. Brit Med J 2:784, 1965.

4. Baum, S., Nusbaum, M.: The control of gastrointestinal hemorrhage by selective mesenteric arterial infusion of vasopressin. Radiology 98:497, 1971.

5. Malt, R.A.: Control of upper gastrointestinal hemorrhage. New Engl J Med 286:1043, 1972.

6. Dagradi, A.E.: Management of major gastrointestinal hemorrhage. Mount Sinai J of Med 43:338, 1976.

7. Law, D.H., Gregory, D.H.: Gastrointestinal bleeding. Gastrointestinal Disease edited by Sleisenger, M.H., Fordtran, J.S. Philadelphia. W.B. Saunders Co., pp. 195-215, 1973.

8. Papp, J.P.: Endoscopic experience in 100 consecutive cases with the Olympus GIF endoscopy. Am J Gastroenterol 60:466-472, 1973.

9. Papp, J.P.: Endoscopic electrocoagulation in upper gastrointestinal hemorrhage. JAMA 230:1172-1173, 1974.

10. Yellin, A.E., Dwyer, R.M., et al: Endoscopic Argon-Ion laser phototherapy of bleeding gastric lesions. Arch Surg 111:750-755, 1976.

B: THE ACUTE ABDOMEN
by Arvey I. Rogers, M.D.

"The abdomen is like a stage
Enclosed within a fleshy cage
The symptoms are the actors who
Although they are a motley crew
Act often with consummate art
The major or the minor part;
Nor do they usually say
Who is the author of the play
That is for you to try and guess,
A problem which I must confess
Is seldom made less easy from the fact
You seldom see the opening act,
Any by the time that you arrive
The victim may be just alive."

"The leading or principal symptoms are four,
They often are fewer and seldom are more,
Though infrequently minor ones come in and out
And make things more difficult, without a doubt.
The 'big' four I mention whom you must watch well
More clearly the site of their author to tell
Come right off the tongue in a simple refrain-
DISTENTION, RIGIDITY, VOMITING, PAIN."

Zeta (Z.C.)
M.K. Lewis and Company,
Ltd., 1962
London

DEFINITION

The patient with severe abdominal pain requiring acute decisions has an acute abdomen. Although the Dorland Medical Dictionary defines the acute abdomen as "medical slang for any acute condition within the abdomen demanding immediate operation", it is important to recall that abdominal pain may not be of primary abdominal origin, and most certainly not require surgical intervention.

APPROACH

The more urgent the clinical problem, the greater the need for acute and astute decisions and the greater the risk for error in the decision-making process when irrational action supersedes a logical approach. Underlying whatever approach the physician in charge applies to the management of the patient with an acute abdomen is the need to ask the right questions and to gather the data necessary to provide accurate or reasonably accurate answers. Some of the more important questions follow:

1. Does the patient have an intra-abdominal catastrophe requiring urgent surgical intervention? What evidence do I have presently that this exists? What evidence do I have to the contrary?

2. What additional subjective and/or objective data do I require to include or exclude more definitely the possibility of a "surgical abdomen"?

3. What pre-existing or acutely-induced medical conditions are present which may be associated with the simulation of a surgical abdomen or complicate its management?

4. What needs to be done to better prepare the patient for urgent surgery should this become necessary within the next several hours?

5. Have I gotten the help I need from colleagues to shed further light on the immediate problem?

The sections which follow should facilitate the process of providing answers and directing appropriate management.

GUIDING PRINCIPLES

1. Every acute abdominal condition should challenge the physician or surgeon to make an early and accurate diagnosis, for the prognosis depends on the early institution of appropriate therapy.

2. Morbidity and mortality increase in direct proportion to the delay in surgical management of a ruptured viscus, yet the early signs and symptoms of such a catastrophe may be so slight that continued observation seems justified.

3. The onus rests on the first physician seeing the patient to make as accurate an assessment as possible, principally to decide whether an acute abdominal emergency has developed.

4. Early diagnosis is often impeded by the fact that many acute conditions have their onset at night and patients attribute them to some sort of dietary indiscretion which has led to milder symptoms usually present at the onset and to the resultant delay in seeking medical assistance.

5. "The general rule can be laid down that the majority of severe abdominal pains which ensue in patients who have been previously fairly well, and which last as long as six hours, are caused by conditions of surgical import". (Cope)

ABDOMINAL PAIN

It is certainly unnecessary to understand the anatomical aspects of abdominal pain to evaluate properly the patient presenting with acute pain. Nonetheless, it is essential to recall that two general types of pain predominate in this setting, namely true visceral pain and referred pain.

True visceral pain is encountered early when the disorder is still mild; referred pain is noted when the condition worsens. The pain sequences mentioned may be observed in acute obstructive appendicitis which progresses from mild to severe disease:

1. Distention of the viscus (appendix) produces midline, periumbilical or low epigastric pain - true visceral pain.

2. Inflammation of the viscus results in lateralizing pain to the right lower abdominal quadrant - referred pain; and, finally.

3. Inflammation of the overlying peritoneum results in localized pain at the site of inflammation with muscle guarding and rigidity-referred pain.

REFERRED PAIN

An understanding of classic referral patterns for visceral pain is essential to arriving at early, accurate diagnoses by ordering appropriate diagnostic procedures suggested by the observed pain referral. Some clinically important patterns follows:

1. Renal pain referring to the testis

2. Referral of testicular pain to areas as high as T10 in addition to areas along L1-2 and S2-4; applies also to ovaries and tubes

3. Referral of appendiceal pain to the testis

4. Lesions irritating the peripheral portion of the diaphragm refer to the lateral chest wall near the costal margin.

5. Irritation of the central portion of the diaphragm refers pain to the upper border of the trapezius muscle on the top of the shoulder and lateral aspect of the neck

6. Midline diaphragm irritation refers pain to the tops of both shoulders

7. Structures derived from the embryological foregut as stomach, and duodenum pancreas and biliary tract refer pain to the epigastrium

8. Mid-gut derived structures as small bowel and colon (to mid-transverse region), inclusive of the appendix, refer pain to the periumbilical region

9. Hind-gut derived structures as the remaining colon, sigmoid colon, bladder and uterus localized pain to the suprapublic or hypogastric region

10. Pain arising from the cervix, prostate, and bladder neck is referred to the saddle area of the perineum.

DIFFERENTIAL DIAGNOSIS

Three categories of abdominal pain enter the differential diagnosis and should be recalled early in the approach to this problem:

1. Intra-abdominal lesions usually requiring surgical intervention;
2. Intra-abdominal conditions usually not requiring urgent surgery;
3. Medical conditions simulating the acute abdomen.

Tables I, II and III present examples of conditions in each of the categories.

The most accurate differential diagnosis is established by careful attention to (1) age and sex; (2) past medical history; (3) precipitating factors; (4) the pain itself; (5) associated features of vomiting, alteration of bowel habit, and the presence of chills and fever; (6) features on general physical examination; and (7) physical examination of the abdomen. It then becomes possible to be more logical and selective in the use of the laboratory and radiology departments.

AGE AND SEX:

1. Males have a greater incidence of perforated peptic ulcer and myocardial infarction

2. Females are more likely to have acute cholecystitis and (obviously) gynecologic disorders

3. In a child, think of appendicitis, mesenteric adenitis, Meckel's diverticulitis, vascular disease, pancreatitis, cholecystitis, and myocardial infarction

PAST MEDICAL HISTORY:

1. Prior abdominal surgery might suggest adhesions or recurrence of the original condition resulting in surgery

2. A history of established or suspected (periodic, rhythmic epigastric distress) peptic ulcer disease could suggest ulcer perforation or pancreatitis

3. Symptoms compatible with biliary colic (episodic, epigastric pain) suggest possible <u>acute cholecystitis</u>

4. A history of alcoholism, known biliary tract disease, or a prior history of <u>acute pancreatitis</u> always should suggest that possibility.

5. Prior episodes of abdominal pain in association with <u>diabetic ketoacidosis</u> should prompt a search for this problem in a known diabetic or in a patient with symptoms suggesting diabetes

6. A prior history of painful irritable colon syndrome or known colonic diverticulosis should suggest <u>possible diverticulitis</u>

7. A creamy vaginal discharge in a patient with possible exposure to venereal disease should suggest <u>pelvic inflammatory disease</u>

8. Recent amenorrhea in a regularly menstruating female suggests a <u>ruptured ectopic pregnancy</u>

9. A history of known rheumatic heart disease with mitral valve pathology suggests a <u>mesenteric vascular disease</u>

10. <u>Drug ingestion</u>? Thiazides, steroids, azathioprine (pancreatitis); anticoagulants (pancreatitis, rectus sheath hematoma, submucosal bowel hematoma, retroperitoneal bleeding); barbiturates (porphyrial); antibiotics (allergic reaction; Henoch-Schonlein purpura); oral contraceptives (pancreatitis).

A past medical history of abdominal pain of proven etiology can provide invaluable information when a similar presentation and pain pattern recur.

TABLE I
CONDITIONS USUALLY REQUIRING SURGICAL INTERVENTION

1. Acute appendicitis
2. Acute intestinal obstruction
3. Free perforation
4. Acute cholecystitis with peritonitis
5. Torsion: ovarian cyst, fibroid, omentum, tumor, diverticulum, appendices epiploicae
6. Rupture: Ectopic pregnancy, corpus luteum cyst
7. Rupture: Diverticulum, cyst, viscus
8. Mesenteric occlusion, ruptured aneurysm
9. Embolism at aortic bifurcation
10. Infarction of omentum or intestine

TABLE II
CONDITIONS USUALLY NOT REQUIRING SURGICAL INTERVENTION

1. Acute pancreatitis
2. Acute gastritis
3. Acute hepatitis
4. Gonococcal periphepatitis
5. Acute pelvic inflammatory disease
6. Painful ovulation
7. Medical condition resulting in 'peritonitis'
8. Retroperitoneal hemorrhage
9. Intramural bowel hemorrhage
10. Acute inflammatory bowel disease
11. Abdominal allergy

TABLE III
MEDICAL CONDITIONS SIMULATING AN ACUTE ABDOMEN

1. CARDIOVASCULAR LESIONS

   a) myocardial infarction
   b) vascular emboli
   c) acute pericarditis
   d) passive congestion of the liver
   e) periarteritis nodosa

2. CHEST LESIONS

   a) pneumonia
   b) pulmonary infarct
   c) pneumothorax
   d) pleurisy
   e) acute mediastinitis
   f) esophageal rupture*
   g) strangulated hiatal hernia*

3. OTHER MEDICAL CONDITIONS

   a) diabetic ketoacidosis
   b) tabetic crisis
   c) black widow spider-bite
   d) sickle cell disease
   e) Henoch-Schonlein purpura
   f) heavy metal poisoning
   g) Addisonian crisis
   h) familial hyperlipoproteinemia
   i) herpes zoster
   j) acute porphyria

* often require surgery

PRECIPITATING FACTORS OR ASSOCIATED EVENTS: Historical details preceding the onset of acute abdominal pain by hours or days could suggest precipitating factors and specific etiologies. For example:

1. Abdominal trauma might suggest a rectus hematoma, a ruptured viscus, internal or retroperitoneal hemorrhage; pancreatitis, or a vascular accident

2. An upper respiratory infection raises the possibility of pneumonia or pleurisy; mesenteric adenitis or childhood peritonitis

3. Heavy alcohol intake suggests pancreatitis or gastritis

4. Heart failure (especially right-sided) suggests passive congestion of the liver

5. Strenuous exertion could precipitate a myocardial infarction or a pneumothorax

6. A recent "insect bite" suggests possible arachnidism (black-widow spider bite)

7. Recent onset of vaginal discharge or known venereal disease suggests pelvic inflammatory disease or gonococcal perihepatitis

8. Associated joint symptoms suggest acute rheumatic fever, collagen vascular disease, sickle cell disease, inflammatory bowel disease, pancreatitis, lead intoxication (saturnine) viral hepatitis, or pelvic inflammatory disease (gonococcal)

9. Recent onset of skin lesions suggests inflammatory bowel disease or rheumatic fever (erythema nodosum); pancreatitis (fat necrosis); drug reaction or collagen vascular disease (macular eruption); herpes zoster (painful vesicular eruptions); hepatitis, Henoch-Schonlein purpura, drug reaction (urticaria)

10. Associated neurologic symptoms? Think of porphyria, lead intoxication.

The important elements in the initial evaluation of the patient with an acute abdominal pain are depicted in Figure 3.1 which emphasizes historical features.

THE PRIMARY SYMPTOM OF PAIN (Table IV): The pain itself obviously provides the most specific clues as to its etiology. Figure 3.2 illustrates the important characteristics of pain, an accurate description of which is most likely to result in a correct preoperative or nonoperative diagnosis. The following axioms may be applied to these characteristics:

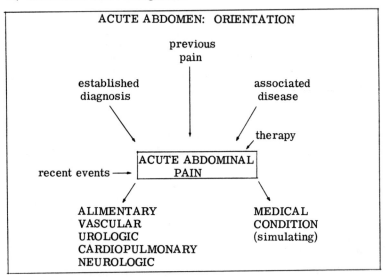

FIG. 3.1

TABLE IV
ACUTE ABDOMEN: NATURE OF ONSET

1. SUDDEN

    A. Viscus perforation
    B. Hollow tube occlusion (usually
       by a stone)
    C. Vascular supply occlusion
       (1) strangulation
       (2) volvulus
       (3) embolism

2. INSIDIOUS

    A. Appendicitis
    B. Cholecystitis
    C. Diverticulitis
    D. Bowel obstruction

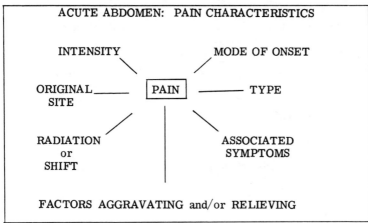

FIG. 3.2

1. When the patient can pin-point the onset of pain to a specific time or activity, or if it awakens him from sleep, or be of such severity as to cause him to faint, the usual causes are:
   a) a perforated viscus
   b) a ruptured aortic aneurysm
   c) a mesenteric infarction

2. And when the same immediate onset of pain builds up over several hours to a peak, think of:
   a) appendicitis
   b) diverticulitis
   c) ruptured ectopic pregnancy
   d) biliary, renal, or ureteral colic
   e) high intestinal obstruction

3. While pain of more gradual onset with the patient being unable to pin-point exact time which increases in intensity over days or weeks should suggest:
   a) appendicitis
   b) low intestinal obstruction
   c) incarcerating hernia
   d) urinary tract infection
   e) ectopic pregnancy

4. And do not forget that medical conditions as:
   a) myocardial infarction
   b) porphyria
   c) tabetic crisis
   d) sickle cell crisis
   e) acute passive congestion of the liver

   as well as others may present similar immediate onset type pain (see Table IV).

5. The original site of pain onset or the location of maximal, fully-developed pain may localize the lesion. Table V indicates conditions by common pain site.

TABLE V
ACUTE ABDOMEN: AREA AND COMMON CAUSES

I: EPIGASTRIC:

    Duodenal or gastric ulcer
    Duodenitis or gastritis
    Cholecystitis, cholangitis
    Pancreatitis
    Appendicitis (early)
    High small bowel or gastric outlet obstruction
    Subphrenic abscess
    Pleurisy, pneumonia, pneumothorax, pericarditis
    Myocardial infarction

II: PERIUMBILICAL OR MID-ABDOMINAL:

    Appendicitis (early)
    Small bowel obstruction or gangrene
    Pancreatitis
    Gastroenteritis

III. LOWER ABDOMEN OR SUPRAPUBIC:

    Colon obstruction or gangrene
    Appendicitis (right lower)
    Diverticulitis (left lower)
    Salpingitis
    Cystitis
    Mittelschmerz
    Torsion of ovarian cyst
    Ectopic pregnancy

6. The four basic types of pain, i.e., cramps, constant ache, intermittent colicky, and constant colicky each suggest possible etiologies:
   a) cramps should suggest inflammation, irritation, or obstruction of viscera or vasculature
   b) a constant ache, especially when increasing in intensity, should suggest peritoneal soiling and is also seen with inflammation of a solid viscus, marked overdistention of hollow viscus, or with impending or actual gangrene
   c) intermittent colicky pain is commonly encountered in early mechanical obstruction of the intestine

d) constant colicky pain is encountered late with obstruction to
a hollow viscus (biliary or renal calculi, small bowel obstruction and intestinal strangulation)

7. Classic posterior referral patterns include:
a) RIGHT SHOULDER: perforated duodenal ulcer, pancreatitis,
diaphragm irritation from other causes
b) LEFT SHOULDER: pancreatitis, ruptured spleen
c) RIGHT SUBSCAPULAR: cholecystitis
d) MIDLINE: penetrating duodenal ulcer (T10-12); pancreatitis
and renal colic (L3-4); and rectum (pre-sacral)

8. A writhing patient usually suggests colic from a hollow viscus,
while lying perfectly still should suggest peritonitis

9. Antecedent abdominal pain of a more chronic nature could suggest
an etiology for an acute process, such as:
a) PEPTIC ULCER: periodic, rhythmic epigastric pain
b) BILIARY TRACT: episodic, epigastric pain
c) MESENTERIC VASCULATURE: diffuse, mid-abdominal
pain 1-3 hours post-prandially

10. The association of vomiting with acute abdominal pain often points
to specific etiologies; important associations are illustrated in
Table VI.

11. The presence of diarrhea should suggest inflammatory bowel disease, an acute, infectious gastroenteritis, or a paradoxical
response around an obstructing colonic lesion.

12. The occurrence of chills and fever at the outset of abdominal pain
suggest an extra-abdominal cause as pneumonia or pyelonephritis.

GENERAL PHYSICAL EXAMINATION: Findings on extra-abdominal
examination frequently provide clues to a specific etiology for the
pain and, therefore, should be looked for carefully. Table VII emphasizes some of the more important findings and suggested diagnoses for abdominal pain.

EXAMINATION OF THE ABDOMEN: The ten most important elements
of the abdominal examination are listed in Table VIII. Especially important to remember are:

1. An immobile patient, abdominal wall rigidity, and absent bowel
sounds provide strong evidence for the diagnosis of peritonitis.

2. Muscle guarding may mimic rigidity.

3. The elderly patient presents special problems in the evaluation of
abdominal findings (Table IX).

4. The absence of bowel sounds is of ominous significance; listen long enough before you reach this conclusion.

5. Auscultate before you palpate and listen for bruit and friction rubs as well as bowel sounds suggesting obstruction (especially when occurring in association with crescendo pain).

6. Muscle guarding may preclude satisfactory palpation; soaping the patient's abdomen or immersion in a tub filled with warm water often relaxes abdominal musculature.

7. Rebound tenderness suggests peritonitis; it may be elicited over distended loops of bowel, however.

8. The iliopsoas test can be used to diagnose a perforated extra-pelvic appendix, while the obturator test may diagnose a perforated intrapelvic appendix; Murphy's sign is most often utilized to diagnose cholecystitis or hepatic congestion or inflammation (Consult Reference #2 for details on technique).

TABLE VI
ACUTE ABDOMEN: VOMITING

1. TIMING
 	
    A. EARLY: Pancreatitis*
                  Cyst pedicle torsion*
                  Bowel strangulation
                  Duodenal obstruction
                  Ureteral obstruction*
                  Biliary obstruction*
    B. DELAYED: Lower GI Tract**
 	
2. ABSENCE
 	
    A. Perforated ulcer
    B. Intraperitoneal hemorrhage
 	
3. ABSENCE OF BILE
 	
    A. Pyloric obstruction
 	
  * prolonged vomiting
** feculent vomiting

TABLE VII
ACUTE ABDOMEN: GENERAL EXAMINATION

IN ASSOCIATION WITH:	THINK OF:
1. Hypertension	a) Myocardial infarction b) Pulmonary embolus c) Pericardial tamponade d) Ruptured aneurysm e) Heart failure f) Mesenteric infarction g) Severe pancreatitis
2. Arrhythmia	a) Myocardiopathy b) Myocardial infarction c) Mesenteric occlusion d) Heart failure
3. Fever	a) Pneumonia b) Pyelonephritis c) Peritonitis/abscess d) Cholecystitis/cholangitis e) Mediterranean fever f) Porphyria g) Bowel gangrene
4. Pleural fluid; rales or friction rub of heart or lungs:	a) Pericarditis b) Congestive heart failure c) Pulmonary embolus/infarct d) Pneumonia e) Pancreatitis f) Myocardial infarction
5. Jaundice	a) Hepatitis b) Hepatoma; metastases c) Pancreatitis; biliary tract disease d) Hemolysis
6. Pharyngitis	a) Infectious mononucleosis b) Rheumatic fever
7. Significant adenopathy	a) Infectious mononucleosis b) Hematologic disease
8. Lipemia retinalis	a) Pancreatitis
9. Neuropathology	a) Porphyria b) Lead poisoning c) Tabes dorsalis

TABLE VIII
ACUTE ABDOMEN: ABDOMINAL EXAM

1. Inspection: Contour   Discoloration
              Scars   Peristalsis
              Herniae   Vascular pattern

2. Localization by patient

3. Systematic, graded palpation

4. Visceromegaly

5. Rebound tenderness; guarding

6. Skin hyperesthesia

7. Evidence of free fluid

8. Bowel sounds, rubs, bruit

9. Special signs: Ileopsoas
                 Obturator
                 Murphy's

10. Peritoneal tap

TABLE IX
SPECIAL CONSIDERATION IN THE ELDERLY PATIENT

1. Reduced awareness 2^O ASCVD

2. Degenerative conditions impairing communication

3. Stoicism; inability to localize process

4. Influence of steroid therapy

5. Improper attention to acute exacerbation of chronic pain

6. Inapparent physical findings 2^O flaccid abdominal abdominal wall and reduced inflammatory response

The rectal and pelvic examinations complete the physical examination and must never be omitted in the complete evaluation of the patient with an acute abdomen. Important points follow:

1. The prostate and seminal vesicles may be the focus of abdominal pain

2. The cul-de-sac may harbor tumor, abscess, or blood

3. Lateralization of pain may help localize an intra-abdominal or pelvic process

4. The finding of blood in the stool could suggest bowel cancer, an intussusception, or mesenteric infarct

5. Uterine size and contour, adnexal masses and tenderness, and the appearance of the cervix may suggest fibroid disease, ovarian cyst pathology, and ectopic pregnancy, or the presence of gonococcal or non-gonococcal pelvic inflammatory disease.

DIAGNOSTIC PERITONEAL TAP (Table X)

This procedure should be employed selectively. Techniques vary from institution to institution and relate usually to site of needle insertion and method of peritoneal lavage. Table X describes the indications and precautions applicable to the technique. The following facts are worth remembering:

1. The finding of pus or blood has the greatest diagnostic significance

2. An acid pH suggests a perforated duodenal ulcer

3. The finding of bile-stained fluid in a non-icteric subject suggests a perforated duodenal ulcer or a gallbladder rupture

4. Fluid high in amylase (2-3X higher than serum) suggests pancreatitis but may also be seen in perforated duodenal ulcer, small bowel obstruction, and mesenteric thrombosis

5. Fluid with no abnormal findings suggests a medical cause for the acute abdomen.

RADIOLOGY (Table XI)

Chest and abdomen films are routine in all patients with an acute abdomen. Table XI indicates the more important findings utilizing these readily available, non-invasive techniques. Films of initially poor quality should be repeated rather than utilized, because incorrect diagnoses may be made and you have a poor baseline for subsequent comparison. Repeat films within 12-24 hours may serve to clarify equivocal findings and simplify further evaluation. Radiographic studies other than chest and abdominal films should be selected based on suspected diagnoses:

1. An intravenous cholangiogram may establish an obstructed cystic duct in a suspected cholecystitis

2. Intravenous pyelography may reveal calculous ureteral obstruction

3. A barium enema may be necessary to confirm and manage a sigmoid volvulus

4. A lung scan may be required to exclude a pulmonary embolus; and a lung-liver scan essential to establish the diagnosis of a subphrenic process, possibly abscess

5. Abdominal ultrasound can detect aneurysmal dissection, calculous gallbladder disease; and pancreatic and ovarian cysts and other pelvic pathology

6. A gastrografin$^{(R)}$ upper GI series may diagnose an ulcer perforation.

TABLE X
ACUTE ABDOMEN: PERITONEAL TAP (or Lavage)

1. INDICATIONS:
   A. Blunt trauma
   B. Comatose patients with possible blunt trauma
   C. Confusing abdominal problems (high-risk patients)
 	
2. PRECAUTIONS: Scars
                 Inf. epig. vessels
                 Liver, kidney, spleen
                 Empty bladder
 	
3. INTERPRETATION: Appearance
                        WBC, RBC
                        Gram Stain
                        Amylase
                        pH
 	
4. COMMENTS:
   A. Greatest value when hemorrhage is suspected
   B. 25-30% false negative incidence
   C. Positive tap of immense value
   D. False positive tap may be seen with aspiration of retroperitoneal hematoma
   E. Intraperitoneal blood doesn't clot
   F. Saline lavage may be helpful

TABLE XI
ACUTE ABDOMEN: RADIOLOGY
1. Chest films 2. Abdomen films; Supine Decubitus Upright LOOK FOR: Pneumonia Pleural effusion (s) Cardiomegaly Dilated bowel Pneumoperitoneum Ascites Calculi; vascular calcifications Absent psoas shadow Visceral or solid organ prominence 3. IVP 4. IVC 5. UGI series 6. BE 7. Echograms

LABORATORY AIDS

An electrocardiogram is an absolute necessity to exclude myocardial or pericardial disease contributing to or a consequence of an acute abdomen. Basic laboratory evaluation should include a complete blood count and differential; a platelet count; urinalysis; coagulation studies; a blood glucose and BUN; serum electrolytes; a liver profile; and a serum amylase and lipase. These are all the tests usually required to evaluate the patient with an acute abdomen along with the other approaches already outlined. Serial studies are often required to clarify an equivocal process. More specific tests would be suggested by the possibility of less obvious etiologies for abdominal pain with or without associated peritonitis and are usually dictated by the patient's sex, age, color, and past history.

MANAGEMENT

The clinician's obligations to assure appropriate management of the patient with acute abdominal pain are:

1. Exclude peritonitis

2. Establish the status of coexistent diseases and manage them appropriately
3. Assure that a cardiopulmonary insult has not complicated the underlying process or its management
4. Exclude a medical cause for the acute abdominal pain
5. Work with quality radiologic and laboratory tools, repeating them whenever in doubt about their validity and as frequently as required to establish 'direction'
6. Consider the surgeon and radiologist equal members of the evaluation team along with you
7. Apply basic principles in the management of peritonitis felt to be present:
   a) Nasogastric tube for gastrointestinal decompression
   b) Intravenous fluids for rehydration and venous pressure monitoring
   c) Whole blood or volume expanders for massive protein and/or volume depletion
   d) Urinary catheter for accurate output measurements
   e) Removal of source of peritoneal contamination or prevention of continued contamination
   f) Removal of purulent material, blood, or intraperitoneal foreign bodies
   g) Drainage of purulent collections
   h) Appropriate antibiotics for systemic as well as intraperitoneal use.

Table XII lists some general management guidelines for the patient with acute abdomen.

This paper concludes with forty 'fun' axioms which are considered generally useful in diagnosing acute abdominal pain problems.

TABLE XII
ACUTE ABDOMEN: MANAGEMENT
1. Structured approach 2. Avoid 'snap' diagnoses 3. Admit to hospital 4. Careful Hx/Px 5. Basic laboratory 6. Chest and abdomen films 7. EKG 8. NG suctioning 9. Correct dehydration/shock 10. Consider medical conditions
WHEN IN DOUBT, REMEMBER THAT THE CONSEQUENCES OF FAILING TO OPERATE UPON A CONDITION REQUIRING SURGICAL INTERVENTION ARE MORE SERIOUS THAN THOSE OF PERFORMING A Dx LAPAROTOMY

AXIOMS APPLIED TO DIAGNOSIS

1. Think of extra-abdominal metabolic and inflammatory causes or you may undertake unnecessary surgery

2. Retroperitoneal disease will commonly produce anterior abdominal pain

3. Alcoholic hepatitis or viral hepatitis may present as an acute abdomen; congestive hepatomegaly may do the same

4. Non-penetrating abdominal trauma may produce intra-abdominal injury without causing a contusion of the abdominal wall

5. Attempt to examine the abdomen before analgesics are given, but do not withhold analgesics to the detriment of considerable suffering and obliteration of valuable abdominal findings

6. The development of severe abdominal pain and shock suggests a perforated viscus or strangulated obstruction; a ruptured aortic aneurysm should be considered as well

7. In reflex ileus, the abdomen remains quiet; in mechanical ileus, some sounds will be heard until bowel compromise develops

8. When classic peritoneal signs are present, ignore the white blood count if it is normal

9. In the obese or elderly, muscle guarding of peritonitis may be minimal

10. The patient with severe abdominal pain who lies perfectly still generally has peritonitis; the one who moves usually suffers from a migrating calculus

11. A bulge in the anterior rectal wall by digital examination may signal the need to empty the urinary bladder

12. When an injured person is unconscious, watch for signs of intra-abdominal hemorrhage or perforation

13. The shorter the interval between the onset of abdominal pain and vomiting, the less likely it is to be on a obstructive basis

14. The rapid onset of abdominal pain in a patient with mitral valve disease, atrial fibrillation, or an endocarditis with mural thrombus suggests mesenteric vascular embolization

15. Multiple abdominal scars suggests intestinal obstruction as the basis for abdominal pain

16. In a child with fever, a recent URI, abdominal pain, and tenderness, think of pneumococcal peritonitis

17. In a cirrhotic patient with ascites who develops abdominal pain,
think of spontaneous peritonitis

18. The abrupt onset of abdominal pain and rapidly enlarging liver
with ascites suggests hepatic vein occlusion; inability to induce
a hepato-jugular reflux response is confirmatory

19. A past history of episodic epigastric pain culminating in the de-
development of colicky abdominal pain, abdominal distention,
vomiting, and obstipation in an elderly patient should suggest
the possible diagnosis of gallstone ileus

20. The development of abdominal distention and pain in association
with bloody diarrhea suggests toxic megacolon complicating
ulcerative colitis or amebiasis

21. A past history of post-prandial diffuse abdominal discomfort
with or without back radiation culminating in severe abdominal
pain, hypotension, and bloody stools with dilated small bowel
suggests mesenteric vascular occlusion

22. Chronic constipation and recurring abdominal distention and discomfort culminating in obstipation and acute symptoms suggests
sigmoid volvulus; a plain film is diagnostic and a sigmoidscopy,
Ewald tube via rectum, or BE may be therapeutic

23. Pain which originates in the epigastrium and further localizes
to the RLQ with signs of peritoneal irritation suggests appendicitis, perforated peptic ulcer or acute pancreatitis

24. Abdominal pain in association with tender splenomegaly suggests
ruptured spleen, infectious mononucleosis, leukemia or pancreatitis

25. In a child younger than two, sudden abdominal pain, pallor, intermittent peristalsis with or without currant jelly rectal bleeding suggests intussusception

26. Lower abdominal pain with testicular radiation and unimpress-
ive abdominal findings suggests ureteral colic

27. Intense abdominal pain, vomiting, collapse, marked pallor, and
marked tenderness without significant guarding in a woman of
child bearing age suggests a ruptured ectopic pregnancy; culde-
centesis should reveal non-clotting blood

28. Repeated attacks of fever lasting a day or two associated with
peritoneal signs suggest familial Mediterranean fever

29. Abdominal pain precipitated by barbiturates suggests porphyria

30. The abrupt onset of right hypogastric pain, possibly precipitated by a cough in a woman over 40 on anticoagulants should suggest the diagnosis of a ruptured rectus abdominis muscle

31. Post-partum collapse with shock suggests a ruptured splenic artery

32. Bloody peritoneal fluid may be seen in hemorrhagic pancreatitis, mesenteric vascular occlusion, and hemoperitoneum complicating hepatoma

33. Abdominal pain and hyperamylasemia may be encountered in biliary tract disease, pancreatitis, parotitis, bowel infarct, ectopic pregnancy, perforated peptic ulcer, and intestinal obstruction.

34. Unexplained exudative ascites with abdominal pain should suggest pancreatic ascites; should amylase content be considerably higher than that of the serum, pseudocyst or pancreatic duct rupture is suggested

35. The occurrence of acute abdominal pain in a patient with cutaneous papulosis (Degos' syndrome) should suggest small bowel perforation and peritonitis

36. The finding of lipemia retinalis in a patient with severe abdominal pain may suggest hyperchylomicronemia and possible pancreatitis

37. Severe abdominal pain developing in a patient treated for diabetic ketoacidosis may indicate fatty liver

38. Relief of abdominal pain on sitting up (Deninger's sign) suggests pancreatitis or phlegmonous gastritis

39. The development of RUQ pain in a female with a past history of venereal disease suggests Fitzhugh-Curtis syndrome of gonococcal perihepatitis diagnosable by peritoneoscopy

40. Abdominal pain referred to the top of a shoulder suggests liver abscess, subphrenic abscess, pleurisy, perforated ulcer, pancreatitis, ruptured spleen and, rarely, appendicitis with peritonitis.

REFERENCES

1. Zeta, Z.C.: The Acute Abdomen in Rhyme, H.K. Lewis and Co., Ltd., London, 1962.

2. Cope, Sir Z.: The Early Diagnosis of the Acute Abdomen, ed. 13, Oxford University Press, London, 1968.

3. A.H. Robins Company series: GI SERIES, Part 5, Abdominal Pain; Part 6. Differential Diagnosis of Abdominal Disorders in Physical Examination of the Abdomen, A.H. Robins Co., Richmond, Virginia 23220.

4. Bockus, H.L., in Bockus, H.L. (Editor): Gastroenterology, ed. 3, Philadelphia, W.B. Saunders Company, 1976, Volume IV, Chapter 145. The Acute Abdomen.

5. Steinheber, F.U.: Diagnosis of the Medical Acute Abdomen. Hospital Medicine, June 1975, pp. 74-89.

6. Taft, D.A. and Viar, W.N.: Acute Peritonitis. Hospital Medicine. December, 1975, pp. 50-60.

7. Jones, R.S.: Differential Diagnosis of Severe Abdominal Pain. In: Gastrointestinal Disease by Sleisenger, M.H. and Fordtran, J.S., W.B. Saunders Company, Philadelphia, 1973, Chapter 25, p. 339.

8. Botsford, T.W. and Wilson, R.E.: The Acute Abdomen. Volume X of Major Problems in Clinical Surgery, ed. J.E. Dunphy. W.B. Saunders Company, Philadelphia, 1969.

C: FULMINANT HEPATIC FAILURE
by Harold O. Conn, M.D.

Fulminant hepatitis is one extreme of a spectrum of related diseases.
I plan to discuss the whole spectrum rather than just the one end,
which at the present time is a dead end--and a rare one at that.

Acute hepatitis is a physician's dream. It comes, it goes and in the
great majority of patients, it leaves few traces. For practical purposes acute hepatitis is acute viral hepatitis, but acute hepatitis of
any clinical type or severity can also be induced by drugs, and probably by other agents. In 90% of the cases the disease is anicteric and
largely unrecognized (Table I). In 85% of the jaundiced patients it is
a benign disease. In 10% it is more severe, but usually ends well.
In about 1% of the icteric cases it is fulminant, i.e. it is associated
with impending or full blown hepatic coma and 75% mortality rate.

TABLE I
CLINICAL DISTRIBUTION OF 1000 CASES OF ACUTE VIRAL HEPATITIS*

ANICTERIC	900
ICTERIC	100
Benign	85
Severe	10
Fulminant	1
Chronic Persistent	2
Chronic Active	2
*THESE ESTIMATES SUBJECT TO CHANGE WITH NOTICE.	

Actually, the outcome of fulminant hepatitis may be related to the
cause of the disease, e.g. viral hepatitis appears have a somewhat
better prognosis than halothane hepatitis [1]. Only a minute percentage of patients with viral hepatitis develop the fulminant form, while
a large fraction, perhaps one-third of those with halothane hepatitis
will have the fulminant type. Once fulminant hepatitis has developed,
however, the prognosis is equally grim for both etiologies.

What is this terrible disease? It has been defined as acute liver disease of progressive severity associated with profound encephalopathy.
Literally fulminant means "explosive", and clearly this disease is
sudden, severe, and explosive. It sometimes develops de novo, but

more frequently it occurs as abrupt deterioration of otherwise unremarkable liver disease. For example, a patient with viral hepatitis of moderate severity may suddenly on the eighth day of illness begin to act peculiarly, become confused within the next 24 hours, and die three or four days later. In general, the hepatitis which subsequently becomes fulminant, is more severe in terms of laboratory abnormalities than that which remains benign [2].

Diverse etiologic agents have been incriminated in fulminant hepatic failure. The incidence of individual etiologies can be calculated from groups of cases reported by Trey [3], Williams [4] and Sherlock [5] and their associates (Table II).

TABLE II		
ETIOLOGY OF FULMINANT HEPATIC FAILURE[3, 4, 5]		
VIRAL HEPATITIS	222	59%
DRUGS	107	28%
PREGNANCY	9	2%
MISC. & UNKNOWN	39	11%
	377	100%

Viral hepatitis makes up about 60% of the total, and two-thirds of the cases of fulminant hepatitis appear to be associated with hepatitis B virus (HBV) while the remainder are associated with hepatitis A virus, and probably with other hepatitis viruses, such as cytomegalic inclusion virus or herpes simplex virus [6, 7]. The second most common cause is drug-induced hepatic injury which may be caused by either idiosyncratic reactions, i.e. hypersensitivity, or by intrinsic hepatic injury. Halothane appears to be the single most common drug [1]. Only a minute fraction of patients who receive halothane anesthesia--usually several exposures--develop this hypersensitivity-like idiosyncratic, hepatotoxic response. For reasons that aren't clear, halothane-associated hepatitis is especially lethal and more than one-quarter of those in whom the syndrome is recognized die [8, 9]. Several other drugs such as α-methyldopa, isoniazid and ipronazid may induce a similar syndrome, which, unlike halothane hepatitis, only occurs in its fulminant form in a very small percentage. Other drugs, which are intrinsically hepatotoxic, such as carbon tetrachloride or acetaminophen can also induce fulminant hepatic failure. The latter agent, commonly implicated in suicide attempts in England where it is known as paracetamol, causes a large fraction of the cases of fulminant hepatic failure seen there. Carbon tetrachloride, which induces fulminant nephrohepatic failure, is no longer a contender for the title. Mitchell and his associates have recently presented evidence that isoniazid and, probably, iproniazid as well, usually cause intrinsic hepatotoxicity and only occasionally hyper-sensitivity-induced hepatotoxicity [10]. The remainder of the cases of fulminant hepatic failure are made up of a variety of causes such as toadstool toxins, fatty liver of pregnancy, hepatic artery ligation, postoperative hepatic failure and terminal stages of a number of liver diseases. Alcohol cannot be exonerated as a frequent cause of fulminant hepatic failure, but acute alcoholic hepatitis, which is fatal in about one-third of cases [11], is not usually classified as fulminant.

It is not usually possible to examine the hepatic histologic features. Prior to the development of the encephalopathy that characterizes it, there is little reason to have performed liver biopsy. Once it has declared itself to be fulminant, the prolonged prothrombin time prevents the performance of biopsy. Tissue obtained after the disease has run its course may not reflect the earlier abnormality. In those who survive, regeneration may obliterate the previous pattern. In those who don't, postmortem liver tissue may show only the lesion at its most advanced, altered by the effects of treatment, agonal alterations and autolysis. If there is some characteristic histologic pattern present to predict the development of fulminance, it has not yet been recognized. The presence of massive or submassive necrosis is, however, ominous.

Very little is known about the pathogenesis of fulminant hepatic failure. It has been reasoned that the syndrome is caused either by the accumulation of toxic substances not metabolized by the injured liver or by the absence of essential, hepatically-synthesized substances. No such substance has been identified although many metabolic derangements have been recognized and many candidate compounds have been nominated.

Although it is not standard practice to consider prognosis before surgery, in this disorder in which treatment is tentative and empiric, the factors which affect prognosis may provide clues to management. The prognosis of fulminant hepatic failure is extremely poor. Three-fourths of patients with this syndrome die, and survival appears to be independent of the type of treatment. The single most important prognosis factor is age. Redeker and his colleagues report that none of the patients over 40 years of age have survived at the John Wesley Hospital [2]. Trey found the prognosis significantly worse in patients over 40 than in those under 40 [3]. Survival appears to be associated with the regenerative capacity of the patient, and this is greatest in the young. Other investigators have found that a number of hepatically-synthesized substances are reasonable accurate prognostic indicators of death, e.g. serum albumin concentration of < 3.0 gm%, excessive prolongation of prothrombin time, and decreased plasma levels of α-1 antitrypsin [12]. Redeker, et al, have found that an increase in serum levels of α-fetoprotein may be the first detectable sign of recovery. The association of α-fetoprotein with hepatic regeneration suggests that recovery from fulminant hepatitis is a function of hepatic regenerative capacity, and that youth is the best ally one can have in this struggle. Indeed, the most spectacular recoveries have occurred in children. The original paper of Trey and his colleagues in South Africa [13], which reported impressive benefits of exchange transfusion, was based primarily on pediatric patients. In retrospect, the progressively declining survival rate with exchange transfusions as the number of cases so treated increased, appears to be related to the increasing mean age of the sample [1].

Treatment has run the gamut from completely rational to last resort, unfounded heroics. The most rational therapy so far attempted is immunotherapy of hepatitis B virus-induced fulminant hepatitis. In a cooperative, double blind, controlled clinical trial involving 28 American hospitals directed by James Mosley [14], 53 patients were randomly selected to receive hepatitis B antibody (Anti-HBs) or a placebo. Exogenous antibody had no effect on survival, and did not even abolish antigenemia (Table III).

TABLE III			
HEPATITIS B ANTIBODY IN FULMINANT HEPATITIS [14]			
	NO.	SURVIVED	DIED
HEPATITIS B ANTIBODY	25	9	16 (64%)
PLACEBO	28	9	19 (67%)

Cross Circulation trials between patients and volunteer subjects have been promising but the technical and ethical hazards are almost overwhelming [15]. Perfusion of patients' blood through human cadaver livers and with bovine and porcine livers has not improved survival although they have been associated with occasional recoveries, and more frequent transient remissions. Exchange transfusion, which may appear encouraging in individual cases [16], was not effective in a small controlled clinical trial [17] (Table IV). Plasma exchange does not appear to offer much more [18]. Total body washout, which was initially enthusiastically proclaimed [19], has quietly passed from view. Each of these forms of therapy has been sustained by occasional dramatic recoveries and by spectacular, transient improvement in patients who subsequently succumb.

TABLE IV			
EXCHANGE TRANSFUSION IN FULMINANT HEPATITIS [17]			
	NO.	SURVIVED	DIED
EXCHANGE TRANSFUSION	8	0	8 (100%)
CONVENTIONAL THERAPY	13	4	9 (69%)

Artificial support systems offer the most rational approach to the problem [20-22] and may provide the best means of establishing the nature of this disorder and of treating it effectively. Unfortunately, the encouraging results initially reported by Gazzard and his colleagues at the King's College Hospital in London [23], were not sustained. A change in the manufacture of the coated resin resulted in absorbtion of platelets, thrombocytopenia, and death. Despite this reversal, it seems clear that the rational removal of toxic materials must eventually play the major role in this drama.

Adrenocorticosteroid therapy, the last therapeutic resort for many difficult diseases, has, of course, been used in fulminant hepatic failure in conventional and in massive doses [24]. As usually happens, the results are much better in subjective reports than in objective, randomized, controlled trials. In a small study of fulminant hepatitis, steroid therapy did not enhance survival [25]. Bywaters has said, and I paraphrase, "Those who have enthusiasm have no controls; those who have controls have no enthusiasm." Steroids have failed to improve survival in most studies of viral hepatitis (Table V). Evans, et al, in controlled investigations, found that ACTH does not improve the survival, course or consequences of run-of-the-mill viral hepatitis [26]. Recently, Gregory and his associates found that in patients with clinically severe viral hepatitis (HBsAg-positive), most of whom had bridging hepatic necrosis [27], steroid therapy not only failed to improve survival, but appeared to diminish it [28].

TABLE V			
EFFECT OF STEROID THERAPY ON HEPATITIS			
DISEASE	SENIOR AUTHOR	REFERENCE	EFFECT
ACUTE VIRAL HEPATITIS			
Average	Evans	(26)	None
Severe	Gregory	(28)	None ?Adverse
Fulminant	Ware	(25)	None
CHRONIC PERSISTENT HEPATITIS	—	—	Not Studied
CHRONIC ACTIVE LIVER DISEASE			
Mild	—	—	Not Studied
Severe	Soloway	(29)	Excellent

I believe that there is no effective, definitive therapy for fulminant hepatic failure at the present time. I assume whenever I see ful-minant hepatic failure that it is pseudo-fulminant hepatic failure, which I define as non-fulminant hepatic failure with non-hepato-genous encephalopathy.

Pseudo-fulminant hepatic failure may occur, for example, in benign cases of hepatitis in whom severe hypoglycemia is present. Ad-ministration of glucose converts "fulminant" hepatitis to ordinary, benign hepatitis. Failure to recognize or treat the hypoglycemia may result in another fulminant death. Incidentally, steroid treat-ment or exchange transfusions might conceivably save such patients by raising blood sugar levels, although for the wrong reasons.

Pseudo-fulminant hepatic failure may also result from benign liver disease plus hyperammonemia. McDermott reported a patient with ureterosigmoid implants who developed viral hepatitis, and then, suddenly, nitrogenous encephalopathy[33]. Antiammonia therapy reversed the disease. Constipation in a patient with hepatitis may cause nitrogenous encephalopathy. I have seen such a case re-versed by enemas. Sedatives, analgesics and tranquilizers in the presence of modest liver damage may induce disproportionately severe depression of the central nervous system. More recognition of the pharmaceutical contribution to the encephalopathy alters prog-nosis and therapy. Incidentally, Schenker and his associates have shown that oxazepam, which can be metabolized normally by patients with hepatic parenchymal injury, unlike diazepam, which cannot[35], is the ideal tranquilizer for patients with liver disease. It is prob-ably the safest agent available for hyperactive patients with active parenchymal liver disease. Other potential, encephalopathogenic agents must be avoided in patients with liver disease and sought as possible precipitators of false fulminant hepatic failure. In addition, nonspecific therapy in such patients must maintain blood volume, blood pressure and oxygen-carrying capacity. Electrolyte abnor-malities and acid-base derangements must be corrected. Azotemia and hyperammonemia must be minimized by a low protein diet and by neomycin, lactulose or both (Table VI). Pneumonitis must be pre-vented or, when present, treated vigorously. Finally one must pre-vent and treat cerebral edema which is frequent in fulminant hepa-titis, and may often be the cause of death[33]. Unfortunately, safe, effective treatment of this complication is not available.

The number of dramatic forms of therapy available attest to the in-efficacy of all. The first law of pharmacology states that the number of drugs advocated for the treatment of a disease is inversely pro-portional to the effectiveness of any. The ever-proliferating number of treatments of fulminant hepatic failure tell us that none is effective.

TABLE VI
CONSERVATIVE MANAGEMENT OF FULMINANT HEPATIC FAILURE

1. Treat hepatic encephalopathy (protein restriction, neomycin lactulose)

2. Identify and treat non-hepatic causes of encephalopathy (hypoglycemia, renal failure, sepsis)

3. Avoid Central Nervous System depressants

4. Maintain blood volume and cardiac output

5. Treat electrolyte abnormalities (hyponatremia, hypokalemia)

REFERENCES

1. Trey, C., Lipworth, L., Chalmers, T., et al: Fulminant hepatic failure: Presumable contribution of halothane. N Engl J. Med 279:798-801, 1968.

2. Redeker, A.G.: Fulminant hepatitis. In: The Liver and Its Diseases, ed. by Schaffner, F., Sherlock, S., Leevy, C.M. Intercontinental Med Book Co., pp. 149-155, 1974.

3. Trey, C.: The fulminant hepatic failure surveillance study: Brief review of the effects of presumed etiology and age of survival. Can Med Assoc J 106:525-527, 1972.

4. Gazzard, B.G., et al: Charcoal haemoperfusion in the treatment of fulminant hepatic failure. Lancet 1:1301-1307, 1974.

5. Sherlock, S.: Acute (Fulminant) hepatic failure. In: Diseases of the Liver and Biliary Tract, 4th Edition. Blackwell Scientific Publications, London, pp. 107-121, 1975.

6. Burnell, J.M., et al: Observations on cross circulation in man. Am J Med 38:832-841, 1965.

7. Anuras, S., Summers, R.: Fulminant herpes simplex hepatitis in an adult: Report of a case in a renal transplant recipient. Gastroenterology 70:425-428, 1976.

8. Conn, H.O.: Halothane-associated hepatitis: A disease of medical progress. Isr J Med Sci 10:404-414, 1974.

9. Walton, B., et al: Unexplained hepatitis following halothane. Br Med J 2:1171-1176, 1976.

10. Mitchell, J.R., Jollow, D.J.: Metabolic activation of drugs to toxic substances. Gastroenterology 68:392-410, 1975.

11. Blitzer, B.L., et al: Adrenocorticosteroid therapy in alcoholic hepatitis: A prospective, double-blind randomized study. Am J Dig Dis 22: (April) 1977

12. Rueff, B., et al: Alpha antitrypsin and fulminant hepatitis. Gastroenterology 68:1084, 1975.

13. Trey, C., et al: Treatment of hepatic coma by exchange blood transfusion. N Engl J Med 274:473-481, 1966.

14. Acute Hepatic Failure Study Group: Failure of specific immunotherapy in fulminant type B hepatitis. Ann Intern Med (in press) 1977.

15. Burnell, J.M., et al: Acute hepatic failure treated by cross circulation. Arch Intern Med 132:493-498, 1973.

16. Lewis, J.D., et al: Exchange transfusion in hepatic coma: Factors affecting results, with long-term follow-up data. Am J Surg 129:125-129, 1975.

17. Redeker, A.G., Yamahiro, H.S.: Controlled trial of exchange-transfusion therapy in fulminant hepatitis. Lancet 1:3-6, 1973.

18. Lepore, M.J., Martel, A.J.: Plasmapheresis with plasma exchange in hepatic coma: methods and results in five patients with acute fulminant hepatic necrosis. Ann Intern Med 72:164-174, 1970.

19. Klebanoff, G., et al: Total-body washout in hepatic coma. N Engl J Med 289:807, 1973.

20. Willson, R.A. et al: Toward an artificial liver. II Removal of cholephilic anions from dogs with biliary obstruction, by hemoperfusion through charged and uncharged resins. Gastroenterology 66:95-107, 1974.

21. Weston, M.J., et al: Effects of haemoperfusion through charcoal or XAD-2 resin on an animal model of fulminant liver failure. Gut 15:482-486, 1974.

22. Williams, R.: Artificial liver support in fulminant hepatic failure. Bull NY Acad Med 51:508-518, 1975.

23. Gazzard, B.G., et al: Charcoal haemoperfusion in the treatment of fulminant hepatic failure. Lancet 1:1301-1305, 1974.

24. Ducci, H., Katz, R.: Cortisone, ACTH and antibiotics in fulminant hepatitis. Gastroenterology 21:357-374, 1952.

25. Ware, A.J., et al: A controlled trial of steroid therapy in massive hepatic necrosis. Am J Gastroenterol 62:130-133, 1974.

26. Evans, A.S., et al: Adrenal hormone therapy in viral hepatitis. 1. The effect of ACTH in the acute disease. Ann Intern Med 38:1115-1133,1953.

27. Klatskin, G.: Subacute hepatic necrosis and postnecrotic cirrhosis due to anicteric infections with the hepatitis virus. Am J Med 25:333-358, 1958.

28. Gregory, P.B., et al: Steroid therapy in severe viral hepatitis: a double-blind, randomized trial of methylprednisolone versus placebo. N Engl J Med 70:425-428, 1976.

29. Soloway, R.D., et al: Clinical biochemical and histological remission of severe chronic active liver disease: A controlled study of treatments and early prognosis. Gastroenterology 63: 820-833, 1972.

30. Porter, H., et al: Corticosteroid therapy in severe alcoholic hepatitis: A double-blind drug trial. N Engl J Med 284:1350-1355, 1971.

31. Campra, J., et al: Prednisone therapy of acute alcoholic hepatitis: Report of a controlled trial. Ann Intern Med 79:625-631, 1973.

32. Helman, R., et al: Alcoholic hepatitis: Natural history and evaluation of prednisolone therapy. Ann Intern Med 74:311-321, 1971.

33. McDermott, W.V. Jr.: Diversion of urine to the intestines as a factor in ammoniagenic coma. N Engl J Med 256:460-462, 1957.

34. Shull, H.J. Jr., et al: Normal disposition of oxazepam in acute viral hepatitis and cirrhosis. Ann Intern Med 84:420-425 , 1976.

D: ACUTE PANCREATITIS
by Francis J. Tedesco, M.D.

Pancreatitis is an acute inflammatory process whose pathogenesis remains unclear. This inflammatory response varies from mild edematous pancreatitis to a life threatening acute hemorrhagic necrotic pancreatitis. It has been reported that the acute hemorrhagic necrotic pancreatitis has a mortality as high as 80%. This considerable mortality may now be less since the advent of more aggressive fluid therapy, careful patient monitoring, peritoneal dialysis and, on occasion, surgical intervention. The exact role peritoneal dialysis and/or surgery plays in the management of acute hemorrhagic pancreatitis awaits careful, prospective evaluations.

The major clinical signs (Table I) of acute pancreatitis are nausea, vomiting and abdominal pain.

TABLE I
CLINICAL SYMPTOMS AND SIGNS
1. Nausea
2. Vomiting
3. Abdominal pain
4. Hypotension
5. Tachycardia
6. Abdominal tenderness ± rebound
7. Decreased to absent bowel signs
8. Cullen's sign
9. Gray Turner's sign

The pain has been described as sharp, boring, abrupt and severe. Depending on the site and severity of the inflamed area, the pain may be in the epigastrium, over the entire abdomen, left lower thorax, or radiating into the back.

The physical findings are varied. Abdominal tenderness, again depending upon the severity of involvement, may vary from minimal to extremely severe with rebound tenderness. A boardlike abdomen, connotating free perforation, is usually not found. Bowel sounds are decreased to absent. The patient may be febrile, hypotensive with significant tachycardia, dyspneic and extremely apprehensive. Other less common clinical signs are tender, nodular erythematous skin lesions secondary to fat necrosis, Gray-Turner's sign (bluish discoloration of the flanks), Cullen's sign (periumbilical discoloration) and arthritis.

Laboratory evaluation (Table II) demonstrates an elevation of serum amylase, lipase, glucose and occasional bilirubin. Urinary amylase likewise is usually elevated. A more sensitive and specific test is an elevation of the amylase/creatinine clearance ratio in patients with hyperamylasemia secondary to pancreatitis. This ratio is calculated as follows:

$$\frac{\text{Amylase clearance}}{\text{Creatine clearance}} = \frac{\text{Urine Amylase}}{\text{Serum Amylase}} \times \frac{\text{Serum Creatinine}}{\text{Urine Creatinine}} \times 100$$

The upper limit of normal clearance being approximately 5.5 per cent.

TABLE II
LABORATORY FINDINGS
Serum amylase – ↑
Serum lipase – ↑
Serum glucose – ↑
Urinary amylase – ↑
Amylase/creatinine clearance ratio – ↑

Roentgenographic findings can be supportive and help eliminate other causes of acute abdomen. One can see sentinel loops, pancreatic calcifications, pleural effusions, and elevation of the left diaphragm. With barium studies, mucosal pattern can be defined, and compression or distortion by a pseudocyst may be elicited.

The Treatment of Acute Pancreatitis (Table III):

1. Maintenance of blood volume: This is the single most important step in the management of patients with acute pancreatitis. One must remember that large quantities of fluid are lost into the retroperitoneal space and abdomen. The magnitude of fluid losses are comparable to those that occur in severe burn patients. With patients who are severely hypotensive and hemoconcentrated, treatment may include plasma, albumin, low molecular-weight dextran and, at times, blood. Electrolyte solutions (i.e., normal

saline, Ringer's lactate) alone may not be adequate to maintain circulating volume. Implicit in the replacement of large amounts of volume is the need for careful and continuous monitoring of central venous pressure.

2. Nasogastric suction: The rational for nasogastric suctioning is (a) decreased pancreatic secretions and (b) diminished abdominal distention. A recent study dealing with patients with alcoholic pancreatitis was unable to prove that nasogastric suction altered the clinical course, narcotic requirement or duration of amylase elevation when compared to patients without nasogastric suction.

TABLE III
TREATMENT
1. Volume replacement
2. Nasogastric suction
3. Calcium gluconate
4. Glucagon, Trasylol
5. Peritoneal dialysis
6. Surgery

3. Other considerations which still need further controlled prospective evaluations are:
   (a) Glucagon: the basis for its use lies in the fact that glucagon suppresses pancreatic exocrine secretion.

   (b) Trasylol (aprotinin): a peptidase inhibitor which is extracted from bovine parotid glands. The postulated mechanism of action is that trasylol is a kallikrein-trypsin inhibitor. The importance of this is the postulation that the kallikreins release kinins, which increase vascular permeability and continued damage to the pancreas. A recent prospective study seemed to demonstrate a decreased mortality in the trasylol-treated group. Further evaluations are necessary.

   (c) Steroids: unproven modality which is used to decrease pancreatic inflammation.

4. Calcium gluconate: May be necessary to treat the neuromuscular irritability secondary to hypocalcemia. The cause of the hypocalcemia is, in a large part, due to the formation of calcium soaps.

5. Insulin: In severe attacks, marked hyperglycemia may occur. Small doses of insulin can be utilized to alter hyperosmolar and hyperglycemic effects.

6. Antibiotics: The routine is controversial. Several recent papers have failed to demonstrate benefit in acute pancreatitis.

7. Peritoneal dialysis: The role of peritoneal dialysis is, as yet, not defined. The postulation is that peritoneal lavage would remove the toxic products (circulating proteolytic enzymes and vasoactive polypeptides) from the peritoneal cavity and ameliorate the disease process. In uncontrolled observations, dramatic responses have been reported. Further controlled evaluations are needed.

8. Surgery: The role of surgery with respect to relative risks and benefits is undefined. Certain centers have advocated extensive surgical intervention. Like peritoneal lavage, this modality of treatment needs prospective controlled evaluation.

In summary, much of what we do for patients with pancreatitis is mainly supportive and the other therapeutic endeavors need more careful, controlled evaluations.

REFERENCES

1. Levant, J.A., et al: Nasogastric suction in the treatment of alcoholic pancreatitis. JAMA 229:51, 1974.

2. Banks, P.A.: Acute Pancreatitis. Gastroenterology 61:382, 1971.

3. Trapnell, J.E., et al: A controlled trial of trasylol in acute pancreatitis. Br J Surg 61:177, 1974.

4. Nugent, F.W., et al: Comprehensive treatment of acute hemorrhagic pancreatitis. Amer J Gastro 47:511, 1967.

5. Rosato, E.E., et al: Peritoneal lavage therapy in hemorrhagic pancreatitis. Surgery 47:511, 1967.

6. Gjessing, J.: Peritoneal dialysis in severe acute hemorrhagic pancreatitis. Acta Chic Scand 133:645, 1967.

7. Ronson, J.H., et al: Prognostic signs and non-operative peritoneal lavage in acute pancreatitis. S G & O 143:209, 1976.

8. Lawson, D.W., et al: Surgical treatment of acute necrotizing pancreatitis. Annals Surg 172:605, 1970.

9. Warshaw, A.L., et al: Increased renal clearance of amylase in diagnosis of acute pancreatitis. NEJM 292:325, 1975.

CHAPTER 4: HEMATOLOGIC EMERGENCIES

A: HEMORRHAGIC DISORDERS
by R. Judith Ratzan, M.D.

The acute hemorrhagic disorders include a variety of bleeding
emergencies of both acquired and hereditary etiologies. A complete understanding of primary hemostasis, secondary hemostasis
and fibrinolysis is important in evaluating these situations.

Primary hemostasis refers to the ability of the blood vessel to contract and activate platelets by exposure to collagen. The activated
platelets aggregate, degranulate and finally, release endogenous
ADP, recruiting other platelets and causing irreversible aggregation and the formation of a platelet clot.

Secondary hemostasis refers to the activation of the coagulation cascade by such things as collagen or platelet phospholipid (see Fig. 4.1).
The end result is the production of a fibrin clot.

It is important to note that concomitant with the initiation of coagulation is the initiation of fibrinolysis. A delicate balance is maintained between these two processes.

The emergency evaluation of the patient who presents acutely bleeding must include the differentiation of bleeding due to: 1) trauma or
blood vessel disruption, 2) a platelet abnormality, 3) a coagulation
factor abnormality, and 4) excessive fibrinolysis or a combination
of 3 and 4 in such disorders as disseminated intravascular coagulation (DIC).

1. BLEEDING DUE TO TRAUMA OR BLOOD VESSEL DISRUPTION:
This is usually easy to identify and is frequently associated with
massive blood loss. Treatment obviously includes control of bleeding, maintenance of volume and prevention of shock. This may require massive blood replacement with possible consequences. (Table I).

TABLE I		
	FRESH BLOOD	STORED BLOOD
RBC	+	+
Normal 2, 3, DPG	+	-
WBC	+	-
Platelets	+	-
Factor V	+	-
Factor VIII	+	-
Other clotting factors	+	+

Fresh blood has all the blood components necessary for adequate hemostasis. Stored blood, however, does not and if large amounts of stored whole blood are given to a patient with massive bleeding, it is understandable that after the blood volume has been replaced, the now circulating blood will be deficient in platelets, Factor V and VIII, producing a secondary bleeding diathesis. This generally requires 18-20 units of blood. It is thus recommended that when a patient requires such massive transfusion every fourth unit should be given as fresh blood.

In addition to the dilution effect, during the storage of blood, platelets and leukocytes become adhesive and form aggregates. These develop maximally within a few hours after heparin anticoagulation and within one to seven days of ACD anticoagulation. These aggregates range in size from 10 u to over 200 u. After one week of storage there may be as many as $140,000/mm^3$ aggregates measuring 10-164 u. Since the standard blood filter has a pore size of 170 u significant numbers would be infused and have been shown to account for the syndrome of post-traumatic pulmonary insufficiency. This syndrome may occur in trauma patients without evidence of chest trauma. After massive blood transfusion they die of pulmonary insufficiency with pathologic evidence of amorphous material and aggregates occluding the pulmonary capillaries and arterioles. There is evidence that this can be prevented by using a 40 u filter instead of the standard blood filter in cases where massive transfusion must be given.

2. BLEEDING DUE TO PLATELET DISORDERS: These disorders may be hereditary or acquired and generally are due to decreased numbers of platelets or abnormal function. The hemorrhagic disorder of thrombocytopenia is usually that of petechial bleeding into the skin, but significant life-threatening gastrointestinal, genitourinary, or intracerebral bleeding can occur. Also, the bleeding defect in thrombocytopenia may be further aggravated by the use of drugs which impair platelet function.

It becomes of therapeutic importance to determine whether low platelet numbers are due to increased destruction or decreased production. The simplest means of determining this is to do a bone marrow aspiration for evaluation of megakaryocytes. The finding of increased megakaryocytes in the presence of a low platelet count indicates either immune destruction or hypersplenism.

In the presence of a normal platelet count, the bleeding time is the best screening test to evaluate platelet function. Platelet function abnormalities may be present on a congenital basis such as in von Willebrand's disease or the primary thrombocytopathies or on an acquired basis such as in association with hematologic neoplasms, uremia, drug effect, etc.

The complete evaluation of platelets includes:

1) Platelet count
2) Bone marrow
3) Bleeding time
4) Platelet aggregation studies
5) Platelet Factor III release
6) Platelet adhesiveness

In order to control bleeding associated with a platelet function abnormality or thrombocytopenia due to decreased production, it may be necessary to give platelet transfusions. In immune thrombocytopenia platelet transfusions are of little value, but steroids and/or splenectomy may be indicated. Thus, it is of great importance to make a specific diagnosis.

3. COAGULATION FACTOR ABNORMALITIES: Coagulation factor abnormalities may be due to: a) congenital hemophilic state, b) liver disease, c) vitamin K deficiency, d) an acquired inhibitor to a coagulation factor, e) consumption of coagulation factors (Table II). This last category will be discussed separately.

TABLE II
EVALUATION OF COAGULATION FACTORS
1. Prothrombin time 2. PTT 3. Recalcification time 4. Thrombin time 5. Prothrombin consumption time 6. Plasma fibrinogen 7. Thromboplastin generation time 8. Specific factor assays 9. Fibrin stability test 10. Fibrin split products 11. Euglobulin lysis 12. Protamine sulfate

By the use of the above tests a coagulation abnormality can be specifically identified. The screening tests are the prothrombin time which is a measure of the extrinsic system and the PTT which evaluates the intrinsic system. (See Fig. 4.1). From these, specific abnormalities can be identified by the use of specific assays. The fibrin stability test evaluates Factor XIII.

Patients with hemophilia have a problem in secondary hemostasis as do patients with other forms of coagulation factor abnormalities. Frequently, there are spontaneous bleeding episodes and insignificant trauma can lead to life-threatening situations. When a patient comes in with an acute hemorrhagic problem that is not traumatic, the history is extremely important in making the diagnosis of hemophilia.

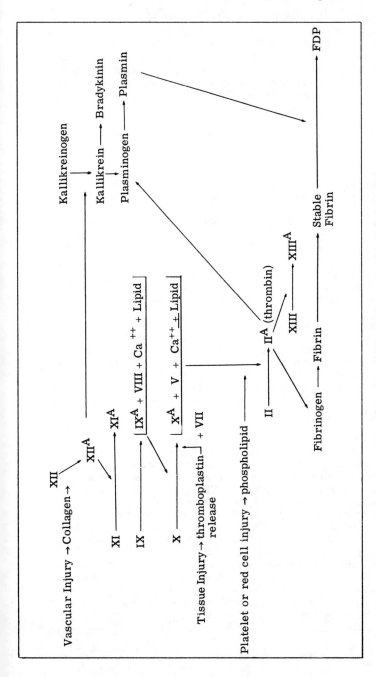

FIG. 4.1: SCHEMA OF COAGULATION AND FIBRINOLYSIS

Of particular importance is the family history, i.e. sex-linked recessive pattern of Factor VIII or IX deficiency vs. the autosomal dominant pattern of von Willebrand's, and the history of previous surgical procedures. Very severe congenital hemophiliacs usually know what disease they have so that diagnosis is not usually a problem. With the better diagnostic techniques available today all patients with suspected Factor VIII, IX or von Willebrand's disease should be re-evaluated.

Therapy of the hemophiliac with an acute hemorrhagic problem requires replacement of the inactive factor and evaluation for a possible inhibitor (see below). Replacement can be with a specific factor concentrate such as cryoprecipitate or lyophilized Factor VIII in hemophilia A or von Willebrand's, or prothrombin Complex for Factor IX, or with fresh frozen plasma for any deficient factor.

Liver disease should not be difficult to diagnose if one's coagulation abnormalities are on this basis. Essentially one has hepatic failure with inability to produce Factors II, V, VII, IX, and X. Severe bleeding in a cirrhotic may be controlled with prothrombin complex, a concentrate containing the vitamin K dependent Factors II, VII, IX, and X. However, Factor V may have to be given as well and would be available from fresh frozen plasma.

Deficiency of vitamin K produces deficiency in Factors II, VII, IX, and X. Coumadin accomplishes the same purpose. In these circumstances treatment of an acute hemorrhagic episode should be with vitamin K rather than prothrombin complex unless the bleeding is life-threatening. Only use Aquamephyton and Synkayvite (K_3) since the latter takes 2-3 days to work. This is because the commercially available prothrombin complex is made from pooled plasma and carries a high risk of serum hepatitis.

Inhibitors to coagulation factors are present in some patients with hemophilia A in which case the inhibitor is to Factor VIII. They may also be present in a wide variety of disorders including rheumatoid arthritis, ulcerative colitis, lupus erythematosus, pregnancy, old age, and idiopathic. This may result in a syndrome similar to hemophilia with spontaneous bleeding, but is acquired. The inhibitor is usually an IgG antibody. Giving the factor against which the antibody is directed only serves to increase the level of antibody. In some cases of life-threatening bleeding and very low antibody levels, very high levels of factor will be given. Exchange transfusions and immunosuppressive therapy especially with cyclophosphamide have been tried with some success. Recently it has been reported that there has also been success in treating individuals with Factor VIII hemophilia and an inhibitor with prothrombin complex with resolution of their bleeding.

4. DISSEMINATED INTRAVASCULAR COAGULATION (DIC) (Coagulopathy and fibrinolysis): DIC or consumption coagulopathy is a disorder that causes acute hemorrhagic problems involving both platelets and coagulation factors. (Table III). This is a disorder triggered by one of many mechanisms producing activation of the coagulation cascade with consumption of platelets and coagulation factors. This consumption leads to a secondary hemorrhagic state. The fibrin that is generated is broken down into fibrin split products or fibrin degradation products (FDP) which inhibit the action of thrombin taking fibrinogen to fibrin thus enhancing the tendency toward hemorrhage. In addition, the fibrin strands that are produced in small blood vessels cause fragmentation of erythrocytes, leading to hemolysis and a typical peripheral blood smear.

One should consider DIC and/or fibrinolysis in the right clinical setting when bleeding and an abnormal coagulation profile are present. The most helpful tests immediately are the platelet count, prothrombin time and fibrin degradation products (Table IV).

Primary fibrinolysis is a disorder that rarely occurs. In most cases fibrinolysis is secondary to consumption. Using the coagulation tests shown in Table IV, one can distinguish between primary fibrinolysis and secondary fibrinolysis. Of particular help is the platelet count, and protime which are normal in primary fibrinolysis.

Treatment of DIC remains the treatment of the underlying disease. However, consumption may be controlled by the prevention of further coagulation. This is best done by the use of heparin. Clotting factors may be replaced or epsilon amino caproic acid (amicar), an inhibitor of fibrinolysis, may be given but only after the patient has been adequately heparinized.

Thus, the field of hemorrhagic emergencies is quite inclusive. Since the treatment is relatively specific, diagnosis and the proper use of blood components become important (Table V).

TABLE III
CLINICAL CONDITIONS ASSOCIATED WITH DIC

Obstetric
    amniotic fluid embolism
    retained fetus
    abruptio placenta
Intravascular hemolysis
Neoplasia
Burns
Snake bites
Hemolytic-uremic syndrome, TTP
Glomerulonephritis
Microangiopathic hemolytic anemia
Infections
    gram negative
    meningococcal
    pneumococcal
Low cardiac output states
Liver disease

TABLE IV
COAGULATION TESTS IN DIC

TEST	NORMAL VALUE	DIC
Plt x 10^3	200-400	↓
PT	10 sec	↑
PTT	30-45 sec	↑
FDP	negative	+++
TT	12-15 sec	↑
Protamine sulfate	negative	+++
Fibrinogen	200-400 mg%	↓
Factor V	70-140%	↓
Factor VIII	50-200%	↓

TABLE V: ABNORMALITIES IN COAGULATION TESTS IN ACQUIRED COAGULATION DISORDERS

ABNORMAL COAGULATION PROCESS	PT	PTT	THROMBIN TIME	PLATELET COUNT	THERAPY
Coumadin	↑↑	↑	N	N	Vitamin K_1
Liver Disease	↑↑	↑	N, ↑	N, ↓	FFP[1] Prothrombin Complex
Malabsorption - Vitamin K Deficiency	↑↑	N, ↑	N	N	Vitamin K_1
Aspirin	↑	N	N	N	D/C Aspirin
DIC	↑↑	↑	↑↑	↓	Heparin Rx Cause
1° Fibrinolysis	N	N		N	EACA[2]
Massive Blood Transfusions	↑	↑	↑	↓	FFP Platelets

[1]FFP = Fresh Frozen Plasma

[2]EACA = Epsilon Amino Caprioc Acid

REFERENCES

1. Abildgaard, C.F., et al: Prothrombin complex concentrate in the treatment of hemophilic patients with Factor VIII inhibitors. J. Pediatrics 88:200, 1976.

2. Bick, R.L., et al: Prothrombin complex concentrate: Use in controlling the hemorrhagic diathesis of chronic liver disease. Digestive Diseases 20:741, 1975.

3. Colman, R.W., et al: Disseminated intravascular coagulation (DIC): An approach. Am J Med 52:679, 1972.

4. Graw, R.G. Jr., et al: Normal granulocyte transfusion therapy. NEJM 8:367, 1972.

5. Levine, A.S., et al: Management of infection in patients with leukemia and lymphoma: Current concepts and experimental approaches. Sem Hemat 9:141, 1972.

6. McKay, D.G., et al: Therapeutic implications of disseminated intravascular coagulation. Am J Cardiol 20:392, 1967.

7. Miller, R.D., et al: Coagulation defects associated with massive blood transfusion. Ann Surg 174:794, 1971.

8. Reul, G.J. Jr., et al: Prevention of posttraumatic pulmonary insufficiency. Arch Surg 106:386, 1972.

B: ACUTE LEUKEMIA
by R. Judith Ratzan, M.D.

Although a diagnosis of acute leukemia connotes a psycho-social emergency for the patient and family, it does not usually constitute a medical emergency. There is generally ample time to make the diagnosis and treat accordingly. However, there are several clinical situations associated with acute leukemia that are medical emergencies.

Included in the discussion of acute leukemia is a heterogeneous group of bone marrow neoplasms in which the malignant cell is a precursor of either the lymphoid or the granuloid-monocyte series. The pathophysiology of the disease predicts the major problems. Replacement of normal bone marrow with malignant cells affects granulocyte production and/or differentiation,thus predisposing patients to infection. A decrease in megakaryocytes predisposes to hemorrhage. In addition, unrestrained cell growth produces syndromes or consequences in and of itself.

The following emergency situations associated with acute leukemia must be recognized and dealt with accordingly: 1) infection, 2) hemorrhage, 3) neurologic complications, 4) leukostasis, 5) hyperuricemia and uric acid nephropathy.

1. INFECTION: The leading cause of death in patients with leukemia is infection. This includes bacterial infections associated with abnormal humoral immunity or absence of adequate phagocytic cells; and viral, fungal, or protozoal infections associated with a defect in cell-mediated immunity.

The bacterial infections which are particularly common are the gram-negatives, notably pseudomonas aeruginosa. It is important to recognize this on an emergency basis as treatment must be initiated immediately to prevent overwhelming sepsis, shock and death. One generally has more time to assess a possible opportunistic fungal or protozoan infection. Thus any new significant febrile episode must be treated initially as if caused by bacteria.

a) If there is an obvious source of infection, then cultures are obtained and broad spectrum antibiotics begun to cover the likely possibilities and then adjusted when the causal agent is known.

b) If there are adequate granulocytes and no obvious source of infection, then after cultures are obtained, treatment should be initiated with an aminoglycoside and cephalosporin.

c) If there are less than 500 granulocytes per mm^3 then add carbenicillin to the aminoglycoside and cephalosporin.

d) White blood cell transfusions can be considered in addition to antibiotics in the agranulocytic patient. These may be obtained by differential centrifugation or filtration leukopheresis. They should be given daily for at least four days. Graw et al (1972) have shown that under these circumstances a patient's chance of surviving an acute infectious episode approaches 100% versus 26% for controls.

2. HEMORRHAGE: This is the second major cause of death in patients with acute leukemia. Hemorrhage is due to thrombocytopenia, dysfunctional platelets or associated consumption coagulopathy.

a) Thrombocytopenia, thrombocytopathy: Thrombocytopenia is a major problem in patients with acute leukemia. It is due in part to marrow replacement by malignant cells as well as to the use of myelotoxic drugs in the treatment of leukemia. Platelets that are produced are frequently abnormal.

In the presence of fever and infection, platelet half-life is diminished and the platelet count may fall even lower than expected. In general, spontaneous bleeding may be expected to occur when the platelet count falls below 20,000/cu mm.

If bleeding is due to or associated with thrombocytopenia then treatment includes identification of the lesion and platelet transfusion in addition to red blood cells. Although in the routine situation care is not taken to provide platelets of the same HLA type as the patient, if he is refractory to random platelets because of numerous platelet transfusions in the past, then HLA matched platelets become desirable.

b) Consumption coagulopathy (DIC): This occurs with increased incidence with acute promyelocytic leukemia. It also may occur with endotoxemia and gram negative sepsis or following initiation of chemotherapy and release of thromboplastic substances.

Diagnosis of DIC may be difficult because 1) thrombocytopenia may be related to other causes, 2) factor VIII level may be normal and 3) fibrinogen may be normal.

The prothrombin time and thrombin time are the most useful laboratory tests in diagnosing DIC in acute leukemia.

Adequate treatment of the DIC includes therapy of leukemia or other underlying causes of the DIC. Heparinization may be hazardous because of the low platelet counts and tendency to bleed even without DIC.

3. CENTRAL NERVOUS SYSTEM LEUKEMIA: There are several neurologic syndromes associated with acute leukemia that require immediate recognition and treatment. The central nervous system

(CNS) is considered a sanctuary for leukemic cells. With the exception of prednisone, the drugs used in treating leukemia do not cross the blood-brain barrier. Common syndromes that develop include leukemic meningitis, cranial nerve palsies, hypothalamic-obesity syndrome and tumors along the spinal cord or within the brain.

The clinical syndrome that occurs with CNS leukemia is a manifestation of increased intracranial pressure. Nausea, vomiting, lethargy, headache, convulsions, cranial nerve palsies of III, IV and VI and papilledema may be present.

Treatment includes a lumbar puncture for diagnostic purposes as well as to instill methotrexate 10 mg/M^2 which is an effective agent in treatment. Once this syndrome occurs, it requires repeated therapy to control it. The use of an Omaya reservoir may facilitate this.

Prevention of this complication is quite effective in patients with acute lymphoblastic leukemia (ALL). 2400 rads to the cranium combined with five doses of intrathecal methotrexate are given prophylactically with a marked reduction in this problem.

The hypothalamic-obesity syndrome is a variant of CNS leukemia generally associated with ALL. These patients develop hyperphagia with resultant excessive weight gain. Histologically hypothalamic infiltration by leukemic cells can usually be demonstrated. Some cases without observable leukemic infiltration are apparently due to dilation of the third ventricle causing hypothalamic damage.

In acute granulocytic leukemia prophylactic therapy has not been proven to be of value in large measure due to the fact that hematologic remissions are not prolonged.

4. LEUKOSTASIS: This is another emergency situation which is more readily prevented than treated. This is a syndrome in which patients develop a very specific type of central nervous system bleeding and death.

This syndrome was reported by Freireich, et al (1960), who noted that of 18 patients with acute leukemia who died of cerebral hemorrhage 9 had WBC of 300,000 mm^3. The other nine had WBC of less than 100,000/mm^3 and bleeding was due to subarachnoid or subdural hemorrhage associated with thrombocytopenia. The group with counts of 300,000/mm^3 or higher had unique lesions described as leukemic nodules present in white matter and surrounded by hemorrhage. The pathogenesis of these lesions is as follows:

a) Intravascular leukostasis occurs and intracerebral vessels become dilated and filled with dividing leukemic cells.

b) These blood vessels are destroyed leaving leukemic nodules in the white matter.

c) Hemorrhage occurs about the leukemic nodules.

The significant features predisposing to this syndrome are the height of the white blood count and the percentage of blasts. Tissue infiltration involving the lungs, leading to respiratory insufficiency has also been described when the WBC is high.

It is therefore of utmost importance when encountering a patient with a very high white count and a high blast count to treat very aggressively to bring the count down to less than 100,000. This is most effectively done by chemotherapy. One must be particularly careful though, when acutely reducing a big cell load not to cause the final emergency problem to be considered namely, uric acid nephropathy.

5. URIC ACID NEPHROPATHY: Leukemia is one of the major causes of secondary gout. A life-threatening situation may arise, generally provoked by chemotherapy, in which the uric acid load is so great that uric acid crystals precipitate in the terminal portions of the nephron and renal collecting system producing a functional obstructive uropathy. The course of uric acid nephropathy is rapidly progressive to renal insufficiency. This is compared to the typical gouty nephropathy which is a very slowly progressive disease with urates present in the interstitial tissue with an associated foreign body reaction.

To treat the uric acid nephropathy in leukemia one must: (a) hydrate the patient well, (b) alkalinize the urine with $NaHCO_3$ and Diamox and (c) if necessary, acutely hemodialyze the patient.

Prevention is of prime importance. The initiation of chemotherapy especially with a large tumor load necessitates the use of the xanthine oxidase inhibitor, allopurinol 300-600 mg/day, hydration and alkalinization.

Thus, the medical emergencies which arise in association with acute leukemia must be immediately recognized and treated. Whenever possible they should be prevented.

REFERENCES

1. Cowan, P.H., and Haut, M.J.: Platelet function in acute leukemia. J Lab Clin Med 79:893, 1972.

2. Freireich, E.J., et al: A distinctive type of intracerebral hemorrhage associated with "blastic crisis" in patients with leukemia. Cancer 13:146, 1960.

3. Graw, R.G. Jr.: Normal granulocyte transfusion therapy. N Eng J Med 287:367, 1972.

4. Leavy, R.A., et al: Disseminated intravascular coagulation. A complication of chemotherapy in acute myelomonocytic leukemia. Cancer 26:142, 1970.

5. Levine, A.S., et al: Management of infections in patients with leukemia and lymphoma: Current concepts and experimental approaches. Sem Hemat IX:141, 1972.

6. Pochedly, C.: Neurologic manifestations in acute leukemia. I. Symptoms due to increased cerebrospinal fluid pressure and hemorrhage. N.Y.S. Jour Med 75:575, 1975.

7. Pochedly, C.: Neurologic manifestations in acute leukemia. II. Involvement of cranial nerves and hypothalamus. N.Y.S. Jour Med 75:715, 1975.

8. Shaw, R., et al: Meningeal leukemia. A syndrome resulting from increased intracranial pressure in patients with acute leukemia. Neurology 10:623, 1960.

C: ACUTE HEMOLYTIC ANEMIA
by Adel A. Yunis, M.D.

DEFINITION AND CLASSIFICATION OF HEMOLYTIC ANEMIA

Under normal, steady state conditions 1/100th of the red cell mass is destroyed daily and replaced by new cells from the bone marrow. In response to excessive red cell destruction the marrow is capable of increasing its production 6-8 fold. Anemia results when this maximal marrow capacity is exceeded.

Increased hemolysis (hemolytic anemia) may be due to extracorpuscular or intracorpuscular factors.

HEMOLYTIC ANEMIA

I. DUE TO EXTRACORPUSCULAR FACTORS:

Immune Hemolytic Anemia
        Secondary
        Idiopathic
Infections, chemicals, toxins
Physical and Mechanical Injury

II. DUE TO INTRACORPUSCULAR DEFECTS:

Hereditary:
        Hereditary Spherocytosis
        Hemoglobinopathies
        Enzyme Defects
        Thalassemias
Acquired:
        Paroxysmal Nocturnal Hemoglobinuria (PNH)

LABORATORY MANIFESTATIONS OF INCREASED HEMOLYSIS

Increased red cell destruction is associated with characteristic laboratory manifestations consequent to hemoglobin degradation and compensatory increase in bone marrow activity. (Table I)

Hemolysis may occur predominantly extravascularly or intravascularly. In the latter case, the classical features of intravascular hemolysis might be expected: hemoglobinemia, hemoglobinuria, methemalbuminemia, hemosiderinuria, decreased plasma haptoglobin and decreased plasma hemopexin. However, the distinction between intra- and extravascular hemolysis is not always sharp, as any severe hemolysis may be accompanied by these laboratory findings. Bilirubinemia occurs when the capacity of the liver to excrete the increased bilirubin load is exceeded. The increased excretion of bilirubin results in increased fecal excretion of urobilin.

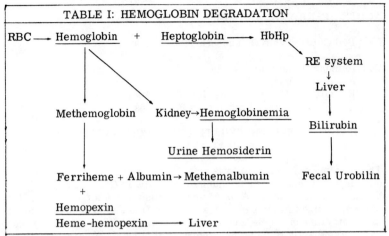

TABLE I: HEMOGLOBIN DEGRADATION

SIGNS OF INCREASED BONE MARROW ERYTHYROID ACTIVITY:
(1) Erythyroid hyperplasia of bone marrow, (2) Reticulocytosis.

CLINICAL CONSIDERATIONS: For the clinician the diagnostic problem in hemolytic anemia is twofold: the demonstration of increased
red cell destruction and determination of the cause. Only then can
a rational course of management be charted. Thus, in addition to
the laboratory approach a thorough history and physical examination
are paramount. Detailed history should include: family history of
anemia or other blood diseases, ethnic origin, exposure to drugs, chemical or physical agents, infections, symptoms of underlying primary
disease (collagen vascular disease, chronic lymphocytic leukemia, infectious mononucleosis, cardiac and microangiopathic etiology, etc.).

The Peripheral Blood Smear in Hemolytic Anemia often provides important information to guide the clinician in the choice of further
diagnostic work-up. Indeed it should be considered part of the physical examination. Some abnormalities which should be looked for
include: polychromasia (indicates presence of young red cells and
therefore, increased marrow erythroid activity), spherocytosis
(hereditary spherocytosis, autoimmune hemolytic anemia), baso-
philic stipplings (β-thalassemia, lead poisoning), hypochromia
(chronic intravascular hemolysis with iron loss, β-thalassemia,
lead poisoning), target cells (liver disease, Hb C, thalassemia, etc.),
schistocytes (microangiopathic hemolytic anemia), ovalocytes (ovalo-
cytosis), acanthocytes, burr cells, spur cells (liver disease, uremia,
microangiopathic hemolytic anemia, PNH, and postsplenectomy).

ACUTE HEMOLYTIC ANEMIA

Many hemolytic anemias have a chronic insidious course, particularly those which are secondary to an underlying disease. In this
review, we will consider only those hemolytic anemias which most
often follow an acute course.

ACUTE HEMOLYTIC ANEMIA:

I.   Red Cell Enzyme Defect - G6PD

II. Immune Hemolytic Anemia
     A. Autoimmune
     B. Drug-Induced Immune Hemolytic Anemia
     C. Alloimmune - Transfusion Reactions

I.   GLUCOSE-6-PHOSPHATE DEHYDROGENASE (G6PD)
     DEFICIENCY

This enzyme deficiency follows an x-linked recessive mode of inheritance. There is a large number of unstable G6PD variants but
the most common is the A or African variant which affects about 10
percent of black American males. A less frequent B variant is found
in Mediterranean people and is usually a more severe deficiency,red
cell enzyme activity being 0-10 percent of normal. Characteristic
of this deficiency is acute hemolysis after the ingestion of fava beans.
Since G6PD deficiency is x-linked, deficient males are usually more
severely affected. Deficiency is only partially expressed in females,
some cells being deficient, others normal, depending upon which of
the two chromosomes is inactive (Lyon's hypothesis).

Mechanisms of Hemolysis: In both the A and B variants, hemolysis
typically follows the intake of certain oxidant drugs or during severe
infections. The G6PD deficient red cells cannot generate adequate
amounts of NAPDH to keep glutathione in the reduced state. Reduced glutathione is necessary to counteract the effect of hydrogen
peroxide produced by the interaction of drug with oxyhemoglobin or
by the granulocytes during infection (which then presumably diffuses
into the red cells). The excess of H_2O_2 causes hemoglobin denatu-
ration, and precipitation as Heinz bodies and oxidation of membrane
SH groups, resulting in membrane damage.

Clinical Features: The severity of hemolysis depends on the degree
of enzyme deficiency, and the amount and type of drug taken. Normally G6PD activity falls as erythrocytes become old. In G6PD deficiency the red cells enzyme activity is low to begin with and is lost
more rapidly as the cell ages. Under redox stress (administration
of oxidant drug) the level of G6PD activity required to preserve red
cell membrane integrity is higher. Hence older cells are more susceptible to destruction. Typically then, hemolysis is self limited
and hemoglobin level stabilizes as the old cells are replaced by young
ones. Since young cells have higher G6PD activity, enzyme assay
at this time may be within normal limits and diagnosis difficult. This
may be circumvented by centrifugation of the blood and performing
the assay on the bottom red cell layer (older cells).

Treatment consists of reducing the dosage or altogether discontinuing
the offending drug. In the case of hemolytic anemia precipitated by
infection,treatment of the underlying infection is needed.

II. IMMUNE HEMOLYTIC ANEMIA

A. AUTOIMMUNE HEMOLYTIC ANEMIA (AIHA): This hemolytic
anemia results from the production by the host of autoantibody directed against his own red cells. The production of such antibodies
may be triggered by an underlying condition such as collagen vascular disease or diseases of the lymphoreticular system, but in a
large number of cases AIHA is idiopathic.

Mechanisms of Hemolysis: The site and severity of red cell destruction are determined by the type of antibody produced and whether
or not complement is fixed. Complete activation of the complement
system usually results in severe intravascular hemolysis. When
complement activation is incomplete or lacking, hemolysis occurs
largely extravascularly by a process of erythrophagocytosis and red
cell fragmentation in the spleen and liver. Macrophages possess
specific receptor sites for the N-terminal part of the Fc fragment
of immunoglobins IgG_1 and IgG_3 which comprise the majority of IgG
antibodies. Red cells coated with these antibodies are thus easily
recognized by splenic and hepatic macrophages with resultant phagocytosis and fragmentation. Macrophage receptors to IgM and complement have also been described. There is recent evidence that
red cells may also be lysed by sensitized lymphoid cells.

AIHA can be classified into three types as determined by the nature
of antibody:

1. Warm antibody hemolytic anemia - most common
2. Cold agglutinin hemolytic anemia
3. Paroxysmal cold hemoglobinuria - rare

1. Warm Antibody Hemolytic Anemia: This is a common immune
hemolytic anemia caused by IgG warm (37°C) reacting antibodies.
It may be idiopathic or secondary. The secondary forms occur
in association with lymphoproliferative diseases, connective
tissue disorders, malignant or benign tumors, infections, and
granulomatous diseases. The incidence of the primary or idiopathic variety has ranged from 70 percent in earlier series to
less than 50 percent more recently.

Clinical Features: This anemia may occur at any age although it is
less common in young children. It is more common in women.
Hemolysis may be acute and severe or may follow a chronic course
with exacerbations and remissions. Symptoms are usually attributed
to anemia or, in the secondary cases, to the underlying disease.
Physical findings include pallor, splenomegaly, less frequently hepatomegaly and lymphadenopathy. Jaundice and fever may be present.

Laboratory Findings: The laboratory manifestations of hemolytic disease have been discussed under general considerations. Anemia and
reticulocytosis are usually present. The peripheral blood smear
may show spherocytes, red cell fragmentation and nucleated red cells.

Leukocytosis is not uncommon and thrombocytopenia may coexist with immune hemolytic anemia (Evans Syndrome). Unconjugated bilirubinemia and decreased serum hepatoglobin may be present.

A positive Coombs' test is the rule. In the direct Coombs' test antiglobulin serum detects antibody coating the red cells. The indirect Coombs' detects antibody in the serum. Specific Coombs' sera are now available for IgG, IgA, IgM, and complement. The antibody in this disease is usually an IgG, nonagglutinating and non-complement fixing. It binds optimally at 37°C and reacts with the Rh antigens (c, D, e).

Treatment: AIHA may present to the clinician as a chronic process with mild to moderate anemia in which case appropriate therapy may be selected in an elective manner. Not infrequently however, AIHA presents with acute severe hemolysis and life threatening anemia requiring emergency transfusions.

Transfusions: The patient with AIHA is serologically incompatible with his own red cells and those of most blood donors rendering cross matching difficult if not impossible. Here the clinician must decide on the absolute necessity for the patients to receive blood and the blood bank must decide on the compatibility of the donor's blood. It is absolutely necessary for the clinician and the blood bank to maintain an excellent system of communication to arrive at the best decision.

Since approximately 75 percent of patients with idiopathic AIHA will show prompt response to steroids, the question often is whether one can or cannot afford wait for response. Thus the clinician must ask himself two important questions: Does the patient need blood desperately to save his life and if so, what is the minimum amount of packed red cells needed? Infused red cells are destroyed at an exponential rate and the more that is given the more is destroyed and the greater is the possibility of complications such as acute renal failure and disseminated intravascular coagulation. It is best to transfuse the minimum amount of type specific packed red cells showing minimal incompatibility keeping in mind that the degree of incompatibility in vitro does not always correlate with that in vivo.

Steroids: Prednisone (60-100 mg daily) is the initial treatment of choice in warm antibody hemolytic anemia and usually results in prompt and dramatic reduction in hemolysis in about 80 percent of idiopathic cases. Hematologic response occurs rapidly with a median of about 7 days. If there is no evidence of response in 3 weeks, further steroid treatment is rarely warranted. Once hematologic remission is achieved, prednisone dose should be reduced slowly at the rate of 5 mg per week. About 20 percent of patients will remain in remission after prednisone has been discontinued, 40 percent can be maintained in remission on small doses (5 - 15 mg OD) and 30-40 percent will relapse and require other therapeutic alternatives. Splenectomy is the alternative of choice. Patients who relapse after splenectomy or in whom surgery is contraindicated may respond to immunosuppressive treatment with or without small doses of prednisone.

At least 3 mechanisms have been postulated to explain the action of corticosteroids in hemolytic anemia. 1. Inhibition of antibody synthesis. 2. Altering antigen-antibody affinity. 3. Delaying the clearance of antibody-coated red cells by macrophages possibly by inhibiting the synthesis of Fc receptor sites on the macrophage membrane.

In secondary AIHA, treatment of the underlying disease should be undertaken but steroid therapy for the hemolytic anemia is often also necessary.

2. Cold Agglutinin Hemolytic Anemia: This hemolytic anemia is characterized by antibodies which react with red cells optimally at 0-4°C and cause agglutination, thus the term cold agglutinin disease. Normal serum contains cold agglutinins in low titers. In this disease titers may range in the millions. The antibody is usually an IgM and reacts with the I or i antigen of red cells. It fixes complement sublytically and may dissociate from the cells at 37°C. Complement lysis is often minimal, hemolysis occurring predominantly extravascularly in the liver and spleen by a process involving binding of red cells to IgM and C_3 receptors on macrophages and consequent erythrophagocytosis.

Clinical Features: The cold agglutinin syndrome may be idiopathic or secondary to underlying disease. The secondary forms occur in association with mycoplasma pneumonia, influenza, infectious mononucleosis and lymphoproliferative diseases. The IgM antibody associated with mycoplasma and infectious mononucleosis is polyclonal and is directed against the I (in mycoplasma) or i antigen (infectious mononucleosis). In the latter case little agglutination of the red cells is expected since only a small amount of i antigen is detectable on red cells of adults.

The mechanisms by which the infection induces antibody production is not clear.

A chronic cold agglutinin syndrome occurs in the elderly and is often idiopathic. The antibody is usually a monoclonal IgM. The bone marrow may exhibit lymphocytosis and peripheral blood lymphocytes have been shown to possess receptors which react with erythrocyte I and i antigens thus suggesting that chronic cold agglutinin disease may be a true lymphoproliferative disorder.

The anemia in cold agglutinin disease is often milder than that of the warm antibody type. However, significant hemolysis may be seen especially related to exposure to cold. Because of the characteristics of the cold agglutinin, intolerance to cold, peripheral venous sludging, acrocyanosis and Raynaud's phenomenon may be observed. There is usually splenomegaly and less frequently lymphadenopathy.

Laboratory Findings: Elevated titers of cold agglutinins are found. Identification of the clonal characteristics may help in determining the etiology (polyclonal in association with infection and monoclonal in the chronic cold agglutinin syndrome). Since the antibody dissociates at 37°C leaving the complement attached, the Coombs' test is frequently positive with anti-C_3 and anti-C_4 Coombs' serum. The indirect Coombs' test is positive if the red cells are cooled to allow antibody attachment and complement fixation and then rewarmed to permit the IgM to elute.

Treatment: Cold agglutinin disease secondary to mycoplasma is normally self-limited, requiring no therapy. In the chronic form in the elderly, avoidance of cold is often helpful. Response to steroids and/or splenectomy is poor. In severe cases a 3-6 month trial of cytotoxic therapy with cyclophosphamide or chlorambucil may be of benefit. In cases of acute severe hemolysis plasmapheresis should probably be tried since IgM is predominantly intravascular and the antibody concentration can thus be lowered rapidly. Plasmapheresis should be carried out at warm temperatures.

3. Paroxysmal Cold Hemoglobinuria (PCH): PCH is a rare disorder which occurs in association with syphilis and some viral infections. The antibody is an IgG which binds optimally at 0°-4°C and causes lysis at 37°C (Donath Landsteiner), has specificity for P antigen of red cells and fixes complement causing immediate intravascular hemolysis. The most common symptom is hemoglobinuria after exposure to cold which may be accompanied by chills, myalgia and urticaria. On physical examination the patient may have jaundice and splenomegaly. Laboratory evidence of intravascular hemolysis is usually present: hemoglobinuria and hemosiderinuria, and serum haptoglobin depletion.

Treatment is usually unsatisfactory. PCH in association with syphilis will respond to treatment with penicillin. Avoidance of cold is necessary in all cases. Steroids are occasionally helpful. PCH in association with viral illness is often self-limited.

B. DRUG-INDUCED IMMUNE HEMOLYTIC ANEMIA: Many drugs are capable of causing a positive direct antiglobulin test with or without hemolytic anemia. By far the most common drugs to cause immune hemolytic anemia are penicillin and α methyldopa (Aldomet).

The mechanism of erythrocyte sensitization of drug-related antibody is variable. Generally four mechanisms by which a drug can cause a positive direct antiglobulin test have been recognized, each one exemplified by one or more drugs:

1. Immune Complex Absorption to Red Cells (innocent bystander mechanism): This mechanism is probably applicable to most drugs that cause immune hemolytic anemia and is exemplified by the drugs quinidine and quinine. Antibody produced against the drug combines with it to form a drug-antibody complex. This complex then is absorbed on the red cell membrane often resulting in complement activation and acute intravascular hemolysis with hemoglobinemia and hemoglobinuria and frequent renal failure.

The antibody is IgM and is capable of fixing complement. The Coombs' test is positive with anticomplement Coombs' serum since the antibody-drug complex dissociates easily from the cell membrane leaving complement attached. The ready dissociation of antibody-drug complex from one cell to react with another explains why a very small amount of drug is capable of producing extensive hemolysis. Demonstration of the reaction in vitro requires drug, patient serum and red cells.

2. Drug Absorbed onto Red Cells (hapten mechanism): This type of mechanism is best exemplified by penicillin. Because of its tendency to bind to proteins, penicillin can be detected on the red cell membranes of most patients receiving high doses of the drug. About 3 percent of patients on massive intravenous doses of penicillin will develop a positive antiglobulin test and a small percentage of these will have hemolytic anemia. Antipenicillin antibody, an IgG, present in the plasma combines with penicillin bound to the red cell membrane causing sensitization usually without complement fixation. The IgG sensitized red cells are destroyed by the reticuloendothelial system. Occasionally complement activation occurs.

Hemolysis usually develops only in patients who are on penicillin doses exceeding 10 million units daily for a week or more. Although the degree of hemolysis may not be as severe as that caused by quinine, it can be life threatening if unrecognized and if penicillin administration is continued.

The direct antiglobulin test is positive with anti IgG Coombs' serum and rarely with anticomplement serum. Antibody eluted from the patient's red cells will react only with red cells which have been coated with penicillin. The patient usually has a high titer of antipencillin antibody.

Treatment consists of early recognition and prompt discontinuation of penicillin. Complete recovery follows although some hemolysis may persist for several weeks.

3. Drug-Induced Autoantibody to Red Cells: Methyldopa (Aldomet) is the most common cause of drug-induced positive antiglobulin test and of drug-induced autoimmune hemolytic anemia. About 15 percent (range 10-36 percent) of patients receiving Aldomet will develop a positive direct antiglobulin test, but only an average of about 1 percent will have hemolytic anemia. The incidence of positive antiglobulin test seems to correlate with dose and also varies in racial groups being highest in caucasian and almost absent in blacks. The exact mechanism by which methyldopa causes red cell autosensitization remains unclear.

All patients with Aldomet-induced hemolytic anemia will have a strongly positive antiglobulin test. The autoantibody is an IgG and the serology is often indistinguishable from that of idiopathic warm AIHA. Striking hematological improvement will occur 1-2 weeks following discontinuation of Aldomet although the antiglobulin test may remain positive for as long as two years.

Two other drugs have been described to cause a positive antiglobulin test by a mechanism similar to that of α-methyldopa: L-dopa and mefanimic acid. The incidence appears to be much lower.

4. Non-immunological Absorption of Protein to Red Cell: A positive direct antiglobulin test has been described following the administration of Cephalothin (Keflin). Three different mechanisms have been proposed. a) Cephalothin modifies red cell membrane allowing non specific absorption of plasma proteins. (Nonimmunological). b) Antibody to penicillin will cross react with cephalothin bound to red cell membrane. c) Antibody produced against cephalothin itself will react similarly.

Since cephalothin causes nonspecific absorption of various plasma proteins to red cell membrane, it is important to remember that a positive antiglobulin test is very common in association with this drug, particularly when crude Coombs' antiserum is employed. However, hemolytic anemia from cephalothin is much rarer than that from penicillin.

Some points to remember in the work up of suspected drug-induced immune hemolytic anemia are as follows:

1. Careful and detailed history of drug ingestion is paramount.

2. Direct antiglobulin test using monospecific antisera against IgG (penicillin, α methyldopa) and C_3 (quinine, quinidine) should always be done; when cephalothin is the suspected drug use antisera against other plasma proteins as well.

3. Indirect antiglobulin test should be done against normal and enzyme (trypsin) treated cells. In the latter case nearly all idiopathic warm AIHA and α-methyldopa hemolytic anemia have antibody in serum. The presence of autoantibody in the serum excludes drugs such as penicillin, cephalothin or quinine.

4. If patient's serum contains no autoantibody and the red cell eluate is also nonreactive against normal red cells, then a drug-induced hemolytic anemia is strongly indicated; the penicillin group of drugs are the most common.

C. ALLOIMMUNE HEMOLYTIC ANEMIA - HEMOLYTIC TRANS-FUSION REACTIONS: Hemolytic transfusion reactions have become rare in recent years because of rapid progress in our understanding of the various blood group systems and the advances in our serologic techniques. Thus, most of the hemolytic transfusion reactions are caused by technical or clerical errors which are entirely avoidable.

Pathologic Physiology: The administration of incompatible blood results in rapid red cell destruction which in turn evokes a series of serious adverse reactions emanating from complement activation. A red cell sensitized with the appropriate antibody will initiate a sequence of complement activation beginning with C_1 and continuing to C_4, C_2, C_3, C_5, C_6, C_7 and finally C_8 and C_9 which leads to lysis and liberation of intracellular constituents. During this sequence of events a number of biologically active peptides are released, the action of which account to a large extent for the pathologic and clinical consequences of hemolytic transfusion reactions. These biologically active factors include:

1. Kinin-like vasoactive peptide (released following interaction of C_1, C_4 and C_2) which cause tissue swelling (pain, fever).

2. Two peptides, C_{3a} and C_{5a} released from C_3 and C_5 respectively. These are both chemotactic for leukocytes and are anaphylotoxins (fever and shock)

3. Activated C_3 (C_{3b}) formed by release of C_{3a} remains bound on the cell membrane. Red cells with bound C_{3b} are susceptible to phagocytosis by macrophages of the RE system which possess C_3 receptors on their membranes (extravascular red cell destruction).

4. Hemoglobin released from intravascular red cell lysis, with additional factors as shock, leads to acute renal failure (mechanism not completely understood).

5. Activation of coagulation cascade: The antigen-antibody complex activates Hageman factor and initiates a platelet release reaction

(platelet factor 3). This plus the liberation of thromboplastic material from hemolyzed red cells accounts for the disseminated intravascular coagulation often observed in hemolytic transfusion reactions.

Clinical Features: Depending on the type and nature of antibody, symptoms may be minor in the form of chills and fever or more often dramatic with shaking chills, fever, pain along the injected vein, flushing pain and pressure in the chest and lower back, dyspnea and circulatory collapse.

Laboratory evidence for intravascular hemolysis is usually easily obtained (hemoglobinemia, hemoglobinuria, hemosiderinuria, etc.).

Investigation of Hemolytic Transfusion Reaction: It is very important to approach this problem in a systematic and efficient manner.

1. Stop further transfusions immediately and check that the correct blood has been given to the recipient. Also check if the donor's blood has been frozen, overheated, stored too long or has been infected. (In all these instances gross hemolysis and free hemoglobin are demonstrable in donor's blood).

2. Collect the following samples for investigation. (a) Pre and post transfusion blood from recipient. (b) Post transfusion urine sample from recipient. (c) Donor's blood and (d) Blood from container.

3. Examine (samples a and c) for hemolysis.

4. Repeat ABO and Rh on all blood samples.

5. Do Coombs' test on sample a.

6. Check cross match report, patient and donor identification.

Often more than one antibody may be present in the serum of a multitransfused patient or following multiple pregnancies in which identification may be difficult. Under these circumstances it may be useful to perform a complete genotype on receipient's red cells since this will exclude antibodies to the antigens present.

It is evident from the foregoing that for the solution of the problem and its appropriate management, a qualified blood bank is needed with which the clinician must maintain an excellent communication system.

Management of Hemolytic Transfusion Reactions:

1. Stop and withhold further transfusion
2. Investigate as above
3. Start an IV drip of normal saline

4. Maintain blood pressure and promote diuresis. Generally one must avoid vasopressors because they restrict blood flow to the kidneys.
5. Maintain urine flow at 1-3 ml/minute (Give 100 ml of 25% mannitol IV and 1 liter of saline with 45 mEq of $NaHCO_3$)
6. If diuresis ensues, continue with 5 percent mannitol matching renal output.
7. If no diuresis - Acute tubular necrosis is probably present. Treat accordingly.
8. If disseminated intravascular coagulation develops, heparin treatment may be indicated.

Preventive measures such as the proper labelling and identification of all cross match blood samples and release of properly cross matched blood only to the recipient for whom it is intended cannot be overemphasized.

Delayed Transfusion Reactions: Occasionally signs and symptoms of a hemolytic reaction make their appearance a week following transfusion. This is usually due to a secondary immune response of the recipient to a donor's antigen to which he has been exposed previously. The antigen is usually of the Rh - Hr system or of the Kidd system. Treatment is essentially the same as for the immediate reaction.

REFERENCES

1. Immune Hemolytic Anemias. Seminars in Hematology, Vol. 13, No. 4, Oct. 1976.

2. Hemolytic Anemias. Clinics in Hematology, Vol. 4, No. 1, Feb. 1975.

3. Blood Transfusions and Blood Products. Clinics in Hematology, Vol. 5, No. 1, Feb. 1976.

D: TREATMENT OF SICKLE CELL CRISIS
by Donald R. Harkness, M.D.

Sickle cell hemoglobin (Hb S) arises from a specific mutation which directs the insertion of valine in place of glutamic acid in the sixth residue of the B chain. This region of the B chain is on the surface of the molecule and the structural change alters the next charge on the hemoglobin tetramer, explaining the ease with which normal adult hemoglobin (Hb A) and Hb S are separated by electrophoresis. More importantly, the presence of the valine somehow disturbs the configuration in that region of the molecule rendering the hemoglobin less soluble and, when deoxygenated, able to form intermolecular aggregates. The linear aggregates, composed of alternating A and B chains, bond together in groups of seven to form rigid fibrils called tactoids. The shortened survival and abnormal flow properties of these cells result in hemolytic and vaso-occlusive phenomena which account for a majority of the clinical manifestations of the sickling disorders.

Persons heterozygous for Hb S and Hb A are referred to as having sickle cell trait. In a majority of persons with S trait the erythrocytes contain from 30 to 45% Hb S, normal amounts of Hb A_2 and Hb F and over 50% Hb A. A small proportion of persons with S trait have less than 30% Hb S in their red blood cells. Persons who inherit the gene for Hb S from both parents have homozygous sickle cell disease or sickle cell anemia. Their erythrocytes contain predominantly Hb S, normal amounts of Hb A_2, variable amounts of Hb F (sometimes as much as 20%) and no Hb A. Persons who receive a gene for Hb S from one parent and a gene for some other structural mutation of the B chain (double heterozygotes) may have clinically significant disease (e.g. SC, SD, SO$_{arab}$). The clinical and laboratory features of homozygous S disease, the S variants and a thalassemia are compared in Table I.

S TRAIT (A/S)

This is usually a completely benign condition, of importance primarily in predicting the genotype of offspring (e.g., if both parents are A/S, for any given pregnancy the chances are 1 in 4 that the child will be A/A, 1 in 4 that the child will be S/S, and 2 in 4 that he will be A/S).

Persons with A/S are not anemic; their reticulocyte count and red cell survival are normal. They have a normal life expectancy, and only under very unusual circumstances do they suffer any of the vaso-occlusive phenomena associated with S/S. Women with S trait may have a slightly increased incidence of bacteriuria during pregnancy.

TABLE I: COMPARISON OF CLINICAL AND LABORATORY FEATURES OF SICKLE CELL ANEMIA, SICKLE VARIANTS AND β-THALASSEMIA

GENOTYPE	ANEMIA	PERIPHERAL SMEAR	SPLENO-MEGALY	CLINICAL SEVERITY	OTHER CLINICAL FEATURES	REMARKS
A/S	0	normal	none	benign	usually none	hematuria; rare sickling when hypoxic or acidotic; less than 50% Hgb S.
S/S	4+	sickle cells target cells polychromasia Howell-Jolly bodies	usually only in childhood	usually severe	painful crises, infections, leg ulcers, gallstones	progressive organ damage; life expectancy ~ 25 years; ↑ fetal and maternal mortality.
S/C	2-3+	target cells sickle cells polychromasia	usual	usually mild	mild painful crises, retinopathy	↑ fetal and maternal mortality; life expectancy ~ 40 years; gallstones; retinopathy.
C/C	2+	4+ target cells mild hypochromia	mild	mild	usually none	mild hemolytic anemia when C trait and β-thal-interact.
S/β^+-thal	2-3+	hypochromia anisopoikilo-cytosis target cells	usual	mild to severe	mild crises	over 50% Hgb S; ↑ A_2; symptoms correlate with amount of Hgb S present
S/β^0-thal	3-4+	sickle cells target cells hypochromia	usual	moderate to severe	similar to SS	no Hgb A; similar to SS; ↑ A_2; low MCHC.

TABLE I: COMPARISON OF CLINICAL AND LABORATORY FEATURES OF SICKLE CELL ANEMIA, SICKLE VARIANTS AND β-THALASSEMIA (Continued)

GENOTYPE	ANEMIA	PERIPHERAL SMEAR	SPLENO-MEGALY	CLINICAL SEVERITY	OTHER CLINICAL FEATURES	REMARKS
S/O arab	4+	sickle cells anisopoikilocytosis Howell–Jolly bodies	usually only in childhood	usually severe	similar to SS	O arab migrates like Hgb C at pH 8.6; identify on agar at pH 6.2.
S/D	2-3+	sickle cells target cells polychromasia	usual	mild to severe	arthralgias	D migrates like S at pH 8.6; separates from S on agar gel, pH 6.2 or by solubility.
β-thal trait	2-3+	hypochromia microcytosis target cells	occasional	mild	usually none	smear looks like Fe deficiency; diagnosed by ↑ A_2 and F; low MCHC.
β-thal major (homozygous)	3-4+	severe hypochromia microcytosis target cells, anisopoikilocytosis	usually marked	severe	gallstones, usually require transfusions	markedly shortened life expectancy; death usually due to iron-loading from transfusions.

Persons with A/S are not anemic; their reticulocyte count and red cell survival are normal. They have a normal life expectancy, and only under very unusual circumstances do they suffer any of the vaso-occlusive phenomena associated with S/S. Women with S trait may have a slightly increased incidence of bacteriuria during pregnancy.

A small percent of individuals with S trait (under 5%) have one or more episodes of unilateral bleeding from the kidney, most often from the left. The source is thought to be submucosal collateral vessels which develop after sickling in, and occlusion of, small arterioles in the renal medulla. The bleeding may be microscopic or gross and may last for only a few days or be prolonged. Patients with significant bleeding should be placed at bed rest and fluid intake should be sufficient to maintain daily urinary output above 3 liters. The urine should be kept alkaline, which usually requires from 0.1 to 0.2 gram $NaHCO_3$ orally per kg. body weight daily in divided doses. The urine pH should be monitored and more alkali given if necessary. If bleeding is brisk, blood transfusions may be indicated. Occasionally bleeding is prolonged and results in iron deficiency. The use of epsilonaminocaproic acid (Amicar) to inhibit clot lysis by urokinase has been advocated by some. Recently in a large number of patients the length of bleeding appeared to be significantly shortened by this therapy [3]. An initial oral dose of 5 grams is given, followed by 1 gram hourly for 8 hours and then 2.5 grams every 4 to 6 hours for 2 or 3 days. The initial 5 gram loading dose may also be given intravenously. Nephrectomy should not be considered except in prolonged, severe bleeding. At least with the initial episode, other causes of hematuria should be considered.

There have been rare occurrences of splenic infarction reported in persons with S trait when at high altitudes, such as when traveling over mountain passes or flying in unpressurized aircraft. There is no contraindication to flying on commercial pressurized airplanes.

Collapse, shock, and death have been reported in several persons with A/S after vigorous exercise, usually at high altitudes. At autopsy, the spleen, liver, and kidneys were found to be congested with sickled erythrocytes. Although death in these cases was attributed to the presence of S trait, this has not been firmly established. Congestion and sickling may have been merely agonal and post-mortem phenomena.

Similarly, unexpected death during general anesthesia has been reported in a few A/S persons. Here, too, the relationship of S trait to death is unclear. I see no necessity to diagnose S trait prior to the use of general anesthetics, because no patient should be allowed to become hypoxic during anesthesia. If tourniquets are to be used in surgery or on an extremity, an exsanguinating technique should be employed.

SICKLE CELL ANEMIA (S/S DISEASE)

Based upon the 8% frequency of the S gene in the black American population, it is estimated that approximately one child out of every 600 in this group will have S/S disease. The actual prevalence of S/S disease in the black population is only about 1 in 1800 because of the shortened longevity.

Although the average life expectancy in sickle cell anemia is probably less than 25 years, many patients survive for four, five, and even six decades. A major factor contributing to the shortened life expectancy is that many succumb to infections in the first decade of life. The clinical course of patients with S/S disease is highly variable -- some patients require hospitalization several times a year and are so disabled by their disease that they are unable to work, whereas others are, for the most part, asymptomatic and able to lead nearly normal lives. Some of these patients with "benign" sickle cell anemia have a high Hb F but many do not. The major clinical problems in S/S disease may be grouped into the following three categories: anemia, vaso-occlusive phenomena, and bacterial infections.

I. ANEMIA:

In S/S disease the hemoglobin level is usually between 6 and 9 grams per 100 ml. Red cell survival is markedly shortened and the reticulocyte count is increased. The serum bilirubin is usually elevated and, in contrast to other forms of hemolytic disease, there is often an almost equal distribution between direct and indirect bilirubin. In general the patients tolerate this degree of anemia very well, and transfusions are indicated only if the hemoglobin drops significantly below the individual's usual level.

As in any patient with chronic hemolytic anemia, the hemoglobin level drops rapidly if marrow production is diminished by such factors as infection (particularly viral), folic acid deficiency, or renal failure. This sequence of events has been called an aplastic crisis. We routinely prescribe folic acid, 1 mg. per day, to all our patients.

At one time it was thought that iron deficiency was extremely rare in hereditary hemolytic anemias because of increased iron absorption somehow related to the marrow erythroid hyperplasia. At the end of a recent clinical trial conducted here, in which an average of 75 ml of blood was drawn monthly over a two year period, marrow iron was absent or markedly diminished in 14 of 17 patients. A recent report of the autopsy findings in four patients with S/S disease revealed that 2 had no iron in the marrow and two had only trace amounts but all had significant iron-loading in other tissues [4]. The absence of iron in the marrow probably results from both urinary loss of iron secondary to intravascular hemolysis [5] and rapid utilization of iron transported to the marrow. When diagnosed, iron deficiency should be corrected.

Autoimmune hemolytic anemia and transfusion reactions, including those of the delayed type, have been reported and are treated the same way as in any other patient. Although episodes of increased hemolysis ("hyperhemolytic crisis") have been described, I have never observed this in a patient with S/S disease in whom the hemolysis could not be explained by mechanisms other than the disease itself. I suspect that these periods of increased hemolysis are rare, if they occur at all.

II. VASO-OCCLUSIVE PHENOMENA:

A. PAINFUL CRISIS: The most typical presentation of a patient with S/S disease is the painful crisis presumably caused by local hypoxia resulting from occlusion of small blood vessels by sickled erythrocytes. The pain may be localized in one site but usually occurs in multiple sites, commonly in the legs, arms, chest, lower back, or abdomen. Fever and leukocytosis frequently accompany such episodes. Other causes of pain must always be considered. For any given patient the pattern of development and distribution of pain is frequently similar with each crisis, and we find this particularly helpful in our initial evaluation. Adult patients can usually state whether they are having a crisis or if there is something different about the pain that brought them to the hospital on that occasion. Patients and physicians should be aware of the common association of crisis with infections, fever, dehydration, overrexertion, exposure to cold (sometimes even a cold shower or swimming in a cold pool), excessive use of alcoholic beverages, and emotional trauma.

1. Care at home: It is not uncommon for patients with S/S disease to have very mild crises which can be treated successfully at home with acetaminophen (Tylenol), salicylates, or propoxyphene (Darvon). Other patients have more severe pains and may require the judicious use of pentazocine (Talwin), oxycodone hydrochloride (Percodan), or codeine. The prescription of such medications must be individualized. When pain occurs, patients are instructed to suspend activities, take pain medication, and increase their fluid intake. If the pain has not subsided within 4 to 6 hours, if there is anything atypical about the pain, or if there are any signs or symptoms of infection, our patients are instructed to report to the emergency room.

2. The Emergency Room:

a) Evaluation: A short history and physical examination are performed immediately so that appropriate therapy can be initiated as promptly as possible. The findings dictate what diagnostic procedures need be carried out. If the patient has chest pain or physical findings suggestive of pneumonia or embolization, a chest film and blood gases are indicated. Joint effusions should be tapped and the fluid examined and cultured. A complete blood count, including a reticulocyte count, is mandatory. Reticulocytopenia is an indication for hospital admission. Fever and leukocytosis commonly accompany crises and alone are not an indication for blood cultures. If, in addition, the patient has had chills, cultures should be obtained. Urinary tract symptoms are an indication for a clean-catch specimen for examination and culture.

b) Therapy:

1) Fluids: The most important single therapeutic measure is the administration of ample fluids. Although we encourage oral fluids at home, once a patient is ill enough to come to the emergency room we feel that intravenous fluids are indicated. We employ 0.45% (1/2 isotonic) saline solution in doses of approximately 5 ml. per kg. body weight per hour. The amount of fluid given must be individualized, depending upon cardiac and renal status and degree of dehydration; 1 ampule (44 mEq.) $NaHCO_3$ is added to each liter of the initial fluids.

2) Treatment for pain: In our experience, patients with crises who require an emergency room visit or hospitalization seldom obtain sufficient relief of pain from oral medication. We usually begin with 50 mg. of meperidine (Demerol) with or without 25 mg. promethazine hydrochloride (Phenergan) intramuscularly every 4 hours as needed. If there is sufficient relief of pain, larger doses may be given or the medication can be given at shorter intervals. Patients should be given adequate medication to keep them comfortable. If a patient is worried about whether he will be given sufficient relief of pain, he may stay away from the emergency room or may not respond as rapidly to other therapeutic measures. Care, of course, must be used to avoid depression of respiratory function. As the crisis subsides, we switch to oral medication.

3) Oxygen Therapy: We routinely administer oxygen at 2 to 4 liters per minute by mask, catheter, or nasal prongs, at least during the first 24 hours. There is no good experimental evidence to suggest that this form of therapy is worthwhile. It has been demonstrated recently that the number of circulating sickled cells is decreased during general anesthesia and this is thought to be secondary to the increased oxygen administered[6]. The patient is kept warm and care is taken to place him in a room away from air conditioner vents, fans, or open windows.

If the aforementioned procedures do not bring about recovery in 8 to 10 hours, or if there are other indications, the patient is admitted to the hospital.

3. Therapy for the Hospitalized Patient: The therapeutic measures are simply a continuation of those already instituted. Fluids are continued at the same rate of administration for at least the first 24 hours, but we usually switch to 0.45% saline with 5% dextrose. Thereafter sufficient fluids are given to maintain a urine output of about 3 liters per day. This usually requires 4 or 5 liters of fluid daily. As the patient improves, this may be given in part or totally by mouth. At this time we encourage adequate food intake, begin ambulation, and switch to oral pain medication. A common cause of rehospitalization is the premature discharge of a patient recovering from crisis. Patients should be relatively free of pain for a period of 12 to 24 hours prior to discharge.

Blood transfusions are not employed in uncomplicated crises. Occasionally when pain persists for over 5 to 7 days, we administer fresh packed cells or carry out a limited exchange transfusion.

We do not employ tolazoline hydrochloride (Priscoline) or papaverine in the treatment of sickle cell crises. Intravenous urea has been discounted as providing any therapeutic usefulness. There are few contraindications to the use of other therapeutic agents deemed necessary for treatment of complications or other disease. Use of acidifying medications should be avoided. Diuretics should be used with caution since the blood viscosity of persons with S/S disease increases dramatically with increasing hematocrit.

B. SEQUESTRATION CRISIS: Although in S/S disease the spleen may be enlarged in early childhood, it later becomes functionless and fibroses to an organ weighing but a few grams, a result of repeated infarction. Until the spleen does become fibrotic, the child may experience episodes of sudden massive splenic enlargement owing to sequestration of sickled cells. Death may ensue rapidly from hypovolemic shock. This is a medical emergency and requires the immediate infusion of plasma expanders followed by whole blood. The cause of this complication is unknown. Since the mortality is high splenectomy should be considered if more than one episode occurs. We saw one child who had survived several episodes before the age of two. Preferring not to remove the spleen this early in life, we placed the child on monthly blood transfusions and he has had no further difficulty. Transfusions will be discontinued at age 4 and if splenic sequestration recurs the spleen will be removed. This form of management requires further evaluation. Similar sequestration may occur in the liver, but sufficient blood cannot be trapped in this organ to produce shock.

C. PRIAPISM: This complication is painful and threatening for the patient and frustrating for the physician. There is no satisfactory treatment. Priapism may occur before the age of 2, and many patients continue experiencing it in their thirties and forties. Usually

138/ Hematologic Emergencies

patients with this complication have repeated attacks. Many forms of therapy have been tried such as corporal aspiration, spinal anesthesia, exchange transfusions, and administration of estrogens. We use bed rest, sedation, narcotics for pain, and hydration. Our anesthesiologists claim that spinal anesthesia may induce detumescence if employed within the first 12 to 24 hours. Our experience in several patients has not substantiated this claim but this may be the only measure that will relieve the pain in some cases. Valium, taken shortly before retiring, dramatically diminished the frequency and severity of attacks in two of our patients who experienced priapism almost nightly.

Surgical shunting procedures may be indicated in some patients; we prefer the shunt between the corpus cavernosum penis and the corpus cavernosum urethrae. If the shunt is successful, it leads to impotence in the majority of cases. The patient should be made thoroughly aware of this prior to surgery. The physician should be cognizant of the fact that fear of experiencing an episode of priapism may also lead to impotence in some of these patients.

D. OTHER VASO-OCCLUSIVE AND EMBOLIC EVENTS: In S/S disease multiple small and even large vessel occlusions may occur in any part of the body and result in organ damage. Renal papillary necrosis, cerebral infarction, bone marrow infarction, and aseptic necrosis of the femoral head are perhaps the most common. Pulmonary emboli and fat embolization from areas of necrotic marrow also occur frequently. Vitreous hemorrhage, retinal detachment, microinfarction of the retina, and central vein thrombosis are seen in the eye.

Treatment of these complications is no different from that of other patients. Some have suggested exchange transfusion to prevent extension of the area of infarction after cerebrovascular accidents. Children who have suffered one CVA are at great risk of experiencing a second. When placed on a chronic exchange transfusion program to maintain the Hb A levels above 60%, second attacks have been reduced dramatically [7].

Total hip replacement has been used with good results in aseptic necrosis of the femoral head. Vascular proliferation ("sea fan") usually precedes vitreous hemorrhage; vessels leading to these lesions can be photocoagulated, preventing this complication.

III. INFECTIONS:

Factors responsible for the increased susceptibility of persons with sickle cell anemia to bacterial infections are not fully understood and are probably multiple. Functional asplenia, inability to fully activate the alternate pathway of complement, and reticuloendothelial blockade probably all play a role. Pneumococcal infections are very common throughout life but are particularly lethal in the preschool child.

In this age group infections caused by Hemophilus influenzae are also common. In the older child and adult, osteomyelitis is common, a much higher proportion being caused by Salmonella organisms than in patients without sickle cell anemia. It is often impossible to differentiate pneumonia from pulmonary infarction. Urinary tract infections are particularly common in women.

After the necessary cultures have been obtained, appropriate vigorous antibiotic therapy should be instituted immediately. This is especially important in young children. Blood transfusions should be given if the hemoglobin level drops or if the patient fails to improve as rapidly as expected. There is no contraindication to the use of chloramphenicol or amphotericin B as long as the hemoglobin level is maintained by transfusion.

IV. OTHER COMPLICATIONS:

A. LEG ULCERS: This complication, usually confined to the medial and lateral aspects of the ankles, most frequently appears during the midteens and may be a recurrent problem for life. Treatment should be prompt -- before the ulcers become large, deep, and infected. The ulcers should be cleansed and, if necessary, debrided either surgically or with enzymes. Previously our best results were with bed rest and warm wet soaks for 1/2 hour three times daily, covering the ulcer with a thin application of petrolatum or lanolin and gauze flats between soaks. More recently we have had success in some patients using karaya powder and in others using the Unna boot. If infected, systemic antibiotics are more successful than those applied topically. If healing is poor, the patient is transfused with fresh whole cells and maintained at a hematocrit of 35 to 40%. Results with various types of surgical grafting have been discouraging.

B. PREGNANCY AND CONTRACEPTION: Fetal wastage and maternal morbidity and mortality are much higher in sickle cell anemia than in the normal population. We prescribe folic acid, 2 mg. per day, and give supplemental iron only if iron deficiency is demonstrated.

All patients are followed at frequent intervals in both the High Risk Obstetrics Clinic and the Hematology Clinic. For many years some have advocated the use of blood transfusions during the third trimester of pregnancy and we have done this routinely at our institution. Several controlled studies are underway. The published results of one recent study indicate that transfusion decreases maternal morbidity and mortality and increases the birth weight of the child[8].

Patients should be advised of the risks of pregnancy. Although we prefer the use of intrauterine devices we prescribe oral contraceptives for patients who do not tolerate this method of contraception.

C. SURGERY AND ANESTHESIA: Prior to major surgery and general anesthesia, we carry out a limited exchange transfusion over a period of 48 hours. This is accomplished in adults by placing the patient at bed rest, removing 500 ml. of blood, administering 250 ml. normal saline, removing another 500 ml. of blood, and then slowly administering 2 to 5 units of packed cells. By this simple means an exchange of well over 50% is accomplished. We prefer to have our patients go to surgery with a hemoglobin level between 10 and 11 mg.%.

The choice of anesthetic agent apparently makes little difference. Patients usually tolerate general anesthesia well, but special care must be taken during the postoperative period to maintain adequate fluid intake, blood pressure, and oxygenation. If a tourniquet is employed, both a limited exchange and exsanguination of the leg prior to inflation are advisable.

D. GALLSTONES: Gallstones eventually develop in most patients with sickle cell anemia. We do not remove them unless they are symptomatic. We also advise cholecystectomy in patients who experience frequent abdominal crises associated with hepatic engorgement with sickled cells, right upper quadrant tenderness and increasing levels of bilirubin. Such episodes usually continue after surgery, but biliary obstruction no longer need be considered.

CURRENT RESEARCH ON THERAPY OF SICKLE CELL ANEMIA

For the last decade the major emphasis in research on sickle cell anemia has centered on attempts to decrease the number of children born with the disease and on the development of forms of therapy that would abolish or minimize the frequency of painful crises. The government has funded large programs designed to educate the public about the disease and its mode of inheritance. An important aspect of these programs has been voluntary testing and genetic counseling of couples at risk of having offspring with sickle cell diseases. The impact of these programs remains to be ascertained, but it seems unlikely that education alone will lead to a significant decrease in the incidence of this disease.

Another approach has been to develop methods for prenatal diagnosis during the first trimester of pregnancy. The present techniques for obtaining fetal blood and making the diagnosis may yield erroneous results, are potentially harmful to the fetus, are exceedingly expensive, and are available only in a few centers [9]. It is obvious that these methods need improvement before prenatal diagnosis can be made generally available.

The value of urea for prevention and/or treatment of painful crises has been discounted. The most promising drug, sodium cyanate, has been shown to be too toxic when taken orally [10]. It is currently being evaluated in a program in which the blood is treated extracorporeally and then returned to the patient. Although the initial studies appear encouraging [11] this form of treatment is time-consuming and unlikely to ever be widely employed.

Zinc has been proposed as a useful therapeutic agent in sickle cell anemia and a double-blind study is being conducted. Plasma and red cell zinc levels in patients with S/S disease are lower than in normal persons, and increased amounts of zinc are excreted in the urine [12]. Oral zinc acetate causes a decrease in the number of circulating irreversibly sickled cells (cells which are permanently sickled) [13]. Although there is no clear relationship of the numbers of irreversibly sickled cells to clinical severity or painful crises there is an impressive correlation with red cell survival. The mode of action of zinc is not established. Irreversibly sickled cells contain a three-fold increase of calcium over reversibly sickled cells (cells which revert to normal when exposed to high oxygen tensions) and a ten-fold excess over the calcium in unsickled cells. It is proposed that this excess calcium plays a role in decreasing the deformability of the erythrocyte. One mechanism proposed for the action of zinc is that it competes with calcium for entry into the red blood cell.

There is some evidence that thrombosis plays a role in the pathogenesis of sickle cell crises. The use of anti-platelet aggregating drugs is being advocated by some, but no satisfactory clinical trial has been reported thus far. Androgens cause a significant increase in red cell mass but the patients experience more frequent crises, probably because of increased blood viscosity [14].

Theoretically the most useful approach to therapy of sickle cell anemia would be prevention of the switch from fetal to adult hemoglobin. Although this is the subject of investigation in numerous laboratories, there have been no promising results. Bone marrow transplantation has been suggested but is unlikely to be attempted until significant improvement in the treatment, or prevention of graft-versus-host disease is achieved.

OTHER FORMS OF SICKLE CELL DISEASE

In general the comments concerning S/S disease are applicable to the other forms of sickle cell disease such as S/β^0 thal, S/β^+ thal, S/C and S/O_{arab}. Clinically S/O_{arab} and S/S are very similar, whereas the other forms of sickle cell disease are less severe. Retinal disease is more common in persons with S/C disease than in S/S disease, and the hazards of pregnancy are similar. Splenic sequestration, infarction and rupture may occur in those diseases in which the spleen is enlarged (S/C, $S\beta^0$ thal and S/β^+ thal).

In this article we have considered only the treatment of those conditions which result primarily from the hemoglobinopathy, but it is essential that these persons be given good general medical and dental care. It is important also that these persons be educated concerning their disease. It would be ideal if each patient could receive sympathetic management by a single physician who is aware of the patient's social and emotional, as well as his medical, needs.

It is disappointing that, despite our vast knowledge of the sickle cell diseases, no suitable form of therapy has been developed. Considering the enormous amount of research effort being expended on these diseases at the present time, it is highly likely that a successful form of treatment will become available within the next decade.

REFERENCES

1. Shaeffer, J.R., et al.: Hemoglobin synthesis studies of a family with α-thalassemia trait and sickle cell trait. Biochem Genet 13:783-788, 1975.

2. Steinberg, M.H., et al.: Alpha thalassemia in adults with sickle cell trait. Brit J Haemat 30:31-37, 1975.

3. Black, W.D., et al.: Aminocaproic acid in prolonged hematuria of patients with sicklemia. Arch Intern Med 136:678-681, 1976.

4. Popescu, E.R., and Martelo, O.J.: Iron metabolism in sickle cell anemia. Abstracts of the IXXth annual meeting of the American Society of Hematology (Boston), abstract #505, p. 222.

5. Washington, R., and Boggs, D.R.: Urinary iron in patients with sickle cell anemia. J Lab Clin Med 86:17-23, 1975.

6. Maduska, A.L., et al.: Sickling dynamics of red blood cells and other physiologic studies during anesthesia. Anesth Analg 54:361-365, 1975.

7. Lusher, J.M., et al.: A prophylactic transfusion program for children with sickle cell anemia complicated by CNS infarction. Am J Hemat 1:265-273, 1976.

8. Morrison, J.C., and Wiser, W.L.: The effect of maternal partial exchange transfusion on the infants of patients with sickle cell anemia. J Pediatr 89:286-289, 1976.

9. Alter, B.P., et al.: Prenatal diagnosis of hemoglobinopathies: a review of 15 cases. N Engl J Med 295:1437-1443, 1976.

10. Harkness, D.R., and Roth, S.: Clinical evaluation of cyanate in sickle cell anemia. In Brown, E.B. (ed): Progress in Hematology, Vol. 9, New York, Grune & Stratton, pp. 157-184, 1975.

11. Diederich, D.A., et al.: Hematologic and clinical responses
    in patients with sickle cell anemia after chronic extracorporeal
    red cell carbamylation. J Clin Invest 58:642-653, 1976.

12. Prasad, A.S., et al.: Trace elements in sickle cell disease.
    JAMA 235:2396-2398, 1976.

13. Brewer, G.J., et al.: Zinc in sickle cell anemia, in Brewer,
    G.J. (ed): Erythrocyte Structure and Function: Progress in
    Clinical and Biological Research. New York, Alan R. Liss,
    Inc., Vol. I, pp. 417-432, 1975.

14. Zanger, B., et al.: The effects of dromostanolone in sickle
    cell anemia. J Lab Clin Med 84:889-901, 1974.

CHAPTER 5: HYPERTENSIVE EMERGENCIES
by Eliseo C. Perez-Stable, M.D.

A hypertensive emergency or crisis is defined as a sudden, life threatening elevation of the arterial pressure, usually but not always with diastolic levels over 130 mm Hg, a situation in which it is a necessity to lower the arterial pressure rapidly and effectively. Most hypertensive crises constitute a failure of medical care and can be prevented by proper antihypertensive chemotherapy. Although they are now less frequently seen than before the clinical application of effective antihypertensive drug therapy, they still represent a major problem for the primary care physician.

Hypertensive emergencies are divided in two groups. The first includes situations demanding immediate reduction in arterial pressure. This reduction must be accomplished in minutes or hours. The second includes accelerated and malignant hypertension. These patients must be considered medical emergencies but the arterial pressure can be reduced in hours or days. Table 1 presents a list of the most common clinical conditions of the two groups.

Usually hypertensive crisis occurs when extremely high arterial pressure poses a threat to the cardiovascular system, as in hypertensive encephalopathy. Also, when abruptness of rise in arterial pressure rather than the absolute level is crucial, as in acute glomerulonephritis. On other occasions, the clinical setting is such that makes even moderate hypertension dangerous, as in cerebral hemorrhage or severe hypertension immediately after major surgery.

All hypertensive emergencies require immediate and intensive treatment. Therapy takes precedence over time consuming diagnostic procedures. The degree of reversibility in hypertensive crisis is a function of how soon treatment is effective. This concept applies also to malignant and accelerated hypertension. Each day without adequate control of hypertension in the presence of retinal hemorrhage, exudates and papilledema leads to additional and potentially irreversible damage to arterioles, and serious complications such as hypertensive encephalopathy, intracranial hemorrhage and acute left ventricular failure can appear at any time.

144

TABLE 1
CLASSIFICATION OF HYPERTENSIVE CRISES

I. Situations demanding immediate reduction in arterial pressure
    (minutes - hours)

    - Hypertensive encephalopathy
    - Hypertension with aortic dissection
    - Hypertension with subarachnoid or intracerebral hemorrhage
    - Severe hypertension with ischemic cerebrovascular accident
    - Severe hypertension with acute heart failure
    - Severe hypertension with myocardial infarction
    - Uremia with severe hypertension
    - Eclampsia
    - Severe "catecholamine-dependent" hypertension

II. Situations that require prompt reduction in arterial pressure
    (hours - days)

    - Accelerated hypertension (hypertension associated with retinal
      hemorrhages and exudates)
    - Malignant hypertension (hypertension associated with retinal
      hemorrhages, exudates and papilledema)

HYPERTENSIVE MECHANISMS

The ideal situation in the treatment of hypertension should be to
identify the cause of the hypertension, suppress it and cure the patient. Unfortunately, this can be done infrequently. However, in
many instances, we can characterize the hypertensive mechanism
operating in the individual patients and accordingly select the most
appropriate therapy. This approach should be preferred over the
empirical use of antihypertensive chemotherapy.

Arterial pressure is the product of cardiac output multiplied by peripheral resistance. An elevation of the arterial pressure may reflect
an increase in cardiac output or in peripheral resistance or in both.
Blood volume is a major determinant of cardiac output. An expansion of intravascular volume is followed by an increase in cardiac
output and elevation of the arterial pressure, unless there is a pro-
portional decrease in peripheral resistance. This type of hypertension is known as "volume-dependent". The best way to correct
this hypertension is reducing plasma volume. If the renal function
is preserved, this can be accomplished with a diuretic drug. In the
presence of advanced renal failure, the use of a dialytic technique
is the only practical method to achieve a volume reduction.

Very important to the clinician is the recognition of a "volume-dependent" hypertension induced by vasodilator or sympathicolytic
drugs. The renal response to a reduction in blood pressure with

these drugs is characterized by sodium retention and secondary plasma volume expansion. In this situation, the patient may become refractory to drug treatment, but in reality this a "false" refractoriness because the hypertension is now due to an expanded volume and would respond to a volume reduction. In other words, the patient initially was a "vasoconstriction-dependent" hypertensive and with treatment, was transformed into a "volume-dependent" hypertensive.

The second mechanism involved in elevation of the arterial pressure is an increase in vasoconstriction. Arteriolar contraction may be mediated by catecholamines which may be released in excess during certain drug interactions. Clonidine withdrawal hypertension may be secondary to central sympathetic outflow and post-operative hypertension is probably secondary to a sympathetic reflex. In all these situations, the hypertension may be considered as "catecholamine-dependent". The combined use of alpha and beta blocking agents has been suggested as the ideal treatment of this type of hypertension.

In other circumstances, the mediator of the vasoconstriction has been identified as angiotensin II and in these clinical situations, the hypertension may be considered to be "angiotensin-dependent". Recently, two inhibitors of angiotensin II have become available. One is specifically an antibody to angiotensin II which blocks its effect on the arteriolar smooth muscle. The other is a specific chemical analogue of angiotensin II, saralasin (1-sar-8-ala-angiotensin II) which is a weak vasoactive substance. A saralasin infusion test has been developed to identify patients who have the hypertension mediated by an increased vasoconstriction due to an excess of angiotensin II. Saralasin is not yet available to the practicing physician. However, its application in other instances of how a more specific therapy may be used in the future is forthcoming.

ANTIHYPERTENSIVE DRUG THERAPY

Many drugs have been used in the past to reduce arterial pressure in hypertensive emergencies, but at the present time sodium nitroprusside and diazoxide are the more commonly used. The choice between the two will depend on the specific type of hypertensive crisis being treated and the availability of continuous monitoring of arterial pressure.

Sodium nitroprusside (nipride) is generally considered to be the most effective antihypertensive agent available for the treatment of hypertensive crises. It is almost ideal to treat emergencies because of its rapid action; specific effect on arteriolar and venous smooth muscle; immediate reversibility; lack of effect on the central or autonomic nervous system; no tachyphylaxis; and high potency and low toxic-therapeutic ratio. In mechanism of action, nitroprusside differs from all the other vasodilators in that it relaxes both arteriolar resistance vessels and venous capacitance vessels. This produces a fall in peripheral resistance without increasing venous return, and therefore without a reflex increase in cardiac output.

Nitroprusside does not increase cardiac work and it is not contraindicated in patients with coronary artery occlusive disease. It decreases both the cardiac preload and afterload. By dilating the venous compartment it decreases the preload and by decreasing the arteriolar resistance it decreases the afterload.

Conversion of nitroprusside to thiocyanate occurs rapidly in vivo. Thiocyanate is handled like a halogen ion. It is relatively nontoxic at levels below 10 mgs. per dl of plasma. At higher levels it is associated with chills, nausea, dizziness, weakness, arthralgias, muscle spasms, agitation, confusion, and toxic psychosis. Thiocyanate levels should be monitored in all patients receiving nitroprusside for more than 48-hours. Since thiocyanate is excreted in the urine, it tends to accumulate in patients who have reduced renal function.

As with other direct vasodilators, nitroprusside-induced hypotension tends to cause sodium and water retention, with resultant expansion of plasma and extracellular fluid volume, weight gain, and edema formation. This effect is not due to decrease in renal blood flow or glomerular filtration rate, both of which are generally increased or unchanged during nitroprusside therapy. It results from reduction in arterial pressure, and may be mediated both by a direct renal mechanism and by the renin-angiotensin-aldosterone system.

The administration of nitroprusside, which comes in 50 mg ampules, requires the intensive care setting with continuous monitoring of arterial pressure. An ampule can be dissolved in 500 ml of 5% dextrose in water and adjusted to a concentration of 100 mcg per ml. The effective dose may range from 35 to 600 mcg per minute. It is advantageous to give nitroprusside with an infusion pump, which allows the regulation of the dose in mcg per minute, instead of ml per minute. This method prevents the administration of excessive fluid when the dosage required is high.

In summary, nitroprusside in several ways is almost an ideal agent to treat hypertensive crises. Its action is rapid, of short duration and acts specifically on peripheral resistance with no central nervous system action and a low toxic-therapeutic ratio.

Diazoxide (hyperstat), a nondiuretic thiazide-like compound, is a potent, rapidly acting antihypertensive agent. It reduces peripheral resistance by producing direct relaxation of arteriolar smooth muscle. As a consequence, diazoxide-induced hypotension is associated with reflex increase in heart rate, stroke volume and cardiac output.

These cardiac effects are reflex mediated, since the drug has no direct stimulatory effect on the myocardium. This adrenergic response is an undesirable effect in patients with aortic dissection and "catecholamine-dependent" hypertensives. In the presence of coronary arterial occlusive disease it may cause severe arrhythmias, angina pectoris and even sudden death. If there is a previous history of myocardial infarction or angina pectoris, the use of diazoxide should be avoided.

Reducing the arterial pressure with diazoxide is associated with sodium retention. The drug also affects nonvascular smooth muscle causing transient reduction in gastrointestinal motility and relaxation of the uterus. It causes hyperglycemia and hyperuricemia. Some clinicians combine the use of diazoxide with furosemide to prevent volume expansion. Sometimes it is necessary to use insulin or tolbutamide to prevent or treat the hyperglycemia. Significant hypotensive reactions are uncommon with diazoxide alone, but they may occur if the drug is combined with beta blockers and diuretics.

Diazoxide is heavily bound to serum albumin. A rapid injection is desirable to ensure that a high concentration of unbound, active dosage reaches the receptor sites on arteriolar smooth muscle. The usual dosage is 300 mg in 20 ml (one ampule), of 5 mg per kg body weight which is administered intravenously undiluted within 15 seconds. Maximum reduction of arterial pressure returns gradually to the original level over 4 to 12 hours. Diazoxide is unique among antihypertensive drugs in acting both rapidly and for a long period. Monitoring of the patient is needed only for the first 30-minutes.

In our opinion, nitroprusside is superior to diazoxide in the treatment of most hypertensive crises. However, diazoxide is an effective and safe drug which could be used when continuous monitoring of arterial pressure is feasible.

Trimethaphan (arfonad) is a ganglionic blocking agent which was the drug of choice for treating hypertensive emergencies before the advent of diazoxide and nitroprusside. It acts immediately and so briefly that it must be given by continuous intravenous infusion. Trimethaphan relaxes capacitance vessels and blocks sympathetic motor reflexes, lowering the arterial pressure by decreasing peripheral resistance and cardiac output. The antihypertensive effect is augmented by the patient's degree of angle compared to the horizontal. Sometimes it is essential for adequate arterial pressure control to elevate the head of the bed on blocks.

All side effects of ganglionic blockade are common during trimethaphan therapy. Tolerance is seen after 48 to 72 hours. Side effects may be a limiting factor, particularly dry mouth, ileus, loss of accommodation, and urinary retention. The dosage ranges from .5

to 20 mg per minute. It comes in ampules of 500 mg which may be diluted in 500 ml of dextrose 5% in water or even better administered with an infusion pump in a reduced volume.

It causes sodium retention and its continuous use induces intravascular volume expansion.

Hydralazine (apresoline) is a direct arteriolar smooth muscle relaxant. It reduces arterial pressure,decreasing peripheral resistance, but also induces a reflex sympathetic tachycardia with increase in cardiac output. It is much less potent than diazoxide. When used intramuscularly in doses of 10 to 20 mg, the onset of action is 10 to 30 minutes and the duration of action from 2 to 6 hours.

Hemodynamic studies have demonstrated that all four drugs lower peripheral resistance and reflexly increase heart rate but only diazoxide and hydralazine increase cardiac output and left ventricular ejection rate. This myocardial stimulation may lessen the danger of hypotension after the drug decreases peripheral resistance but we suggest caution in its use in patients with congestive failure, coronary arterial occlusive disease or dissection of the aorta. The four favor sodium retention and volume expansion after being used for more than 24 hours, and adding a diuretic may be necessary. In Table 2 is summarized the effect of these four drugs on cardiac output, ventricular rate, arterial pressure, peripheral resistance and ventricular ejection rate.

Reserpine and methyldopa (aldomet) are drugs with a period of time of 1 to 3 hours to start their antihypertensive action and in our opinion, should not be used in the treatment of hypertensive crises.

After the immediate control of the elevated arterial pressure with the use of sodium nitroprusside or diazoxide, the patient should be changed to oral drugs as soon as possible. We prefer for the treatment of severe hypertension the combined use of diuretics, beta blockers and direct vasodilators. The diuretic usually is a thiazide-derivative given in doses equivalent to 100 mg of hydrochlorothiazide. In the presence of reduced glomerular filtration rate a more potent natriuretic such as furosemide in doses of 40 to 160 mg is necessary to obtain the desired reduction in plasma volume. Propranolol (inderal) in doses of 80 to 320 mg and sometimes as much as 640 mg is the second step in treatment. We are now giving propranolol twice a day. As a direct vasodilator, the physician now has available hydralazine (apresoline) or prazosin (minipress) as oral agents.   If this treatment does not control the arterial pressure, then the clinician may add guanethidine, clonidine or aldomet. Minoxidil is an interesting investigational drug with a potent vasodilator effect. Several studies have shown dramatic effects of this drug in patients with accelerated or malignant hypertension who were resistant to other medications.

TABLE 2

HEMODYNAMIC EFFECTS OF DRUGS USED TO TREAT HYPERTENSIVE CRISIS

	ARTERIAL PRESSURE	HEART RATE	PERIPHERAL RESISTANCE	CARDIAC OUTPUT	VENTRICULAR EJECTION RATE
Nitroprusside	↓	↑	↓	↑↓	↓
Diazoxide	↓	↑	↓↓	↑	↑
Trimethaphan	↓	↑	↓	↓	↓
Hydralazine	↓	↑	↓	↑	↑

SPECIAL CLINICAL SITUATIONS

I. Hypertensive encephalopathy: The term hypertensive encephalopathy should be reserved for discrete and "self limited" episodes which result either in death or (if arterial pressure is reduced) complete recovery within a few days.

Hypertensive encephalopathy is seen in patients with essential hypertension or hypertension secondary to renal parenchymal disease, renovascular hypertension, pheochromocytoma or toxemia of pregnancy. Characteristically, the arterial pressure is spectacularly high, usually above 250 mm Hg systolic and 150 mm Hg diastolic. The manifestations of hypertensive encephalopathy appear at lower levels of arterial pressure when hypertension develops suddenly, as in children and adolescents with acute glomerulonephritis or in women with toxemia of pregnancy.

The process of cerebral autoregulation is important in order to understand the mechanism of hypertensive encephalopathy. This is a normal process by which the lumen of the cerebral arteries varies with changes in systemic arterial pressure in such a way as to prevent alterations in cerebral blood flow. If the arterial pressure is reduced, the arterial vessels dilate in order to prevent a reduction in cerebral blood flow. When the arterial pressure increases, then the arterial vessels contract, to prevent an increase in cerebral blood flow. In patients with chronic hypertension, both the arterial pressure below which flow decreases and that above which cerebral blood flow increases, are abnormally elevated. It has been suggested that in patients with hypertensive encephalopathy, the first abnormality is a breakthrough of cerebral autoregulation with a resulting hyperperfusion and facilitation of cerebral edema. However, when the clinician sees the patient, the cerebral vascular resistance has increased to such a degree that the cerebral blood flow is normal or even below normal. At any rate, the goal of therapy is to decrease the arterial pressure as soon and as effectively as possible.

Hypertensive encephalopathy is characterized clinically by subacute onset of altered consciousness, progressing from drowsiness to stupor to coma, accompanied by headache, nausea, vomiting, visual blurring and transient neurological disturbances, including seizures.

Whenever the diagnosis is established or suspected, the patient should be treated energetically with antihypertensive drugs to levels around 180 mm Hg systolic and 100 to 110 mm Hg diastolic. Nitroprusside is the drug of choice, although excellent results have been obtained with diazoxide.

II. Subarachnoid or intracerebral hemorrhage: In these patients, reduction of the arterial pressure is usually well-tolerated and sometimes attainment of low normal or even slightly hypotensive levels is beneficial. However, a recent study has shown no benefits of antihypertensive therapy in patients with ruptured berry aneurysms. If clinical deterioration is observed with reduction of arterial pressure, then use of a less aggressive approach is warranted. Drugs which alter mental status should not be used (methyldopa, reserpine). Some experts consider trimethaphan the drug of choice, but we prefer nitroprusside.

III. Ischemic cerebrovascular accident: When severe hypertension occurs as a complication in patients with this disorder, the situation is difficult to handle. A rapid reduction of arterial pressure may aggravate the cerebral ischemia and increase the neurologic deficit. Always avoid drugs which tend to either lower cardiac output (trimethaphan, guanethidine) or alter mental status (reserpine, methyldopa). A moderate and gradual reduction of arterial pressure is usually well-tolerated, but if clinical status deteriorates as arterial pressure decreases, discontinue antihypertensive medication.

IV. Hypertension associated with acute heart failure: In the presence of acute left ventricular failure with severe hypertension, the work load of the heart must be reduced. Nitroprusside decreasing cardiac pre and after load is the drug of choice. In addition, natriuretic agents should be used to decrease the expanded intravascular volume and prevent any sodium retention secondary to the reduction in arterial pressure.

V. Hypertension complicated by aortic dissection: Acute dissecting aortic aneurysm in the hypertensive patient is an important indication for lowering the arterial pressure rapidly. The goal of therapy is not only reduction in arterial pressure, but also to reduce shearing forces on the aortic wall, turbulence and sharpness of the pulse wave, which are thought to propagate the dissection. Avoid agents which stimulate the force of cardiac contraction (hydralazine, diazoxide). The accepted regimen now consists of the use of trimethaphan and reserpine parenterally and guanethidine and propranolol orally. However, the combined use of nitroprusside and propranolol appears to be as effective.

VI. Acute myocardial infarction with severe hypertension: This association is not common. In this situation, the clinician must attempt to avoid the use of agents which tend to increase cardiac work (diazoxide, hydralazine). Nitroprusside and trimethaphan have been used with success and it has been claimed that if used early enough, antihypertensive therapy may reduce the size of the infarction.

VII. Uremia with severe hypertension: In the vast majority of patients with severe hypertension associated with end-stage renal failure, the hypertension is "volume-dependent" and only after adequate reduction of blood volume, the hypertension can be controlled. In a small number of patients the hypertension is "vasoconstriction-dependent" and a crisis can be precipitated by dialysis.

VII. Eclampsia: When eclampsia (hypertension, edema, convulsions proteinuria) occurs, early delivery is essential. Whether one should also rapidly lower the arterial pressure of the mother in this situation is controversial, however. Some believe any reduction of arterial pressure will-diminish placental blood flow and jeopardize the fetus. Others consider rapid lowering of the arterial pressure will not have an adverse effect in the fetus and may protect the mother from serious cardiovascular complications. Eclampsia has been successfully treated with diazoxide and furosemide, while delivery plans are carried out. Some obstetricians favor the use of magnesium sulfate to control seizures.

IX. Catecholamine-dependent hypertension: A sudden release of catecholamines from a pheochromocytoma, or from ingestion of tyramine-containing foods by patients taking monoamine oxidase inhibitors or sudden discontinuance of clonidine may produce a life-threatening hypertension. This situation is theoretically best treated by intravenous administration of the alpha-adrenergic blocking agent, phentolamine (regitine). Because the beta-adrenergic stimulation of the heart by catecholamines is not suppressed by phentolamine, the occurrence of extreme tachycardia or arrhythmias must be treated simultaneously with the beta blocker propranolol (inderal). The intravenous injection of phentolamine lasts for only 15 to 20 minutes and sometimes it is necessary to maintain a continuous infusion of phentolamine at a rate of .2 to .5 mg per minute. Nitroprusside is equally effective in controlling the elevated arterial pressure due to an excess of circulating catecholamines. If tachycardia or arrhythmias occur, then propranolol should be added.

REFERENCES

1. Koch-Weser, J.: Hypertensive Emergencies, N Engl J Med 290, 211, 1974.

2. Palmer, R. P.: Sodium Nitroprusside, N Engl J Med 292, 294, 1975.

3. Johansson, B., et al.: Supplement I to Circulation Research 34, I-167, 1974. On the Pathogenesis of Hypertensive Encephalopathy.

4. Bhatia, S.K., and Frohlick, E.D.: Hemodynamic comparison of agents useful in hypertensive emergencies. American Heart Journal, 367, 1973.

5. Freis, E.D.: Hypertensive Crisis, JAMA, 208, 1969.

6. Streeten, D.H.P., et al.: Angiotensin blockade: Its Clinical Significance, Am J Med 60, 817, 1976.

7. Baer, L., et al.: Detection of renovascular hypertension with angiotensin II blockade, Ann Intern Med 86, 257, 1977.

ANAPHYLACTIC REACTIONS
by Jay H. Sanders, M.D.

An anaphylactic reaction represents one of the most dramatic and emergent situations in medicine. It is essential that the physician be aware of the signs and symptoms and immediately initiate therapy to avert a disastrous outcome. Within seconds following the injection of an antibiotic or perhaps the sting of a bee, the patient becomes apprehensive and flushed, complaining of "air hunger" and chest discomfort. Shortly cyanosis ensues, wheezing is heard, and the blood pressure falls. Respiratory arrest or cardiovascular collapse results in the death of the patient.

Pathogenesis of the Anaphylactic Reaction: A variety of mechanisms have been identified that can lead to an anaphylactic reaction. The most common of these in man is mediated by IgE antibody and is called Cytotrophic Anaphylaxis. This type of reaction is known to be responsible for the anaphylaxis seen with exposure of heterologous protein, antibiotics and insect stings. IgE is a specialized immunoglobulin capable of fixing to and interacting with certain target cells such as basophils and mast cells. Subsequent contact of the IgE molecules with an antigen to which it was previously sensitized leads to the release, activation and/or synthesis of chemical mediators that act to increase vascular permeability, contract smooth muscle in the bronchi, cause peripheral vasodilatation and inflammatory cell chemotaxis (Table I). Complement is not required for this reaction.

TABLE I
CHEMICAL MEDIATORS OF ANAPHYLAXIS
Histamine - Bronchial Constriction ↑ Capillary Permeability Vasodilatation SRS - A - Bronchoconstriction Eosinophilic Chemotactic Factor Platelet Aggregation Factor

Modulation of the release mechanism is effected by changes in the intracellular levels of cyclic nucleotides. Increasing cyclic AMP by beta-adrenergic receptor activation (epinephrine, isuprel) or phosphodiesterase inhibition (methylxanthines) will inhibit release of the mediators. Conversely, decreasing cyclic AMP by beta-receptor blockade (propranolol) or alpha-receptor activation (phenylephrine) will facilitate release of the vasoactive substances. Cholinergic receptor activation (acetylcholine) eventuates in an increase in cellular cyclic GMP and enhancement of the release mechanism. (Figure 6.1)

Another immunologically mediated hypersensitivity reaction is Cytotoxic Anaphylaxis. In this mechanism circulating antibody reacts with the sensitizing antigen which is part of the cell wall of the target cell. This antibody, which is either of the IgG or IgM class, causes direct cellular damage. Complement is generally required for cytotoxic anaphylaxis. The acute hemolytic transfusion reaction is an example of this type of hypersensitivity response.

A third mechanism which does not require antigen-antibody reactions or prior sensitization is called the Anaphylactoid Reaction. Substances such as non-steroidal anti-inflammatory agents have the capacity in the "genetically prone" individual to induce release of the chemical mediators of anaphylaxis. Since certain prostaglandins can stimulate an increase in intracellular cyclic AMP, it is postulated that the non-steroidal anti-inflammatory agents, by their ability to inhibit prostaglandin synthesis, effect a net decrease in cyclic AMP. Other agents, such as radiopaque dyes, can cause degranulation of mast cells and thus elicit a reaction without the need for prior sensitization.

Precipitating Causes of Anaphylaxis: While the list of potential agents capable of inducing an anaphylactic reaction are quite numerous, antibiotics, contrast dye and insect stings constitute the most frequent initiating factors.

Penicillin alone accounts for approximately 300 fatal anaphylactic reactions per year. The incidence of allergy to insect stings is estimated to be about 8 of 1000 people, and 4 of the 8 have severe reactions. Although about 40 deaths per year are ascribed to anaphylaxis from insect stings it is probable that the figure is much higher as many patients are misdiagnosed as having myocardial infarction.

Clinical Manifestations of Anaphylaxis: While the clinical manifestations of the anaphylactic reaction are diverse it is important to remember that the two main shock organs are the respiratory and cardiovascular systems. The physician should be aware that the chronology of the onset of the reaction may vary from seconds to hours. In general, the more immediate the reaction the greater the severity.

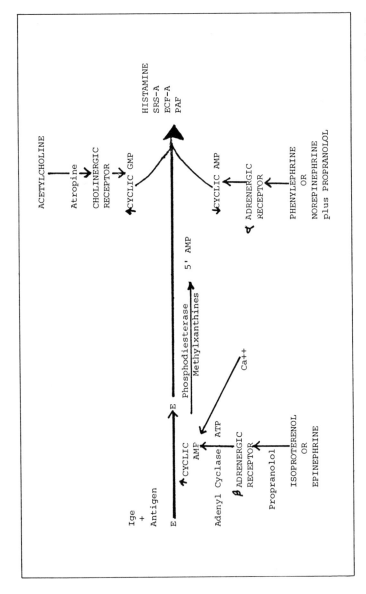

FIG. 6.1: Pharmacological controls of the immunologic release of chemical mediators. Adapted from Internal Medicine, 1977, with permission from K. Frank Austen, M. D.

Involvement of the Respiratory System may be limited to sneezing, nasal congestion and cough. However, it should be appreciated that these symptoms generally precede the more dangerous complications of laryngeal edema and/or bronchospasm. Hypoxia leads to secondary vascular collapse. At postmortem examination obstruction of the upper airway has been noted with edema of the tongue, hypopharynx, and larynx. The lungs may demonstrate emphysematous changes.

Cardiovascular collapse may be secondary to the respiratory failure, but importantly, can evolve in the absence of any respiratory symptoms. Hypotension, as a result of decreased peripheral vascular resistance and increased capillary permeability, is the hallmark of this stage. Activation of the kallikrein system is thought to mediate this reaction. Tachycardia, arrhythmias and cardiac arrest follow shortly. Cutaneous manifestations are very common and are important to recognize as they commonly precede the more severe respiratory and cardiovascular involvement. Facial flushing, pruritus and an urticarial reaction constitute the more frequent manifestations. The development of angioedema should be viewed with great concern as it can lead to edema of the tongue, larynx and hypopharynx causing airway obstruction and hypoxia.

Nausea, vomiting and crampy abdominal pain characterize the gastro-intestinal manifestations. It is probable that these symptoms are caused by the same process evoking the cutaneous urticaria. One can demonstrate edema of the wall of the small bowel that mimics the urticarial reaction. Diarrhea that occasionally is bloody has also been described.

Treatment: Obviously the most critical determinant of the prognosis of an anaphylactic reaction relates to early recognition. Therapy should be begun immediately with beta adrenergic agents, in particular, epinephrine,to reverse the urticaria, bronchospasm and hypotension. The route of administration should be based on the severity of the reaction. Intramuscular or sublingual injections into the posterior ventral vascular plexus of 0.3-0.5cc of 1:1000 aqueous epinephrine should be employed for most reactions involving respiratory or cardiovascular symptomatology. Subcutaneous injections are appropriate for the milder cutaneous reactions, but this route should not be used if the patient is hypotensive. If the sublingual route is unavailable because of seizures or if there is profound cardiovascular collapse intravenous epinephrine can be given although cardiac arrhythmias may be induced.

In an occasional patient, B-stimulatory agents such as epinephrine or isuprel are not effective as a result of the patient being on a B-blocking drug. In this situation, calcium gluconate (10 m I.V. of a 10% solution) will bypass the epinephrine resistance and result in a similar therapeutic response.

If the anaphylactic reaction has occurred as a result of an injection of a drug or an insect sting, the application of a tourniquet above the site, and injection of epinephrine at the site is recommended.

When bronchospasm is not alleviated by epinephrine alone the adjunctive use of a methylxanthine such as aminophylline in a dosage of 250-500 mg IV over a 10 minute period is advisable. Caution should be taken in using aminophylline if the only manifestation of the reaction is cardiovascular collapse for it may decrease peripheral vascular resistance with resultant aggravation of the hypotensive state. It should be emphasized that antihistamines and corticosteroids are secondary drugs. They should not be used instead of epinephrine and are of no value in preventing the acute respiratory or cardiovascular collapse. They do serve however, to forestall continued effects of the chemical mediators but their onset of action precludes an immediate response. (Table II)

TABLE II
TREATMENT OF THE ANAPHYLACTIC REACTION
Epinephrine Aminophylline Antihistamines Corticosteroids Vasopressors Barbiturates

General supportive therapy in addition to specific pharmacologic intervention is equally as important. If laryngeal edema is leading to severe hypoxia, O_2 should be given and a tracheostomy performed if an oral airway cannot be placed. Hypotension not responsive to epinephrine dictates the need for vasopressors, such as levophed, placing the patient in the Trendelenburg position, and, if necessary utilizing plasma expanders. If seizures occur barbiturates can be used. Should cardiac arrest ensue the usual procedures for cardiopulmonary resuscitation are initiated. (Table III)

TABLE III
TREATMENT OF THE ANAPHYLACTIC REACTION
GENERAL MEASURES Oxygen Maintain Oral Airway Trendelenburg Position Plasma Expanders Tourniquet CPR

<u>Diagnosis and Prevention</u>: A careful history to elicit previous drug exposure or sensitivity should be sought. An atopic diathesis as a child or a family history of drug sensitivity are important clues for both diagnosis and prevention. Usually the clinical picture unfolds with such a characteristic pattern and speed that diagnosis is not difficult.

Skin testing can be done, and in the case of penicillin and hymenoptera stings, bees, wasps, yellow jack, etc. where the sensitizing antigens have been clearly identified, the correlation is quite good. Caution should prevail, however, as skin testing procedures have caused anaphylactic reactions.

A new procedure called the radioallergosorbent test which can demonstrate increased levels of IgE antibody in the blood against the sensitizing antigen should aid considerably in diagnosis. In this test serum from the patient is incubated with the antigen attached chemically to inert cellulose disks. The disks are then exposed to radioactive anti-IgE antibody and are counted in a gamma counter.

Perhaps the most critical aspect of a program of prevention is to educate the patient and his family as to what he should avoid and how he should treat an evolving reaction. An emergency kit should be kept available at all times - in the home, in the car, and at work, particularly for those who are allergic to insect stings. The kit should contain a pre-loaded syringe of epinephrine, a tourniquet, an antihistamine and a barbiturate. A medical warning tag should be worn.

Immunotherapeutic programs utilizing desensitization procedures have been employed and, while of considerable help, have not been totally effective. Improvement in this treatment modality should occur as the specific sensitizing antigens are isolated and purified for use. The recently purified specific venoms from the hymenoptera species will provide a more rational desensitization program to match their successful application as a diagnostic procedure.

Finally, an exciting new immunotherapeutic approach is unravelling as a result of experiments in mice. Mice, previously sensitized to penicillin were made tolerant to it following the intravenous injections of isologous gamma-globulin coupled to benzyl penicilloyl (BPO) which is the main antigen causing penicillin sensitivity. It is presumed that BPO-conjugate has the capacity to bind to B lymphocytes impairing their ability to respond to the sensitizing antigen. Alternatively, it is possible that the hapten (BPO) - carrier molecule (gamma globulin) has the capacity to stimulate a population of T suppressor cells which inhibit IgE synthesis by B lymphocytes. Preliminary experiments in man have begun, and if successful will open a new era in the immunotherapeutic approach to hypersensitivity states.

REFERENCES

1. Lewis, J.P. Jr., Austen, F.K.: Fatal Systemic Anaphylaxis in Man. NEJM 12:597-603, 1964.

2. Kaliner, M.: Immunologic Release of Chemical Mediators From Human Nasal Polyps. NEJM 6:277-281, 1973.

3. Lewis, R.A., et al.: The Release of Four Mediators of Immediate Hypersensitivity From Human Leukemic Basophils. J. Immunol 1:87-92, 1975.

4. Corbascio, A.N.: Countermeasures for Anaphylactic Reactions. Drug Therapy, July 1976.

5. Patterson, R., et al.: Classification of Hypersensitivity Reactions. NEJM 5:277-278, 1976.

6. Austen, F.K.: Systemic Anaphylaxis in the Human Being. NEJM 13:661-664, 1974.

7. Quend, J.T., McGovern, J.P.: Acute Anaphylaxis. Hospital Medicine 31-34, September 1976.

8. Frick, O.L.: Immediate Hypersensitivity. Basic & Clinical Immunology (Fudenberg, H.H., Stites, D.P., Caldwell, J.L., Wells, J.V.) California, Lange Medical Publications, 1976.

9. Van Dellen, R.G., Gleich, G.J.: Penicillin Skin Test in Predictive and Diagnostic Aids in Penicillin Allergy. Med Clin No Amer 54:997-1007, July 1970.

10. Immunological Tolerance to Treat Penicillin Allergy. Lancet, October 1976.

11. Hunt, K.J., et al.: Diagnosis of Allergy to Stinging Insects by Skin Test with Hymenoptera Venoms. Ann Int Med 85:56-59, 1976.

12. Frazier, C.A.: Insect Stings - A Medical Emergency. JAMA, 22:2410-2411, 1976.

CHAPTER 7: INFECTIOUS DISEASE EMERGENCIES

A: EMERGENCY TREATMENT OF INFECTIVE ENDOCARDITIS
    by Arnold N. Weinberg, M.D.

A discussion of emergency therapy in infective endocarditis requires
consideration of three aspects: recognition of the likelihood of this
diagnosis; a reasonable estimate of the causative agent; assessment
of the need for early surgical intervention - which almost always
signifies intractable congestive heart failure secondary to valvular
destruction or malfunction of a heart valve prosthesis.

In the following sections I'll deal with each of these areas and then
devote attention to specific therapeutic considerations, both medical
and surgical, as they pertain to the emergency situation.

DIAGNOSIS OF ENDOCARDITIS: In general acute problems occur
most often in infections of the aortic valve.[5] Patients can present
with high fever without heart murmurs or peripheral manifestations
of infection, a major challenge to our clinical skills. Other patients
may have known valvular heart disease and murmurs, the habit of
drug addiction or previous surgery for replacement of a deformed
valve with one of the several available prostheses. In addition, a
number of other factors enter into the complexity of recognizing
acute endocarditis, and these are summarized in Table I.

TABLE I
PITFALLS IN THE DIAGNOSIS OF ACUTE INFECTIVE ENDOCARDITIS

NORMAL VS. VALVULAR DISEASE
YOUNG   VS. OLDER PATIENTS
MAIN LINE ADDICT
PATIENTS WITH PROSTHESES
CARDIAC DISEASE DOMINANT: CHF, Pericarditis
CNS DISEASE DOMINANT: Meningitis, Abscess
LUNG DISEASE DOMINANT: Multiple Infiltrates,
                                         Emboli
EMBOLIC DISEASE DOMINANT: Large Vessel
                                         Occlusion

The normal heart valves of young and old individuals are susceptible to colonization and infection by virulent organisms (e.g. Staphylococcus aureus),[8] and rapid destruction of local tissue plus metastatic infection can lead to functional derangement of cardiac and other organs. Often no murmur is discernible when initially examining such individuals. Older patients may have complex and distracting chronic problems that make the diagnosis of endocarditis difficult, especially if there is no pedigree of valvular heart disease or an insignificant sounding murmur.[7] Occasionally, unexplained left or right-sided congestive heart failure or an acute purulent pericarditis may be principle manifestations of cardiac sepsis and demand therapeutic interventions directed towards correcting altered physiology.

It should be appreciated that non-cardiac aspects may dominate the clinical picture, making the unifying diagnosis of endocarditis difficult to establish (See Table I). Thus, acute S. aureus meningitis in an individual without a history of recent head trauma or neurosurgery should always raise for strong consideration the sequence of subclinical bacteremia, acute endocarditis and subsequent metastatic spread to the meninges. Encephalitis with a predominant polymorphonuclear inflammatory reaction and impaired local neurological function secondary to brain abscess may also occur and overshadow an underlying endocarditis. When acute pneumococcal pneumonia is associated with meningitis, the triad that includes endocarditis should be considered and treatment directed accordingly.

When the acute infectious process involves one of the valves of the right side of the heart the major manifestations can be pulmonary. Septic infarcts, with or without cavitation, multifocal bronchopneumonia, pleurisy with acute inflammatory effusions or right-sided congestive heart failure may be clues to the diagnosis of tricuspid valve endocarditis. If the patient has a history of intravenous drug abuse it makes such a possibility even more likely. Since heart murmurs occur in only about one-third of such individuals where the infection is localized to the tricuspid valve the involvement of the heart may not be obvious.[2]

Occasionally a large vessel embolus will initiate the acute clinical illness. Ordinarily embolic complications of endocarditis occur in minor arteries, consistent with occlusion by small vegetations. Bulky emboli are seen in S. aureus infections but are especially characteristic of yeast or fungal endocarditis. Because impairment of the blood supply is dramatic when a large vessel is occluded, emergency embolectomy is often performed. The central diagnosis of endocarditis, including etiology, can be made from the microscopic characteristics of the embolus as well as results from culturing the clot.

It should be apparent from the above discussion and the features listed in Table I that acute endocarditis may not always be diagnosed immediately.[3] Distracting features and obscure presenting complaints in complex patients can delay an appreciation of the correct diagnosis. In this setting we should exploit another area of physical diagnosis in looking for clues to help make the diagnosis. We're all familiar with the classic peripheral manifestations of bacterial endocarditis, most of which are now considered to be caused by local vasculitis secondary to immune complexes[9]. There is great variation in reported frequencies of conjunctival hemorrhages and Roth spots, splinter hemorrhages and cutaneous petechiae. These lesions are dynamic in the rapidity of their emergence, transient presence and disappearance without therapy. Our experience is replete with examples of the discovery of these characteristic lesions resulting in clarification of previously obscure clinical problems. The presence of conjunctival petechiae below the upper eye lid, a Roth spot several discs diameters from the nerve head or a pustular petechial lesion emerging on clear skin can be dramatic physical clues bringing a previously obscure clinical diagnosis into clear focus as endocarditis.

INITIAL ASSESSMENT OF ETIOLOGY PRIOR TO CULTURE RESULTS: Decisions about initial antibiotic therapy in acute endocarditis should be made as soon as the diagnosis is seriously considered and after approximately 3 pairs of blood cultures are obtained during a period of 15 to 30 minutes. In arriving at a rational choice of drugs, I use an information base gathered from large numbers of patients with acute endocarditis. If these patients are separated into three groups the choices become clearer.

The largest group are patients with no history of heart disease or those having known valvular or degenerative lesions. In these individuals the most common organisms producing an acute, potentially destructive process, are included in Table II.

There are some constant themes in this group of patients in regard to bacterial isolates. Approximately two out of three patients were infected with S. aureus. There is often a history of minor skin sepsis, like a furuncle or the presence of a percutaneous catheter line, but in the absence of an obvious focus or portal of entry, the etiologic agent can sometimes be suspected from observing pustular petechiae that contain characteristic gram positive cocci in clusters. While most individuals with Group A streptococcal and pneumococcal endocarditis had antecedent upper or lower respiratory tract disease, those patients with enterococcal infection most often were elderly males who had genitourinary instrumentation. Although the total number of hospitalized patients with Gram negative bacteremia has increased in the past several decades the number associated with acute endocarditis remains low, in the range of 7-8% in our experience. Most of our patients with Gram negative pathogens had some focal process like urinary tract sepsis or hepatobiliary disease. Thus, in the patient with

acute endocarditis associated with a previous normal background or
valvular or degenerative heart disease, initial decisions regarding
therapy would focus primarily on the Gram positive cocci, especially
S. aureus but include the other pyogenic cocci. Under appropriate
circumstances, in the presence of a localized Gram negative rod infection, we would add coverage for these organisms. In our experience that would be the case in less than 1 in 10 initial decisions.

TABLE II
ISOLATES FROM PATIENTS WITH ACUTE BACTERIAL ENDOCARDITIS MASSACHUSETTS GENERAL HOSPITAL, BOSTON *

S. aureus	107
S. epidermidis	1
Pneumococci	16
Enterococci	9
Gp A Streptococci	7
Gm Neg. Bacilli	13
Other Strep	6

* 1944 - 1973 inclusive

The main-line drug addict population represents a special risk subset
that is fortunately small in number. Although infections and other
febrile diseases appear frequently among this group the spectre of
endocarditis must always be considered, clinical clues looked for and
appropriate blood cultures taken[2]. Table III contains a summary of a
number of series of isolates of documented endocarditis in the addict
population. In comparison with the previously mentioned group of
patients the etiologic agents causing valvular infections in this unfortunate group differs in a number of ways. S. aureus is the major
pathogen but fully one quarter of infections are due to Gram negative
bacilli like Pseudomonas aeruginosa and Serratia marcescens. Also,
approximately one in ten patients has Candida species as the causative
agent. Given a history of intravenous use of heroin and other drugs
the physician must seriously consider S. aureus and Gram negative
rods that are highly resistant to antibiotics, and alert the laboratory
to the possibility of a yeast infection as well.

Finally, the third group of patients that we must consider separately
are those with prosthetic valves in place. Well over 10,000 new valves are inserted successfully each year and patients are living full
and active lives as a result of this type of surgery. The potential un-
toward consequences of the presence of a foreign body in the circulation includes colonization by bacteria, resulting in prosthetic endocarditis. A large variety of virulent and avirulent organisms have
been responsible for prosthetic valve infections, reflecting the enhanced susceptibility of host tissues in the presence of this type of

foreign body. The species of bacteria involved and their frequency differs depending on whether the infection is acquired in proximity to the surgery, within 60 days, or later. Early and late cases include a wide variety of pathogens, including some of very low virulence that rarely infect the natural valve whether diseased or normal [4]. Table IV lists the major isolates from the group of patients extensively studied by Dr. A.W. Karchmer and his colleagues at Massachusetts General Hospital. In the early cases there were only 4 isolates of streptococci. The largest numbers of pathogens included some that are rarely involved in non-prosthetic patients, including S. epidermidis and diphtheroids. In addition, the nine patients with Gram negative organisms and eight with various types of yeast present major problems in design of initial therapy. Undoubtedly this wide variety of organisms reflects the influence of the proximity to surgery, the hospital environment, antibiotics and post-surgical complications.

TABLE III
ETIOLOGY OF ENDOCARDITIS IN DRUG ADDICTS

Pneumococcus	0%
Viridans Streptococci	0%
Other Streptococci	14%
S. aureus	48%
Gram Neg. Bacilli	24%
Candida Sp.	10%
Unknown	4%

Those patients who do well after surgery and develop infective prosthetic endocarditis months to years later have a different mix of infecting organisms that can be of help in early decision making about antibiotics. Almost half of the isolates are a mixture of antibiotic sensitive streptococci that are found in natural valve infection. Both S. aureus and S. epidermidis are frequent and challenging pathogens in this group, as are a wide variety of Gram negative rods and a small number of isolates of diphtheroids. Yeasts however, are not frequent once the valve has been in place beyond a few months and removed from the environmental influences of the hospital and antibiotic exposure.

In making initial decisions about antibiotic therapy in this group we need to establish a number of guidelines: the acuteness of the process, clues from obvious primary or secondary foci (like micro-abscesses in skin) and proximity to prosthetic surgery are of help.

TABLE IV		
ISOLATES FROM PROSTHETIC VALVE ENDOCARDITIS MASSACHUSETTS GENERAL HOSPITAL *		
	EARLY	LATE
Streptococci	4	18
Enterococcus	1	3
S. aureus	3	6
S. epidermidis and Micrococcus Sp.	5	4
Gram Neg. Bacteria	9	7
Bacilli	9	3
Hemophilus Sp.	-	3
Vibrio fetus	-	1
Diphtheroids	6	4
Candida Sp.	8	1
*Through July 1973. Data courtesy of Dr. A.W. Karchmer		

EVALUATION FOR EARLY SURGERY: Any discussion of emergency therapy in infective endocarditis must include recognition of the need for surgical intervention in selected patients, within hours to days of presentation to the hospital[6]. Although vigorous medical therapy may improve the manifestations of congestive heart failure and low cardiac output, some patients need emergency surgery. This is especially true when an acute infection on a normal aortic valve leads to early insufficiency and extreme cardiac dilatation. We have sent patients to surgery within 24 hours of clinical presentation of endocarditis, with successful results, but delayed that decision too long in other patients, with tragic consequences. I'm convinced from 15 years of experience with such patients that appropriate bactericidal antibiotic therapy coupled with early surgery is the treatment of choice when initial intensive efforts to improve myocardial function are not successful, especially in acute aortic valve endocarditis. The problem is patient selection and timing, and that requires constant assessment of cardiac function and size while therapy proceeds, as well as clinical judgment.

A second indication for emergency surgery in endocarditis is large vessel occlusion due to a bulky embolus. As mentioned earlier,

embolectomy may establish the etiologic diagnosis from microscopic
study and culture of the removed embolus in addition to returning
continuity to the peripheral circulation.

Occasionally patients with prosthetic valve infections will require
emergency surgery in close proximity to their presentation with
acute endocarditis. Interference with valve function can lead to
acute heart failure and drastically reduced cardiac output. Paravalvular leaks may also be associated with serious impairment of
cardiac function and massive hemolysis, requiring immediate surgical correction [4].

Having dealt with the initial considerations of diagnosis, etiologic
agents and assessment of the need for early surgery, I will focus
my final remarks on the general and specific aspects of medical and
surgical therapy in natural valve and prosthetic infections.

MEDICAL THERAPY - INITIAL DECISIONS: My remarks will concentrate on early decisions in patients with acute endocarditis, patients who are very ill and getting worse. After blood cultures are
taken, over a period of 15 to 30 minutes, therapy should be instituted,
guided by clinical clues and special circumstances of the patient.
Table V summarizes the initial choice of antibiotics I personally
make based upon the acute pace of the infection and the characteristics of the patient. Antibiotic therapy should be given in maximum
doses by the intravenous route with attention to renal function to
avoid toxic concentrations. When an organism is isolated its sensitivity must be quantitated for the most effective bactericidal agent
or combination found. The efficacy of therapy should then be checked
by establishing that serum inhibits the patient's organism in vitro,
even when diluted out eight to sixteen fold. Long-term antibiotic considerations will not be discussed here, nor will the medical treatment
of yeast or fungus infections require our attention in this discussion
of emergency therapy.

SURGICAL THERAPY - INITIAL CONSIDERATIONS: Progress in
anesthesia and cardiac surgical technology have allowed a much
more vigorous approach to surgery in patients with endocarditis.
In addition, the natural history of acute valve infections has been
studied by cardiologists and infectious disease specialists, and from
their observations an appreciation of the need for surgical intervention at an earlier time in selected patients has developed [5]. In Table
VI I've included those problem areas that may require early surgical intervention. Many are controversial and of unproven benefit
but all focus on problems that to date have met no solution by medical efforts alone.

TABLE V		
INITIAL ANTIBIOTIC DECISIONS IN INFECTIVE ENDOCARDITIS		
TYPE OF PATIENT	ORGANISM(S) SUSPECT	ANTIBIOTIC(S)
Normal	S. aureus	Nafcillin
Genito-urinary problems	Enterococcus or S. aureus	Nafcillin + Gentamicin
Gyn. problems	Streptococci incl. Enterococci	Ampicillin + Gentamicin
Percutaneous lines	S. aureus or non-fermentor Gram neg.	Nafcillin + Tobramycin or Amikacin
Drug addict	S. aureus or Gram neg.	Nafcillin + Tobramycin
Prosthetic Valve	Staphylococci or Gram neg. rods others	Nafcillin + Tobramycin

TABLE VI
EMERGENCY SURGERY IN ENDOCARDITIS

Intractable Heart Failure
Myocardial or valve ring abscess
  EKG changes; A-V dissociation,
  wide P-R interval
Large Vessel Emboli
Mycotic Aneurysm
Resistant Organisms: Yeast, Fungi, Tricus-
  pid Valve Location
Prosthetic Valve Problems

As discussed in an earlier section, unresponsive heart failure and large vessel emboli constitute the two common indications for emergency surgery. An expanding or ruptured mycotic aneurysm, especially in an extracranial location, likewise requires immediate surgical attention. At present the approach to intracerebral mycotic aneurysms is uncertain. Rupture constitutes catastrophy but some lesions heal spontaneously without rupture, some are multiple and others are too centrally placed to be treated surgically without unacceptable morbidity.

While surgical correction of an incompetent valve causing intractable failure is effective in a large number of patients, those with progressive valve ring or myocardial abscesses constitute a group that does poorly. Continuing fever, pericarditis and electrocardiographic changes of heart block are some of the associated findings[9]. Current knowledge encourages a more vigorous attack on such lesions since these patients do poorly, even if treated with the correct bactericidal antibiotics. Unfortunately, technology is not refined enough to definitively pinpoint the location and size of these, so there is understandable reluctance to proceed to early surgery without assurances of an anatomically correctable situation. These patients constitute a potentially curable group and demand our attention in seeking methods to define their problem more clearly.

Resistant organisms, especially yeast and fungi, can most effectively be treated by a combination of medical therapy and valve debridgement or replacement since antifungal drugs are very toxic and fungal vegetations are bulky and less well penetrated by available drugs. Relatively resistant organisms, like Psuedomonas aeruginosa, can be eradicated by appropriate combinations of antibiotics[1]. When the tricuspid valve is involved primarily it can be surgically removed without adding the additional surgical time and risk of a prosthetic valve, and such patients seem to do very well with free tricuspid regurgitation. Except for these unusual circumstances surgical extirpation of infected valvular tissue, to cure antibiotic resistant endocarditis, will not be successful and should be avoided.

Surgical therapy in prosthetic valve endocarditis is a special problem. Mechanical difficulties with the valve or severe paravalvular regurgitation may require immediate surgical attention even in the presence of acute infection. In the absence of such problems, in early or late occurring infections, results of medical therapy alone have been rewarding in individual patients. A major problem relates to selection of individuals for medical therapy vs. combined medical-surgical approach. Under ordinary circumstances, when not pushed by acute mechanical problems, these decisions can be delayed for an initial 7 to 10 day period. My colleagues at the Massachusetts General Hospital have been studying this problem, focusing on clues that will aid decision making regarding surgical intervention at the earliest time. There is a suggestion that prolonged fever (beyond a week of optimal antibiotic therapy), newly developed paravalvular leak and congestive heart failure constitute important findings that argue against continuing medical therapy alone as the treatment of choice. If further analysis of their data can help to develop treatment guidelines for earlier surgical intervention then immediate combined medical and operative treatment may at times become an accepted method of therapy for prosthetic valve infections.

In conclusion, I would like to emphasize the need for early recognition of endocarditis, in patients with obscure backgrounds as well as those with obvious valvular disease or prosthetic devices.   The pedigree of the patient can help in making initial antibiotic decisions prior to results of cultures. An important aspect of therapy in many of these patients is surgical correction of local and metastatic infections and destructive lesions. Our cardiac surgical colleagues should be consulted at the time such patients come to the hospital to help in decision making. Even though emergency treatment suggests a desperate situation and effort, the combined benefits of medical and surgical inputs can often lead to successful therapy in acutely ill patients who may have completely reversible disease.

ACKNOWLEDGEMENT: the author wishes to thank Dr. A. W. Karchmer of the Infectious Disease Unit at Massachusetts General Hospital for his counsel.

REFERENCES

1. Carruthers, M. M. and Kanokvechayant, R. :   Pseudomonas aeruginosa endocarditis. Amer J Med 55:811, 1973.

2. Cherubin, C. E., et al.: Infective endocarditis in narcotic addicts. Ann Int Med 69:1091, 1968.

3. Cooper, E. S., et al.: Pitfalls in the diagnosis of bacterial endocarditis. Arch Int Med 118:55, 1966.

4. Dismukes, W. E., et al.: Prosthetic valve endocarditis. Circulation 48:365, 1973.

5. Manhas, D. R., et al.: Experience with surgical management of primary infective endocarditis: A collected review of 139 patients. Amer Ht J 84:738, 1972.

6. Okies, J. E., et al.: Valve replacement in bacterial endocarditis. Chest 63:898, 1973.

7. Thell, R., et al.: Bacterial endocarditis in subjects 60 years of age and older. Circulation 51:174, 1975.

8. Watanakunakorn, C., et al.: Some salient features of Staphylococcus aureus endocarditis. Amer J Med 54:473, 1975.

9. Weinstein, L. and Schlesinger, J. J.: Pathoanatomic, pathophysiologic and clinical correlations in endocarditis (2 parts), New Eng J Med 291:832, 1122, 1974.

B: BACTERIAL MENINGITIS AND SYNDROMES WITH
MENINGEAL REACTIONS
by Thomas A. Hoffman, M.D.

Bacterial meningitis continues to be an important medical emergency, even though the use of effective antimicrobial agents has clearly improved the prognosis of this disease. Early recognition of acute bacterial meningitis, correct identification of the causative organism and use of specific antibiotic therapy remain essential steps in the management of meningitis.

The symptoms and signs expected in adults with bacterial meningitis are well-known and include headache, fever and nuchal rigidity. Various changes in the level of consciousness ranging from irritability or marked hyperactivity with delirium to stupor or coma may occur. The illness may take the course of a fulminant process resulting in marked clinical progression within a few hours of onset. In other patients, the process progresses more slowly over several days. The course appears to depend more upon the intensity of infection and failure of the host response rather than the causative agent.

Streptococcus pneumoniae, Hemophilus influenzae and Neisseria meningitis account for approximately 70% of the cases of bacterial meningitis. The organism recovered most frequently from adults with bacterial meningitis is the pneumococcus. This finding probably reflects the fact that there are several serological types of pneumococci and immunity is type-specific. Pneumococcal meningitis may result by metastatic spread from a pulmonary focus. This combination of pneumococcal pneumonia and meningitis should suggest the presence of endocarditis. More commonly, pneumococcal meningitis occurs in association with otitis media, sinusitis or a cranial defect in the paranasal sinuses.

The principal causative organism in the pediatric age group is Hemophilus influenzae type b. The capsule of type b strains consists of polyribophosphate, a polysaccharide capable of inducing a type-specific immune response. Although all persons over 10 years of age were formerly considered immune to H. influenzae, recent studies have shown that a significant proportion of our present adult population lack bactericidal antibodies against this organism. This finding may explain the occasional occurrence of H. influenzae meningitis in adults, although an immunoglobulin deficiency state must also be considered. It has recently been noted that some H. influenzae causing meningitis have the capability of producing a beta-lactamase which rapidly inactivates both penicillin and ampicillin.

Meningococcal infection occurs in children and young adults (especially military recruits). Pathogenic strains of Neisseria meningitis can be divided into several sero-groups (A, B, C and Y) depending upon the presence of a group-specific capsular polysaccharide. Immunity to meningococcal infection has been shown to be group-specific; vaccination with the group C polysaccharide is effective in reducing the incidence of group C meningococcal disease. Less common agents causing pyogenic meningitis are Staphylococcus aureus, streptococci, E. coli and other gram-negative enteric bacilli; Listeria monocytogenes and Acinetobacter calcoaceticus var. lwoffi. Although Acinetobacter calcoaceticus is a rare cause of meningitis, its appearance may mimic the meningococcus in smears. Listeria monocytogenes is an occasional cause of pyogenic meningitis. The finding that a diphtheroid has been isolated from spinal fluid suggests that the causative agent is Listeria. This type of meningitis is seen in normal individuals at the extremes of life and in patients with impaired cell-mediated immunity. Recent reports have indicated that meningitis due to gram-negative bacilli and Pseudomonas is increasing in frequency. These infections may result from a bacteremia, central nervous system trauma, or following surgical procedures on the brain or its contiguous structures.

Lumbar puncture and careful examination of the cerebrospinal fluid (CSF) are the essential steps in the evaluation of every patient suspected of having meningitis. The number of cells in infected spinal fluid may vary widely. However, the counts range from 1,000 to 10,000 polymorphonuclear leukocytes per cubic millimeter of spinal fluid in the majority of patients with bacterial meningitis. There is no relationship between the height of the CSF pleocytosis and the clinical outcome. The CSF protein is usually increased in proportion to the number of cells present; elevated levels are seen in most patients with bacterial meningitis. The finding of a CSF sugar that is less than 50% of the simultaneously obtained blood sugar usually suggests the presence of bacterial meningitis. Lowered values, however, are also seen in tuberculosis and mycotic meningitis and occasionally with carcinomatous meningitis or viral meningoencephalitis. It has been observed that the CSF sugar is significantly decreased in only one-half of the patients with bacteriologic-proven meningitis.

Recently, counterimmunoelectrophoresis has been used for the rapid and specific identification of organisms in infected CSF. The specific capsular antigen of the three common causative agents can be detected in concentrations of 0.02 ug/ml by this technique.

The factors influencing mortality in bacterial meningitis are advanced age, coexisting illness, coma, delay in instituting therapy and the presence of bacteremia. Bacteremia can be demonstrated in approximately 50% of patients with meningitis and in all of the fatal cases. In meningococcal disease, fatalities occur in a high proportion of patients with fulminant meningococcemia or meningoencephalopathy.

In fulminant meningococcemia, there is evidence of disseminated intravascular coagulation which may lead to a hemorrhagic diathesis or oliguric renal failure. Among the three major types of meningitis, the mortality in pneumococcal meningitis is generally considered to be the highest despite the use of effective antibiotics. When meningitis and pneumonia are caused by Type III Streptococcus pneumoniae, the mortality has been reported to approach 50%.

Repeated episodes of bacterial meningitis suggest the presence of a gross anatomical defect, a parameningeal focus of infection or impairment of the immune response. Parameningeal foci include chronic infections of the mastoids and sinuses or abscesses of the epidural or subdural space. Surgical eradication of these anatomic defects constitutes the definitive treatment for these conditions.

Treatment of bacterial meningitis is based upon the administration of a specific antibiotic in sufficient dosage to obtain levels in the cerebrospinal fluid that inhibit the causative agent (Table 1). Use of penicillin provides therapeutic efficacy in pneumococcal and meningococcal meningitis that equals or exceeds that of other antimicrobial agents. Alternative antibiotics in penicillin-allergic patients are erythromycin and chloramphenicol, respectively. Cephalothin is inactivated in CSF and should never be used in bacterial meningitis.

The antibiotics currently available for the treatment of gram-negative baciliary meningitis in adults include ampicillin, carbenicillin, chloramphenicol and gentamicin. Of these, gentamicin does not diffuse into CSF reliably and must be given by the intrathecal as well as by the parenteral route. The recommended intrathecal dose of gentamicin is 4 mg every 12 hours. Pseudomonas meningitis poses a difficult treatment problem since the concentration of carbenicillin required to inhibit the majority of Pseudomonas strains is higher than the level which diffuses into cerebrospinal fluid when it is administered parenterally. Some cases have responded successfully to parenteral therapy combined with intrathecal administration by means of the Ommaya shunt, a subcutaneous cerebrospinal fluid reservoir.

A frequently discussed problem of antibiotic selection concerns the treatment recommendations for bacterial meningitis when no organisms are identified on gram stain of the CSF. It must be stressed that gram stain of the CSF usually reveals the causative organism in most cases of culture-proven bacterial meningitis. Antibiotic therapy, however, should not be delayed if the clinical picture and other findings in the CSF are consistent with bacterial meningitis. Treatment in this situation is begun empirically based upon the likely causative organism. Most adults with bacterial meningitis acquired in the community setting can be treated with penicillin G alone since this type of bacterial meningitis is almost always caused by penicillin-

TABLE 1		
RECOMMENDED INITIAL TREATMENT OF BACTERIAL MENINGITIS		
CAUSATIVE ORGANISM	ANTIBIOTIC	DOSAGE FOR ADULTS
S. pneumoniae N. meningitides L. monocytogenes	Penicillin G	2×10^6 u every 2 hr iv
H. influenzae Gram negative rod	Chloramphenicol*	1g every 6 hr iv
S. aureus	Methicillin	2g every 4 hr iv
Ps. aeruginosa[+]	Carbenicillin[+]	5g every 4 hr iv

* drug may be changed after identification of the causative organism and determination of its antibiotic susceptibility pattern.

[+] intrathecal administration is usually required; an aminoglycoside may also be needed.

sensitive organisms. Children with community-acquired bacterial meningitis in localities where ampicillin-resistant H. influenzae has been identified should be treated with chloramphenicol until the microbiology laboratory identifies the causative organism and its antibiotic susceptibility pattern. Although hospital-acquired cases of bacterial meningitis occur infrequently, these cases must be individually evaluated because of the multitude of causative organisms and influence of previous antibiotic therapy upon the likely causative agent. Chloramphenicol is often a useful antibiotic in adults with hospital-acquired types of bacterial meningitis, but intrathecal therapy with an aminoglycoside antibiotic may be necessary in patients with meningitis caused by multiply-resistant strains of gram-negative enteric organisms.

Tuberculosis meningitis may occur as part of the primary infection by Mycobacterium tuberculosis. This form occurs in young children in whom radiographic evidence of active pulmonary disease is invariably present. Tuberculous meningitis in adults is seen in miliary tuberculosis as the result of hematogenous dissemination of organisms from a pulmonary focus, but it more commonly occurs from reactivation of a previously dormant focus of infection within the brain. Consequently, there may not be radiographic evidence of pulmonary tuberculosis in adults with tuberculous meningitis. The adult form of the disease often presents in a subacute manner with headaches, signs of meningitis and cranial nerve defects. The CSF in tuberculous meningitis is characterized by an increase in pressure, an increase in total protein, a reduction in glucose and from 100 to 1,000 WBC which are predominantly lymphocytes. Special techniques for concentrating CSF are usually required to permit identification of the organism by acid fast stain. Culture proof of the diagnosis requires 6 to 8 weeks. Therapy consists of two antituberculous drugs including isoniazid, which penetrates well in CSF. Ethambutol and rifampin have also been shown to attain therapeutic levels in the CSF and either of these drugs may be used.

Cryptococcal meningitis (torulosis) is the most common type of mycotic meningitis. Although Hodgkin's disease and steroid therapy seem to predispose to this infection, most cases of cryptococcal meningitis occur in previously normal individuals. The course is typically indolent and protracted; since there may be relatively few symptoms and minimal changes in the CSF. Examination of the CSF usually reveals an increased number of lymphocytes (usually 50 to 500/mm^3) and an increased protein. The CSF sugar is reduced and the pressure is elevated in about half of the cases of cryptococcal meningitis. Definite diagnosis depends upon growth of the organism or detection of cryptococcal antigen in CSF. The organism may be seen on direct gram stain of the CSF, but India ink preparations are useful for outlining the large capsule of this organism. Therapy for cryptococcal meningitis consists of intravenous amphotericin, but the addition of 5-fluorocytosine may be advantageous.

Another type of mycotic meningitis is coccidioidal meningitis which may also have an indolent course. It is often difficult to recover the organism from CSF and the diagnosis usually depends upon the identification of complement-fixing antibody to Coccidioides immitis in the CSF. Treatment of this type of mycotic meningitis requires intrathecal amphotericin.

Amoebic organisms of the genus Naegleria have been responsible for the few reported cases of amoebic meningoencephalitis. This infection is usually acquired in fresh water lakes and motile trophozoites can be seen in CSF. Treatment with amphotericin B may be beneficial since this agent is amoebicidal.

Several different viruses may cause a clinical picture of meningitis. The viruses most commonly associated with aseptic meningitis syndrome are the enteroviruses, mumps virus and arboviruses. Herpes simplex type 2 has been an occasional cause of this syndrome. An infrequent cause of this syndrome is lymphocytic choriomeningitis (LCM) virus. Examination of the CSF usually reveals fewer than 500 leukocytes (mostly lymphocytes) per mm^3; however, neutrophils may be the predominant cell in the early stages of viral meningitis. It is usually possible to differentiate viral meningitis from bacterial meningitis by a subsequent examination of CSF in 8 hours.

Other causes of an aseptic meningitis syndrome are secondary
syphilis, leptospirosis and relapsing fever (caused by Borrelia re-
currentis).

Viral encephalitis may also be associated with a meningeal reaction,
resulting in a pleocytosis of the CSF.

Herpes simplex type I is known to cause an encephalitis which is
either diffuse or more characteristically localized to a hemorrhagic
area of necrosis in one temporal lobe. The disease usually begins
insidiously with headache, fever, psychotic behavior and lethargy.
Convulsions, paralysis and coma frequently occur; clinical and
radiographic evidence of an expanding temporal lobe lesion are
usually present. CSF may show a lymphocytic pleocytosis, elevated protein content and often an increased number of red blood
cells. Herpes simplex encephalitis carries a very high mortality
rate. Specific antiviral chemotherapy with adenyl arabinoside
(Ara-A) may have beneficial effects but the toxicity of parenteral
idoxyuridine (IDU) is unacceptably high. Dissemination of localized
herpes zoster infection can occur in patients with malignancies.
Encephalitis is an infrequent but serious complication of disseminated herpes zoster. Cytosine arabinoside (Ara-C) has been shown
to prolong the period of viral dissemination and is not recommended
for treatment of viral infection.

Finally, there are several important bacterial processes that may
present with a clinical picture compatible with meningitis. Bacterial
endocarditis may be associated with inflammatory, thrombotic or
hemorrhagic changes in the meninges. Organisms are rarely cultured from CSF in patients with endocarditis even though examination of the CSF may be indicative of an inflammatory reaction in the
meninges. Other causes for an inflammatory reaction in the meninges even though the CSF is sterile are an intracranial brain abscess, subdural empyema and an extradural abscess. These parameningeal foci of infections are frequently associated with a pleocytosis of the CSF and focal neurological defects. The appropriate
management of these three conditions usually includes prompt appropriate antibiotic therapy and surgical intervention for drainage.

REFERENCES

1. Swartz, M.N., Dodge, P.R.: Bacterial Meningitis - A Review
    of selected aspects. New Engl J Med 272:725-731, 779-787,
    842-848, 898-902, 954-960, 1003-1010, 1965.

2. Sampson, D.S., Clark, K.: A current review of brain abscess.
    Amer J Med 54:201-210, 1973.

3. Farmer, T.W., Wise, G.R.: Subdural empyema in infants,
    children and adults. Neurology 23:254-261, 1973.

4. Youmans, G. P.: CNS Infections: General considerations, Chap. 33. The Biologic and Clinical Basis of Infectious Diseases (Youmans, G.P., Paterson, P.Y. and Sommers, H.M.), W.B. Saunders, 1975.

5. Paterson, .R.Y.: Neisseria meningitidis and meningococcal disease, Chap. 33. Ibid.

6. Carruthers, M.: Viral meningitis and encephalitis, Chap. 35. Ibid.

C: SEPTIC SHOCK
by Arnold N. Weinberg, M.D.

The shock syndrome associated with acute infections is all too familiar in the experience of most physicians and surgeons who care for critically ill hospitalized patients. The variety of underlying predisposing conditions of afflicted patients, multiplicity of etiologic agents involved and the variable expressions of the syndrome in relation to alterations in pathophysiology contribute to the problems of managing these patients clinically. [4]

When it was recognized that Gram-negative bacteria were frequently causal in this condition, and that cell wall products ("endotoxins" or lipopolysaccharides) of these organisms could produce a similar picture in experimental animals, the use of the term "endotoxic shock" became synonomous with septic shock. This unfortunate situation, which began in the early 1950's, turned attention from the more general concept of septic shock associated with a variety of Gram-positive as well as Gram-negative bacterial infections and probably narrowed our vision concerning mechanisms. In fact, during the zenith of the primacy of the endotoxic theory of septic shock, it was felt by some investigators that such factors as skin temperature and color as well as presence or absence of perspiration could be used as indicators of the specificity of a particular group of Gram-negative organisms. The contemporary experience with septic shock argues for a more general approach to etiology initially, and the finding of Staphylococcus aureus septicemia is as compatible with this syndrome as is Escherichia coli infection.

GENERAL FEATURES OF THE CLINICAL SYNDROME: The fundamental feature of this syndrome is hypotension, but often there are a variety of findings that support and amplify the diagnosis. Table I lists the major features that are associated with this syndrome.

TABLE I
CLINICAL FEATURES - SEPTIC SHOCK
Hypotension Fever, Chills Tachypnea, Hyperpnea with Respiratory Alkalosis Mental Torpor Oliguria Thrombopenia (with or without DIC syndrome) Leukopenia Local organ disease - Genitourinary, biliary, respiratory Skin lesions - petechiae, ecthyma gangrenosum

It should be emphasized that respiratory findings are not necessarily associated with pulmonary or cardiac disease and may relate to direct stimulation of the respiratory center or to increased pulmonary capillary permeability. Mental changes probably reflect diminished cerebral blood flow and metabolic consequences of shock, and occur most often in elderly patients. While oliguria usually reflects volume depletion and diminished renal blood flow, it may be a symptom of obstructive uropathy. Changes in platelet numbers can be seen independent of the syndrome of diffuse intra-vascular coagulation, in Gram-positive as well as Gram-negative bacterial infections. Leukopenia also may reflect overwhelming sepsis of varied causes. It can be produced in experimental animals by giving endotoxic lipopolysaccharides intravenously to non-tolerant subjects and is seen clinically in both Gram-negative and Gram-positive infections. Underlying diseases and therapeutic efforts as well as nutritional factors can cause chronically lowered white blood counts and must be taken into consideration in individual patients. Skin lesions accompany a variety of bacterial infections. Direct involvement of the skin may reflect the underlying bacterial pathogen as in pustular petechiae of S. aureus infection or ecthyma gangrenosa of Pseudomonas aeruginosa septicemia. [8]   Petechiae and ecchymoses can occur secondary to depression of platelets or interference with the clotting mechanism of the host, as in the consumption coagulopathy syndrome.

In the differential diagnosis of shock the possibility of sepsis must be entertained. While fever and a known infectious focus in a susceptible patient may be present, there are exceptions to this situation. Thus, fever, that vital clue to infection, may be absent due to metabolic conditions like uremia or ketoacidosis, endocrine factors such as hypoglycemia, hypothyroidism or Cushing's syndrome or uncertain factors in very young or elderly individuals. The clinical expression of infectious inflammation may be masked by certain drugs, like corticosteroids, and intraabdominal sepsis (especially renal or hepatobiliary) or endocarditis may be occult and hence escape early detection.

The background of the patient is frequently the major factor in susceptibility to sepsis and the shock syndrome, as well as the difficulty in arriving at the etiologic diagnosis. In approximately 25% of cases the patient is admitted to the hospital in septic shock, and a clearly related problem, like prostatic hypertrophy with urinary infection is apparent. Of the 75% of individuals who develop this syndrome while in the hospital many have complex illnesses and a background of procedures and therapeutic interventions that both predispose to sepsis and obscure its cause.

The following section will deal with an evaluation of the predisposing conditions of major importance that alter host defense mechanisms and predispose to bacteremic shock.

PREDISPOSING FACTORS AND ASSOCIATED PATHOGENS: Overwhelming septicemias, including those due to the meningococcus,
Gp. A Beta hemolytic streptococcus and S. aureus, may be accompanied by hypotension without any underlying predisposing conditions.
Thus, inherent toxicity (virulence) of microorganisms can produce
this syndrome in previously healthy individuals. Patients without
underlying causes rarely develop septic shock, so every effort
should be directed towards answering the question, "Why did this
patient develop an infection, and why did shock result?"

Some general features that predispose to the development of shock
in septicemia include: nutritional debility, dehydration, vasomotor
failure secondary to extremes of age or various drugs, obstruction
of natural passages (ureter, bronchus, nasal sinus), cutaneous,
bladder or endotracheal lines or tubes, the hospital environment
and exposure to multiple antibiotics, chemotherapeutic or immunosuppressive agents. Other patients have illnesses that alter immune
mechanisms, depress cellular clearing functions or cause breakdown
of mucous membrane or cutaneous protective barriers. [4] With these
factors as contributing features we can focus on some of the specific
organ system related problems most commonly associated with septic shock, as well as the pathogens that usually are implicated.
Table II summarizes the more important anatomical areas and bacteria found.

TABLE II
PREDISPOSING CONDITIONS - PATHOGENS

Genitourinary	- E. coli, Klebsiella-Enterobacter-Serratia (K-E-S) Proteus sp., Enterococcus, S. aureus
Gastrointestinal	- E. coli, K-E-S, Bacteroides sp., Enterococcus
Biliary	- E. coli, Proteus sp., Enterococcus, Clostridium perfringens
Gynecological	- Bacteroides sp., Enterococcus, E. coli. Other anaerobes incl. streptococci and Clostridia
Cutaneous	- Pseudomonas aeruginosa, Herellea sp., Serratia, S. aureus
Respiratory Primary	- Pneumococcus, Gp. A Beta streptococcus
Secondary	- K-E-S, Pseudomonas, S. aureus

The genitourinary tract is the most frequent organ system associated
with septic shock. Obstruction secondary to prostatic hypertrophy,
stones or tumor is a major factor. Catheterization, instrumentation
and other operative procedures are frequent instigating events.
Ordinarily, the more complicated the urologic history and antibiotic

treatment background of the patient, the less likely that E. coli will be the major pathogen encountered. The most common group of patients entering the hospital with established shock and septicemia are those with GU problems.

When the gastrointestinal tract is the focus for septicemia, the specific lesions are usually focal, in association with diverticular or appendiceal abscesses or following perforation from a neoplasm. Spread of infection, via septic portal thrombophlebitis to the liver may be followed by liver abscess with the shock syndrome secondary to the hepatic focus. Diffuse peritonitis secondary to perforation or bacteremic spread to ascitic fluid in patients with underlying cirrhosis or the nephrotic syndrome can also lead to septic shock. In contrast to genitourinary sepsis,organisms associated with gastrointestinal foci rarely include Pseudomonas, and often involve obligate anaerobes of the normal gastrointestinal flora (See Table II).

The hepatobiliary area represents a special offshoot of the gastrointestinal tract and infections here are the second most common focus for septic shock. Ascending cholangitis or gallbladder sepsis secondary to obstruction in the common or cystic ducts are the major mechanisms predisposing to this situation . Single or multiple liver abscesses can complicate the primary process, or perforation of the gallbladder with resultant peritonitis or subhepatic abscess may result. Although physical findings are usually localized to the right upper quadrant, with accompanying jaundice, occasionally elderly patients have little fever and no localizing manifestations. The most common causal pathogens are facultative organisms of the bowel microflora (See Table II). Occasionally Clostridium perfringens, an obligate anaerobe found in the gastrointestinal tract, can produce acute infection with associated intravascular hemolysis leading to profound anemia and shock without evidence of blood loss.

With the availability of abortion on demand, gynecologically associated septic shock has plummeted to an insignificant level as criminal abortions have almost ceased. This is an example of preventive medicine that is most gratifying since these patients are usually young, healthy and without underlying physical problems. Organisms implicated in septic shock associated with this area include those members of the normal vaginal flora, a significant number of which are obligate anaerobes.

When septic shock is associated with cutaneous foci there often are familiar predictable background circumstances. The patient is usually hospitalized, and has a severe underlying illness often requiring percutaneous lines, antibiotic therapy and other life support measures. In this setting, skin organisms like S. aureus, Pseudomonas aeruginosa and the Mima-Herellea group are important to consider when designing acute treatment. The circumstances that encourage local skin infection, like a percutaneous line, should be removed and local suppurative lesions like thrombophlebitis drained and excised.

Finally, the respiratory tract may be the initial source of infection associated with the shock syndrome. Primary pneumonias like that caused by the pneumococcus can lead to shock in association with septicemia, with or without hypoxia as a major contributing factor. In secondary pneumonias suprainfection of a patient on assisted ventilation with a tracheostomy can be causal, and usually the organisms isolated are relatively antibiotic resistant, like Pseudomonas or Klebsiella.

In the above discussion the focus has been on the organ systems most commonly disturbed by processes leading to local and then systemic infection, with the resultant development of the shock syndrome. General factors that contribute to the susceptibility of individuals developing hypotension were enumerated. The sum of all these circumstances often determine the balance of effect of therapy, i.e., the outcome. Before proceeding to specifics of therapy the pathophysiologic mechanisms that contribute to the development of this morbid state will be reviewed.

PATHOPHYSIOLOGIC MECHANISMS: While numerous investigators have studied the process of shock in sepsis, in laboratory animals including primates as well as in acutely ill patients, there is a great deal of uncertainty as to how various changes relate mechanistically. Undoubtedly part of the difficulty is the multiplicity of factors interplaying, unique differences in different hosts as well as variations related to species of microorganisms. Thus, any discussions of mechanisms implies that a concordance of many factors are operative and different ones may play major or minor roles with changing circumstances, even over a period of minutes to hours in the same patient.[7] The longer an individual remains hypotensive the more complicated the situation may become, as tissue hypoxia, acidosis, vasomotor paralysis and end organ impairment add to existing problems of management, including response to therapeutic measures that earlier might have been effective.

The alterations in normal physiology that are associated with septic shock can develop in a sequential manner as depicted in Table III, although there are no assurances that any single factor is operative in the individual patient, or that they occur in the exact order tabulated.

In many patients the interplay of compensatory mechanisms results in early maintenance of an adequate blood pressure, probably due to increased cardiac output. Eventually hypotension becomes manifest, as factors such as volume depletion, third space losses and fever associated with peripheral vasodilitation and insensible loss of water vapor develop. Diminished blood volume is reflected in low pressure measurements using a central venous catheter or, more accurately, a Swan Ganz line. As tissue perfusion falls the resultant hypoxia leads to local acidosis and eventually a loss of catecholamine stimulated vasomotor tone.

TABLE III
FACTORS ASSOCIATED WITH SEPTIC SHOCK IN MAN

Release of vasoactive kinins like bradykinin

↓   Peripheral arteriolar resistance

↓   Venular resistance

Edema, anoxia, acidosis

↓   Effective blood volume
        loss to extravascular compartment
        relative increase vascular bed capacitance

↓   Venous return

Myocardial failure

Decreased cardiac output after initial increase

In addition to the dynamic changes cited above, eventuating in diminished circulating blood volume, there may be early potent effects of vasoactive kinins, like bradykinin, on the vascular tree.[3]   These kinins may be formed in Gram-negative infections through the release of Factor XII, Hageman factor, by lipopolysaccharide (endotoxic) bacterial products. A cascade of interactions can eventually lead to stimulation of the kallikrein system, and via this pathway bradykinin may be released. Bradykinin acts on peripheral arteriolar structures producing profound vasodilatation and this may eventually be a major factor in the developing shock syndrome, through lowered peripheral resistance.

The effects of bradykinin on venular smooth muscle are much less pronounced so there may be increased venular resistance relative to that of the arteriolar bed, resulting in an augmentation of fluid loss via the capillaries, further aggravating the state of diminishing intravascular volume. The result of these multiple dynamic changes is an ineffective blood volume with inadequate venous return to maintain an optimal cardiac output. Hypotension results from this sequence, intensified by local tissue hypoxia and acidosis.

Finally, there is evidence from physiologic as well as pathologic studies that septicemia may be associated with impairment in myocardial function, especially inotropy.[7] If myocardial failure develops, then central venous pressure will rise even in states of low blood volume, and the shock syndrome will be aggravated further. The biochemical mechanism underlying failure of mycardial function is uncertain but its occurrence in septicemic conditions caused by Gram-positive as well as Gram-negative organisms argues against a specific "endotoxic" factor.

From this review of pathophysiologic alterations associated with septic shock a sound sequential therapeutic approach can be developed. Success or failure remains problematical since differences in individual patients' underlying problems and timing of initiation of therapeutic efforts produces variations in results that cannot be measured with confidence.

TREATMENT OF SEPTIC SHOCK: Considering the complexity of this syndrome and the relatively poor results of therapy in most medical centers, every effort should be made to prevent the development of septic shock by early recognition and vigorous antibiotic treatment of any acute infection. This requires constant vigil of patients with problems that predispose to septicemia, including early surgical intervention to drain abscesses and relieve obstructive lesions. If hypotension develops in the setting of septicemia, sequential efforts based upon known pathophysiologic alterations should be undertaken immediately.[6] These emergency efforts must be augmented by measures that include assessment of bacterial etiology and institution of appropriate antibiotics and surgical procedures, which can influence eventual outcome once the shock syndrome has been treated effectively. Table IV lists these sequential therapeutic efforts that are based upon the known changes enumerated in the previous section.

TABLE IV
THERAPEUTIC CONSIDERATIONS IN SEPTIC SHOCK

IMMEDIATE MANAGEMENT:
 	
    Oxygen
    Normalize hematocrit
    Central venous or Swan Ganz line
        Low pressure → volume
        High pressure → Beta stimulator - dopamine,
                                            isoproterenol
    Bicarbonate if pH < 7.10
    Vasodilators - alpha blockade - Chlorpromazine
    Corticosteroids
 	
CONTINUING MANAGEMENT:
 	
    Antibiotics via intravenous route
    Surgical procedures - relieve obstruction
                                    drain abscess

In the immediate management of these patients oxygenation and the hematocrit should be optimalized. Hypoxia may be the cause of hypotension in an individual with a pulmonary infection or the adult respiratory distress syndrome, and improved oxygen capacity will result from correction of low hemoglobin levels. Usually these patients are volume depleted but it is mandatory to record pulmonary wedge or central venous pressures (CVP) prior to intravenous administration of volume expanders. Occasional patients have early myocardial failure associated with hypotension, and a high CVP is the best indicator that this situation exists. Volume overload under those circumstances may precipitate pulmonary edema. Often in patients with low CVP's the addition of volume alone will reverse the hypotensive episode without the need for pharmacological agents. If volume replacement to high normal central pressures, in the range of 15 cm of water, doesn't correct the hypotension then dopamine therapy should be instituted.[2] Non-alkaline solutions should be used since high pH can inactivate dopamine. This endogenous catecholamine has a primary direct action in increasing myocardial contractility and heart rate via stimulation of beta-adrenergic receptors. In addition dopamine can exert vasodilatory effects on selective vascular beds, with resultant alleviation of local hypoxia and increased renal blood flow, may improve a desperate situation and help reverse the downhill course. If dopamine infusions at low flow rates (less than 20 ug per kilogram per minute) improve myocardial function and renal blood flow then CVP will fall, additional volume may be added more safely and patient survival may be enhanced.

During this acute phase of treatment of septic shock blood pH should be followed closely. If values fall to 7.1 or below then sodium bicarbonate should be added to the regimen. There is evidence that oxygen dissociates more readily from hemoglobin in acidotic states and less readily if the pH moves towards an alkaline range. Since tissue hypoxia is a critical lesion in these hypotensive patients too vigorous use of bicarbonate may lead to pH's that interfere with oxygen dissociation and therefore enhance tissue hypoxia.

The use of alpha adrenergic blocking drugs to produce vascular bed vasodilation has been suggested as a mechanism for improving tissue perfusion in patients that don't respond to the above measures and are becoming profoundly acidotic and oliguric. While dopamine in low doses produces dilation of some vascular areas (see above), the ongoing hypotension may require higher doses of dopamine with consequent vasoconstrictor effects predominating. Phenoxybenzamine is a potent alpha blocking agent that has been used experimentally with some success but isn't readily available. Chlorpromazine has potent alpha blocking properties and has been an available and useful agent. If effective the CVP will fall (enlarged capacitance of the vascular bed), urine output may increase and additional volume may safely be added. The net result can be increasing blood pressure.

Finally, some comments must be made about the use of corticosteroids in septic shock. They are last on the list of immediate management efforts and cause controversy whenever this subject is discussed. Corticosteroids in high doses have been shown to have a salutory effect on myocardial contraction but this effect is not as potent or easily titratable as the action of dopamine. Corticosteroids in high doses also can decrease peripheral resistance and therefore improve tissue perfusion and oxygenation.[1] This may be achieved using low dose dopamine, volume expansion, bicarbonate therapy for pH < 7.1 or agents like chlorpromazine. I would urge the rapid sequential use of those agents and procedures listed in Table IV and if no progress is made during the course of the first hour or two, then corticosteroids should be instituted. A recent report in the Annals of Surgery describes very favorable results with dexamethasone, 3 mgm per kg or methylprednisolone, 30 mgm per kg intravenously as a single bolus over 10 to 20 minutes, repeated once after 4 hours.[5] This seems like a regimen that won't do much harm and the results in this study show significant reduction in mortality. Unfortunately, patient selection and description of the severity of the clinical syndrome was not described in detail. Therefore, it is difficult to judge if this series is comparable to other reports where the results were less favorable. Time and other carefully controlled and described clinical studies should settle this issue. Other studies in the literature present strong cases for and against use of these agents.

In addition to these emergency measures, the rational choice of antibiotics and assessment of the patient for the need for surgical intervention are essential steps to be taken. If the patient has a genitourinary, pelvic or intraabdominal source for the septic process that precipitated the shock syndrome then obstruction and localized abscess must be considered, and early appropriate surgery undertaken as soon as the cardiovascular problem has been stabilized.

Antibiotic therapy must be promptly administered via the intravenous route. The choice of drugs should be guided by the results of gram-staining exudates or data from previous blood and other cultures. In the absence of this information the likely causal agent or agents, based on the location of the septic focus and the background of the patient, can be anticipated. Based on data from Gram stains the choices of antibiotics can be divided into those directed towards Gram-positive pathogens and those directed towards Gram-negative organisms. Table V and VI list the most frequent bacterial species encountered and the antibiotics currently of choice at our institution. Since antibiotic sensitivity characteristics vary from region to region and hospital to hospital these recommendations should be considered as guidelines only.

TABLE V
ANTIBIOTIC THERAPY - GRAM-NEGATIVE PATHOGENS

E. coli	-	Ampicillin, Aminoglycoside, Chloramphenicol
Kleb-Enterob-Serratia	-	Aminoglycoside, Cephalosporin, Chloramphenicol
P. mirabilis	-	Ampicillin, Aminoglycoside, Cephalosporin
Proteus sp.	-	Aminoglycoside, Carbenicillin
Pseudomonas	-	Carbenicillin + Tobramycin or Gentamicin
Herellea	-	Kanamycin, Amikacin, Polymixin
Meningococcus	-	Penicillin, Erythromycin, Chloramphenicol

TABLE VI
ANTIBIOTIC THERAPY - GRAM-POSITIVE PATHOGENS

Pneumococcus	-	Penicillin, erythromycin
Streptococcus	-	Penicillin, erythromycin
Enterococcus	-	Penicillin + Gentamicin, Vancomycin
S. aureus	-	Nafcillin, Vancomycin, Cephalosporin
Clostridium perfringens	-	Penicillin, erythromycin

In most large series of septic shock Gram-negative pathogens are
causal in approximately two-thirds of patients.[4] From information
available on the likely primary site of infection, antibiotic history
and relationship to hospitalization an intelligent guess can be made
in deciding on the likely pathogen and appropriate therapy. An acute
renal infection in a patient without a history of chronic recurrent
pyelonephritis or instrumentation will be caused by E. coli or Pro-
teus mirabilis in approximately 85% of cases. Ampicillin is an
effective drug to choose. In contrast, an individual with a complex
chronic renal problem developing acute septic shock following prolonged hospitalization may have a Klebsiella or Enterobacter infection and an aminoglycoside like gentamicin should be prescribed.

If Pseudomonas septicemia is suspected from finding lesions of ecthyma gangrenosa in a leukemic patient with a percutaneous catheter, then carbenicillin and tobramycin therapy should be instituted. In like manner, we can use the pedigree of the patient, location of the septic focus or route of spread and information from the Gram stain to initiate therapy in most situations.

Gram-positive pathogens can often be identified by characteristics of location of the primary infection. Pneumococcal septicemia often originates in a respiratory focus and may be complicated by invasion of the meninges. Group A Beta hemolytic streptococci produce acute edematous cellulitis, pneumonitis with early pleural effusions and characteristically appear as long chains of cocci. S. aureus septicemia may be reflected by pustular petechiae or abscess formation and the organisms appear as clumps of cocci. If the infection is in the urinary tract and organisms present on Gram staining are chains of cocci, the enterococcus should be most strongly considered. Clostridial septicemia can follow gastrointestinal or gynecological infection or surgery and intravascular hemolysis can be an important clue to the etiologic diagnosis. Therapy, as outlined in Table VI can be instituted appropriately once consideration is given to the clinical situation and the results of Gram stains.

PROGNOSIS IN SEPTIC SHOCK: Patients with this syndrome vary widely in their underlying diseases and the circumstances in which septicemia occurs. If the measures to support blood pressure are intelligently and vigorously applied, and surgical intervention is timely, then outcome often relates to appropriate selection of antibiotics and the patient's primary disease. Dr. William McCabe has summarized his extensive experience in terms of survival related to these factors.[4] In patients with rapidly fatal underlying diseases approximately 40% survive. Those with ultimately fatal disease have a 70% survival and 93% of individuals with non-fatal illnesses will recover. When the antibiotic therapy is not well chosen then these survival figures fall to 10%, 50% and 66% respectively. This type of information emphasizes the importance of appropriate antibiotic therapy to survival, although the initial management of the shock syndrome will eventually determine if the patient will remain alive long enough to benefit from the agents used.

By individualizing therapy according to the specific indications from clues in the history, physical exam and laboratory data, appropriate antibiotics can be selected. With careful monitoring of blood volume, pH, oxygenation of blood and urine output, a sequential pattern of therapy of the shock syndrome can be developed. When simple measures work then complex therapies can be avoided. Dopamine, other catecholamines, alpha-blocking agents and corticosteroids are available if necessary and may be effective in treating this potentially reversible syndrome.

The relatively poor results encountered in this syndrome stand as a major challenge to us to prevent the development of septic shock, or to deal rationally and vigorously with it when confronted with this difficult clinical problem.

REFERENCES

1. Christy, J.H. : Treatment of Gram-negative shock. Am J Med 50:77, 1971.

2. Goldberg, L.I.: Dopamine - Clinical uses of an endogenous catecholamine. New Engl J Med 291: 707, 1974.

3. Mason, J.W. , Kleiberg, V. , et al.: Plasma kallikrein and Hageman factor in Gram-negative bacteremia. Ann Intern Med 73:545, 1970.

4. McCabe, W.R.: Gram-negative Bacteremia. Disease-a-Month. Year Book Medical Publish., Inc. Chicago, Dec. 1973.

5. Schumer, W.: Steroids in the treatment of clinical septic shock. Ann Surg 184:333, 1976.

6. Treatment of shock associated with bacterial sepsis. Medical Letter 11:93, 1969.

7. Udhoji, V.N. , and Weil, M.H.: Hemodynamic and metabolic studies associated with bacteremia. Ann Int Med 62:966, 1965.

8. Weinberg, A.N. , and Swartz, M.N.: Gram-Negative coccal and bacillary infections, In: Dermatology in General Medicine, Thomas B. Fitzpatrick, ed. , McGraw Hill, Inc. , New York, 1971, p. 1713.

9. Winslow, E.J. , Loeb, H.S. , et al.: Hemodynamic studies and results of therapy in 50 patients with bacteremic shock. Amer J Med 54:421, 1973.

CHAPTER 8: METABOLIC EMERGENCIES
by Andrew Taylor, M.D.

HYPERCALCEMIA

Hypercalcemia is one of the true emergency conditions encountered
in Internal Medicine. This problem historically has been in the pur-
vue of the endocrinologist ever since Fuller Albright's time, even
though endocrine causes constitute a minority of situations in
which the serum calcium is dangerously elevated.

For the purposes of this discussion, serum calcium will mean total
calcium, both protein bound and ionized, even though it is recognized that it is ionized calcium that is important for membrane,
cellular and physiologic effects. The routine chemistry lab is not
equipped to measure ionized calcium, and fortunately total calcium
does give reliable information on ionized calcium as long as the
serum albumin is normal. There are a few exceptions to this situation. Local protein bound calcium concentrations may rise by
0.5-1 mg% with prolonged tourniquet application, para-proteins
associated with myeloma may bind calcium, and such situations are
usually not overlooked.

There are various symptoms and signs that should suggest clinically
important hypercalcemia, which are listed below in approximate decreasing frequency.

1. weakness, lethargy
2. anorexia, nausea
3. polyuria, thirst, dehydration
4. constipation
5. myopathy
6. arrhythmias, heart block
7. mental disturbance, somnolence
8. coma

There seldom are symptoms from hypercalcemia when levels are
below 11.5 mg%. Their frequency increases, however, with very
high calcium levels (above 15 mg%), particularly if the level is
rapidly rising and if there is an ↑ in the ionized fraction as is seen
in acidemic states.

The most common and least specific indication of hypercalcemia is
insidious lethargy, sometimes with frank objective weakness from
proximal myopathy. The lethargy may arise from central effects of
calcium on mental processes as well as elevation of the threshold for

190

depolarization of muscles. Anorexia, nausea and vomiting are very frequent, arise probably from central nervous system effects, but the associated hyperacidity and pylorospasm may contribute to it.

The succeeding symptoms become somewhat more specific indicators of hypercalcemia. Hypercalcemia results in a solute diuresis as well as net free water loss. The former results from inhibiting sodium reabsorption as well as by water loss accompanying the calciuresis. Hypercalcemia also causes vasopressin unresponsive loss of distal tubular concentrating ability, through inhibition of adenyl cyclase, so free water is lost. The resulting dehydration, (as might happen from associated nausea), if not balanced by water intake, would lead to severe dehydration and a fall in renal blood flow and GFR. This would remove renal excretion of calcium as a mechanism of partial compensation for hypercalcemia, and a rapid rise in calcium level would ensue. While several diseases with chronic hypercalcemia are associated with hypertension the "cause and effect" relationship is not clear. It is well recognized, however, that acute calcium elevation may increase cardiac output and increase peripheral resistance together resulting in transient dangerous blood pressure elevation.

After substantiating the suspicion of hypercalcemia, concern should be directed at lowering the level of calcium if any of the more serious symptoms are present or if the level is over 14 mg %, even before one searches for causes. Only when one is assured that the calcium is progressively falling are definitive diagnostic procedures appropriate.

The mainstay of therapy clearly remains rehydration or overhydration, both to dilute the calcium in extracellular fluid, and to promote renal filtration and calcium excretion. Often this maneuver does not completely normalize calcium but like many therapies for hypercalcemia, lowers the level to less critical levels. Hydration is appropriate for mild or severe hypercalcemia alike, but in the latter case with associated severe nausea and dehydration, parenteral saline must be used. In the majority of situations intravenous saline is all that is required for general therapy of the hypercalcemia and to replenish prior sodium losses. In many situations, however, additional maneuvers must be resorted to as shown below.

1. Hydration (saline)
2. Glucocorticoids
3. Forced diuresis
4. Phosphate (oral or IV)
5. Calcitonin
6. Mithramycin
7. EDTA
8. Hemodialysis

The choice among these possibilities is quite straightforward today. For nearly all situations the first four treatments are satisfactory.

Glucocorticoids (40-60 mg Prednisone) have specific and unique usefulness in treating the hypercalcemia of saroid and vitamin D intoxication as they inhibit the vitamin D effect of promoting gastrointestinal Ca++ absorption. Glucocorticoids are also partially effective in hypercalcemia caused by some cancers, but other therapies have become more useful in these situations. It should be noted that it has little if any effect on the ↑ Ca++ of primary hyperparathyroidism.

Recent experience with a forced diuresis combining saline and a potent diuretic such as furosemide (not thiazides) has shown this approach to be very effective in enhancing renal excretion of calcium. Old enthusiasm for sodium sulfate solutions has not continued since the calciuresis and serum calcium lowering effect is entirely related to the sodium diuresis, and much higher losses are possible with furosemide and saline. When a rapid diuresis is initiated as proposed by Suki et al [2], close observation and supervision, preferably in an intensive care unit, is mandatory. One must overhydrate the patient before giving furosemide and closely assess urine flow and sodium losses to prevent inducing dehydration and potentially re-elevation of the serum calcium. A CVP line should be placed. The Suki regimen of 100 mg furosemide with saline and D5W (in a ratio of 4:1) matching output every 2 hours can result in 5 mEq sodium excretion per minute and 4000 mg calcium excretion per 24 hours-8 times that of rehydration with saline alone, and approaching that of hemodialysis (6000 mg calcium per 8 hours). The serum calcium generally is lowered to safe (if not normal) levels in 12-24 hours. Potassium must be added to each liter of saline, and serum phosphorus and magnesium assessed every 6 hours. One must recall that it is not the furosemide itself which results in this procedure being much more effective than saline alone, it is the ensuing saline and calcium diuresis. If there is renal failure or no diuresis, the procedure will not work (and may be dangerous for a weakened circulation). The need for close attention to cardiovascular status and electrolyte losses somewhat limits the practical use of this method, but more modest furosemide doses and diuresis often are sufficient.

Phosphate (sodium and potassium salt) therapy has been an old mainstay of therapy, [3], yet less used today than a forced diuresis. Phosphate rapidly causes complexing of calcium in bone and activates osteoblasts. A slower effect is to decrease the activation of Vitamin D and decrease intestinal calcium absorbtion. Intravenous phosphate is rapidly effective (8-10 hr) and generally regarded to be safe in modest doses as suggested by Goldsmith et al [4], but oral doses of 2-4 g per day are effective for subacute situations. There has been much concern, largely unsubstantiated, of precipitation of calcium-phosphate complexes in extra skeletal sites such as lung, heart and kidney with intravenous phosphate, and undoubtedly this theoretically could happen. But, with adherence to standard doses (100 mM/6 hr repeated each day as needed) this risk is minimized.[3]

Recent experience with salmon calcitonin[5, 6] and Mithramycin[7] indicates that these drugs may become the treatment of choice when one can safely wait 18-26 hours for full effectiveness. They both appear potentially safer than phosphate and long-term glucocorticoids. Both, as yet are not approved for use in hypercalcemia although Mithramycin is approved as an antitumor agent and can be used for cancer induced hypercalcemia[8]. Calcitonin is available, but for use only in Paget's disease.

Calcitonin promotes osteoblastic activity and bone uptake of calcium. When used at 8 units per kg per day in divided doses it is effective in lowering extremely elevated calcium levels from varied causes (cancer, Vitamin D intoxication, hyperparathyroidism, thyrotoxicosis) within a day. There has been concern over development of resistance (antibodies) to continued use of calcitonin, but this is less with salmon then porcine varieties. Addition of small doses of glucocorticoids, too small to themselves have hypocalcemic effects, seem to retard the development of antibodies to salmon calcitonin.

Small doses of Mithramycin (25 μ g/kg) given as a single parenteral injection may after one to two days control the calcium for several days. Side effects are largely avoided at this dosage and the simplicity of this regimen together with hydration is appealing particularly when chronic therapy may be anticipated.

EDTA, as a chelator of calcium, is seldom used today, because of the availability of other less toxic agents, and the difficulty in obtaining it. However, it remains, together with rehydration, the most rapid acting agent, and if renal excretion is normal (not frequent with the highest calcium levels!) and less than 10 grams are used in a 24 hour period, it still may occasionally be useful.

Hemodialysis rarely is used and only if renal failure interdicts forced diuresis or phosphate administration. Calcium removal is only slightly better than with a furosemide forced diuresis.

After hydration and perhaps use of one of the acute modalities to lower the calcium below 14 mg%, definitive diagnosis of the cause of hypercalcemia should be instituted. Sarcoid, thyrotoxicosis, Vitamin D intoxication, post-acute renal failure (especially rhabdomialysis), milk-alkali syndrome (very rare with non-absorbable antacids) are readily diagnosed by history and simple laboratory tests. Thiazide diuretics never cause hypercalcemia in an otherwise normal individual, and even in a person with hypercalciuria it can only result in slight hypercalcemia. Hyperparathyroidism [8] may be much harder to diagnosis. PHT radioimmunoassays with localizing catheterization of venous blood PTH are helpful in defining and localizing parathyroid adenomas. Chronic therapy for hypercalcemia in cancer generally is afforded by Mithramycin, meticulous hydration, phosphate, or occasionally glucocorticoids. Surgery is the only appropriate therapy for hyperparathyroidism.

REFERENCES

1. Popovtzer, M.M., et al.: The acute effect of chlorothiazide on serum-ionized calcium. J Clin Invest 55:1295, 1975.

2. Suki, W.N., et al.: Acute treatment of hypercalcemia with furosemide. New Engl J Med 283:836, 1970.

3. Fulmer, D.H., et al.: Treatment of hypercalcemia: comparison of phosphate, sulfate, and cortisone. Arch Intern Med 129:923, 1972.

4. Goldsmith, R.S., et al.: Inorganic phosphate treatment of hypercalcemia of diverse etiologies. New Engl J Med 274:1, 1966.

5. Au, W.Y.W.: Calcitonin treatment of hypercalcemia due to parathyroid carcinoma. Arch Intern Med 135:1594, 1975.

6. Silva, O.L., Becker, K.L.: Salmon calcitonin in the treatment of hypercalcemia. Arch Intern Med 132:337, 1973.

7. Elias, E.G.: Control of hypercalcemia with Mithramycin. Ann Surg 175:431, 1972.

8. Brewer, H.B.: Osteoclastic bone resorption and the hypercalcemia of cancer. New Engl J Med 291:1081, 1974.

CHAPTER 9: NEUROLOGICAL EMERGENCIES
by Robert J. Schwartzman, M.D.

Because the brain is encased in a bony box which is incapable of expanding,any process that increases volume in the skull causes an increase in intracranial pressure. Increased intracranial pressure in turn causes: (1) loss of cerebral autoregulation of blood flow; (2) direct pressure on brain stem structures, and (3) compression of the brain stem's blood supply. The increased volume causes a further increase in brain edema and finally, hemorrhages into the brain stem itself. Almost all serious vascular diseases of the brain are associated with cerebral edema, an increase in intracranial pressure, and the possibility of cingulate gyrus or transtentorial herniation.

The following will be a brief clinical description of the most common vascular structure lesions that cause acute neurological emergencies.

SUBDURAL HEMATOMA: Alcoholics and elderly patients constitute the majority of subdural hematoma patients in the adult population. Any medical problem that interferes with clotting mechanisms predisposes a patient to a subdural hematoma. The most common examples are uremia, disseminated intravascular coagulation, hepatic failure, hemophilia, blood dyscrasias and iatrogenic anticoagulation. The hematoma is formed from venous bleeding caused by rupture of cortical bridging veins which extend from the dura to the cerebral gyri or from direct damage to the cortical veins themselves. Subdurals increase in size from rebleeding of the heavily vascularized subdural membrane. There is an antecedent history of head trauma in only approximately 50% of patients.

Often conscious patients complain of headache which may be localized directly over a subdural collection. This headache is often exacerbated by any change of position, but in my experience particularly by standing The patient is paretic, not plegic, and has no visual field deficit. Frequently, these patients are quiet and lethargic. As the subdural collection matures, it may calcify or gradually resorb with resolution of the patient's symptoms.

Alternatively, if there is rebleeding and the subdural rapidly increases in size, the patient may quickly become obtunded. The physical examination then reveals the pupil on the side of the subdural to be larger and less briskly reactive to light than the other. The patient demonstrates central neurogenic hyperventilation, (rapid steady breathing between 20-40/minute), and often decorticate posturing ipsilateral to the lesion and decerebrate posturing contralateral to the lesion. As the intracranial pressure continues to increase, the ipsilateral pupil becomes fixed and dilated and the patient develops a complete third nerve paralysis. The eye is deviated out and down and the pupil is fixed to light and is dilated. Often the eye

is midline and the pupil is dilated at 3mm. The patient demonstrates decerebrate posturing in both upper and lower extremities.
The longer the patient is allowed to remain in this stage of coma,
the less chance there is of a meaningful recovery. The treatment
of a subdural hematoma is immediate drainage by a neurosurgeon.
All neurosurgeons are aware of the possibilities for bilateral subdural hematomas.

SUBARACHNOID HEMORRHAGE: There are both medical and surgical conditions associated with blood in the subarachnoid space.
A common cause of acute subarachnoid hemorrhage is the leakage
or bursting of an aneurysm of a vessel of the circle of Willis. The
most common sites for congenital aneurysms are at the origin of
the anterior communicating artery and the anterior cerebral artery,
and the origin of the posterior communicating and internal carotid
artery. These congenital aneurysms are located at branching points
of vessels where there is a deficit in the media and elastic membranes of the vessel wall. Peripheral aneurysms, those located
distal to the circle of Willis, are secondary to SBE, atrial myxoma
or trauma. Eighty-five percent of all congenital aneurysms are
found in the anterior circulation. Aneurysms of the posterior circulation are found: (1) at the tip of the basilar artery, the origin of
both posterior cerebral arteries; (2) the basilar artery itself, the
aneurysm being either fusiform or saccular; (3) the origin of the
posterior inferior cerebellar artery from the vertebral artery; or
(4) rarely, the origin of the anterior inferior cerebellar artery
from the basilar artery.

Medical conditions commonly associated with aneurysms are poly-
cystic kidney disease, Turner's syndrome and coarctation of the
aorta. There are families with a high incidence of multiple aneurysms. The Marfan syndrome and homocystinuria may be associated with large-vessel extracranial aneurysms. There are three
ways for an aneurysm to become symptomatic: (1) enlarging and
acting as a mass lesion; (2) eroding the pituitary fossa; and (3)
most commonly by bursting and causing subarachnoid hemorrhage.
Aneurysmal rupture is associated with vasospasm of the artery
upon which the aneurysm was located, hematoma formation, and
rarely with subdural collections of blood.

Clinically, the patient who presents with a burst aneurysm, if still
conscious,complains of a blinding headache that reaches maximum
intensity immediately. There is pain in the neck and back and usually nausea and vomiting. These symptoms are secondary to meningeal irritation and the sudden increase of intracranial pressure.
The patient may become comatose with or without focal signs.
There is often a characteristic presentation for each type of aneurysm depending upon its location in general, rupture of an anterior
communicating artery aneurysm may be characterized by person-
ality change, agitation and belligerence, or a peculiar indifference

to the patient's surroundings. Usually, the patient is lethargic or obtunded. There may be no focal neurologic signs. If a jet of blood from an anterior communicating aneurysm ruptures the lamina terminalis and bursts into the third ventricle, the patient may lapse into sudden coma, become decerebrate with pin-point pupils and expire. Complete third nerve paralysis is the hallmark of aneurysmal rupture at the junction of the posterior communicating and posterior cerebral artery. These patients have a flaccid ptosis, the pupil is dilated and the eye is out and down. They have no other sensory or motor signs. Rupture of an aneurysm at the junction of the internal carotid artery and posterior communicating artery is also associated with third nerve paralysis and a hemiplegia on the opposite side. Middle cerebral artery aneurysms may present with a similar picture, however, the pupillary abnormalities are late and are a consequence of temporal lobe swelling with pressure on the nerve by the uncus of the hippocampal gyrus.

Posterior circulation aneurysms cause symptoms in one of the following ways: (1) acute subarachnoid hemorrhage; (2) cranial nerve and brain stem signs and symptoms; (3) or obstruction of spinal fluid pathways with consequent hydrocephalus. Instead of headache, these patients may first complain of severe neck and midscapular back pain. Basilar artery aneurysmal rupture causes death within a matter of minutes or seconds. These patients are comatose, have pin-point pupils (which may be unresponsive to light), are decerebrate bilaterally with Babinski signs and demonstrate central neurogenic hyperventilation (deep sustained respiration at 20-40/minute). Aneurysms at the tip of the basilar artery, the origin of the two posterior cerebral arteries, may be associated with migraine-like visual symptoms or actual occipital lobe visual field deficits. However, when this aneurysm ruptures the patient may die because of ischemia to thalamic and midbrain areas which are supplied by the first one third of the posterior cerebral artery. The most benign of the posterior circulation aneurysms are those found at the junction of the vertebral and posterior inferior artery. Rupture may cause vasospasm of the posterior inferior cerebellar artery (PICA) which leads to ischemia of the lateral aspect of the medulla. These patients are dizzy, have a sudden onset of vertigo, nausea and vomiting, ataxia on the side of the lesion and dysphagia. Examination reveals a Horner's syndrome on the affected side associated with a decrease of facial sensation to pinprick and temperature on the ipsilateral side of the face, as well as on the contralateral side of the body below the clavicle. There is ipsilateral course nystagmus on the side of the lesion and finer jerk nystagmus to the opposite side. Patients are often lethargic and complain of severe back and neck pain as well as crushing headache. Aneurysms at the junction of the anterior inferior cerebellar artery and the basilar artery are exceedingly rare. All aneurysms that have ruptured may cause severe back pain due to irritation of the spinal meninges by blood. A helpful clinical sign in any patient who is unconscious and is suspected of having a leaking aneurysm is the presence of a subhyaloid hemorrhage in the retina. This is probably due to the rupture of retinal veins by the sudden increase of intracranial pressure. The hemorrhage is formed by blood under Decemet's membrane which changes position with different head posture.

Lumbar puncture after aneurysmal rupture reveals increased pressure, usually greater than 200,000 RBCs a number of WBCs equivalent to the ratio of one WBC to 700 RBCs and a modest increase of protein (1 mg of protein to 1000 RBC). The sugar is usually normal, but occasionally after a week to 10 days very low CSF sugars have been reported. This is thought to be due to release of enzymes from extravasated RBCs. The diagnosis is confirmed by arteriography. All vessels should be explored by a femoral artery approach as soon as possible. There is a 25% incidence of multiple aneurysms. If this is the case, the largest aneurysm, a multiloculated aneurysm, or an aneurysm with a small projection (Murphy's tit) or one close to an intracerebral hematoma is the one that bled. Another helpful sign is arterial vasospasm in the arterial distribution of the aneurysm that burst.

Rebleeds characteristically occur within the first 10 days to two weeks and then again within the first 3 weeks. The patient should have an immediate neurosurgical consultation and surgery if he meets their surgical criteria. The patient should be at absolute bedrest, and have special attention to good bowel care to avoid straining at stool. The patient's blood pressure should be kept at 120/80, if possible. Not all agree with the above approach.

Summary: the sudden onset of a blinding headache, lethargy, stiff neck associated with focal neurological signs.

BASAL GANGLIONIC HEMORRHAGE: Perhaps the most common neurologic emergency that leads to death if not properly managed is basal ganglionic hemorrhage. Almost all of these patients have severe hypertension that has not been adequately managed. These hemorrhages occur in characteristic locations and may be distinguished by clinical presentation. The most common sites of deep intracranial hemorrhage are the lenticulo-striate arteries which arise from the proximal segment of the middle cerebral artery. Medial and lateral branches of these arteries supply the internal capsule and thalamus. A medial lenticulostriate hemorrhage is characterized by the rapid onset of coma, flaccid paralysis, hemisensory deficit, and homonymous hemianopsia on the side opposite the lesion. The patient has Cheyne-Stokes respiration and his blood pressure is in the neighborhood of 24/120 mm hg - 220/110 mm hg. His head and eyes are often deviated to the side of the lesion. The deep tendon reflexes are hypoactive on the paralyzed side and he may demonstrate bilateral Babinski signs. As intracranial pressure increases due to both extravasated blood and cerebral edema there is increased pressure on the brainstem. The blood may also start to track down descending fiber pathways into the midbrain. The eyes are below the horizontal plane and adducted as if looking toward the patient's nose if there is primary thalamic destruction. Otherwise they are in mid-position below the horizontal plane. There is often skew deviation. The patient rapidly loses upgaze to both the Doll's head maneuver and ice-water calorics. The pupils are 2-3 mm in diameter and are usually reactive to light before third nerve paralysis is seen. If the process continues and intracranial pressure continues to rise the patient dies of transtentorial herniation. If on the other hand the hemorrhage is from a lateral lenticulostriate artery, the patient develops a headache, remains conscious for hours and slowly develops a hemiparesis. Blood dissects away from the internal capsule and into the basal ganglia, primarily the globus pallidus and putamen. As the hematoma enlarges with consequent further increase of vasogenic cerebral edema, the patient becomes lethargic and then obtunded, the hemiparesis is more severe and hyperreflexia is seen on the side opposite the lesion. A helpful clinical sign that may differentiate this lesion from a more medial one is increased tone on the paralyzed side. These patients also have Cheyne-Stokes respiration and small pupils. Another variant of lenticulostriate hemorrhage is that which rapidly dissects into the ventricular system. These patients often have a sudden increase of temperature from 103° - 106°, are decerebrate and die rapidly.

At the present time there is no effective surgical treatment for deep medial hemorrhage particularly in the dominant hemisphere. However, if the bleed is lateral, on the right side, and is acting predominantly as a mass lesion, surgical decompression may lead to a useful recovery. Surgical decompression and evacuation are also successful for subcortical frontal and temporal lobe hematomas, but unfortunately, these are much rarer than the deeper lesions. The emergency treatment for the deep lesions is the treatment for increased intracranial pressure. Mannitol, glycerol, diuretics, steroids, controlled hyperventilation and hypothermia have all been used successfully. The treatment for any patient with incipient or early transtentorial herniation is immediate intubation, Mannitol 12.5 grams by I.V. push (may be repeated in 3 hours), dexamethasone 8 mg. I.V. push and 80 mg of I.V. lasix. Almost all patients will improve for at least several hours which will enable thorough evaluation and possible neurosurgical intervention if indicated.

Summary: A hypertensive patient, admission B.P. 245/120, Cheyne-Stokes respiration, head and eyes deviated to the side of the lesion, contralateral hemiparesis, hemisensory deficit, and visual field deficit.

CEREBELLAR HEMATOMA: Approximately 10%-20% of all intracranial hematomas occur in the posterior fossa. Most of these are in the cerebellum. The superior cerebellar artery ruptures most frequently. This complication is most often seen in the poorly controlled hypertensive. Diagnosis and treatment must be accomplished within 4 hours to avert irreversible coma and death. The classic patient is a middle-aged hypertensive male who suddenly develops a severe occipital headache and rapidly falls to the ground. If examined immediately he demonstrates dysarthria and is ataxic. He is quadriparetic but is able to move all extremities. A few patients have a central facial paralysis and are hemiparetic. The patient then slips into coma due to the rapid development of pressure on the brain stem reticular activating system. The patient may demonstrate 2-3 mm pupils which are reactive to light. There is a conjugate gaze preference away from the side of the lesion. Due to the tight tentorial covering of the cerebellum, there is no place for expansion of the hematoma, except through the tentorium (upward herniation) or by herniation of the cerebellar tonsils into the foramen magnum. This form of herniation may be associated with a stiff neck and anesthesia of the occiput secondary to compression of the upper cervical nerves. If immediate treatment is not administered successfully the patient has a respiratory and then vasomotor collapse. The EMI scan allows for rapid diagnosis, and immediate surgical decompression is the treatment of choice. If an EMI scan is not readily available a rapidly performed carotid arteriogram will demonstrate severe hydrocephalus with no other significant intracranial shifts. A spinal tap should not be performed if this diagnosis is suspected.

Summary: hypertensive patient, occipital headache, inability to stand, nausea and vomiting, dysarthria, ataxia, nystagmus and quadriparesis. Frequently mistaken for brainstem stroke.

THROMBOTIC CEREBRAL VASCULAR ACCIDENTS: Patients may have a seizure at the onset of a complete carotid occlusion and frequently demonstrate a varying level of consciousness that may be confused with that produced by a subdural hematoma. The extent of collateral circulation through the circle of Willis determines the neurological deficit the patient suffers. There may be a Horner's syndrome on the side of the occlusion (ptosis, enophthalmos and miosis) generally associated with a hemiparesis, hemisensory loss and visual field deficit on the contralateral side of the body. Within the first few hours after the infarction there is a gaze preference or horizontal deviation of the eyes to the side of the lesion. Early, arm, leg and face are paralyzed to the same degree. This type of occlusion most often occurs in elderly patients who have severe generalized arteriosclerotic disease. Both anterior cerebral arteries may have taken origin from the infarcted internal carotid artery which then leads to hemispheric infarction, deep coma and death. Infarction of the middle central artery results in greater paralysis of the distal upper extremity and face than the leg, although the extensors of the foot are usually affected. If the occlusion is on the left side and involves a superior branch of the middle cerebral artery, a Broca's aphasia (inability to initiate speech) is prominent. If the inferior branch is occluded, a Wernicke's aphasia (receptive aphasia) is seen. The patient with an inferior branch occlusion may have a mild hemiparesis early, but has a marked inability to comprehend the spoken word.

Infarction of the anterior cerebral artery presents with paralysis of the leg with minimal involvement of the shoulder and preserved function of the hand. Characteristically, the patient has no Broca's aphasia and no visual field deficit. However, if both anterior cerebral arteries have taken origin from the same anterior communication artery segment, the cingulate gyrus, a critical relay of the limbic system, may be infarcted. The patient may then gradually slip into an akinetic mute state and demonstrate a peculiar flexed posture of the lower extremities.

The distinguishing feature of a posterior cerebral artery occlusion is a severe homonymous (congruent) field deficit. The visual field deficit is dense, and the defect from each field may be exactly superimposed. The proximal one third of the posterior cerebral artery supplies part of the thalamus, midbrain and internal capsule. Therefore, infarction of this part of the artery results in hemiparesis, a hemisensory loss and a congruent field deficit.

The immediate emergency management of these patients usually involves the treatment of severe cerebral edema. Infarction of the carotid artery is followed by severe cerebral edema within the first 12-24 hours. Infarction of the proximal segment of the middle cerebral artery causes severe cerebral edema usually on the second and third day. The patient becomes progressively obtunded to comatose and if not treated may succumb to transtentorial herniation. The treatment of cerebral edema is exactly the same as that for those patients suffering from basal ganglionic hemorrhage. This consists of intubation, I.V. mannitol, steroids and diuretics. Complete infarction of the basilar artery usually results in death within a few seconds to 5 minutes. The patient loses consciousness because of the destruction of the ascending reticular activating system. The patient presents with pinpoint pupils that may not respond to light, and a gaze preference or horizontal deviation of the eyes to the side opposite the infarction. The patient is also paralyzed on the side opposite the infarction; therefore the eyes are deviated to the paralyzed side. There are usually bilateral long tract motor and sensory signs with cranial nerve involvement associated with brainstem infarction. Frequently central neurogenic hyperventilation and bilateral Babinski signs are evident. Vertebral artery infarction is rarely an isolated event and is often associated with basilar artery ischemia. Therefore, many of the same signs are seen with this type of infarction as are seen with basilar artery disease. In general, coarse nystagmus with a rotary component to the side of the lesion and finer nystagmus to the opposite side are seen with vertebral artery disease in association with ataxia, dysarthria, dysphagia and quadriparesis. Bilateral nystagmus to upgaze is characteristic of

brainstem disease and is seen with both basilar and vertebral artery
disease. Many drugs, particularly tranquilizers, phenobarbital and
dilantin all cause upgaze nystagmus. Many of the above described
patients who have suffered severe infarctions of the vertebrobasilar
system and are comatose do amazingly well with good medical care.

The emergency treatment of the patient who has suffered vertebro-
basilar artery infarction is fourfold: (1) the patient must be protected from aspiration. (2) blood pressure must be maintained at
normotensive levels but somewhat higher in known hypertensive
patients. (3) anticoagulation therapy with heparin should be instituted
if the infarction is progressive and the patient has less than 50 red
blood cells in his cerebrospinal fluid. (4) other contributing factors,
such as cardiac arrhythmia, diabetes mellitus, hyperlipidemias,
hypercholesterolemia, polycythemia vera, Waldenstrom's macro-
globulinemia and other dysproteinemias must be diagnosed and
treated. Posterior inferior cerebellar artery and anterior inferior
cerebellar artery infarctions rarely present as neurological emergencies.

Summary: (a) Carotid occlusion - Horner's syndrome, arm, face
and leg equally involved early on the contralateral side, hemiparesis,
hemisensory and visual field deficits. May be initiated by a seizure
and cause lethargy or changing levels of consciousness. (b) Middle
cerebral artery - arm and face more involved than leg. (c) Posterior
cerebral artery - dense contralateral visual field deficit and hemiparesis. (d) Basilar artery - nausea, vomiting, cranial nerve dysfunction, internuclear ophthalmoplegia, nystagmus, bilateral motor
signs and sensory signs.

TRANSIENT ISCHEMIC ATTACKS: A transient ischemic attack is
a neurologic deficit that totally clears without residua within 24
hours. Some authorities believe that these episodes must clear
within 6-12 hours or the episode is a complete stroke. In general,
TIA's are thought to be caused by emboli from either the carotid-
vertebral arteries or the heart. In specific rare instances embolic
material may break off from the arch of the aorta. Transient intracranial hypotension and vasospasm may be causative of posterior
circulation TIA's. Clinically, symptoms of anterior circulation
TIA's (carotid, anterior and middle cerebral arteries) are unilateral.
The patient complains of a hemisensory, hemiparesis or speech impairment. Amaurosis fugax (transient monocular blindness) associated with contralateral motor or sensory deficit is suggestive of
disease in the internal carotid artery that supplies the affected eye
through the ophthalmic artery. Loss of consciousness is extremely
rare during anterior circulation TIA's.

The vertebro-basilar arterial system is affected during posterior
circulation TIA's. Dizziness and vertigo are prominent at the start
of an attack and may be followed by momentary bilateral blindness,

diplopia, dysphagia, peripheral numbness and an occipital headache. Sensory and motor symptoms may affect alternate sides of the body during different attacks. Occasionally a patient may complain of numbness of one half of the face and the opposite side of the body, ataxia or drop attacks. A drop attack is a momentary sudden loss of postural tone which causes the patient to fall to the ground usually without loss of consciousness.

Patients who are suffering a flurry of TIA's should be hospitalized. If they have no severe medical contraindications to anticoagulation they should be anticoagulated with I.V. heparin. Most authorities feel that anticoagulation does not stop an impending stroke but may reduce the number of attacks. If the attacks are in the distribution of a carotid artery, the patient should undergo immediate trans-femoral angiography. If a 50% reduction of the carotid artery is detected or if a burst plaque is seen the patient should undergo immediate emergency carotid endarterectomy. The usefulness of aspirin or an anticoagulant for cerebrovascular disease is presently under investigation.

Summary: A neurologic symptom that must clear within 24 hours. (a) Carotid, ipsilateral monocular blindness, contralateral motor or sensory symptoms. Usually just blindness of the ipsilateral eye, that lasts for 1-2 minutes.

CEREBRAL EMBOLUS: Most emboli come from the heart or an ulcerated plaque in the internal carotid artery. Cardiac emboli are most often seen in patients who have chronic atrial fibrillation, mitral stenosis, artificial heart valves or intermittent cardiac arrhythmias. An occasional patient will embolize from a floppy mitral valve. Any patient with acute or subacute bacterial endocarditis is a prime candidate for a cerebral embolus. Approximately 5% of patients who have suffered a myocardial infarction may also embolize. Other rare causes of cardiac emboli are ball valve thrombi, atrial and ventricular myxomas, marantic endocarditis, congenital right-to-left intracardiac shunts and air during open heart surgery. The hallmarks of embolic disease are: (1) the proper clinical setting; (2) a neurological deficit immediately after the event; (3) some neurologic improvement within 2 to 24 hours; (4) headache; (5) seizures (15-40%);and (6) blood in the CSF (50% of patients) usually in the range of 50,000 RBCs. The artery that is occluded, how close the obstruction is to the artery's origin from the circle of Willis and the collateral circulation that develops all determine the severity of the deficit.

The emergency treatment of these patients is directed at (1) seizure control; (2) treatment of increased intracranial pressure that may develop; and (3) a search for the cause of the embolus. Patients with SBE or any other infected emboli should not be anticoagulated.

Patients with cardiac causes of emboli such as atrial fibrillation should be anticoagulated if the CSF has fewer than 50 RBCs and there are no other medical contraindications. In my experience the major cause of disaster in this situation is anticoagulating a hypertensive patient.

Summary: The proper setting, i.e., cardiac arrhythmia, carotid disease, following myocardial infarction, sudden onset of symptoms that improve within several hours. Seizures, loss of consciousness or headache approximately 40-50% of the time.

HYPERTENSIVE ENCEPHALOPATHY: Hypertensive encephalopathy is most often seen in patients who have severe poorly controlled hypertension and who have had a recent exacerbation of their blood pressure. Characteristically, the diastolic pressure is over 120 mm Hg and often is in the 140 mm Hg range. All of these patients have severe hypertensive retinopathy with hemorrhages, exudates and severe arterial spasm. Papilledema is often seen but is not essential for the diagnosis. The patients are lethargic or obtunded, and may have blindness, seizures or any focal neurological signs. The spinal fluid is under pressure, demonstrates a high protein content (about 90 mg%) and often a few hundred RBCs are seen. The treatment is immediate lowering of the blood pressure. The patient should be placed in an intensive care unit, nitroprusside should be used to lower the pressure to 180/110 for several hours before it is lowered to 140/90. Special care must be taken to avoid renal failure secondary to decreased perfusion pressure. Electrolytes, BUN and creatinine should be monitored closely. The pathology of the disease is cerebral edema, petechial hemorrhages into the substance of the brain as well as a necrotizing endarteritis of the intracranial vessels. The neurological damage may be permanent, but blindness usually clears.

A real error in the management of patients who have suffered a stroke from poorly controlled hypertensive disease is to confuse these patients with those suffering from hypertensive encephalopathy. In general, patients with hypertensive encephalopathy have papilledema, severe retinopathy, evidence of less severe central nervous system damage and a higher blood pressure (250/150mm Hg) than those patients who have suffered a cerebral hemorrhage from hypertension and have increased intracranial pressure secondary to cerebral edema. This latter group of patients usually have an obvious hemiparesis, no papilledema and are not as encephalopathic as those patients with hypertension due to the Cushing reflex (pressure on the brain stem vasomotor center from the hemorrhage), are unstable, and often minimal amounts of antihypertensive medication cause a catastrophic drop in blood pressure which further increases the damage caused by the initial vascular insult. These patients need their pressure lowered slowly and carefully and treatment for increased intracranial pressure if it is indicated. I prefer apresoline and bed rest to lower the pressure. Phenobarbital and Aldomet should not be used because they both depress the patient's mental status which makes continual neurological assessment impossible.

Summary: Hypertensive patients 240/120 mm Hg, lethargic, focal neurologic signs that may change. Occasional seizure. Rarely dense stroke-like picture.

STATUS EPILEPTICUS: Status epilepticus usually occurs secondary to severe metabolic brain disease as well as in those patients who suddenly stop taking anticonvulsant medication. Almost any severe infection, poisoning or structural disease of the brain may cause this emergency. Frontal lobe brain tumors may present in this manner. By definition, status epilepticus is one seizure after another without a clear interictal period. However, this is a totally unrealistic view of seizure activity, since there may be electrical seizure activity with possible brain damage without movement. Practically, any patient with 3 major motor convulsions within 1 hour should be treated for status epilepticus. Patients die from aspiration, cardiac arrhythmia, anoxia and rare neurogenic pulmonary edema. Any patient in major motor status epilepticus should be intubated. Often the seizures may have to be broken initially with I.V. valium 10-20mg in order to intubate the patient. Once intubated the patient should receive 1 gram to 1.5 gram of Dilantin I.V., 100 mg/minute. If this is not effective, phenobarbital 200-400 mg I.V. push over 15 minutes every 4 hours may be given to a total of 1 gram - 2 grams per day. If this is not effective the next drug that has been used very effectively is paraldehyde. This also should be given I.V. There has been some question as to microcrystal formation in Dilantin glucose mixtures. This does occur and Dilantin is best given in a drip mixed with regular saline. If Dilantin phenobarbital, and paraldehyde do not stop the seizure activity patients may have to undergo general anesthesia or hyperthermia. Patients must be well oxygenated, kept in excellent electrolyte balance, and particular attention must be paid to possible calcium and magnesium depletion. Temporal lobe status and petit mal status may be difficult to stop but are not neurological emergencies.

Summary: At least 3 tonic-clonic seizures within 30 minutes. Temporal lobe status - obtunded or lethargic patient with lip smacking or eye blinking. Petit mal status - multiple lapses, eye blinks, and myoclonic jerks. Occasional urinary incontinence.

GUILLAIN-BARRÉ SYNDROME: The Guillain-Barré Syndrome (GBS) is a paralytic disorder that usually follows a viral illness. Patients complain of numbness or tingling in the feet and hands which is quickly followed by ascending weakness affecting legs, arms, trunk muscles and lower facial musculature. Bowel and bladder are affected 1-2% of the time. Patients die of respiratory arrest or cardiac arrhythmias. No patient should die of the GBS if it is correctly diagnosed and treated. In the past, patients who had only a minimal depression of vital capacity were allowed to remain in a private room or an open ward. A patient with vital capacity may quickly decrease from 3 liter-minute to less than 1 liter/minute without his awareness. The patient may simultaneously develop life threatening cardiac arrhythmias from the anoxia. The GBS itself may be associated with primary involvement of the autonomic nervous system (including demyelinization of cardiac nerves) and thus cause paroxysmal cardiac arrhythmias rather than respiratory failure. Placement of the GBS patient in an intensive care unit as soon as his vital capacity falls below 3 liters/minute or if he develops cardiac arrhythmias and paroxysmal hyper or hypotension will save almost every patient. I personally believe that both I.V. ACTH and oral steroids are beneficial in this disease.

Summary: Rather sudden onset of tingling paresthesias in feet and hands. Rapidly followed by ascending paralysis. No reflexes in affected muscles, sensation intact. Bowel and bladder rarely affected.

MYASTHENIA GRAVIS: Both steroid treatment and thymectomy have completely altered the life of myasthenia patients. Neurological emergencies with this disease process almost always concern respiratory failure. The myasthenic may quickly go into crisis following a severe viral infection, medication error, severe emotional crisis or for reasons that are not well understood. If a myasthenic patient has difficulty with swallowing, the physician should be aware of a possible respiratory crisis. Intubation should always be done rather than tracheostomy. Once a myasthenic patient with breathing problems (and/or) a vital capacity at or less than 1.5 liter/minute should be hospitalized in an intensive care unit. He should be tested with tensilon to see if he is either over or under medicated with anticholinesterase medication. The use of intubation and steroids or I.V. ACTH usually allows the myasthenic patient to escape a tracheostomy and return to a normal life. The threat of a cardiac arrhythmia is always present in any anoxic myasthenic patient. The other major medical problem in the intubated myasthenic is gastrointestinal hemorrhage, which may be exacerbated both by steroids or ACTH, although there is controversy concerning the role of steroids in G.I. bleeding. Patients must be given antacids and potassium supplementation if they are on steroids or ACTH.

Summary: Weakness and severe extraocular muscle palsies. No sensory loss, pupils react normally, reflexes are normo or hyperactive.

REFERENCES

VASCULAR DISEASE:

1. Adams, R.D., and Eecken, H.M. Vander: Vascular Disease of the Brain; Ann Rev Med 4:213, 1958.
2. Baker, A.B., and Iannone, A.: Cerebrovascular Disease. II The smaller intracerebral arteries Neurology 9:391, 1959.

3. Berry, R.G.: Discussion of collateral circulation of the brain. Neurology 11:20, 1961.
4. Reinmuth, O.M.: Prologue to guidelines for stroke care. Stroke: 5:109-111, 1974.
5. Toole, J.F., and Patel, A.N.: Cerebrovascular Disorders. 2nd Ed., McGraw Hill, New York, p. 412.
6. Yates, P.O.: The pathological basis for cerebral ischemia. Mod Trends Neurol 4:180-192, 1967.
7. Report of the Joint Committee for Stroke Facilities. V.: Clinical Presentation of Stroke. Strokes 3, 3:803-825, 1972.
8. Freis, E.D.: The Veterans Administration Cooperative Study on antihypertensive agents. Duplications for Stroke prevention. Stroke, 5:76-77, 1974.
9. Gifford, R.W., Jr. and Westbrook, E.: Hypertensive encephalopathy: Mechanisms, Clinical features, and treatment. Prog. Cardiovasc. Dis., 17:115-124, 1974.
10. Report of the Joint Committee for Stroke Facilities. XI. Transient focal cerebral ischaemia: Epidemiological and clinical aspects. Stroke 5:275-287, 1974.
11. Whisnant, J.P., et al.: The effect of anticoagulant therapy on the prognosis of patients with transient cerebral ischaemic attacks in a community. Rochester, Minn. 1955-1969. Mayo Clin Proc 48:844-849, 1973.
12. McDowell, F.H.: Cerebral embolism. In: Handbook of Clinical Neurology Vascular Diseases of the Nervous System, Part I. Vol. II, edited by P.J. Vinken and G.W. Bruyn, Chapter 15, American Elsevier, New York, pp. 386-414.
13. Browne, T.R., III, and Poskanzer, D.C.: Treatment of strokes (second of two parts). N Engl J Med 281:650-657.
14. Ziegler, D.K.: Hypertensive Vascular Diseases of the Brain. In: Handbook of Clinical Neurology; Vascular Diseases of the Nervous System, Part I. Vol. II, edited by P.J. Vinken and G.W. Bruyn, American Elsevier, New York, Chapter 20, pp. 552-577.

SEIZURE DISORDERS:

1. Penfield, W., and Jasper, H.: Epilepsy and the Functional Anatomy of the Human Brain, Little Brown & Co., Boston, 1954.
2. Tower, D.B.: Arrest of seizure activity. Biochemical Aspects and Pharmacology. Epilepsia 6:141-155, 1965.
3. Symonds, C.: Classification of the epilepsies. Brit Med J 1:1235-1238, 1955.
4. Bell, P.S.: Dangers of treatment of status epilepticus with diazepam. Brit Med J 1:159, 1969.
5. Cobb, S.: Causes of epilepsy, Arch Neurol Psychiat. 27:1245, 1932.

6. Hunter, R.A.: Status epilepticus: History, Incidence and problems. Epilepsia 1:172, 1959.
7. Naquet, R., et al.: First Attempt at Treatment of Experimental Status Epilepticus in Man with Diazepam (Valium), Electroenceph Clin Neurophysiol 18:427, 1965.
8. Nicol, C.O., et al.: Parenteral diazepam in status epilepticus, Neurol 19:332, 1969.

MYASTHENIA GRAVIS:

1. Rowland, L.P., et al.: Myasthenic Syndromes, Res Publ Assoc Res Nerv Ment Dis 38:548, 1961.
2. Osserman, K.E., and Whipple, H.E.: Myasthenia Gravis, Ann N.Y. Acad Sci 135:1, 1966.
3. Namba, T., et al.: Neonatal Myasthenia Gravis: Report of two cases and review of the literature, Pediatrics 45:488, 1970.

GUILLAIN-BARRE SYNDROME:

1. Haymaker, W.E., and Kernshaw, J.W.: The Landry-Guillain-Barré Syndrome: A clinico-pathologic report of 50 fatal cases and a critique of the literature. Medicine 28:59, 1949.
2. Wiederholt, W.C., et al.: The Landry-Guillain-Barré, Strohl syndrome of polyradiculoneuropathy: Historical review, report of 97 patients, and present concepts, Mayo Clin Proc 39:427, 1964.

CHAPTER 10: PHARMACOLOGIC EMERGENCIES

A: ALCOHOL WITHDRAWAL SYNDROMES
by Bernard I. Elser, M.D.

Mood altering drugs are popular in our society today. Substances such as Marihuana, Cocaine, Heroin, etc. are being used with increasing frequency. Nevertheless, alcohol remains as THE favorite and its consumption grows annually. It is estimated that there are ten (10) million alcoholics residing in the United States today, and if the present trend continues, this number will rise.

The alcoholic is subject to a multitude of different medical problems. Some of these are the result of the toxic effects of the alcohol itself or its metabolites, (i.e., alcoholic cardiomyopathy, alcoholic hepatitis, alcoholic pancreatitis). Others are often the result of the lifestyle of the alcoholic (i.e., trauma, malnutrition, infection, etc.) One of the most common disorders seen in alcoholics first becomes manifest when there is an absolute or relative decrease in alcohol consumption. Although more common in the sporadic or binge drinker, it may also be seen in the steady drinker who, for any number of reasons has suddenly decreased his intake of alcohol.

The various disorders seen in the alcohol withdrawal syndrome are directly related to the withdrawal of alcohol and are not a toxic effect of the alcohol or its metabolites. The symptoms of alcohol toxicity - slurred speech, staggering gait, stupor, etc., are quite different from those seen in the alcohol withdrawal syndrome and are associated with elevated blood alcohol levels. The signs and symptoms of alcohol withdrawal, on the other hand, may be reversed by the administration of alcohol. Nor is the alcohol withdrawal syndrome related to malnutrition, vitamin, or mineral deficiency. Withdrawal occurs in volunteers who are fed adequate amounts of vitamins, minerals, and other essential nutrients. The signs and symptoms of alcohol withdrawal will subside without supplemental vitamins, minerals or other nutrients, although their use is recommended.

The immediate cause of the alcohol withdrawal syndrome is the predominance of the compensatory neurophysiological effects which are induced in the nervous system to counteract the chronic effects of the ethanol:

A) EFFECT OF ALCOHOL:
   1) Depression of Neuronal excitability
   2) Depression of Impulse Conduction
   3) Inhibition of Transmitter Release
   4) Elevation of Seizure Threshold

B) COMPENSATORY EFFECT:
   1) Hyperexcitability of Sensory Modalities
   2) Hyperreflexia
   3) Increased Muscle Tension
   4) Anxiety
   5) Insomnia
   6) Decreased Seizure Threshold

Upon withdrawal of the alcohol, the compensatory effect predominates and produces the sign and symptoms of the alcohol withdrawal syndrome!

ALCOHOL WITHDRAWAL STATES:
A) Tremulousness
B) Alcoholic Hallucinosis
C) Alcohol Withdrawal Seizures: "Rum fits"
D) Delirium Tremens

The alcohol withdrawal syndrome is a symptom complex. Each component of the syndrome may occur in relatively pure form, although they are usually seen in various combinations. Their appearance is related to the amount and duration of alcohol ingested prior to withdrawal; tremulousness for example, may appear following the withdrawal from the daily consumption of a liter of 86 proof whiskey, 2-3 liters of wine or their equivalent for as short a period of time as one week whereas delirium tremens may become manifest following withdrawal after consumption of a similar amount of alcohol over a period of approximately six weeks. Individual susceptibility and tolerance also play a large role.

A) TREMULOUSNESS: Tremulousness is the most common component of the alcohol abstinence syndrome, and frequently coexists with other components of the syndrome. It may appear after a few days of drinking and a period of abstinence represented by a night's sleep. When the patient awakens in the morning he feels very nervous and tremulous. He is alert but may startle easily. The tremor which is noted is usually coarse and irregular and increases with stress or motor activity. It is very distressing to the patient as he may not be able to stand, speak, or feed himself, and he soon learns that a drink will reverse these symptoms. This cycle repeats itself for days or weeks until such time as there is complete alcohol withdrawal, brought about by nausea, vomiting, abdominal pain, trauma, lack of funds or another reason. There may then be progression to one or more of the other components of the syndrome, or the tremulousness may resolve without progression within a few days. The tremor may not disappear completely for up to 2 weeks. Occasionally, there is no objective evidence of a tremor, the patient complaining of an inner tremulousness, of being shaky inside, and not being able to sleep well. The clinical course of this component of the alcohol withdrawal syndrome is usually benign. It must, however, be treated aggressively. If the tremor continues and interferes with the patient's activities, he will continue to drink, if only to ameliorate these symptoms.

B) ALCOHOLIC HALLUCINOSIS: The second component or second stage of the alcohol withdrawal syndrome is characterized by disorders of perception. Most commonly, sensory stimuli, such as faces, shadows, etc. are misperceived. Despite these illusions, the patient may be completely oriented to time, place, and person, and be quite coherent. There may be hallucinations, which are most commonly visual but also may be auditory, olfactory, or even tactile. They may assume animate or inanimate form and may be pleasant or frightening to the patient. None are specific or pathognomonic for alcohol withdrawal. Depending on the nature of the perceptual disorder, the patient may react appropriately to it. He may be fearful of, or aggressive against, the deprecating voices he hears. He may even become suicidal or homicidal and have to be restrained.

These perceptual disorders usually appear within 24 hours of alcohol withdrawal and can remain for up to one week or longer. As the patient's condition improves he rapidly realizes the true nature of the hallucinations. Rarely, after repeated episodes, they may become chronic, and difficult to differentiate from schizophrenia.

C) ALCOHOL WITHDRAWAL SEIZURES: "Rum Fits": One of the most distressing components of the alcohol withdrawal syndrome is the alcohol withdrawal seizure, or "Rum Fit". Although alcohol has been shown to be an effective anticonvulsant in animals, capable of suppressing drug and/or electroshock induced seizures, the dosage of alcohol required to achieve this effect is large and causes generalized central nervous system depression. This anticonvulsant effect is followed by a period of hyperexcitability that lasts from 12 hours (after a single dose) to several days (following chronic alcohol intake). During this interval, seizure threshold is reduced to normal and seizure activity is more readily elicited.

Clinically, the seizures are usually grand mal and often multiple, but only rarely do they progress to status epilepticus. Focal seizures suggest the possibility of a focal lesion and should prompt a thorough search for another possible cause of the seizure. The seizures usually occur within 12-24 hours following alcohol withdrawal and most fall within 48 hours of withdrawal. On rare occasions, they may occur up to 2-3 weeks later. Clinically, they are indistinguishable from seizures brought about by other conditions, (posttraumatic, idiopathic, etc.) but other stigmata of alcohol withdrawal may coexist or develop shortly therafter.

There are two features which may help to distinguish "Rum Fits" from other grand mal seizures. Except for that period of time during the ingestion of alcohol or during the immediate withdrawal period, the EEG is usually normal in the patient with alcohol withdrawal seizures as opposed to the patient with posttraumatic or idiopathic epilepsy, many of whom demonstrate EEG abnormalities even during the inter-seizure period.

The patient undergoing alcohol withdrawal is also very sensitive to photic stimulation. The strobe light effect will induce myoclonic jerks, and grand mal seizures in many of these patients. In contrast, however, this will rarely if ever be seen in patients with other forms of epilepsy.

Although "Rum Fits" are probably not a variant of true epilepsy, the patient with other forms of epilepsy is even more likely to develop seizures upon alcohol withdrawal and must be advised against any consumption of alcoholic beverages. There may be a sudden increase in the incidence of epileptic attacks in the previously well controlled epileptic who drinks even for short periods of time. As might be expected, most of these seizures occur in the withdrawal phase.

D) DELIRIUM TREMENS: Delirium tremens is the most dramatic, and serious manifestation of the alcohol withdrawal syndrome. Although the term has often been used loosely in the past, it should be reserved for those patients who demonstrate the following signs and symptoms.

a) Confusion, agitation, insomnia, restlessness
b) Disordered perception, illusions, hallucinations, delusions, and
c) Signs of autonomic nervous system hyperactivity, including tachycardia, fever, sweating and mydriasis.

When defined this way, the incidence is probably less than ten percent of all alcohol related hospital admissions.

The mortality rate, depending on the series, varies between 10 and 40 percent, with patients succumbing to associated disorders, such as infection, trauma, electrolyte imbalance, etc. Other stigmata of alcohol withdrawal may coexist. D.T.'s may develop de novo or may temporarily follow the other components of the alcohol withdrawal syndrome.

Clinically, the affected patient is restless and agitated. He often has a coarse tremor which increases with activity. Speech may be tremulous and unintelligible. It is difficult to communicate with the patient, he is confused and disoriented. He cannot concentrate and is easily distracted. He seems to be preoccupied with other things. His hallucinations and illusions are obvious and his mood may change abruptly from one of friendliness and joy to that of fear or anger. The patient is often unable to stand or sit still and dominates his surroundings by virtue of his loudness and hyperactivity.

The D. T.'s usually end abruptly with the patient exhausted, going into a long sleep. When he awakens, he is weak and hungry and does not recall previous events. Rarely there may be relapses after several days of lucidity. The onset of delirium tremens is usually 3-5 days after discontinuing a long (usually weeks) period of heavy alcohol ingestion. Most cases resolve within 72 hours of onset.

DIAGNOSIS

There are no laboratory tests which are specific for alcohol withdrawal. A frequent finding is hypomagnesemia, whose signs (tremor, hyperreflexia, seizures) may mimic those of alcohol withdrawal. Replacement of magnesium will abolish the signs related to the hypomagnesemia but will have no effect on those related to alcohol withdrawal. Another frequent finding is respiratory alkalosis. Chronic alcohol stimulation leads to decreased sensitivity to endogenous CO_2 and during withdrawal, there is increased sensitivity, leading to hyperventilation and the production of respiratory alkalosis. Both of these findings tend to increase CNS irritability during alcohol withdrawal and may potentiate some of the other signs and symptoms of alcohol withdrawal.

TREATMENT

The treatment of alcohol withdrawal is basically supportive. The aim of therapy is to: 1) Protect the patient from injuring himself, 2) treat associated disorders, and 3) blunt the hyperkinetic state to reduce exhaustion.

The patient in withdrawal, often agitated and confused, must be protected from injuring himself. His labile mood and the hallucinations and delusions which dominate his consciousness often evoke aggressive or self-mutilating impulses from which he must be protected. This may be effected physically with restraints and/or with the use of appropriate medications (Table 1).

There are many other disorders which may be present but are hidden by these dominating signs and symptoms; associated occult infections, especially pneumonia and meningitis; occult or overt trauma (subdural hematoma); fluid and electrolyte disorders; and malnutrition, including vitamins, minerals and other essential nutrients. These must be considered, investigated and treated appropriately and aggressively.

One of the most difficult components to treat is the hyperkinetic agitated state. It is important to emphasize that sedating drugs have no effect on the metabolism of ethanol or on the course of the alcohol withdrawal syndrome. The aim of therapy is to blunt the agitated state and thereby decrease exhaustion, as well as to enable medical and paramedical personnel to care for the patient. Attempts at completely suppressing agitation require dosages of drugs with their own serious complications.

TABLE 1. DRUG TREATMENT OF ALCOHOL WITHDRAWAL		
DRUG	DOSAGE	COMMENTS

1. Benzodiazepines
  a. Chlordiazepoxide
    (Librium^R)
  b. Diazepam
    (Valium^R)
  c. Oxazepam
    (Serax^R)
	25-150 mg.
	
	5- 25 mg.
	
	10- 30 mg.
		Effective against anxiety, tremors and withdrawal seizures; metabolized by liver; long half life necessitates decreasing doses. (except Oxazepam)

2. Barbiturates
  a. Short-acting
    Pentobarbital
  b. Long-acting
    Phenobarbital
	30-100 mg.
	
	30-100 mg.
		Cross dependence with alcohol; liver is principle site of biotransformation

3. Paraldehyde	8 - 12 mg.	Predominant hepatic biotransformation
4. Chloral Hydrate	250-1500 mg total	only available orally

5. Phenothiazines
  a. Chlorpromazine
  b. Trifluoperazine
	100-800 mg/daily
	4- 15 mg/daily
		Alpha blocking activity (hypotension; EPMS and other neurological side effects

6. Butyrophenones
  a. Haloperidol
    (Haldol^R)
	2 - 6 mg/daily	lowers convulsive threshold; high incidence EPMS reactions

7. Antihistamines
  a. Diphenhydramine
    (Benadryl^R)
  b. Hydroxyzine
    (Vistaril^R)
  c. Promethazine
    (Phenergan^R)
	25- 50 mg.
	
	25-150 mg.
	
	25- 50 mg.
		less effective in controlling seizures. Anticholinergic activity

8. Ethyl Alcohol	Variable	should only be used in emergent situations (surgery)

DRUG THERAPY: The Benzodiazepines are probably the most commonly used drugs in the treatment of alcohol withdrawal. They include Diazepam (Valium^R) Chlordiazepoxide (Librium^R) and Oxazepam (Serax^R). They are all equally effective against the anxiety, restlessness, and tremors associated with alcohol withdrawal. Significantly, they also are effective in controlling seizures and decreasing their frequency. The former two have long half-lives (1-3 days) with active metabolic degradation products. Dosages must be individually adjusted as repeated daily doses may result in drug cumulation and toxicity. Oxazepam, on the other hand, is rapidly converted to an inactive metabolite, with a half life of eight hours. The initial daily doses of chlordiazepoxide, for example, range from 100-1600 mg. Thereafter, there should be a progressive decrease in dosage to prevent cumulation and toxicity. Both Diazepam and chlordiazepoxide are slowly and incompletely absorbed from intramuscular sites. For a more rapid effect, these drugs must be given intravenously. Significantly lower dosages should be used in those with chronic liver disease to compensate for their decreased hepatic metabolism.

The barbiturates have been used effectively for many years in the treatment of alcohol withdrawal. They have the theoretical advantage of demonstrating cross dependence with alcohol. Patients with significant physical dependence on alcohol may demonstrate reduced mortality and morbidity when these agents are used. Frequently used drugs include phenobarbital, amytal, or pentobarbital, 100 mg, every four hours until the desired effect is achieved. As the liver is the principle site of biotransformation, caution is advised in using these drugs in patients with advanced liver disease.

Paraldehyde is another popular and effective drug. Its rate of administration however, limits its usefulness. It should not be given intravenously because of the danger of respiratory depression. Intramuscular administration should be avoided because it may damage nerves and cause sterile abscesses. It may be administered rectally, but has been known to cause severe proctitis. It may be given orally in doses of 8-12 ml in orange juice but this is limited by the frequently associated nausea and or vomiting in the various alcohol withdrawal states. It also is an effective anticonvulsant, but with predominant hepatic biometabolism of the drug, the same precautions exist in its use as in patients with chronic liver disease.

Chloral hydrate has been used effectively but is limited by its oral route of administration. It cannot be given parenterally.

Phenothiazines have also been used. Although they are generally potent antihallucinatory agents, they have no specific action against alcoholic hallucinations. Major disadvantages of their use include their alpha blocking activity and the resulting hypotension. They also lower seizure threshold.

Butyrophenones, specifically Haloperidol, has been used. It has less prominent autonomic effects than the other antipsychotic agents but has a high incidence of extrapyramidal reactions. It also lowers the convulsive threshold.

There is very little justification for using antihistamines. There is less seizure control than with the benzodiazepines.

Ethyl alcohol itself may be used. However, it is very short acting and has a narrow range of safety. In addition, it is merely delaying and not resolving the problem.

In summary, the treatment of any of the stages of the alcohol withdrawal syndrome is basically supportive and symptomatic. The patient must be protected from harming himself and others, and the physician must use special care in choosing the appropriate drug and dosage in this often difficult to handle patient. Attention must also be given to the other medical problems (metabolic, infectious, traumatic, etc.) which often accompany the alcohol withdrawal syndrome. Finally, after these are resolved, the time may be ripe to treat the drinking problem itself.

REFERENCES

1. Victor, M.: Alcoholism; Clinical Neurology. Baker, A.B., Baker, L.H., Harper & Row. Vol. II, 1975.

2. Victor, M.: Treatment of Alcoholic Intoxication and the Withdrawal Syndrome: a critical analysis of the use of drugs and other forms of therapy. Psychosom Med 28:636-650, 1966.

3. Gross, M.M., et al.: Acute Alcohol Withdrawal Syndrome, Biology of Alcoholism. Vol. 3, Clinical Pathology, Plenum Press, New York, pp. 191-263, 1974.

4. Goodman, L.S. and Gilman, A.: The Pharmacologic basis of therapeutics. Fifth Edition, Macmillan, New York, 1975.

B: ACUTE DRUG OVERDOSE
by Bernard I. Elser, M.D.

The number of patients presenting with drug overdoses has increased substantially over the past twenty years. The drugs may be administered with suicidal or homicidal intentions or may be taken accidentally. Rarely, the depressant effect of a drug may cause the patient to forget that he ingested the drug, leading to the administration of further doses of the drug and toxicity (Drug Automatism). Drugs may be taken individually, in combination with other drugs (up to 35% of cases may involve multiple drug ingestion) or together with other substances (i.e., Ethanol). The additive or synergistic effect of these combinations, or any possible interactions, may hasten, delay or intensify the clinical presentation. The eventual outcome of treatment will be determined by the ability to recognize the patient who presents with an overdose with all its possible clinical presentations, as well as the ability to anticipate and treat any potential complication.

I. GENERAL TREATMENT PRINCIPLES: Supportive therapy is the basis of treatment of all drug overdoses. It must come first and be maintained at all times, independent of other therapeutic modalities which may be available. Valuable time must not be lost with often questionably effective antidotes or stimulants, many of which may do more harm than good. Basic support of vital functions must be provided and maintained at all times.

Attempts should be made to identify the suspected drug(s) or compound(s). Family or friends may be helpful in confirming ingestions, drugs, and dosages. If the suspected substance is available, the Physicians Desk Reference, or the dispensing pharmacy, if known, may aid in identification of the drug and dosage. Consideration must be given to the increasingly frequent incidence of multiple drug overdoses.

If possible, the drug should be evacuated from the stomach. If available the appropriate antidote may be given.

Finally, continued observation of the patient until all the effects of the drug have dissipated is necessary.

It is helpful to classify patients according to their symptoms when initially seen by the physician.

II. ASYMPTOMATIC PATIENT: When confronted by an asymptomatic patient with the history of a drug ingestion, the first question which must be asked is why is the patient asymptomatic. It is dangerous to assume that an insufficient quantity of a drug has been ingested unless one can be reasonably certain of that fact. Hopefully, the amount of time which has elapsed since ingestion has been too short for sufficient absorption (enteric coated tablets, effect of drug, etc). Depending on the drug and the amount taken, symptoms usually manifest themselves within two hours of ingestion. Where there has been absorption of multiple drugs or possibly in combination with ethanol, symptoms may appear earlier. A specimen of blood, urine, or gastric contents may be obtained to confirm drug ingestion and identify the drug.

III. SYMPTOMATIC PATIENT: The clinical presentation of a patient who manifests symptoms of drug(s) ingestion will vary to a great extent upon the specific drug ingested, and elapsed time since administration. There may be alterations of mental status, from mild lethargy to deep coma (Table 1). Vital signs may be depressed.

TABLE 1				
DEPTH OF COMA				
Stages	Mental Status	Reflexes	Blood Pressure	Respirations
0	Arousable	+	NL	NL
1	Withdrawal from pain	+	NL	NL
2	No response	+	NL	NL
3	No response	Absent	NL	NL
4	No response	Absent	↓	↓
(Reed, Ann. Int. Med. - 1952)				

In addition, there may be specific organ failures, although this may not become manifest for days (Table 2).

TABLE 2	
EXAMPLES OF EFFECTS OF VARIOUS DRUGS ON SPECIFIC ORGANS	
Drug	Organ Affected
Acetaminophen, Alcohol	Liver
Tricyclic Antidepressants	Heart
Antibiotics	Kidney
Sedatives, hypnotics, alcohol	Brain, Lung

IV. ASSESSMENT: There are no simple laboratory tests or physical findings which will prove drug ingestion. Toxicological evaluation of blood, urine, or gastric contents will assist in documenting ingestion, following the clinical course and determining prognosis. Evacuation of gastric contents containing recognizable particulate matter may rarely be helpful.

The pupillary reaction may be helpful in differentiating drug-induced coma from that seen with trauma or certain central nervous system vascular catastrophies. The pupillary pathways are relatively resistant to metabolic insults, and the presence or absence of the pupillary light reflex is a key sign in distinguishing metabolic causes of coma from structural causes.

With few exceptions (Atropine, Scopolamine, Glutethimide, barbiturates, in very high doses) the reaction to light in acute drug overdoses is usually preserved although a strong light and careful observation may be necessary. Opiates cause pinpoint pupils and the pupillary light reflex, although difficult to observe, is usually maintained.

Further evaluation will depend on the clinical status of the patient, and the drug(s) ingested, if known. Routine laboratory tests, including CBC, urinalysis, electrolytes, liver and renal function tests, are necessary in the symptomatic patient. A chest radiograph is essential because of the possibility of aspiration, even before the patient's entry into the medical system. Furthermore, an ECG is useful where there has been ingestion of a drug with known cardiac toxicity (tricyclic antidepressants, digitalis preparations) or hypotension. Arterial blood gases are also valuable. They may give an indirect clue to type of drug ingested (mixed metabolic acidosis and respiratory alkalosis seen in significant aspirin (overdoses) and evaluate adequacy of pulmonary function where respiratory depression has occurred.

V. TREATMENT: All patients presenting with suspected or proven drug overdoses must be observed closely. Vital signs must be monitored frequently and therapy directed at support of these functions before any other therapeutic modalities are employed. Only then may symptomatic therapy be instituted.

Support of the respiratory system is obviously critical. The airway must be cleared of dentures and all foreign bodies if there is any alteration of mental status or respiratory function. The patient should be positioned in a semi-prone position to prevent aspiration. If spontaneous respirations are adequate, an oral pharyngeal airway may be inserted to facilitate breathing. When respirations are depressed and inadequate, a cuffed endotracheal tube should be inserted atraumatically and connected to a mechanical respirator. This will also simplify gastric lavage, if appropriate, and prevent aspiration of gastric contents. Chest x-ray (to rule out aspiration), arterial blood gases (to monitor pulmonary function) and respiratory care should be performed routinely.

Cardiovascular function must also be maintained. Depending on the severity, central venous pressure or Swan-Ganz catheters as well as electrocardiographic monitoring may be necessary, certainly where cardio-toxic drugs have been ingested. Monitoring urine output and intravenous fluid administration are often necessary.

After these supportive measures, if necessary, have been instituted, and in the asymptomatic patient, several additional non-specific therapeutic maneuvers may be initiated.

VI. EMESIS: When a drug is taken by mouth, emptying the stomach of the drug, if instituted early may be very effective in limiting further absorption and consequently minimizing any symptoms and their duration. Many drugs by themselves may induce emesis; if not, other measures may be taken to achieve this effect. Induction of emesis, however, is contraindicated where there is coexisting CNS depression or a decreased gag reflex because of the danger of aspiration.

Syrup of Ipecac acts both centrally and locally in the GI tract to cause vomiting. Onset of action averages 15-30 minutes. Dosage is 10-15 ml. P.O. and may be repeated once if no emesis ensues. Vomiting will generally not occur if the stomach is empty so that it is advisable to give 1-2 glasses of water concomitantly. Ipecac has some mild cardiac toxicity in large doses and should be used cautiously in patients with coexisting cardiac disorders. It should not be used together with activated charcoal which may inactivate it. The charcoal may be used following emesis. The fluid extract of Ipecac is more potent, potentially toxic and should never be used.

Apomorphine is a very powerful, rapidly acting emetic which may cause severe emesis. It is administered parenterally and thus may be used in an uncooperative patient. However, it may cause severe emesis and therefore should be reserved for very serious situations (uncooperative suicidal patients). Dosage is 6 mg. administered subcutaneously (0.1 mg/kg in a child). As with Ipecac, it may not be effective when administered to a patient with an empty stomach and thus should be given together with oral fluids. Its central effect usually begins within 3 - 5 minutes and may be blocked with Naloxone (Narcan [R]). This may be necessary in the patient who continues to vomit after the desired effect is achieved or who develops a depressed mental status or gag reflex following administration of the drug but before emesis ensues. It should not be given to any patient whose mental status or gag reflex is known to be depressed.

VII. LAVAGE: Gastric lavage is generally used where emesis cannot be induced or is not effective. Except where contraindicated, it may be used anytime within several hours of ingestion of a drug or even later if there is reason to suspect delayed emptying or absorption (enteric coated tablets, full stomach, etc.).

It is contraindicated with significant central nervous system depression or with an attenuated gag reflex because of the danger of aspiration. In these cases, a cuffed endotracheal tube must be inserted before instituting gastric lavage.

As lavage fluid, cold tap water or normal saline may be used. Approximately 300 cc. is injected through the tube in 1-2 minutes, leaving it in place for another 1-2 minutes and then permitting gravity drainage for 3-4 minutes. Any residual may be aspirated with an aspirating bulb syringe. Lavaging should be continued for several liters after the aspirate clears.

Some of the initially aspirated fluid may be saved for toxicology, if necessary. Other lavage solutions have been used including Tannic Acid, potassium permangenate, and copper sulfate, but accidental aspiration with these substances is so serious that their use is rarely indicated.

After lavage is completed, an antidote, if appropriate and available and/or activated charcoal to prevent further absorption of any residual drug may be administered through the nasogastric tube. A cathartic to speed its passage may also be passed through the tube (see below). Before finally removing the tube, however, it should be rinsed once more with saline to prevent aspiration of any of these substances. The lumen is then pinched off and the tube removed.

There are various adjunctive measures which may be used in addition to those already mentioned.

Activated charcoal is a potent absorbant which is effective against most agents and which can prevent absorption of many drugs. It is effective throughout the GI tract and will not desorb in the lower tract. The dosage is generally 100 gms. or 1-2 tablespoons in a glass of water to make a paste. It should only be used following emesis or lavage and should not be given with Ipecac, which will be neutralized by it. It is not effective against cyanide, but otherwise does form an effective barrier between drugs and the GI mucosa to prevent their absorption. It will also block the entero-hepatic circulation of many drugs.

Cathartics are also valuable in that they may speed passage of the drug through the GI tract. One of the most popular is Magnesium Sulfate (Epsom Salt). Dosage is 5-15 grams and its bitter taste should be masked. It may cause nausea and is slowly and incompletely absorbed. It is usually effective within 3-6 hours and should be given last, following emesis, lavage and charcoal. Renal function must be normal prior to its administration because of the absorption and threat of magnesium toxicity. Magnesium citrate, in a dose of 200 ml. is similarly effective. Castor oil, containing an unsaturated hydroxy fatty acid, in an oral dose of 15-60 cc acts on the small intestine usually within 2-6 hours to give prompt and thorough evacuation.

Forced diuresis is another measure which may be effective with some drug ingestions. Obvious prerequisites for its effectiveness include a significant renal excretory mechanism for the ingested drug and satisfactory renal function in the affected individual. Fluids are administered, usually intravenously, to maintain a urine output of at least 8-14 liters per day and thereby increase excretion of the drug. Electrolyte balance must be carefully maintained. This is effective with overdoses of aspirin and the long acting barbiturates, when used in conjunction with alkalinization of the urine.

Excretion of a drug may also be enhanced by altering the pH of the solution in which it is dissolved, a concept called ion trapping (Table 3). It is based on the fact that many biologically active substances, including drugs, behave in solution as weak acids and bases and thereby exist, to a variable extent, in an ionized form. As most cell membranes, and specifically those of the renal tubules, are less permeable to the ionized form of a drug, any maneuver which increases the concentration of the ionized state of a drug will block its absorption and speed its excretion. Although the extent of ionization of a drug, termed ionization constant, or pK, is a property of the substance itself and cannot be changed, the concentration of the ionized form may be altered by changes in the pH of the solution in which it is disolved.

The effectiveness of this method is decreased where biotransformation is necessary before excretion (e.g. with pentobarbital) or where there is significant protein binding.

This maneuver may be very effective in speeding elimination of a drug. Each unit change in pH will give a ten fold change in the concentration of the ionized form. A change in urinary pH from 7 to 5 for example, will give a one hundred fold change in ionization and depending on other factors, may significantly affect reabsorption of a drug.

Finally, analeptics have been used as adjunctive measure and are mentioned here to recommend that they not be used routinely. Their effectiveness is limited and they may have their own serious adverse effects.

TABLE 3
DRUGS AND ION TRAPPING

A. Definitely effective:

   1. Acids - Alkalinize Urine
     a) Aspirin
     b) Phenobarbital
     c) Phenylbutazone - Butazolidin (R)
     d) Salicylic Acid

   2. Bases - Acidify Urine
     a) Amphetamine
     b) Dextroamphetamine
     c) Meperidine - Demerol (R)
     d) Phencyclidine (PCP)

B. Not Effective or of Limited Clinical Value:

   1. Acids - Alkalinize Urine
     a) Amobarbital
     b) Barbital
     c) Pentobarbital
     d) Secobarbital

   2. Bases - Acidify Urine
     a) Imipramine - Tofranil (R)
     b) Amitriptyline - Elavil (R)
     c) Chlorpromazine - Thorazine (R)

Dialysis, both hemodialysis and peritoneal dialysis is used in severe cases of drug overdose. Indications for its use however, remains controversial. A critical prerequisite is that the drug be dialyzable (Table 4). Renal failure, coma, respiratory failure, and severe hypotension are some of the indications for dialysis. Newer methods including hemoperfusion through activated charcoal, promise an effective method for some of the more potent substances including fat soluble drugs.

Finally, mention must be given to antidotes. There are very few specific antidotes and their availability does not replace the need for support of vital functions. In most cases, they should not be used prophylactically. On occasion, the duration of action of the antidote is significantly shorter than that of the offending drug. In these cases, the patient must be observed carefully and the antidote readministered if needed.

TABLE 4
DIALYZABLE DRUGS

I. BARBITURATES:
1. Barbital
2. Phenobarbital
3. Amobarbital
4. Pentobarbital
5. Butabarbital
6. Secobarbital
7. Cyclobarbital

II. GLUTETHIMIDE: Doriden [R]

III. OTHER TRANQUILIZERS, DEPRESSANTS, SEDATIVES:
1. Diphenylhydantoin
2. Primidone - Mysoline [R]
3. Meprobamate - Miltown [R]
4. Ethchlorynol - Placidyl [R]
5. Methprylon - Noludar [R]
6. Methaqualone - Quaalude [R]
7. Paraldehyde
8. Chloral hydrate - Noctec [R]
9. Chlordiazepoxide - Librium [R]

IV. ANTIDEPRESSANTS:
1. Amphetamine
2. Methamphetamine
3. Tricyclic secondary and tertiary amines
4. MAO inhibitors
5. Pargyline - Eutonyl [R]

V. ALCOHOLS:
1. Ethanol
2. Methanol
3. Isopropanol
4. Ethylene glycol

VI. ANALGESICS:
1. Acetyl Salicyclic Acid
2. Methyl Salicyclic Acid
3. Acetophenetidin
4. Dextropropoxyphene
5. Paracetamol

VIII. OTHERS:
1. Digoxin
2. (Carbon tetracholoride)

One of the more recently introduced specific antidotes is Naloxone (Narcan (R)). It is an opiate antagonist which can be administered IM, IV, or subcutaneously in a dose of 0.4 to 0.8 mg. It will rapidly reverse many of the opiate (including heroin and methadone) effects. Significantly, it is a pure antagonist with few of the agonistic effects seen in previously used opiate antagonists such as nallorphan or levallorphan. It will rapidly reverse the respiratory depressant effect, the hypotensive effect, and the sedating effects of the opiates. Duration of action is one to four hours, significantly shorter than that of heroin and methadone. It is not effective in reversing the respiratory depression induced by ethanol or barbiturates.

Another frequently used antidote is physostigmine (Antilurium (R)). Its use has increased recently as a result of the introduction and use of many new drugs possessing anti-cholinergic activity.

Physostigmine is a rapidly reversible cholinesterase inhibitor which potentiates the effects of endogenous acetyl choline and reverses the effects of drugs and plants possessing anticholinergic properties (Table 5).

TABLE 5
DRUGS AND CHEMICALS CAPABLE OF PRODUCING ANTICHOLINERGIC POISONING

Amitriptyline (Elavil(R), Triavil (R), Etrafon(R))	Mepenzolate Methantheline Methapryiline Nortriptyline (Aventyl(R))
Anisotropine methylbromide	
Atropine	Pipenzolate Bromide
Belladonna	(Piptal(R))
Chlorpheniramine	
Desipramine (Norpramin(R), Pertofrane(R)	Propantheline Protriptyline (Vavactil(R)) Pyrilamine
Diclyclomine	Stramonium
Doxepin (Sinequan(R))	Tricyclic Antidepressants:
Homatropine	(Aventyl(R), Elavil(R),
Hyoscine	(Etrafon(R), Norpramin(R),
Hyoscyamus	Pertofrane(R), Presa-
Imipramine (Tofranil(R), (Presamine(R))	mine(R), Tofranil(R), Triavil(R), Vivactil(R))
Isopropamide	Thioridazine Mellaril(R))

PLANTS CAPABLE OF PRODUCING ANTICHOLINERGIC POISONING:

Amanita muscaria	Jerusalem cherry
Bittersweet	Jimson weed
Black henbane	Lantana
Black nightshade	Potato leaves, sprouts, tubers
Deadly nightshade	Wild tomato

Some of the anticholinergic effects which may be seen in affected individuals include tachycardia, mydriasis, dry skin and mucous membranes, urinary retention, ileus, hyperpyrexia, confusion, disorientation, agitation and coma.

Physostigmine is a tertiary amine and easily crosses the blood-brain barrier. Dosage is 2 mg, IV slowly over two minutes. It may be repeated, if necessary in 30 - 60 minutes up to a total dose of 6 mg.

It may also be given IM. An excellent indicator of its effect is slowing of the pulse. Care must be taken not to overtreat, thereby producing a cholinergic crisis with its associated bronchospasm, laryngospasm, central respiratory paralysis, excess pulmonary secretions, muscle twitching and seizures.

Contraindications include absolute or relative obstruction of the GI or GU tracts, asthma or chronic obstructive lung diseases, and organic heart disease.

Finally, do not do further harm. Be careful not to traumatize the patient while inserting a nasogastric tube, or an endotracheal tube. Pay attention to the patients position in bed so that his extremities will not be traumatized. He should be turned frequently, especially if comatose, and placed in a semiprone position to help prevent aspiration.

VIII. COMPLICATIONS: The complications of acute drug overdose may occur quite independently of the type of drug ingested or may be a direct toxic effect of the drug. Similar effects are seen with many drugs.

Central nervous system depression, from lethargy to coma, may be seen with many different categories of drugs but is most frequently seen with the sedative-hypnotic group overdoses.

Similarly, acute respiratory insufficiency, due to a depressant effect of drugs on the respiratory center, is a serious complication of many drugs.

Hypotension may be caused by a central or peripheral depressant effect of the drug on the heart and vasculature, complicated by an associated volume depletion. Tissue hypoxia and metabolic acidosis are frequent contributory factors.

Acute renal failure, either as a direct toxic effect of a drug, or as a consequence of prolonged hypotension, may also be observed.

Aspiration pneumonia may occur either before the patient is brought to medical attention or thereafter, and may be a serious complication.

The patient's depressed mental status may prevent him from describing the trauma which may have occurred prior to his entry into the medical system. Following that, care must also be exercised to prevent trauma to the patient, often related to hanging extremities or the patient reclining in the same vulnerable position for prolonged periods.

All of these complications must be considered and searched for with the appropriate maneuvers.

It would be impossible to detail individual drugs, the signs and symptoms associated with their overdosage, the prognosis, lethal dosage and recommended therapeutic measures. It is suggested that when the ingested drug is known, the PDR, (Physician's Desk Reference), or a local poison control center (often with toll-free hotline phone numbers) be consulted for specific treatment information. When the drug ingested is not known with any reasonable certainty, supportive measures should be instituted and maintained until all signs and symptoms of the episode have completely disappeared.

REFERENCES

1. Goodman, L. S. and Gilman, A.: "The Pharmacological Basis of Therapeutics", Fifth Edition, Macmillan, 1975.

2. Walker, Wm. E., et al.: "Physostigmine - Its Use and Abuse" JACEP, Vol. 5, No. 6, p. 436

3. Done, Alan K.: "The Toxic Emergency; Setting Traps for Poisons", Emergency Medicine, p. 197, Aug. 1976.

4. Package Insert: "Antilirium(R)", O'Neal, Jones & Feldman, Inc.

CHAPTER 11: RHEUMATOLOGIC EMERGENCIES
by Harvey E. Brown, Jr., M.D., Ph.D.

ACUTE ARTHRITIS

In the discussion to follow special emphasis is placed on synovial fluid analysis as a major aid in prompt diagnosis.

SEPTIC ARTHRITIS: Prompt diagnosis of septic arthritis is crucial and with the exception of gonococcal infections usually is marked by "septic" synovial fluid. As shown in Table I, the fluid is not clear and straw-yellow but turbid, greenish or bloody. The white blood cell count may be as high as $200,000/\text{mm}^3$, with a predominance of polymorphonuclear leukocytes. There are some variations in the fluid findings in the various bacterial infections but generally they are not of diagnostic help. While staphylococcal infection of joints may occur spontaneously, these and other types of infections usually accompany or follow systemic infections or bacteremias. Young children and infants are prone to hemophilus influenzae joint infection, while the elderly are more susceptible to gram-negative organisms.

In most infected joints the synovial fluid sugar is depressed. It is important to measure the blood sugar simultaneously, as the blood/synovial sugar differential is more important than the absolute level.

The Gram stain usually corroborates the clinical impression but if infection is suspected culture should be performed even if the Gram stain is negative.

When aspirating fluid on which cultures are to be done, it is wise to use procaine or a dry syringe. Lidocaine and some other local anesthetics have been shown to have bacteriostatic activity.

Blood cultures are advisable in patients suspected of having an infected joint. This is particularly important in patients with pneumonia or a history of intravenous drug use; at times a septic joint is the first sign of bacterial endocarditis.

Tuberculosis of joints still occurs but in low frequency. Tuberculosis infection is primarily of the juxta-articular bony tissue and is usually a subacute rather than acute process. At times, however, an acute exacerbation of a smoldering process may occur. Skin tests, synovial fluid analysis and x-ray are helpful but biopsy is often required for positive diagnosis.

TABLE I					
SEPTIC FLUID					
Condition	Color	Clarity	Viscosity-Clot With Acetic Acid	WBC/MM^3	Note
Bacterial	Yellow-Green to Bloody	Purulent	Low/Poor	to 200,000	+ Bacteria
Tuber-culous	Yellow	Cloudy	Low/Poor	25,000	+ AFB
Gono-coccal	Yellow to Green	Clear to Purulent	Low/Poor	1 - 50,000	+ Bacteria

Gonococcal arthritis is a result of gonococcal septicemia and often will present with chills, fever and migratory tenosynovitis for several days before settling into one or two joints. About a quarter of patients will present characteristic skin lesions of gonococcal septicemia. There are few too many pustules or hemorrhagic bullae, at times in the general area of the involved joints. The disease was formerly rare in males but is being seen with increasing frequency, especially in the homosexual population. In this setting, a positive pharyngeal or rectal culture may be diagnostic. A history of sexual contact is often hard to obtain. There is a marked tendency for the process to become evident at about the time of the menses or during pregnancy. It may appear at any time during pregnancy, including labor. Acute arthritis in a pregnant woman should be considered gonococcal until an alternate etiology is proven.

Synovial fluid findings in gonococcal arthritis are very variable and at times surprisingly normal. White cell counts less than 1000 and normal sugar levels have been found in joint fluid from which gonococci have been cultured. Blood, pharyngeal, urethral/cervical and rectal cultures as well as synovial fluid cultures are helpful in proving diagnosis.

In spite of reports of increasing resistance to penicillin of gonococcal strains, especially of Asian strains, no resistance problems have been encountered in joint infections and moderate doses of intravenous penicillin for a few days have proven curative.

About a quarter of patients with gonococcal arthritis will have evidence of serositis with EKG or physical findings. In some the EKG may be suggestive of a myocarditis, but serious cardiac complications are very rare if appropriate therapy is given.

GOUT AND PSEUDOGOUT: As seen in Table II, there is considerable overlap between "septic" and "inflammatory" synovial fluid. It is not unusual for gouty or rheumatoid fluids to appear "septic" due to the very high WBC counts seen with severe inflammatory changes in these diseases. While superimposed infection is rare in gout, it is not in pseudogout and rheumatoid arthritis. In a patient with old or newly diagnosed rheumatoid arthritis or pseudogout who is febrile, has chills or presents with one or two extremely tender and inflamed joints, the possibility of infection should be settled by Gram stain and culture of the fluid and blood.

The history is not of much value in differentiating gout from pseudogout (unless a previous diagnosis has been confirmed). Increasing incidence with age, high association with diabetes mellitus and diuretic therapy are seen in both. There is a tendency for pseudogout to occur more rarely in the great toe joints in the initial attacks but the x-ray appearance of chondrocalcinosis in the involved joints (sometimes it is easily demonstrated in the wrists and knees even when they are not clinically involved) is more helpful. Demonstration of the diagnostic needle shaped crystals of urate or the more regular rhomboids of pseudogout is diagnostic. In questionable cases the use of compensated polarized microscopy is of great value. In gout, the urate crystals show weakly negative birefringence, while the calcium pyrophosphate crystals in pseudogout are weakly positive under polarized light.

RHEUMATOID ARTHRITIS: Rheumatoid arthritis in the adult rarely presents as an acute arthritis. (Any adult with known or suspected rheumatoid arthritis who presents in such a fashion must be carefully studied to rule out infections, rheumatic fever, or the other causes of inflammation). In childhood, rheumatoid arthritis and acute onset in one to many joints, often with fever, is more often a problem in differential diagnosis. Young children may present with high fever, WBC counts as high as 50,000 mm^3, generalized lymphadenopathy, hepato-splenomegaly and a typical salmon colored rash. The differential diagnosis between rheumatoid arthritis, rheumatic fever and systemic lupus erythematosus may be difficult especially when carditis is present, as it is common in all three. High titers of anti-streptococcal antibodies may also be confusing, as they are often high in attacks of juvenile rheumatoid arthritis. Response to saliccylates may be similar in all three conditions, as is response to corticosteroids. Signs of valvular involvement point to rheumatic fever; kidney or hematologic involvement and false positive VDRL to lupus. Low to moderate levels of antinuclear antibodies may occur in rheumatoid arthritis but high levels point to lupus. A positive LE prep is almost pathognomonic for lupus.

Rheumatologic Emergencies/ 231

TABLE II: INFLAMMATORY FLUID

CONDITION	COLOR	CLARITY	VISCOSITY/CLOT WITH HAC	WBC/MM^3	NOTE
Rheumatic	Yellow Milky	Clear to Cloudy	Low/Good	15,000	
Pseudo Gout	Yellow	Cloudy	Low/Fair	15,000	Crystals (1)
Gout	Yellow Milky	Cloudy	Low/Fair	50,000	Crystals (2)
Rheumatoid Arthritis	Yellow to Green	Cloudy	Low/Poor	50,000	"RA Cells" (3)
Reiter's	Yellow to Green	Cloudy	Low/Poor	50,000	"Reiter's Cells" (4)
Ankylosing Spondylitis	Yellow	Cloudy	Low/Poor	25,000	
Psoriatic Arthritis	Yellow	Clear to Cloudy	Low/Poor	25,000	
Intermittent Hydroarthrosis	Yellow	Clear	Low/Fair	20,000	

1. Calcium pyrophosphate rhomboids intra + extra-cellular
2. Needle like crystals of sodium urate intra and extra cellularly.
3. "RA CELLS" or ragocytes are polys with refractive inclusions.
4. Reiter's cells are white blood cells with large inclusions.

REITER'S DISEASE: Reiter's disease is primarily a disease of young males. The conjunctivitis and urethritis may be mild or transient and the acute arthritis the major complaint. In this country the diarrheal onset is unusual. The onset of arthritis may be abrupt and the inflammation and tenderness as marked as in a severe attack of gout. There is a tendency to attack the lower extremity joints, especially the ankles. The periarticular cellulitis at times is marked as is involvement of the bursae about the Achilles tendon insertion. Careful search for mucosal lesions on the tongue and palate or the glans penis and keratotic lesions of the navel, toe or soles are important diagnostic clues. There may be sacroiliac involvement or the development of aortic insufficiency in a matter of weeks.

PSORIATIC ARTHRITIS: Psoriatic arthritis may present much as Reiter's disease, again looking and feeling like gout. Careful search for pits in the finger nails, palpable seborrhea and typical plaques on the elbows, knees, or gluteal fold may provide a clue to otherwise puzzling arthritis. Gout and psoriasis may occur together so should be searched for. (For some reason coincident gout and rheumatoid arthritis are extremely rare.)

ANKYLOSING SPONDYLITIS: Adolescent males may have the onset of ankylosing spondylitis as an acute peripheral arthritis usually of a hip or knee. A family history of spondylitis or iritis is at times a helpful clue. Less than expected chest expansion or sacroiliac or lumbosacral motion may be present but asymptomatic. Demonstration of the tissue typing antigen HLA-B-27, makes the diagnosis probable and should be determined in doubtful cases.

DIAGNOSTIC CONSIDERATIONS

Intermittent hydroarthrosis is an acute arthritis with effusion, sometimes with much inflammation. During the first few attacks care must be taken to rule out an infectious etiology.

The conditions causing non-inflammatory effusions as outlined in Table III are generally less acute then those previously discussed. At times, however, arthritis may be the presenting symptom and when a non-inflammatory fluid is obtained from a joint these conditions should be considered.

Special mention should be made of bloody effusions. Hemarthrosis may be the first sign of a bleeding disorder and even with a history of trauma, abnormalities of clotting must be ruled out. In the older patient bleeding in a joint may be a sign of Charcot joint, today more likely diabetic than leutic.

Special clues to be searched for include the skin lesions of erythema nodosum which may be overlooked in the patient with severe ankle arthritis and periarthritis. When found they suggest either sarcoidosis, drug reaction (notably birth control pills) and inflammatory bowel disease.

TABLE III: NON-INFLAMMATORY FLUID CHARACTERISTICS

CONDITION	COLOR	CLARITY	VISCOSITY/CLOT WITH HAC	WBC/MM^3	NOTE
Normal	Straw	Clear	High/Good	<200	
Traumatic	Straw-Bloody	Varies	High/Good	<200	RBCS
Osteo Arthritis	Straw-Yellow	Clear	High/Good	<200	Cartilage Debris
Systemic Lupus	Straw	Clear to Cloudy	Low/Good	<5000	LE Cells
Charcot	Straw to Bloody	Varies	High/Good	<1000	RBS Often
Hypertrophic	Straw	Clear	High/Good	<1000	
Colitis Whipple's	Straw	Clear	Low/Good	<2000	
Sickle Cell Disease	Yellow	Clear	Low/Good	<2000	Sickle Cells
Hypothyroidism	Yellow	Clear	High/Good	<2000	

In the immuno-suppressed patients special care should be taken to search for the "opportunistic" microbiological agents as well as the common and uncommon pathogens.

Consideration of the age of the patient, the accompanying signs and symptoms, appropriate laboratory x-rays and especially careful examination of the synovial fluid should enable one to make a presumptive or definitive diagnosis (or at least a reasonable differential diagnosis) so that prompt and appropriate therapy can be undertaken.

REFERENCES

1. Hollander, J. L. and McCarty, D. J. (Eds): Arthritis and Allied Conditions. 8th Edition, Lea and Febiger, Philadelphia, 1972.

2. Keiser, H., et al.: Clinical forms of gonococcal arthritis. N Engl J Med, 279:234, 1968.

3. Wyngaarden, J. B., and Kelly, W. N.: Gout In: Stanbury, J. B., Wyngaarden, J. B. and Fredrickson, D. S. (Eds): The Metabolic Basis of Inherited Disease. 3rd Edition, McGraw-Hill Book Company, New York, p. 889, 1972.

CHAPTER 12: RENAL EMERGENCIES

A: SEVERE ACID-BASE ABNORMALITIES
by Laurence B. Gardner, M.D.

INTRODUCTION: In assessing the patient with a potential acid base disturbance, obtaining an arterial blood gas is virtually mandatory. The pH (strictly the negative logarithm of the hydrogen ion concentration $[H^+]$, but practically an inverse measurement of $[H^+]$) defines the state of the patients blood (acid or alkaline), the pCO_2 affords important information about alveolar ventilation and CO_2 elimination, the pO_2 tells the physician about hypoxemia, an important cause of acid-base disturbances, and the HCO_3^- (bicarborate concentration) allows us to assess the quantity of circulating buffer. Most important in determining the need for treatment is the pH. If the pH is markedly abnormal, then therapy aimed at returning this value toward normal is usually indicated. If, on the other hand, the patient is suffering from more than one acid base disturbance (see below) and the effect of these multiple disorders is to "cancel each other out" resulting in a normal pH, then therapy is not indicated.

Acid-base disturbances can be broken down into two major categories: respiratory and metabolic. Respiratory disturbances result from an abnormal handling of CO_2 gas - either failure of elimination or inappropriate elimination. The important parameter in assessing respiratory disturbances is the pCO_2 (partial pressure of CO_2 gas in the blood). Metabolic disturbances result from pathological processes which interfere with normal handling of fixed (as opposed to volatile -CO_2) hydrogen ion (H^+). They may involve states of H^+ deficiency or excess, the latter due to either excess production or decreased elimination. Bicarbonate (HCO_3^-) concentration tends to vary inversely with the concentration of fixed H^+ and is the important parameter (after pH) in assessing metabolic disturbances.

The Henderson-Hasselbalch equation: $pH = pK + \log \dfrac{HCO_3^-}{H_2CO_3}$ is of critical importance in understanding acid-base physiology and pathophysiology. The equation can be simplified in two important ways. First, since the pK term is a constant we can eliminate it from our simplified formula, and second, H_2CO_3 (concentration of carbonic acid or dissolved CO_2 gas in the blood) can be expressed as "(0.03) pCO_2". Expressed simply then, this very important equation now becomes:

$$pH = (constant) + \log \frac{HCO_3^-}{(.03)\, pCO_2}$$

ACID-BASE MAP

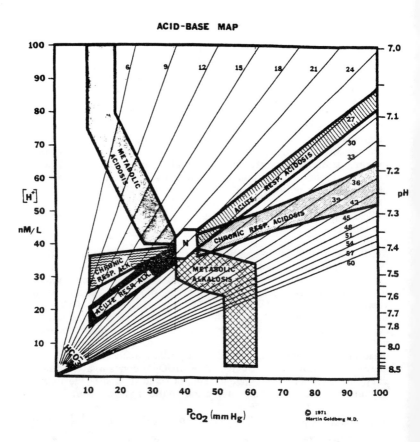

P_{CO_2} (mm Hg)

© 1971
Martin Goldberg M.D.

Thusly, the pH will vary directly with the HCO_3^- concentration (pCO_2 constant) and inversely with the pCO_2, (HCO_3^- constant). From this equation we can predict the directional change in pH with a change in either of these two variables and if we realize that the normal ratio $\dfrac{HCO_3^-}{(.03)\,pCO_2}$ has a numerical value of approximately $20\left(\dfrac{25}{(.03)\ 40}\right)$, then the direction of pH change can be assessed even with simultaneous changes in both pCO_2 and HCO_3. This becomes even more important when we start to consider compensatory processes as well as primary acid-base disorders.

Other important factors to take into consideration in the assessment of acid-base disturbances are severity and chronicity. As a rule acute changes require more aggressive treatment than chronic processes and we must determine, prior to therapy, whether or not a process is ongoing or self-limited.

The serum potassium (K+) concentration is another important factor in the assessment and therapy of acid-base disturbances. In general, the K+ varies inversely with the pH, tending to rise with low pH and fall with increases in pH. A gross prediction of this change can be stated as follows:

a) In acidemia, for each fall of 0.1 units in the pH, the K+ will rise 0.75 mEq/L.

b) In alkalemia, for each elevation of 0.1 units in the pH, the K+ will fall 0.5 mEq/L.

It is obvious that no therapy of severe acid-base disorders can be undertaken without careful consideration of the effect of that therapy upon the serum K+.

OVERALL ACID PRODUCTION AND ACID-BASE BALANCE: Each day, man, in the course of metabolism of foodstuffs, produces acid waste products which if not disposed of efficiently and safely would accumulate with resultant irreparable harm to the organism. The oxidation of fats and carbohydrates, which compose over 80% of the calories ingested each day, results in the generation of 15,000 mM of CO_2 gas referred to as "volatile" acid. This acid is normally eliminated by the lungs during normal respiration and does not require complex metabolic machinery for its disposal.

The metabolism of protein, specifically phosphate and sulfur containing amino acids, results in the formation of approximately 1 mEq of "fixed acid" for each gram of protein ingested (about 75-100 mEq per day for an adult on a normal protein diet). This is strong acid, usually in the form of sulfuric or phosphoric acid, and is immediately buffered by the body's major circulating buffer, sodium bicarbonate ($NaHCO_3$). While this "inactivates" the strong and potentially harmful hydrogen ion (H+), a deficit of HCO_3^- would develop if there were no opposing process. The kidney's role in the maintenance of acid-base balance revolves around the regeneration of this consumed HCO_3^-. This is accomplished by the excretion of H+ into the urine with simultaneous generation of new HCO_3^-. Failure of the lungs or kidneys to match acid excretion with acid production results in a pathologic accumulation or deficit of H+ recognized clinically as acidosis or alkalosis.

DEFINITIONS:

Alkalemia: Blood pH $>$ 7.45

Acidemia: Blood pH $<$ 7.35

Alkalosis: A primary process which, if unopposed by another primary process, will result in alkalemia.

Acidosis: A primary process which, if unopposed by another primary process, will result in acidemia.

Anion Gap: The concentration of anions in the blood unmeasured by the usual electrolyte determinations. Calculated as: Serum Sodium concentration (Na+) minus the sum of the chloride (Cl^-) and HCO_3^- concentrations. Na+ - (Cl^- + HCO_3^-); normal range 4 - 12 mEq/L

Compensatory Processes:
Never named a primary process! Describes changes in ventilation (pCO_2) and buffering capacity (HCO_3^-) which tend to bring pH back toward normal. Virtually never restores the pH to normal.

Simple Acid Base Disturbance:
The primary disease process with its primary and compensatory changes in pH, pCO_2 and HCO_3^-.

The Four Simple Acid Base Disturbances:
(1) Metabolic Acidosis
(2) Metabolic Alkalosis
(3) Respiratory Acidosis
(4) Respiratory Alkalosis

Mixed Acid-Base Disturbance:
Two or more simple disturbances occuring simultaneously.

RESPIRATORY ACIDOSIS: The primary abnormality in respiratory acidosis is CO_2 retention. This is manifested by an elevation of the pCO_2 above normal (40 mmHg) and from our understanding of the Henderson-Hasselbalch equation a decrease in the value of the $\dfrac{HCO_3^-}{(.03)\,pCO_2}$ term and a low pH (acidemic). Compensatory responses to CO_2 retention take two forms: acute (cellular) buffering and chronic (renal) buffering. An illustration of these changes is seen in Table 1.

	Normal	Acute Respiratory Acidosis		Chronic Respiratory Acidosis
		No Compensation	Acute Compensation	
pH	7.40	7.08	7.15	7.30
pCO_2 (mmHg)	40	80	80	80
HCO_3^- (mEq/L)	25	25	30	40

TABLE 1

Notice that buffering occurs by means of an elevation of HCO_3^- concentration, small in the acute phase and more substantial with chronic CO_2 retention. The acute rise in HCO_3^- occurs basically because H+ enters cells and is buffered by intracellular protein and Cl⁻ is exchanged for HCO_3^- across the cell membrane. Although only a small rise in HCO_3^- occurs (2-5 mEq/L this is enough to raise the pH from 7.08 (where it would be with no change in HCO_3^-) to 7.15. Renal compensation takes longer (16-72 hours) but is quantitatively more significant. The elevated pCO_2 "induces" the kidney to generate more HCO_3^-, thus ameliorating the acidemia. Note that one can assess the "acuteness" of respiratory acidosis by the severity of the pH change and the chronicity by the magnitude of the HCO_3^- elevation.

Causes of respiratory acidosis may be divided into two general categories: diseases depressing the respiratory center and diseases directly affecting the lung and respiratory mechanics. Common causes are as follows:

Causes of Respiratory Acidosis:

A. CENTRAL DEPRESSION OF RESPIRATION
   1. Drug Overdose (Narcotics, Barbiturates, etc.)
   2. Central Nervous System Trauma
   3. Infections of the Nervous System (Encephalitis, Meningitis)
   4. Cerebrovascular Accidents
   5. Primary Central Hypoventilation

B. PRIMARY PULMONARY DISEASE
   1. Chronic Obstructive Lung Disease
   2. Status Asthmaticus (severe)
   3. Pulmonary Infections (severe)
   4. Chest Wall Disease
   5. Neurologic Disorders Affecting The Muscles of Respiration
   6. Sleep Disorders

Treatment of respiratory acidosis is aimed at restoring alveolar ventilation and correcting as much of the CO_2 retention as possible. In acute disease states, or those known to be self-limited, endotracheal intubation and assisted ventilation should be employed. Careful attention should be paid to the pH so as not to correct the CO_2 retention too quickly and precipitate alkalemia. With chronic CO_2 retention such as might be seen in end stage lung disease, intubation should be a last resort and conservative management (bronchodilators, pulmonary physiotherapy, antibiotics) should be tried first. However, even here a pCO_2 over 60 mmHg or a pH less than 7.25 may force the physician's hand. Sodium bicarbonate does not have a major role in respiratory acidosis and should only be used for life threatening acidemia (pH $<$ 7.10) if a respirator is not immediately available. These principles of management are as follows:

Treatment of Respiratory Acidosis:

I. ACUTE (OR SELF LIMITED) DISEASE
   A. Treat Primary Condition
   B. Early Endotracheal Intubation and Assisted Ventilation (pCO_2 $>$ 50, pH $<$ 7.30).
   C. Careful Attention to pH and pCO_2

II. CHRONIC CO_2 RETENTION
   A. Conservative Management to Improve Alveolar Ventilation
   B. Intubation For Severe CO_2 Retention And Acidemia (pCO_2 $>$ 60, pH $<$ 7.25)

RESPIRATORY ALKALOSIS: Respiratory alkalosis is characterized by inappropriate hyperventilation resulting in hypocarbia (low pCO_2) and alkalemia. Etiologies, like respiratory acidosis, include both central and pulmonary causes and are as follows:

Etiologies of Respiratory Alkalosis:

I. CENTRAL MECHANISM (via Respiratory Center)
   A. Anxiety
   B. Metabolic Encephalopathy
   C. CNS Infections (Meningitis, Encephalitis)
   D. Cerebrovascular Accidents
   E. Hypoxemia
   F. Gram Negative Septicemia
   G. Salicylate Intoxication

II. PULMONARY MECHANISMS (Reflex Stimulation)
   A. Pneumonia
   B. Asthma
   C. Pulmonary Emboli
   D. Interstitial Lung Disease
   E. Congestive Heart Failure

An acute fall in pCO_2 produces profound alkalemia and compensatory responses again take two forms: cellular buffering (rapid) and renal compensation (slow). Compensation is accomplished by a decrease in the serum HCO_3^- concentration thus returning the pH toward normal. During the first few minutes of hyperventilation the $[HCO_3^-]$ falls a maximum of 4-5 mEq/L. This change results from lactic acid production (perhaps in part from the increased work of ventilation), Na+ for H+ and K+ for H+ exchange across cell membranes. Over the course of the next 24-48 hours the kidney, in response to the low pCO_2, excretes urine with a higher pH and a lower acid content, which results in a further lowering of the plasma $[HCO_3^-]$ and greater protection of the plasma pH. It is not unusual for the $[HCO_3^-]$ to reach 15 mEq/L in chronic respiratory alkalosis. The importance of this compensation is illustrated in Table 2.

TABLE 2				
	Normal	Acute Respiratory Alkalosis		Chronic Respiratory Alkalosis
		No Compensation	Acute Compensation	
pH	7.40	7.70	7.60	7.50
pCO_2 (mmHg)	40	20	20	20
HCO_3^- (mEq/L)	25	25	19	15

Alkalemia may exert a number of deleterious effects. The most important include neuromuscular hyperirritability manifested by carpopedal spasm and trismus (tetany). Classic teaching explained this phenomenon as resulting from an increase in calcium binding by albumin with a subsequent depression of ionized calcium during alkalemia. This change in binding, however, is physiologically insignificant and the tetany is the direct result of a deficiency of H+ on the sarcolemmal membrane. Central effects such as coma and seizures are also seen in alkalemia and may be life-threatening. Although these can occur in metabolic alkalosis as well, they are seen more frequently in respiratory alkalosis, perhaps because the alkalemia is often more severe in this latter state.

Therapy for this condition is unsatisfactory. For the asymptomatic patient with a pH < 7.60, management should be directed not at the alkalemia, but at the primary disorder causing the hypocarbia. The patient who is symptomatic, however, requires therapy. The first approach is to increase the pCO_2 concentration by either a rebreathing device (paper bag, rebreathing mask) or administration of a 95% oxygen - 5% CO_2 gas mixture with careful monitoring of arterial blood gases. If this is not successful, then more hazardous therapy may be required. Administration of small amounts of acid ($NH4Cl$ or HCl) will "help" the patient lower the serum HCO_3^- more rapidly than would be achieved by the usual physiologic compensatory responses. Acetazolamide (Diamox$^{(R)}$), a carbonic anhydrase inhibitor, increases renal bicarbonate excretion and will accomplish similar results. With this latter agent, however, urinary K+ loss is enhanced and pre-existing hypokalemia may be exacerbated. Both of these approaches run the risk of causing acidemia and should only be employed when more conservative measures fail.

Treatment of Respiratory Alkalosis:

I. Patient Asymptomatic, pH < 7.60
  A. Treat primary condition
  B. Follow pH, pCO_2
  C. Administer O_2 if patient hypoxic

II. Patient Symptomatic, or pH > 7.60
  A. Rebreathing Device
  B. Acid Administration (HCl, NH_4Cl)
    1. 20-40 mEq Intravenously per hour
    2. Maximum 100 mEq (will lower HCO_3^- approximately 7 mEq/L)
    3. Careful attention to pH, pCO_2
    4. Have $NaHCO_3$ available in case hyperventilation ceases or pH falls.

  C. Acetazolamide (Diamox$^{(R)}$)
    1. 250 mg IV q 8 h
    2. Administer KCl if K+ < 4.0 and adequate urine output
    3. Follow pH, pCO_2 carefully

METABOLIC ALKALOSIS: Metabolic alkalosis is an acid-base disorder characterized by an elevated serum HCO_3^-, hypochloremia and, almost invariably, hypokalemia. The basic pathophysiologic event involved in the pathogenesis of this disorder is H+ loss from the body. This loss occurs from the stomach, kidney or rarely the colon. Alkali intake may also produce metabolic alkalosis.

Causes of Metabolic Alkalosis:

I. Upper GI H+ Losses
  A. Vomiting
  B. Nasogastric Suction

II. Renal H+ Losses
   A. Diuretic Use
   B. Autonomous Mineralocorticoid Excess (Conn's Syndrome, Cushing's Syndrome)
   C. Severe Hypokalemia

III. Colonic H+ Losses
   A. Chloride Wasting Diarrhea
   B. Villous Adenoma

IV. Excess Alkali Intake
   A. "Absorbable" Antacids (Calcium Carbonate, "Baking Soda")
   B. Sodium Bicarbonate (Intake or Administration)

Pathogenesis: In understanding the pathophysiology of metabolic alkalosis it is important to review separately those mechanisms that are responsible for its inception and those that maintain the already established alkalosis.

Generation: The loss from the extracellular fluid of gastric contents (HCl) results directly in a deficiency of these two ions and in metabolic alkalosis. The parietal cells of the stomach generate H+ by the metabolism of carbonic acid and for each H^+ secreted into the gastric lumen, a HCO_3^- ion is secreted into the blood. Thus, the removal of H+ from the stomach prior to its reaction with pancreatic bicarbonate results in a condition appropriately described as "gastric alkalosis".

When the kidney is responsible for the generation of metabolic alkalosis it means that it is being constrained to excrete more acid (as NH_4^+) than is necessary for the maintenance of acid-base homeostasis.

The metabolic alkalosis frequently accompanying the use of diuretic agents has been referred to as "contraction alkalosis". Until recently, the alkalosis was thought to result from the selective loss of NaCl from the extra-cellular fluid (ECF) and the subsequent contraction of the ECF "around" the remaining $[HCO_3^-]$. Recent evidence refutes this concept and emphasizes that plasma $[HCO_3^-]$ is a function of many variables including the state of nonbicarbonate buffers, so that losses of HCO_3^- poor fluids would only rarely be sufficiently large to result in marked alkalosis. A more tenable explanation for diuretic-induced metabolic alkalosis implicating a renal mechanism has emerged recently. Secondary hyperaldosteronism, resulting either from diuretic-induced volume depletion per se, or from the primary disease process (congestive heart failure, cirrhosis, etc.), coupled with the increased delivery of sodium resulting from the diuretic agent, results in increased distal reabsorption of sodium. The kidney is therefore obligated to excrete excess quantities of potassium, resulting in hypokalemia. As serum and total body potassium content decline, potassium ions shift from the cells to the ECF (and H+ from the ECF into cells), and this intracellular depletion of potassium together with "aldosterone excess" results in enhanced renal H+ secretion (and NH_4^+ excretion) with generation of alkalosis.

Maintenance: It is relatively easy to understand those factors involved in the generation of the above varieties of metabolic alkalosis, but the reasons why the organism is unable to repair this disequilibrium are more complex.

One should consider first the organism's priorities: the overriding requirement is to maintain extracellular fluid volume (reabsorb Na+ from the renal tubule) even at the expense of maintaining an abnormal blood pH. As the chloride concentration in the plasma falls, more and more Na+ is filtered as $NaHCO_3$ rather than NaCl. It is relatively "easy" metabolically for the kidney to reclaim the filtered NaCl with potent sodium pumps in the proximal and distal tubule (chloride following passively) and a potent chloride pump in the ascending limb of the loop of Henle (sodium following passively). To reclaim the Na+ which has been filtered with HCO_3^- is more difficult, since HCO_3^- is a poorly reabsorbable anion and will not cross cell membranes. This process is accomplished by a mechanism located primarily in the distal tubule and early collecting tubule whereby Na+ is reabsorbed and the resultant enhancement of the electrical potential difference facilitates the concomitant secretion of K^+ and H^+. The renal excretion of a H^+ ion results in the return to the blood of a HCO_3^- ion. There are only two salts of sodium which can maintain the ECF volume: NaCl and $NaHCO_3$. When the latter is utilized to a greater than normal extent metabolic alkalosis is the result. In states of hypochloremia and metabolic alkalosis in order to reabsorb Na+ and maintain ECF volume at a normal level the kidney is "forced" to: a) secrete large amounts of potassium in the urine resulting in potassium deficiency and hypokalemia, and b) secrete large quantities of H+, thus maintaining the excessive level of HCO_3^- in the blood. Were the kidney to do otherwise and allow large quantities of $NaHCO_3$ to escape in the urine, serious volume depletion would result and compromise the survival of the organism.

While the stimulus to sodium reabsorption in diuretic induced metabolic alkalosis is clear: (drug-induced sodium loss), there are at least two factors related to volume contraction in gastric alkalosis: 1) some sodium is present in gastric losses (approximately 20 mEq/L) and, 2) early during induction of the alkalosis there is an initial loss of $NaHCO_3$ in the urine as the plasma $[HCO_3]$ rises abruptly. Once sodium depletion occurs, however, sodium retaining stimuli come into play (increased aldosterone secretion, decreased GFR and alteration of peritubular hemodynamics [hydrostatic and oncotic pressures]) and distal tubular reabsorption of Na+ and secretion of H+ and K+ are enhanced.

Hypokalemia in metabolic alkalosis occurs as much, if not more, from accelerated renal loss as it does from the original process causing the alkalosis. In turn the hypokalemia (together with the increased mineralocorticoid activity associated with volume depletion) tends to both generate and perpetuate the alkalosis by enhancing HCO_3^- reabsorption and acid excretion.

The term paradoxical aciduria refers to the finding of acid urine in a patient with metabolic alkalosis. This was attributed first to hypokalemia, later to a decreased availability of easily reabsorbable anions and more recently to concomitant hypovolemia, all of which tend to remove HCO_3^- from the urine.

Several less common etiologies of metabolic alkalosis need to be considered briefly. Mineralocorticoid excess caused by hyperaldosteronism or Cushing's syndrome can result in hypochloremic metabolic alkalosis presumably of primary renal origin. The volume expansion caused by the excess hormone leads to increased delivery to the distal nephron of Na+ and the continued H+ and K+ secretion lead to the genesis and maintenance of the metabolic alkalosis. Note here that extracellular volume is expanded, not contracted, and that the stimulus to renal H+ and K+ secretion is autonomous, not compensatory. A similar situation may pertain in the very rare instances of "saline resistant" metabolic alkalosis. All of these patients have had severe potassium deficiency and evidence of chloride wasting by the kidney. Tubular dysfunction secondary to potassium depletion may be the important factor here.

Post-hypercapneic metabolic alkalosis is seen in patients recovering from respiratory acidosis and hypercarbia. During the renal compensatory phase of respiratory acidosis, the kidney increases chloride excretion while enhancing H+ secretion and HCO_3^- generation. Once the stimulus to HCO_3^- retention has been removed (i.e. the hypercapnia) a true state of chloride depletion exists and unless that ion is replaced metabolic alkalosis will develop.

In summary, chloride depletion, and a volume stimulus or mineralocorticoid "excess" appear necessary for the maintenance of metabolic alkalosis. The kidney "faced with the decision" of maintaining volume or acid-base status chooses the former and inappropriately large amounts of H+ and K+ are lost in the urine. Rarely, renal chloride wasting is seen in association with severe potassium deficiency. These events are summarized in Figure 12.1.

Compensation for metabolic alkalosis is incomplete. Review of the Henderson-Hasselbalch equation reveals that the only compensatory measure is hypoventilation and this the organism seems loathe to do for obvious reasons. Some hypercapnia does occur and although in rare instances it is significant (one case was reported where the PCO_2 reached 75 mm Hg) the PCO_2 rarely exceeds 50-55 mm Hg. Over this level a primary respiratory disturbance should be suspected.

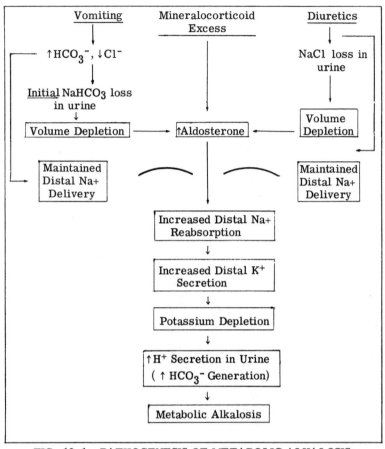

FIG. 12.1: PATHOGENESIS OF METABOLIC ALKALOSIS

Treatment of metabolic alkalosis is quite straightforward once the pathogenetic factors are understood. If sodium depletion is present, saline is administered until normal volume status is achieved, and potassium losses are replaced with KCl. If sodium excess is present, the condition usually responds to KCl alone but occasionally certain acidifying agents such as NH_4Cl (contraindicated in patients with liver disease), arginine hydrochloride or even intravenous HCl may be needed. The alkaline salts (gluconate, acetate, citrate, etc.) of potassium should not be used as treatment for this condition since replacement of the chloride deficit may be as important, or more so, than treatment of the hypokalemia.

Treatment of Metabolic Alkalosis:

I. Asymptomatic, pH $<$ 7.60
    A. Associated With Volume Depletion
       1. Re-expand With Isotonic NaCl
       2. Administer KCl to replete K+ Stores

    B. Associated With Edema
       1. KCl po or IV

II. Symptomatic, pH $>$ 7.60
    A. NH_4Cl or HCl
       1. 20-40 mEq/hr
       2. Each 100 mEq Should Decrease HCO_3^- By 7 mEq/L
       3. Follow pH, pCO_2, HCO_3^- hourly
       4. Stop Once Patient Asymptomatic And pH $<$ 7.60

    B. Acetazolamide (Diamox $^{(R)}$)
       1. Use With Caution Because of Hypokalemia
       2. 250 mg IV q 8 h
       3. Must Administer Large Amounts of KCl
       4. Stop Once Patient Asymptomatic and pH $<$ 7.60

METABOLIC ACIDOSIS: Metabolic acidosis is an acid-base disorder characterized by an excess of fixed H+ and deficiency of HCO_3^-. It results from either H+ over production or failure of elimination of H+ ion. Rarely, loss of $NaHCO_3$ from the body will produce the same result.

Metabolic acidosis may be divided into two major categories: those disorders characterized by an increase in unmeasured anions ("Anion Gap" variety) and those associated with a normal anion gap and hyperchloremia ("Hyperchloremic" acidosis). The common causes are listed below:

Causes of Metabolic Acidosis:

I. Increased Anion Gap
    A. Diabetic Ketoacidosis
    B. Uremic Acidosis
    C. Lactic Acidosis
    D. Alcoholic Ketoacidosis
    E. Poisons and Toxins
       1. Salicylate Intoxication
       2. Methanol
       3. Paraldehyde
       4. Ethylene Glycol

II. Hyperchloremic (Normal Anion Gap)
   A. Diarrhea
   B. Renal Tubular Acidosis
   C. Acetazolamide (Diamox$^{(R)}$)
   D. Ureterosigmoidostomy
   E. Chronic Interstitial Nephritis
   F. Acid Administration (HCl, NH_4Cl)

Anion gap metabolic acidosis is characterized by an increase in unmeasured anions to a value of greater than 16 mEq/L. Virtually all causes of anion gap metabolic acidosis are associated with increased acid production. The sole exception is uremic acidosis where retention of normal quantities of fixed acid causes the decrease in HCO_3^- and increase in unmeasured anions. The pathogenesis of this type of metabolic acidosis is illustrated in Figure 12.2.

	Increased Acid Production ($\uparrow H^+, An^-$)		Decreased Acid Excretion ($\uparrow H^+, An^-$)
		$\uparrow H^+ An^-$	
	Baseline Electrolytes		Electrolytes in Acidosis
Na	140	+	140
K	4.0	Na HCO_3^-	5.0
Cl	105	$\downarrow$	105
		+	
HCO_3^-	25	Na An^-	15
		+	
Anion Gap	10	CO_2 H_2O	25

FIG. 12.2: PATHOGENESIS OF ANION GAP ACIDOSIS

In diabetic and alcoholic ketoacidosis the organic acids produced ($H^+ An^-$) are known: B- hydroxybutyric acid and acetoacetic acid. In lactic acidosis, lactic acid is the major excess acid. Sulfuric and phosphoric acids are the major acids retained in uremic acidosis. The exact nature of the anion gap is less well characterized with the poisons and toxins but probably includes the following: salicylate intoxication (lactic and others); methanol (formic and others), paraldehyde (acetaldehyde) and ethylene glycol (oxalic, glyoxalic, lactic and others).

The more severe the acid production, the larger the anion gap. In lactic acidosis and ethylene glycol intoxication in particular, anion gaps may exceed 30 mEq/L and H^+ production may be greater than 100 mEq/hr. This is particularly impressive when we consider that normal acid production is approximately 70 mEq/day.

Hyperchloremic acidosis is the less common variety of metabolic acidosis and results from three basic processes: 1) $NaHCO_3$ loss, 2) HCl acid (or an analog) administration and 3) a failure of the kidney to regenerate HCO_3^- in an appropriate fashion. (Fig. 12.3)

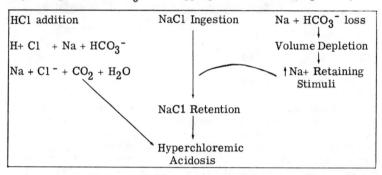

FIG. 12.3: PATHOGENESIS OF HYPERCHLOREMIC ACIDOSIS

Diarrhea, ureterosigmoidostomy, acetazolamide and one variety of renal tubular acidosis (proximal) all result in $NaHCO_3$ loss from the body. Ingestion of NaCl by the patient results in retention of NaCl in response to volume depletion and gradual depression of HCO_3^- and elevation of Cl^-. No pathological organic acid is produced, so an anion gap does not develop.

Distal renal tubular acidosis and chronic interstitial nephritis both result in hyperchloremia and decreased serum bicarbonate by means of the failure of complex physiologic processes involved in the renal production of HCO_3^-. Failure to maximally acidify the urine (distal RTA) or failure to produce normal quantities of NH_3 (chronic interstitial nephritis) results in decreased renal generation of HCO_3^- as the precursors of this buffer are lost into the urine. Functionally, this can be considered another variety of HCO_3^- loss by the kidney.

The administration of chloride containing acid directly reduces the serum HCO_3^- concentration while raising the chloride concentration. No anion gap develops because chloride is a "measured" anion.

Compensation for metabolic acidosis is achieved rapidly and almost immediately by hperventilation. (Table 3) Unlike the primary respiratory disturbances, there is no significant difference between acute and chronic states of metabolic acidosis. The extent and adequacy of the compensatory response depends upon the integrity of the respiratory system's response to blood and CSF acidosis. Patients with lung disease will obviously fail to compensate as adequately as those with normal respiratory mechanics.

	Normal	Metabolic Acidosis		
		No Compensation	Lung Disease	Maximal Compensation
pH	7.40	7.07	7.20	7.30
pCO_2	40	40	30	22
HCO_3^-	25	12	12	12

TABLE 3. COMPENSATION IN METABOLIC ACIDOSIS

The treatment of metabolic acidosis is basically straightforward: the administration of $NaHCO_3$, when indicated. The difficulty here lies in determining when and how much therapy should be initiated. Several important questions must be considered when contemplating therapy. First, how well is the patient compensating? A young patient with diabetic ketoacidosis will be able to lower his pCO_2 (and thus compensate more effectively) far better than an elderly patient with chronic lung disease. Obviously, therapy will be required earlier in the latter patient. Second, is the process ongoing? Remember that blood gases and electrolytes only reflect a static assessment of the patient's acid-base status. An entirely different approach will be taken in the patient whose acidosis has stopped as opposed to one in whom acid production is continuing at a rapid rate. Third, what is the total remaining buffering capacity? A serum HCO_3^- of 8 mEq/L is obviously of more concern than one of 15 mEq/L assuming other factors (pH, K+, etc.) are equal. Finally, what is the patient's sodium status and state of renal function? Administration of sodium bicarbonate to a patient with edema or renal failure must be undertaken with caution as pulmonary edema could result.

Also critical to the therapy of metabolic acidosis is an understanding of the control of compensatory hyperventilation. The best evidence now suggests that cerebrospinal fluid (CSF) pH is the most important stimulus to hyperventilation in acidosis. This finding has important clinical consequences. Since HCO_3^- diffuses poorly into the CSF and CO_2 gas diffuses very rapidly, the CSF pH may remain acid long after the blood pH has been corrected with $NaHCO_3$. This will result in continued hyperventilation even in the face of normal or alkaline blood pH. Hence the amount of $NaHCO_3$ administered must be calculated, at least initially, using the assumption that hyperventilation will not cease (that is, that the pCO_2 will remain unchanged). Then as the pCO_2 gradually rises, additional $NaHCO_3$ can be given if needed.

Example of Using "Constant pCO_2 Assumption" In Planning Treatment of Metabolic Acidosis.

1. Initial Values   pH   7.10
                      pCO_2 20
                      HCO_3^- 6

2. Desired pH (estimate) $\doteq$ 7.30

3. If pCO_2 remains constant, what HCO_3^- concentration is required to reach pH 7.30

4. "Shorthand" Henderson-Hasselbalch Equation

$$\left[H^+ \right] = \frac{25 \times pCO_2;}{HCO_3^-}$$

$\left[\dfrac{H^+}{} \right]$	pH
70	7.10
60	7.20
50	7.30
40	7.40
30	7.50
20	7.60

$$\text{Desired } HCO_3^- = \frac{25 \times pCO_2}{\left[H^+ \right]} = \frac{25 \times 20}{50}$$

$$= \quad 10 \text{ mEq/L}$$

The final important factor to consider in planning the treatment of metabolic acidosis is the nature of the underlying process. When HCO_3^- loss, inorganic acid (HCl) addition or acid retention are etiologic then an <u>estimate</u> of the alkali requirement can be made from a knowledge of the body weight and serum HCO_3^- concentration.

<u>Estimating Alkali Requirements:</u>

Patient's Serum HCO_3^- =   A mEq/L

*Desired Serum HCO_3^- =   B mEq/L

Patient's Weight   =   C kg.

Amount of $Na\,HCO_3$ required to reach desired serum

$$HCO_3^- = (B-A) \times .20\, C \times 2$$

*Note that B must be calculated taking into account desired pH and pCO_2.

When the metabolic acidosis is the result of the accumulation of organic acids(specifically lactic or keto acids) another variable must be considered. Both of these acids are metabolized by the body in such a manner as to result in the addition to the extracellular fluid of 1 milliequivalent (mEq) of HCO_3^- for each mEq of acid consumed. Thus, once the abnormal acid production ceases, these patients "make their own" HCO_3^- and overtreatment with exogenous alkali can be hazardous. These patients can be considered as having their own supply of potential alkali, frequently as reflected by the anion gap.

It should be clear from the above that it is difficult to generalize about the treatment of metabolic acidosis. Some general guidelines can be useful, however.

Guidelines In The Treatment of Metabolic Acidosis:

I. Treat The Underlying Condition
  A. Goal is to shut off acid production

II. If Treatment Is Indicated By Clinical Setting And Blood Gases (pH $<$ 7.20, HCO_3^- $<$ 10 mEq/L)
  A. Calculate desired HCO_3^- using "Constant pCO_2 Assumption"
  B. Calculate alkali requirement as above
  C. Give $\frac{1}{2}$ of requirement and repeat blood gases; recalculate as above
  D. Pay careful attention to K+ concentration
  E. A diuretic may be required if edema is present
  F. Remember CSF pH
  G. Remember "Potential Alkali" in patients with organic acidemia
  H. Avoid correcting pH to $>$ 7.30
  I. Never aim to correct HCO_3^- to normal

MIXED ACID-BASE DISTURBANCES: The simultaneous occurrence of two or three primary acid-base disturbances in the same patient is not rare. The effect of mixed acid-base disturbances on pH is variable. Some disturbances "cancel each other out" resulting in a virtually normal pH, while others may cause severe abnormalities in pH.

Recognizing the presence of mixed acid-base disturbances is not difficult. Remember that compensatory responses do not return the pH to normal. A normal pH in the face of an abnormal HCO_3^-, pCO_2 or anion gap should make one suspect the presence of a mixed disturbance. Similarly, a normal HCO_3^- in the face of a markedly abnormal pH or pCO_2 indicates more than one primary process. Calculation of the anion gap is an important tool in the recognition of mixed disturbances and should be done routinely with every set of electrolytes.

Common clinical settings in which mixed acid-base disturbances occur are as follows:

Common Settings for Mixed Disturbances:

1. Recovery phase of any simple disturbance
2. Renal failure with gastrointestinal losses
3. Hepatorenal syndrome
4. Gram negative septicemia
5. Cardiac arrest
6. A majority of patients with chronic respiratory acidosis

The treatment of mixed disturbances is based on the identification of the predominant process. This is then managed as has been previously discussed, using the pH as the guide to therapy, always keeping in mind that the other process (or processes) may become "uncovered" and affect the pH once the predominant abnormality has been corrected.

The use of an acid base nomogram such as the one included, kindly supplied by Dr. Martin Goldberg of the University of Pennsylvania, facilitates the assessment of acid base abnormalities. Any one of the three acid base parameters can be calculated if the other two are known, thus avoiding the need for mathematical calculations. In addition, this particular nomogram shows the range of normal compensatory responses for each of the four primary acid base disturbances. If a particular set of blood gas values falls outside these areas, a mixed disturbance should be strongly suspected.

ACKNOWLEDGEMENT

I would like to thank Drs. Donna McCurdy and Martin Goldberg for imparting to me some of their vast talent and enthusiasm for the field of acid base physiology. The support and encouragement of Drs. Samuel Thier and Arnold Relman is also gratefully acknowledged.

REFERENCES

1. Emmett, M., Narine, R.G.: Clinical Use of the Anion Gap. Medicine 56:38, 1977.
2. Kassirer, J.P.: Serious Acid-Base Disorders. New Eng J Med 291:773, 1974.
3. Kurtzman, N.A., White, M.G., et al.: Pathophysiology of Metabolic Alkalosis. Arch Intern Med 131:702, 1973.
4. McCurdy, D.K.: Mixed Metabolic and Respiratory Acid-Base Disturbance: Diagnosis and Treatment. Chest 62:355 (Supplement), 1972.
5. Morris, R.C., Jr., et al.: Renal Acidosis. Kid Int 1:322, 1972
6. Oliva, P.B.: Lactic Acidosis. Am J Med 48:209, 1970.
7. Seldin, D.W., Rector, F.C.: The Generation and Maintenance of Metabolic Alkalosis. Kid Int 1:306, 1972.

B: ACUTE RENAL FAILURE
by J. Phillip Pennell, M.D.

INTRODUCTION: Acute renal failure (ARF) is a clinical syndrome of diverse etiologies wherein rapid reduction in excretory renal function leads to accumulation of nitrogenous waste products within the body. Acute renal failure can threaten the life of the patient and yet, if recognized early and treated appropriately, it may be immediately reversible. Perhaps even more importantly, recognition of clinical settings in which acute renal failure is likely to occur may permit the physician to initiate appropriate prophylactic measures that will prevent impairment in renal function.

The prognosis of acute renal failure has not improved in recent years despite the advent of sophisticated diagnostic and therapeutic technologies. The mortality of ARF after surgery or trauma is about 60%, about 30% in association with other medical illness, and about 10-15% for the obstetrical patient.[1] Mortality now is more related to infection and to the primary disease precipitating ARF whereas, prior to the era of widespread use of dialytic therapies, fluid and electrolyte abnormalities and uremia were the leading causes of death. Persistence of the high mortality in part is the result of changing patterns of incidence and causation of ARF as the median age of patients has increased and larger proportions of cases are associated with extensive surgery and serious medical conditions, while the incidence in obstetric cases has declined.[2] Hopefully, both the incidence and mortality of ARF will improve as progress is made in understanding the pathogenesis and pathophysiology of ARF and as there is more widespread appreciation and utilization of prophylactic measures and optimal treatment protocols.

The pathogenesis and pathophysiology of ARF remain hypothetical. Current theories suggest a primary role for alterations in renal blood flow (possibly mediated by the sympathetic nervous system or by the renin-angiotensin system or possibly resulting from vascular endothelial cell swelling secondary to ischemia) leading to diminished glomerular filtration with secondary roles for tubular obstruction by necrotic debris and leakage of glomerular filtrate through necrotic tubular walls. Recent reviews provide details of the pathophysiology of acute renal failure. [1,3]

DEFINITIONS: A few definitions are appropriate before embarking upon a discussion of the clinical management of acute renal failure. Renal insufficiency generally refers to a measurable decrease of renal function, whereas renal failure refers to a later stage with more marked abnormalities of blood chemistries. Uremia is the syndrome of symptomatic renal failure. Oliguria generally is considered to be a daily urine output of 400 ml or less. The rationale for citing less than 400 ml per day of urine as inadequate is that people who eat a normal diet and have an intact maximal urinary concentrating ability must excrete a minimum of 400 ml of urine each day in order to excrete the waste products of food ingested and metabolized. Although the definition of anuria has varied from 0-100 ml of urine per day, in this discussion, anuria will mean virtual absence of urinary excretion, as documented by bladder catheterization.

Acute renal failure is a generic term that refers to the clinical syndrome of a rapid decrease in renal function typically manifested by a correspondingly rapid progression of azotemia and the development of oliguria. The time course designated as "rapid" is quite arbitrary and may vary from a few hours to a few days.

Although frank oliguria is typical, about 20% of patients with ARF are non-oliguric. Nonoliguric ARF occurs more commonly after surgery and exposure to toxins. Its pathophysiology is not understood. Despite speculations that intrinsic renal damage is less severe in nonoliguric ARF, its mortality is about 25%.[4]

Acute tubular necrosis (ATN) is a histopathological term that has been used to refer to the classic clinical syndrome of established parenchymal acute renal failure that is not immediately responsive to diuretics or to volume expansion or to correction of other non-renal factors impairing renal function. Other terms such as vaso-motor nephropathy have been suggested instead of ATN; but this term focuses on the functional aberration in blood flow, just as ATN overemphasizes cellular damage per se. In this discussion, acute renal failure will be used as a generic term while acute tubular necrosis will refer to the clinical syndrome of established renal parenchymal acute renal failure.

The classical clinical course of ATN consists of an insult (such as trauma or shock) followed within a few hours by an oliguric phase lasting 1-2 weeks followed by a diuretic phase of a few days duration heralding the onset of gradual recovery of renal function. Variations of this classical course are common. Oliguria may be delayed in onset or develop gradually over a few days, especially after exposure to toxins or after surgery. The oliguric phase can persist for as long as 4-6 weeks, particularly in elderly or critically ill patients. When oliguria is prolonged for 4-6 weeks, other diagnostic possibilities such as glomerulonephritis, vasculitis, or cortical necrosis should be considered and pursued, for instance by open renal biopsy. The diuretic, or polyuric, phase may be blunted or totally absent especially when fluid balance is well-maintained or when uremia is mild or the patient is well-dialyzed.

There are certain danger periods for the patient. The onset of acute renal failure can go unrecognized or be obscured by failure of oliguria to appear. Hence, the patient's life may be threatened by:

1) fluid overload, 2) hyperkalemia, 3) acidosis, 4) cardiac arrhythmias, 5) hypertension. Onset of recovery usually is manifested by increasing urine volumes preceding improvement in renal function. Hence, during this phase, azotemia progresses despite disappearance of oliguria; and there may be inappropriately fixed urine output, or even frank polyuria, so that the patient is at risk for development of dehydration or depletion of sodium and potassium. The major causes of death late in the course of ATN are sepsis and bleeding, which frequently are associated with severe catabolism.

ETIOLOGY: The major causes of ARF can be subdivided arbitrarily into three categories: 1) pre-renal, 2) post-renal, 3) intrinsic renal.

Pre-Renal: Pre-renal causes of ARF are diverse (Table I), yet all have in common a relative or absolute deficiency in delivery of blood to the kidneys. If the conditions causing pre-renal ARF are recognized and effectively treated before ischemia causes severe or irreversible damage of the renal parenchyma, then the progression of renal failure may be immediately reversed or prevented. In other words, pre-renal ARF represents a phase of incipient intrinsic renal failure. Specific considerations for diagnosis and therapy of each of these conditions are beyond the scope of this discussion. There are certain characteristic clinical and laboratory findings common to pre-renal ARF, and these will be discussed below when considering the differential diagnosis of acute renal failure.

Post-Renal: Post-renal causes of ARF all are characterized by obstruction to the flow of urine through the urinary collecting and drainage system (Table II). In order to produce ARF, obstruction must be bilateral or superimposed on pre-existing renal disease, or there may be obstruction of a solitary kidney. The acuity and severity of impaired renal function secondary to obstruction in general depends on the following factors:

1) degree of luminal obstruction
2) rate of progression of luminal obstruction
3) site, or proximity of the obstructing lesion to the kidneys
4) duration of obstruction
5) presence of urinary tract infection

Acute, within the first 24-48 hours, diminished glomerular filtration is the result of elevated hydraulic pressures proximal to the site of obstruction; but thereafter, even though dilatation permits decompression of the GI tract, decreased glomerular filtration continues because of progressive loss of nephrons primarily due to ischemia as renal blood flow falls precipitously. Yet, if obstruction is relieved within the first week, eventual recovery of renal function may be nearly complete. After two weeks of obstruction, renal function may return to as much as 70% of normal; but recovery of function becomes progressively less for longer periods of obstruction.

TABLE I

CAUSES OF PRE-RENAL ACUTE RENAL FAILURE

A. RENAL VASCULAR OCCLUSION

    1. Arterial: thrombosis, embolism, tumor
    2. Venous: thrombosis, tumor

B. SEVERE VASOCONSTRICTION

    1. Vasculitis
    2. Malignant hypertension
    3. Disseminated intravascular coagulation
    4. Eclampsia and bilateral cortical necrosis

C. DECREASED BLOOD VOLUME

    1. Hemorrhage
    2. GI losses: vomiting, diarrhea
    3. Renal losses: diuretics, diabetic glycosuria
    4. Sweating
    5. Third Spaces: burns, peritonitis, tissue trauma

D. DECREASED "EFFECTIVE" BLOOD VOLUME
(Vasodilatation)

    1. Sepsis
    2. Hepato-renal Syndrome
    3. Antihypertensive Medications

E. IMPAIRED CARDIAC FUNCTION

    1. Congestive Heart Failure
    2. Myocardial Infarction
    3. Pericardial Tamponade or Constriction
    4. Pulmonary Embolism
    5. Arrhythmias

TABLE II
CAUSES OF POST-RENAL ACUTE RENAL FAILURE

OBSTRUCTION AT ANY SITE:

Stones
Papillary Necrosis
Blood Clots
Tumor
Trauma

OBSTRUCTION OF URETERS:

Intrinsic

Stones
Uric acid crystals
Blood clots
Necrotic renal papilla
Edema and inflammation
Tumor

Extrinsic

Tumor: uterine, bladder, prostatic, lymphoma, endo-
metriosis
Retroperitoneal fibrosis or hemorrhage
Pregnancy
Accidental ligation

OBSTRUCTION OF BLADDER

Carcinoma of bladder
Infection
Autonomic nerve dysfunction
Anticholinergic drugs

OBSTRUCTION OF URETHRA

Prostatic hypertrophy and carcinoma
Stricture, post-infectious or post-traumatic
Foreign body

Obstructive uropathy must be considered whenever renal failure occurs without apparent cause or when a patient with underlying chronic renal disease has an unexpected increase in the rate of progression of renal failure. Clinical clues that obstruction may be the cause of acute renal failure include the following:

1) Anuria, polyuria, or intermittent anuria/polyuria
2) Recurrent or refractory urinary tract infection
3) Pain in abdomen, flank, groin, or suprapubic region
4) Hematuria without a large number of casts
5) Crystalluria
6) Bladder symptoms suggestive of infection or residual urine or diminished stream
7) Hypertension, either recent in onset or recently exacerbated
8) Presence of a primary disease predisposing to obstruction such as nephrolithiasis, pelvic disease, autonomic nerve dysfunction, or diseases leading to papillary necrosis such as analgesic abuse, sickle cell disease, diabetes, acute pyelonephritis
9) Masses: abdominal, flank, suprapubic, pelvic
10) Asymmetrical or large kidneys

Because of the critical importance to nephron survival of avoiding or preventing urinary tract infection, every effort should be made to diagnose obstruction using noninvasive methods that avoid instrumentation of the GU tract. Of particular value in this regard are the KUB, nephrotomography, and high-dose intravenous pyelography. If necessary to proceed with retrograde ureteropyelography, finding a patent urinary tract on the side with the more normal kidney should rule out obstruction as the cause of ARF.

The goal of treating urinary tract obstruction is conservation of maximal numbers of nephrons. The principles of treatment are simple:

1) relieve obstruction
2) avoid/treat infection
3) avoid nephrectomy, unless mandatory
4) maintain fluid and electrolyte balance

Post-obstructive diuresis is not common and is seen most often after relief of lower urinary tract obstruction resulting from prostatic disease.

Intrinsic-Renal: Causes of intrinsic renal ARF are legion (Table III). The list includes specific diseases of the renal parenchyma such as glomerulonephritis, vasculitis, interstitial nephritis, pyelonephritis and also involvement of the kidneys by disorders of metabolism and coagulation. The clinical importance of nephrotoxic agents appears to be increasing as more diagnostic and therapeutic agents are being found to damage kidneys by direct toxicity or by hypersensitivity reactions. Of course, any cause of pre-renal, post-renal, or intrinsic-renal ARF can produce the clinical syndrome of ATN providing the causative condition is not relieved before the renal parenchyma is damaged sufficiently to impair its functional integrity.

DIAGNOSIS: Immediate or early recognition of the existence of ARF is of critical importance to the health and prognosis of the patient. Typically, ARF is recognized by the development of oliguria and rising BUN and creatinine, particularly if the patient is hospitalized. However, a substantial number of patients initially present to the hospital with symptoms of either acute renal failure or its complications or with frank uremia. Even among the patients who develop renal failure in the hospital, the clinical suspicion may not be aroused until complications ensue or uremic symptoms appear. Reasons for this include: 1) renal function not being monitored routinely either by blood tests or by daily weights or measurement of intake and output, 2) delayed onset of oliguria, 3) nonoliguric ARF. These considerations emphasize the critical importance of recognizing that acute renal failure can be predicted to occur in certain clinical situations where it should be anticipated by careful monitoring of renal function.

Establishing an etiologic diagnosis is fundamental to appropriate therapy. Once renal failure is recognized, critical questions to consider are: 1) Is the renal failure acute and reversible? 2) Is acute renal failure superimposed on chronic irreversible renal disease? 3) Are there specific remedial therapies for underlying etiologic factors? 4) Is supportive therapy required to sustain life and to permit spontaneous recovery?

METHODS OF ESTABLISHING DIAGNOSIS:

History and Physical Examination: Frequently the history and physical exam suggest the etiology of ARF either by revealing specific precipitating factors or by indicating presence of clinical conditions or systemic disease with which acute renal failure may be associated. If the history initially is not helpful, then specific questions should be directed toward possible exposure to drugs or nephrotoxins. Of particular importance is a critical assessment of the patient's cardiovascular status and a search for evidence of volume depletion or excess. Of course, pelvic and rectal exams must be performed routinely. Presence of one illness with which ARF may be associated (e.g. heart failure) does not rule out the presence of another etiology (e.g. prostatic hypertrophy or malignant hypertension); hence, clinical evaluation of the patient must be thorough.

TABLE III
CAUSES OF INTRINSIC RENAL ARF

ACUTE TUBULAR NECROSIS

<u>Post-Ischemia:</u>

    includes all causes of Pre-Renal ARF

<u>Nephrotoxins:</u>

    Antibiotics: the -mycins, sulfas, cephaloridin,
            amphotericin B
    Anesthetics: methoxyflurane
    Analgesics: phenacetin and aspirin
    Heavy Metals: mercury, bismuth, arsenic, gold, uranium,
            lead, cadium
    Halogenated Hydrocarbons: CCl_4
    Glycols: ethylene glycol
    Iodinated radiographic contrast media
    Miscellaneous: mushroom poison, venoms

<u>Heme Pigments:</u>

    Hemolysis: transfusion reactions, malaria
    Rhabdomyolysis with myoglobinuria: trauma, seizures,
               heat stroke, myopathy

<u>Obstetrical Causes:</u> eclampsia, septic abortion, uterine,
             hemorrhage, DIC, postpartum renal failure,
             bilateral cortical necrosis

INTRA-RENAL OBSTRUCTION

    Hypercalcemia
    Hyperuricemia
    Myoglobinuria, Hemoglobinuria
    Abnormal proteins: myeloma, cryoglobulinemia

OTHER RENAL PARENCHYMAL DISEASES

    Acute glomerulonephritis
    Vasculitis
    Malignant Nephrosclerosis
    Infections: acute pyelonephritis, papillary necrosis
    Acute Interstitial Nephritis: hypersensitivity to antibiotics
                     (penicillins, sulfa), diuretics,
                     (thiazides, furosemide), and
                     other drugs (allopurinol,
                     azothiaprine)

Laboratory Evaluation:

(1) Urine: Urine output must be monitored sufficiently well to establish whether the patient is oliguric, nonoliguric, or anuric. This may require initial, short-term catheterization of the bladder, utilizing strict aseptic techniques. Once the diagnosis of oliguric acute renal failure is established, the indwelling catheter should be removed, urine cultured, and bladder washed with an antiseptic solution, (such as Neosporin GU Irrigant (R)). Anuria suggests occlusion of renal arteries of veins or obstruction of urine outflow and indicates the need for emergent diagnostic studies to evaluate renal blood flow or to rule out obstruction. Occasionally anuria results from acute glomerulonephritis or vasculitis or bilateral cortical necrosis. Sporadic swings in urine output suggest obstruction.

Urinalysis may reveal hematuria and red cell casts indicative of acute glomerulonephritis or vasculitis or may reveal pyuria and bacteriuria indicative of acute urinary tract infection. Urine sediment should be examined for crystals (uric acid or oxalate, the latter due to methoxyflurane anesthesia or ethylene glycol ingestion) and for tissue (sloughed necrotic papillae). Proteinuria is not a distinguishing feature. In pre-renal and post-renal ARF, urinary findings usually are nonspecific (finely granular and hyaline casts and paucity of cellular elements).

(2) Renal Function and Serum Electrolytes: Renal Function Tests must be performed. Whenever timed urine volumes (however brief) are available and especially in patients with nonoliguric ARF, estimates of creatinine clearance may prove to be of great value in documenting the degree of renal functional impairment. Elevation in BUN can result not only from renal failure but also from catabolic states, tissue trauma, and blood in the GI tract; whereas elevation of serum creatinine is indicative of renal failure, though occasionally may be further elevated by massive tissue trauma. In the absence of other non-renal causes of elevated BUN, a BUN: creatinine ratio of greater than 10:1 suggests pre-renal ARF.

Serum electrolytes must be monitored carefully. Hyperkalemia can develop suddenly and be life-threatening, particularly in presence of severe catabolism, hemolysis, and tissue necrosis. Hyperkalemia usually is asymptomatic but may cause drowsiness, weakness, fatigue, or flaccid paralysis. However, in acute renal failure, initial clinical manifestations of hyperkalemia often consist of changes in the electrocardiogram (peaked T-waves or prolonged QRS leading to heart block, ventricular fibrillation, or cardiac arrest). Metabolic acidosis results from failure to excrete acid produced metabolically and is worsened in states of hypercatabolism. Hyponatremia indicates accumulation of excessive water from exogenous or endogenous sources (catabolism provides 300-500 ml of water daily).

The rate of rise of BUN and serum K are good indicators of the level of catabolism. With uncomplicated acute renal failure, daily rises of BUN are around 10 mg% and of serum potassium about 0.5 mEq/L. Severe catabolic states may be manifested by rises in BUN of over 30 mg% per day and rises in serum potassium of 1-2 mEq/L within a few hours.

(3) Radiographic Studies: A plain film of the abdomen should be obtained to look for opaque stones and to determine kidney size. Nephrotomography with infusion of radio-opaque dye is a more reliable technique for determining kidney size. Bilaterally small kidneys indicate chronic renal disease. Asymmetric kidney size could be the result of obstruction or pre-existing unilateral renal diseases. Large kidneys may be seen in obstruction, acute glomerulonephritis, ATN, acute inflammatory diseases, acute renal vein thrombosis, tumors, cysts, and infiltrative diseases.

The primary reason for performing excretory urography in acute renal failure is to evaluate the possibility of obstruction. Contemporary techniques of high-dose infusion urography usually will suffice to make the diagnosis of obstruction even in the face of acute renal failure. [5] Even though the pyelogram per se may not visualize, the infusion nephrogram should be sufficiently dense to permit visualization of dilated calyces.

Also, the infusion nephrogram may assist in the differential diagnosis of pre-renal ARF and ARN. In pre-renal ARF, the nephrographic pattern becomes increasingly dense with time, whereas in ATN the nephrogram becomes dense immediately and persists. [5] Although these patterns are not absolutely distinctive, their recognition renders the infusion nephrogram an even more clinically valuable diagnostic tool in the evaluation of patients with ARF. Importantly, this technique should be employed prior to using retrograde pyelography. Although high-dose infusion urography generally has proven to be well-tolerated and safe, two cautionary notes are in order: (1) the remote possibility of reversible nephrotoxicity in response to the contrast media, especially in patients with diabetes, myeloma, or liver disease and especially in the presence of dehyration or hypotension; (2) the possibility that large doses of contrast media will provide osmotic loads (elevating plasma osmolality by as much as 100 mOsm/L) that may be poorly tolerated, especially in the presence of pre-existing fluid overload or CHF. Patients should not be dehydrated prior to infusion urography, and afterwards their cardiovascular status should be followed carefully.

The use of retrograde pyelography to evaluate possible obstruction already has been discussed above. The possibility of a major vascular occlusion requires arteriography or inferior vena cavogram.

(4) Renal Biopsy: Occasionally, renal biopsy must be used to evaluate ARF, especially when glomerulonephritis, acute interstitial nephritis, or vasculitis are under consideration. Biopsy may help distinguish acute from chronic renal failure and may help in rendering prognosis for recovery of renal function after prolonged episodes of apparent acute renal failure. Biopsy should not be performed if kidneys are small in size.

GUIDELINES FOR DIFFERENTIAL DIAGNOSIS: Specific guidelines to assist in differentiating acute pre-renal ARF from ATN include (1) analysis of "renal failure chemistries" and (2) diagnostic challenges with diuretics or volume expansion. These guidelines are of no value in the presence of chronic renal disease or nonoliguric acute renal failure or recent prior treatment with diuretics. A good general approach when confronted with the patient suspected to have ARF is (1) obtain history and perform physical exam; (2) perform urinalysis; (3) document the presence or absence of oliguria by monitoring hourly urine output, using an aseptically-placed bladder catheter if necessary; (4) send blood to the lab for stat determinations of BUN, creatinine, electrolytes; (5) send urine to the lab for stat determination of Na, creatinine, osmolality and for culture; (6) if necessary, document state of hydration by placement of a CVP line; (7) perform a diagnostic challenge with diuretics or volume expansion or both.

Table IV illustrates the chemical findings to be expected for pre-renal ARF versus ATN. Pre-renal factors causing acute renal failure generally result in a decreased glomerular filtration rate (GFR) per surviving functional nephron, in which case the intact tubules avidly reabsorb both sodium and water resulting in a low urinary concentration of sodium (U_{Na}) and a high urine-to-plasma ratio of creatinine $(U/P)_{Cr}$ and osmolality $(U/P)_{Osm}$. On the other hand, ATN is manifested by diffuse nephron damage, decreased GFR, and nonfunctional tubules so that glomerular filtrate is altered very little as it passes through the nephron. The result is a high urinary concentration of sodium and low urinary-to-plasma creatinine and osmolality ratios. These chemistries do not always reliably distinguish pre-renal ARF from ATN; however, either the "renal failure ratio" $(U_{Na} \div U/P_{Cr})$[6] or the fractional excretion of sodium (FE_{Na}) enhances their specificity.[7] (See Table IV). The most difficult problem is the patient who is in a phase of incipient ATN, when the chemical tests are least reliably distinctive. During the first 24-48 hours of obstruction, the renal failure chemistries may be those of pre-renal failure; but thereafter, the pattern will be that of ATN. Usually these chemistries are of no value in the diagnosis of ARF secondary to obstruction.

If the patient clearly is dehydrated, or volume depleted, and has a low CVP, then cautious expansion of extracellular volume may be reasonable and safe. The patients can be given 500-1000 ml of isotonic saline solution over 1-4 hours or a volume sufficient to elevate a low CVP into the normal range. If volume expansion is to be tried, then use of CVP monitoring is highly recommended.

TABLE IV		
DIAGNOSTIC LABORATORY INDICES FOR DIFFERENTIAL DIAGNOSIS OF PRE-RENAL ARF versus ATN		
LABORATORY TEST	PRE-RENAL ARF	ATN
Urine Sodium (mEq/L)	< 20, often < 10	> 30
(U/P) Creatinine	>20, often > 40	< 20, often <15
(U/P) Osmolality	>1.3	<1.3
U_{Na} $(U/P)_{Cr}$	< 1.1	>1.25
FE_{Na} $(U/P_{Na}$ $U/P_{Cr})$	$< 1\%$	$>1\%$

Unless the patient clearly is volume depleted, an alternative and probably safer diagnostic maneuver is to administer a diuretic. There are enthusiasts for the use of mannitol who advise giving 100 ml of 25% mannitol intravenously over a 5-10 minute period. An increase in urine output to 1.0 ml/min or a doubling of the previous hourly urine volumes favors the diagnosis or pre-renal ARF. The response to mannitol frequently is not distinctive. A second dose of mannitol may be tried, but further use is not recommended because of the dangers of producing or worsening states of fluid overload or of aggravating hypertension and hyponatremia.

Probably a safer diagnostic challenge is to administer a single large dose of furosemide (160-480 mg) I.V. slowly over a few minutes. In pre-renal ARF, there should be a doubling of the previous hourly urine output. A lack of response to a single large I.V. dose of furosemide has been used to define a state of "unresponsive" or "established" ARF, or ATN. The lack of diuretic response is against pre-renal factors causing ARF. A potential danger of using a large dose of diuretic is that of aggravating pre-existing volume depletion. Accordingly, the volume status of the patient must be followed carefully during such a diagnostic maneuver. An alternative test is to give 100 ml of 25% mannitol and a large dose of furosemide simultaneously. Regardless, it must be emphasized that in the absence of a diuretic response to mannitol or furosemide, their continued administration has no intrinsic therapeutic value in curing ARF. If there is a diuretic response to furosemide, then it can be used effectively to manage states of fluid overload or CHF. Use of ethacrynic acid is not recommended in this setting because of the danger of permanent deafness. Furosemide in large doses may cause tinnitus and deafness, which are reversible.

THERAPY: The best treatment is to anticipate and prevent development of ARF in clinical situations where it commonly occurs. The early detection and early treatment of ARF may be life-saving and halt the progression of renal failure before development of ATN per se. The therapeutic regimen must employ a combination of specific therapy aimed at the underlying primary disease plus general measures of supportive therapy for the oliguric patient.

It is recommended that a special flow sheet be used throughout the treatment course of all patients with ARF. Data to be recorded at least daily should include weight, intake and output of all fluids and their electrolyte composition, vital signs including CVP measurements, renal chemistries (BUN, creatinine), serum electrolytes, hematocrit, and notes of major therapeutic interventions (such as drugs, dialysis, procedures, etc.). Additional data may be appropriate depending on the individual patient.

For states of decreased blood volume, restore specific deficits and institute specific measures to combat the underlying illness (See Table I). Heart failure may be a primary problem or a complication of ARF. The combination of cardiac and renal failure requires extreme care in the use of digoxin, and primary efforts should be directed toward relief of fluid overload by use of diuretics or dialysis. The critically ill patient should be in an intensive care unit where cardiotonic drugs such as digoxin or intravenous dopamine and isuprel can be used, if necessary, in conjunction with appropriate monitors of cardiovascular status.

For states of severe vasoconstriction, specific therapy may include steroids or immunosuppressive drugs for vasculitis or potent antihypertensives for malignant hypertension or heparin for states of DIC. The treatment of eclampsia requires antihypertensive agents; the role of heparin in its treatment is controversial and not firmly established as the complications may outweigh the benefits.

Acute treatment of vascular occlusion of the renal arteries or veins by surgery may not be successful and more conservative management using acute and long-term anticoagulation may be the only course of therapy available.

Post-Renal ARF: The successful treatment of obstruction requires a specific diagnosis and otherwise consists of relieving the obstruction and treating (preventing) urinary tract infection.

Intrinsic Renal ARF: Treatment of post-ischemic ATN requires specific attention to the underlying etiology. Nephrotoxins must be identified and the patient's exposure to them must be stopped. There are few specific antidotes for nephrotoxins other than heavy metals where chelating agents (EDTA for lead, BAL for mercury) may be useful. Treatment of hemoglobinuria or myoglobinuria involves alkalinization ($NaHCO_3$) and inducing a diuresis with fluids (saline) and diuretics (furosemide). If acute renal failure is unresponsive to diuretics, then dialysis must be employed to support the patient until there is sufficient recovery of renal function. Similarly, hypercalcemic ARF can be treated with forced diuresis if possible and otherwise by dialysis. Intrarenal obstruction by abnormal proteins (myeloma) requires specific treatment of the underlying disease and supportive therapy plus dialysis if necessary. Drug-induced acute interstitial nephritis requires identifying and stopping the offending drug and supportive therapy plus dialysis if necessary; the efficacy of using steroids is not established and they are not recommended.

Supportive Therapy of the Oliguric Patient: Specific recommendations for supportive therapy of the patient with established oliguric acute renal failure are outlined below.

1) Fluid Restriction: It is essential to strictly monitor intake and output of all fluids and to weigh the patient daily. The electrolyte content of all fluids put out by the patient should be measured. Fluid intake should be restricted to equal the output plus insensible loss (roughly 0.2-0.3 ml/Kg/hour plus an additional 100 ml per degree centigrade elevation in body temperature above normal). The oliguric patient should lose 1.0-1.5 pounds per day, at least, and more if very catabolic. Serum sodium will reflect levels of water excess or deficit and should be maintained in the normal range. In general, patients with acute renal failure should not be given electrolytes in intravenous solution except to replace clearly documented deficits. In the oliguric patient, indwelling Foley catheter drainage of the bladder is contraindicated, and the bladder can be emptied intermittently (every other day) by aseptic insertion of a straight catheter, drainage, and washing of the bladder with an antiseptic GU irrigant.

2) Fluid Overload, Heart Failure, and Hypertension: Prevention is the best treatment. Potent loop diuretics such as furosemide or ethacrynic acid occasionally may improve urine output but generally are useless in the oliguric patient. One or two therapeutic trials of furosemide (80-480 mg I.V.) may be tried, but continued use of diuretics is not indicated unless there is a clear cut response. Occasionally such a diuretic program may convert oliguric to non-oliguric ARF and therefore benefit the patient with fluid overload, or permit infusion of larger quantities of I.V. fluid for nutritional purposes (see below).

The use of digitalis to treat CHF is dangerous in patients with ARF and usually is not needed unless the patient has intrinsic cardiac disease and/or severe CHF not responding to control of fluid balance. Hypertension may be caused by, or aggravated by, fluid overload and may respond simply to control of fluid balance and not require specific antihypertensive therapy. In the oliguric patient, dialysis may be required to manage fluid overload, heart failure, and hypertension.

3) <u>Hyperkalemia:</u> Every effort must be made to prevent hyperkalemia. Adequate nutrition plays a key role in combating hyperkalemia secondary to catabolism. Devitalized tissues must be debrided. G.I. bleeding must be counteracted and measures should be instituted to remove blood from the G.I. tract (e.g. N-G suction). Penicillin G and old bank blood (10 days or older) are external sources of excessive potassium that should be avoided. In the severely catabolic patient, daily hemodialysis may be required. Specific emergency treatment of life-threatening hyperkalemia is discussed in the chapter on electrolyte abnormalities.

Therapeutic measures for hyperkalemia can be categorized as follows:

   a) to counter cardiotoxicity of hyperkalemia, administer calcium gluconate I.V.
   b) to shift potassium from extracellular to intracellular compartments, either administer sodium bicarbonate I.V. and/or give I.V. glucose and insulin
   c) to remove excess potassium from body stores, either use ion-exchange resin Kayexalate or dialyze.

The first two categories provide only temporary relief and can be utilized for short terms until definitive measures for potassium removal can be achieved. The non-dialytic therapy of hyperkalemia involves administration of fluid and/or sodium and may cause fluid overload, edema, heart failure, or hypertension. It must be remembered that the patient may absorb 2-3 mEq of sodium for each gram of Kayexalate given. Hemodialysis is a very efficient means of removing potassium from the body, whereas peritoneal dialysis is much less efficient, even less so than an effective Kayexalate regimen.

4) <u>Nutrition:</u> Although protein restriction is appropriate for patients with acute renal failure, adequate caloric intake is necessary in order to counteract catabolism. If the patient can eat, a diet containing 40 gm of high quality protein (e.g. eggs) and 2000-3000 calories (by means of Karo syrup, ginger ale, butterballs, hard candy low in K) should help keep the patient in nitrogen balance.

When oral feeding is not possible, parenteral nutrition must be provided. A minimum of 400 calories per day will reduce ketosis due to metabolism of fat and will reduce protein catabolism. One liter of 10% dextrose in water will provide 400 calories (or 500 ml of 20% D/W). Parenteral hyperalimentation by means of intravenous infusion of hypertonic glucose and L-amino acids has been found to be benefical in improving survival and achieving more rapid recovery for patients with acute renal failure;[8] however, these results have yet to be confirmed. Commercial preparations of mixtures of essential and non-essential L-amino acids now are available. Programs of total parenteral nutrition are complicated, and a detailed account is beyond the scope of this discussion but may be found in reference(9). It may involve infusing the patient with as much as 2-3 liters of fluid per day as well as administering substantial quantities of potassium and phosphate, both of which enter the cells with glucose to be utilized in the synthesis of new tissue. Hypomagnesemia, hypocalcemia, hypophosphatemia, hypokalemia, hyperosmolality, metabolic acidosis, and fluid overload all are real potential complications of parenteral hyperalimentation that demand vigilant attention. Sepsis is a major life-threatening complication, the source being the indwelling central venous catheter or arteriovenous shunt used for administration of the nutrient solutions. An effective program of total parenteral nutrition may require daily dialysis in order to control fluid and electrolyte balance. Because the problem of effectively combating catabolism remains as a major block to substantially improving survival in the critically ill patient with oliguric ARF, parenteral hyperalimentation is an important adjunct to the management of these patients. However, further clinical studies and refinement in techniques are needed before it will become a routine part of the supportive management of ARF.

The value of routine daily physical therapy for the bedridden immobilized patient should not be underestimated or ignored.

Vitamins should be provided routinely, especially water soluble vitamins for patients receiving dialysis.

5) Infection: Infection should be avoided and treated with specific antibiotics based upon culture and sensitivity data. Catheter drainage of the bladder is contraindicated in the patient with oliguric ARF (ARN) once the diagnosis is established. Prophylactic antibiotics are inappropriate. Nephrotoxic drugs should be avoided when possible and otherwise the dose should be altered as required by level of renal function or by dialysis schedules and as indicated by routine monitoring of drug levels. An excellent guide to usage of drugs in renal failure is available,[10] and the nephrotoxicity of antimicrobial agents recently has been reviewed.[11]

6) GI Bleeding: GI bleeding occurs commonly in patients with ARF and appears to be particularly associated with states of hypercatabolism and is a major cause of hyperkalemia. Uncontrollable GI bleeding not uncommonly is the cause of death in the catabolic, acutely uremic patient. This association heightens the importance of adequate nutrition. Antacids may be used prophylactically but cannot be those that contain absorbable magnesium or calcium. Accordingly, aluminum hydroxide preparations are best to use in presence of acute renal failure. The use of heparin during hemodialysis may aggravate GI bleeding, hence either low-dose heparin protocols or regional heparinization of the dialysis machine are indicated in the bleeding patient.

7) <u>Nausea and Vomiting</u>: Treatment with phenothiazines may help alleviate these symptoms, but repeated doses lead to accumulation of the drug and may cause undesirable side effects of hypotension (making hemodialysis difficult to accomplish) and oculogyric crisis (which responds dramatically to Benadryl).

8) <u>Anemia</u>: Hematocrit may fall rapidly due to hemolysis and blood loss (especially GI bleeding) and bone marrow suppression by uremia. In general, hematocrit can be expected to settle in the mid-to-low 20's in acute renal failure, even in the absence of a bleeding diathesis. Transfusions generally are not indicated to raise hematocrit much above 25% unless there is active bleeding. As a general principle, transfusions should be avoided unless specifically indicated. Frozen red cells should be used as much as possible to minimize incidence of hepatitis. Leuko-poor frozen cells are also indicated for patients with probable chronic renal failure in order to avoid sensitizing them to transplant antigens.

9) <u>Pericarditis</u>: Pericarditis is an unusual complication of ARF. It is an indication for dialysis. Tamponade should be treated by pericardiocentesis.

10) <u>Encephalopathy</u>: Seizures should be treated acutely with I.V. valium or with short acting barbiturates or dilantin. Seizures and other manifestations of uremic encephalopathy should respond to control of uremia by means of dialysis. Etiologies of encephalopathy other than uremia should be actively pursued.

PHASE OF RECOVERY FROM OLIGURIA: In the past, massive diuresis with urinary loss of large quantities of sodium and potassium commonly heralded the phase of recovery from oliguric ARF. Now, probably because of more effective control of uremia by means of dialysis and conservative therapy, massive polyuria occurs infrequently. However, the patient may pass through a phase of fixed output of urine during which dehydration and depletion of sodium or potassium can occur. Hence, during the phase of recovery from oliguria, the physician must be vigilant in monitoring intake and output of fluid and electrolytes. Unless the patient has been permitted to accumulate very high levels of urea and other metabolic waste products, the phase of fixed urine output, or polyuria, should not persist beyond a few days at most. Longer durations of polyuria may be iatrogenic, that is, in response to continued high rates of fluid administration.

DIALYSIS: The conservative non-dialytic management of patients with oliguric ARF can be quite successful for short-term periods if intake of fluid, sodium, and potassium is carefully restricted and basal dietary requirements of protein and calories are provided. Such programs require strict monitoring of the patient and are successful for only limited periods of time and are not adequate

for management of the catabolic patient. Hence, non-dialytic conservative regimens are employed primarily during the incipient
phase of acute renal failure when the patient initially is being evaluated and treated in efforts to forestall development of frank ARF.

Dialysis, either peritoneal or hemo-, is effective in controlling
fluid and electrolyte balance and in controlling uremia and its
symptoms. Indications for dialysis are:

1) hyperkalemia
2) fluid overload: heart failure, hypertension
3) acidosis
4) persistent oliguria
5) uremia, per se
6) hypercatabolism
7) pericarditis
8) uremic encephalopathy
9) hyperuricemic or hypercalcemic nephropathy

Dialysis therapy should be employed early in the treatment of acute
renal failure in an attempt to prevent the development of uremia
and its complications and in order to enhance survival. [4] It is far
better to err in the direction of over-dialysis rather than under-
dialysis. In general, the pre-dialysis BUN should be kept below
100 mg% by use of every other day or daily dialysis, depending
upon the state of catabolism. Dialysis should never be employed as
a substitute for proper medical management. The nephrologist
should be involved in the evaluation and management of the patient
early in the course of acute renal failure.

Factors influencing the choice of peritoneal or hemodialysis in a
given clinical setting are as follows:

1) Advantages of peritoneal dialysis, versus hemodialysis:

   a) Is a safe and effective method of dialysis
   b) Can be performed in any hospital as a nursing procedure
      with physician supervision
   c) Can be performed in patient with low cardiac output
   d) Avoids need to create a chronic blood access route such
      as a shunt
   e) Avoids abrupt alterations in blood volume and electrolyte
      composition
   f) Less incidence of disequilibrium
   g) Does not represent a commitment to long-term chronic
      supportive therapy for renal failure

2) Disadvantages of peritoneal dialysis, versus hemodialysis:

   a) Less efficient and therefore may not be adequate for the
      severely catabolic patient

b) May not be able to perform peritoneal dialysis in patient with recent abdominal surgery because adhesions may prevent successful dialysis or may bind intestines to abdominal wall and enhance danger of intestinal perforation by the trochar
c) Commits patient to bed for prolonged periods of time thereby interfering with pursuit of diagnostic or therapeutic procedures
d) May cause anorexia and decreased ability to tolerate ingestion of food
e) May compromise respiration
f) May cause abdominal pain and discomfort
g) Protein loss may equal 0.5-1.0 gram per liter of dialysate and aggravate negative nitrogen balance
h) Peritonitis may develop, especially if dialysis is continued beyond 48 hours

3) Advantages of Hemodialysis, versus peritoneal:

a) Efficient (may be only way to control severe catabolism)
b) Intermittent - so patient can be free for pursuit of diagnostic and therapeutic procedures
c) Permits less restriction of daily intake of food and fluid (oral or parenteral)

4) Disadvantages of Hemodialysis, versus peritoneal

a) Shunt needed
b) Patient exposed to heparin
c) May require transfer of patient to another hospital.
d) High incidence of disequilibrium syndrome and aggravation of drug toxicity (e.g. digitalis)
e) Difficult to achieve in presence of low cardiac output and shock

The fundamental principles in the management of patients with acute renal failure can be summarized:

1) anticipate and prevent ARF
2) recognize early the existence of ARF, or incipient ARF
3) make a specific etiologic diagnosis, as soon as possible
4) treat the primary illness, correcting those factors causing the renal failure
5) immediately institute appropriate supportive therapy
6) prevent, treat complications of ARF with particular attention to:
    fluid and electrolyte balance
    maintenance of cardiovascular system
    preventing, treating infections
    providing adequate nutrition
    combating catabolism
7) dialyze early and aggressively.

REFERENCES

1. Levinsky, N.G., and Alexander, E.A.: Acute Renal Failure, in The Kidney, W.B. Saunders, Philadelphia, pp. 806-837, 1976.

2. Cattell, W.R.: Acute Renal Failure, in Recent Advances in Renal Disease, edited by N.F. Jones. Churchill Livingstone. New York, pp. 1-47, 1975.

3. Flamenbaum, W.: Pathophysiology of acute renal failure. Arch. Intern Med 131:911, 1973.

4. Kleinknecht, D., et al.: Factors influencing immediate prognosis in acute renal failure with special reference to prophylactic hemodialysis. Adv Nephrology 1:207-230, 1971.

5. Fry, I.K., and Cattell, W.R.: Radiology in the Diagnosis of Renal Failure. Br. Med Bull 27:148-152, 1967.

6. Handa, S.P., and Morrin, P.A.: Diagnostic indices in acute renal failure. Can Med Assoc J 96:78, 1967.

7. Berns, A.S., et al.: Urinary diagnostic indices in acute renal failure. Kidney Int 10:495, 1976.

8. Abel, R.M., et al.: Improved survival from acute renal failure after treatment with intravenous essential L-amino acids and glucose. NEJM 288:695-699, 1973.

9. Shils, M.E.: Guidelines for Total Parenteral Nutrition. JAMA 220:1921-1929, 1972.

10. Bennett, W.M., et al.: A guide to drug therapy in renal failure. JAMA 230:1544-1553, 1974.

11. Appel, G.B., and Neu, H.C.: Nephrotoxicity of Antimicrobial Agents. NEJM 296:663-670, 722-728, 784-787, 1977.

C: SEVERE ELECTROLYTE ABNORMALITIES
by Leon G. Fine, M.B.

In the hectic atmosphere of a busy emergency room, nothing can be less dramatic than the seemingly innocuous recording of an abnormal serum potassium or sodium concentration scrawled on a scrap of paper as results are returned from the laboratory. The prognosis in many instances, is as grave as if the patient had entered the hospital with a stab wound of the chest. This section deals with the rational emergency approach to hyper- and hypokalemia and hyper- and hyponatremia, for it is in the form of an abnormal serum potassium or sodium concentration that the physician is often presented with realization that he is confronting a gravely ill patient.

HYPERKALEMIA

The etiology of an elevated serum potassium (K+) concentration is totally irrelevant to its initial management. In all cases this should include a) an immediate ECG recording and b) a repeat laboratory determination. Common causes of spurious hyperkalemia are 1) hemolysis of drawn blood, 2) tourniquet method of drawing blood with local tissue damage releasing intracellular potassium, and 3) increased WBC or platelet count.

Since sudden death in patients with hyperkalemia is invariably the result of a cardiac complication, the ECG, which represents a physiological appraisal of the electrical events brought about by changes in ion distribution across cell membranes, is more relevant than any absolute value for serum potassium.

The ECG in hyperkalemia initially shows tall peaked T waves (especially in precordial leads) and later a decrease in amplitude and widening of the QRS complex with a prolonged P-R interval. Later the P waves become flattened or even absent. The final result is a merging of the QRS with the tall T wave to give the classic sine-wave form. At this point ventricular arrhythmias are almost inevitable. Neuromuscular manifestations include weakness, paralysis, and mental confusion. These effects are due to a depolarization block, described below, which leads first to hyperexcitability and then to weakness.

In the absence of ECG changes and with potassium concentrations less than 6.5 mEq/L no emergency measures are required other than to bring to the attention of the managing physicians the need to search for a cause, to discontinue drugs which may potentiate potassium retention by the kidneys (e.g. Aldactone(R)) and to limit intake.

If ECG changes are apparent at any level of serum K^+ or if serum K^+ is greater than 7 mEq/L immediate treatment is called for.

The response to therapy will be immediately apparent if the ECG is monitored continuously. Treatment is now aimed at antagonizing the effects of hyperkalemia on cardiac and neuromuscular function. It should be appreciated that the excitability of cardiac or skeletal muscle fiber is dependent not specifically on the concentration of potassium in the ECF but rather on the distribution of potassium between intracellular and extracellular compartments. An elevated potassium concentration in the ECF relative to the ICF leads to a hyperexcitable state, e.g., the resting membrane potential approaches the threshold potential required to initiate contraction. Stabilization and recovery to the resting state (after the action potential) also involves the entry of calcium ions into the cell.

It may therefore be appreciated that immediate reversal of the hyperexcitable state is of primary importance. This is achieved 1) by administering calcium intravenously (as Calcium gluconate or Calcium chloride) and 2) achieving a state of extracellular alkalosis by the administration of sodium bicarbonate intravenously. This latter maneuver, by reducing the hydrogen ion concentration outside of the cells, will cause hydrogen ions to leave the cells down an altered concentration gradient. Potassium ions enter the cells secondarily to maintain electroneutrality and it is this redistribution of potassium into the intracellular compartment that reduces the excitable state. Initial dosage of calcium is usually 1.0 g intravenously, while anywhere from 50 to 100 mEq of bicarbonate are given with careful attention to the ECG. Calcium and bicarbonate should not be given via the same intravenous route.

Another measure which is immediately effective in promoting potassium entry into cells is the administration of intravenous glucose and insulin (approximately 1 unit of regular insulin per 5G glucose). Usually about 50G glucose will be required to achieve an acceptable response. All the aforementioned maneuvers should lead to a reversal of hyperkalemia within a half hour.

In cases where it is impossible to administer fluid for fear of volume overload or where multiple electrolyte abnormalities are present or where it is required to remove significant amounts of potassium from body fluids, the only effective alternative may be hemo- or peritoneal dialysis. Since the logistics of hospital medicine dictate that these procedures take considerable time to organize they should be considered as adjunctive, as must the administration of an ion exchange resin such as sodium polystyrene sulfonate (Kayexalate(R)) which accelerates potassium removal via the gastrointestinal tract. The resin exchanges sodium for potassium and the additional sodium load can be significant in patients with incipient cardiac failure. (Table I)

TABLE I
TREATMENT OF HYPERKALEMIA

A. EMERGENCY MEASURES
   1. IV CaCl (1.0 gram)
   2. IV NaHCO$_3$ (50-100 mEq)
   3. Glucose and insulin
 	
B. DEFINITIVE MEASURES
   1. Treat the primary cause
   2. Ion Exchange Resin
   3. Dialysis

TABLE II
CAUSES OF HYPERKALEMIA

I. K+ redistribution - metabolic acidosis
                            - hyperkalemic periodic paralysis
 	
II. Impaired renal excretion of K+
   1) Reduced functional nephron mass
      - acute renal failure
      - advanced chronic renal failure
 	
   2) Diminished mineralocorticoid activity
      - Hyporeninemic hypoaldosteronism
      - Addison's disease
      - Aldosterone antagonists (spironolactone)
 	
   3) Functional - Volume contraction with diminished
                    distal Na+ delivery
 	
III. Increased entry of K+ in serum
   1) Endogenous - hemolysis
                 - rhabdomyolysis
 	
   2) Exogenous - salt substitutes
                   - potassium penicillin

Once the serum potassium concentration has stabilized around normal levels a cause can be sought from the multitude of possibilities listed in Table II.

HYPOKALEMIA

The danger of sudden death from hypokalemia is no less than with hyperkalemia and the diagnosis is probably overlooked more often. Once again the cardiac and neuromuscular effects predominate. The ECG may show flattening of T waves, the appearance of a U wave, S-T depression and both atrial and ventricular premature beats.

In any hypokalemic patient it should be immediately established whether the patient is on digitalis since the cardiac effects would be expected to be more pronounced in these cases. Neuromuscular excitability is diminished leading to weakness, paralysis, and ileus. In patients with hepatocellular failure, hypokalemia exacerbates encephalopathy. Additional effects of longstanding hypokalemia include a defective urinary concentrating mechanism leading to polyuria, and isolated instances of sodium retention with edema.

The emergency management again requires 1) ECG monitoring, 2) repeating the laboratory measurement of serum K^+, 3) measurement of arterial blood pH and 4) measurement of potassium concentration in a urine aliquot. If urine potassium concentration is low ($<$ 20 mEq/l) the primary cause of the hypokalemia is unlikely to be renal loss (primary or diuretic induced) and suggests a state of chronic depletion in that the low urinary excretion represents the kidneys' attempt to retain potassium maximally.

The treatment of hypokalemia is again determined by the magnitude of the deficit, the extent of the ECG changes and the plasma pH.

A serum potassium of below 3 mEq/liter generally generally represents a loss of at least 200 mEq. Immense losses may occur before patients become symptomatic. The importance of a pH measurement cannot be overemphasized since, as described above, the ECF hydrogen ion concentration determines the relationship between intracellular and extracellular potassium. In any alkalotic state (low H+ concentration) H+ ions will leave the cells down a concentration gradient and will be replaced by potassium ions. Metabolic alkalosis will therefore always be accompanied by some degree of hypokalemia. A rule of thumb estimate indicates that serum K+ will fall 0.5 mEq/liter for every 0.1-unit change in pH. (Correction of the acid-base abnormality alone may correct the serum potassium ion concentration.)

Therapy should be tailored to achieve reversal of the ECG abnormalities (if present) as a short term requirement and replacement of chronic losses over a more prolonged period. Oral treatment is preferred unless the deficit is severe in which case parenteral therapy is indicated. The dangers of administering potassium too rapidly relate to the imbalance which sudden changes in ECG potassium concentration would effect across cell membranes leading to neuromuscular irritability identical with that seen in hyperkalemia. As a general rule, IV potassium replacement should not exceed 40 mEq/hr although occasionally greater quantities may be needed.

The form in which potassium is administered is also important. In alkalotic patients alkaline potassium salts (bicarbonate, citrate) elevate serum bicarbonate further. Since bicarbonate is a poorly reabsorbable anion, an increase in the loss of bicarbonate via the kidneys will further aggravate sodium and potassium loss. <u>Potassium chloride</u> (KCl) should be used in these cases. In acidotic patients potassium bicarbonate or citrate are most effective.

Once the potassium deficit is adequately replaced (as evidenced by a state of external potassium balance) a diagnostic work-up or the cause of hypokalemia should be instituted. Table III lists the causes of hypokalemia.

TABLE III
CAUSES OF HYPOKALEMIA

I. <u>K+ redistribution</u> - Hypokalemic periodic paralysis

II. <u>Loss of K+ from the body</u>
   1) via skin - excessive prolonged sweating
   2) via gastrointestinal tract
      - diarrhea
      - villous adenoma
      - (vomiting)
   3) via kidneys -
      Primary aldosteronism
      a) Exogenous - steroids, licorice
      b) Endogenous - adrenal adenoma, hyperplasia, malignant hypertension, renal artery stenosis, adrenogenital syndrome.

      Secondary aldosteronism plus distal Na+ delivery
      a) Edema states plus diuretics
      b) Edema states plus glycosuria, bicarbonaturia

HYPERNATREMIA

As a rule an elevation or depression of the sodium concentration of the serum has very little to do with sodium homeostasis. Rather, it reflects alterations in water metabolism and since sodium is the predominant ion in the extracellular fluid and, as such, is the most important osmotically active particle, hyponatremia is essentially a hypo-osmolar state, whereas hypernatremia is associated with hyperosmolarity.

The second important principle required to interpret changes in serum sodium concentration relates to the fact that <u>whatever the serum sodium concentration, total body sodium may be normal, increased or decreased.</u> The net result of the loss or gain of sodium and water is dependent only upon the relative proportion of each which enters or leaves body fluids. Hypernatremia may result only from a water deficit or from a loss of sodium and water (the latter being in excess) or a gain of sodium and water in which the former predominates. Since the sodium ion is, for practical purposes, exclusively an extracellular cation, net gain or loss of sodium must be associated with changes in ECF volume. It is important clinically to establish first whether the patient is hypovolemic (tachycardia, absence of neck vein distention in the supine position, postural hypotension, low urine sodium concentration, elevated BUN, loss of tissue turgor).

The causes of hypernatremia according to this clinical separation are listed in Table IV.

TABLE IV
CAUSES OF HYPERNATREMIA (HYPEROSMOLARITY)

I. Normal body sodium: Pure water loss
  1) Insensible - febrile states
               - high ambient temperatures
  2) Renal -
  Central diabetes insipidus
  a) Idiopathic
  b) Neoplastic
  c) Infiltrative

  Nephrogenic Diabetes insipidus
  a) Drugs - Demeclocycline
           - Methoxyflurane anesthesia
           - Lithium carbonate
  b) Hypokalemia
  c) Hypercalcemia
  d) Hereditary

II. Low body sodium: Loss of water and electrolytes in hypotonic
                     proportions
  1) Insensible
  2) Gastrointestinal
  3) Renal - osmotic diuresis (glycosuria, mannitol)

III. High body sodium: Addition of solute in excess of water
  1) Excess sodium as bicarbonate, lactate, chloride intravenously or in dialysis fluid

Once it has been established whether the patient is normovolemic, volume contracted or expanded the appropriate treatment may be administered. Patients with normal body sodium require only water; those with low body sodium will require hypotonic fluids (usually as dextrose and half-normal saline) and those with high body sodium require water only with cessation of the source of excess sodium. If the sodium load has been excessive, diuretics may be employed.

HYPONATREMIA

The approach to the hyponatremic patient rests upon the same principles as are outlined on page 279. The possible causes are multiple and once again require differentiation according to the volume status of the patient (Table V). It is important to realize that edamatous patients, although patently volume overloaded, are physiologically volume contracted i.e. their effective arterial blood volume is reduced. In other words, the volume of blood perfusing some essential (and yet undetermined) compartment in which volume receptors reside, is reduced. In such patients, sodium retention by the kidneys will persist in an attempt to restore this underperfused state to normal.

TABLE V
CAUSES OF HYPONATREMIA (HYPO-OSMOLARITY)

I. Normal body sodium with excess of water
Normal or moderately expanded effective arterial blood volume
1) Chronic inappropriate ADH secretion
   a) Carcinomas
   b) Pulmonary disorders
   c) CNS disorders
   d) Drugs (chlorproparide, clofiltrate)
   e) Metabolic (hypothyroidism, cortisol insufficiency)

II. High body sodium and larger excess of water
Contracted effective arterial blood volume with edema
1) Edema states
   a) Nephrotic syndrome
   b) Hepatic failure
   c) Congestive heart failure

III. Low body sodium and body water
Hypovolemia with dilutional hyponatremia
1) Renal losses
   a) Diuretics
   b) Adrenal insufficiency
   c) Interstitial nephritis
   d) Renal Tubular Acidosis
2) Gastrointestinal loss
   a) Vomiting, diarrhea
   b) Pancreatitis
   c) Intestinal obstruction
3) "Third space" loss
   a) Peritonitis
   b) Burns

A key to the unraveling of the mechanism of the hyponatremia once again requires an assessment of the patient's volume status and measurement of urinary sodium concentration on a "spot" sample. If the patient has a normal body sodium with an expanded effective arterial blood volume due to water retention urinary sodium excretion will be increased (Group I). It is the volume stimulus per se which enhances renal sodium excretion (>25 mEq/l) and treatment requires only restriction of water. In cases where both sodium and water are retained (Group II) i.e. edema states, urinary sodium excretion will be low (<10 mEq/l) in response to the stimulus of a contracted effective arterial blood volume. Once again water should be restricted but together with sodium.

In patients who are volume contracted and hyponatremic (Group III), urinary sodium concentration is usually high (>20 mEq/l) where the loss is renal in origin, whereas, if the loss is extrarenal, urinary sodium concentration will be low. Whatever the cause, the state of overt volume depletion requires treatment with isotonic sodium chloride.

REFERENCES

1. Renal & Electrolyte Disorders, Ed. Schrier, R.W., Little, Brown & Co., 1976.

2. Clinical Disorders of Fluid & Electrolyte Metabolism, Eds. Maxwell, M.H. and Kleeman, C.R., McGraw-Hill Book Co., 1972.

3. The Sea Within Us, Ed. Bricker, N.S., Science and Medicine, Publishing Co., 1975.

CHAPTER 13: RESPIRATORY EMERGENCIES

A: ACUTE RESPIRATORY FAILURE
by Robert Brown, M.D. and
Arthur A. Sasahara, M.D.

ACUTE RESPIRATORY FAILURE (ARF)

DEFINITION: Acute Respiratory Failure (ARF)is the clinical condition characterized by the abrupt deterioration of respiratory function resulting in arterial hypoxemia with or without hypercapnia.

Although the choice is somewhat arbitrary, many authors select an
arterial pO2 (paO2) below 60 mm Hg or an arterial pCO2 (paCO2)
above 49 mm Hg as appropriate to the definition of ARF.[1] It should
be clear that many patients (e.g.,COPD, kyphoscoliosis) have such
blood gas abnormalities chronically. A brief classification of ARF
is presented in Table I. Although some of the conditions noted are
most often characterized by hypoxemia with hypercapnia (e.g.,
COPD, drug overdose) and others by hypoxemia without hypercapnia (e.g., pulmonary embolism, adult respiratory distress syndrome (ARDS) virtually all of them, at one stage or another may
be associated with either pattern.

We will consider some of the pathophysiological mechanisms related to the occurrence of hypoxemia and hypercapnia and from
these derive general principles of treatment. This will be followed
by specific considerations in the management of ARF in COPD,
ARDS and drug overdose.

HYPOXEMIA: There are 5 mechanisms which have been identified
in causing hypoxemia (Table II).

The occurrence of hypoxemia due to reduction in the oxygen concentration of inspired gas such as occurs at high altitude or in jet air-
crafts is not pertinent here, and will not be considered further.

The term "alveolar-capillary block" has been used to imply that
hypoxemia may occur secondary to an anatomic barrier to the
diffusion of oxygen from the alveoli to the pulmonary circulation.[2]
However, it is likely in most disease states that the contributions
of diffusion to hypoxemia is small when compared to that of ventilation-perfusion $(\dot{V}/\dot{Q})$ abnormalities.[3]

TABLE I
CLASSIFICATION OF ACUTE RESPIRATORY FAILURE

NORMAL LUNGS

1) Neuromuscular disorders: myasthenia gravis, amyotrophic lateral sclerosis, Guillain Barré
2) Chest wall: flail chest, kyphoscoliosis
3) CNS depression: drug overdose, head trauma, electrocution
4) Compensation for severe metabolic alkalemia

ABNORMAL LUNGS

1) Obstructive ventilatory disorders
   a) Acute exacerbations of COPD
   b) Status asthmaticus
   c) Cystic fibrosis
   d) Acute pulmonary embolism
2) Acutely stiff lungs
   a) Adult respiratory distress syndrome (ARDS)
   b) Overwhelming pneumonia: bacterial, fungal, etc.
   c) Aspiration pneumonitis
   d) Pulmonary edema (cardiogenic)
   e) Pulmonary hemorrhage

TABLE II
MECHANISMS OF HYPOXEMIA

1) Decreased oxygen concentration in inspired gas, e.g., high altitude
2) Diffusion abnormalities
3) Alveolar hypoventilation
4) Ventilation-perfusion decrease
5) Venous to arterial shunt

Alveolar hypoventilation (characterized by an elevated $paCO_2$) may contribute to hypoxemia in ARF. Figure 13.1a shows the relationship of alveolar pO_2 (paO_2) to alveolar ventilation ($\dot{V}A$) and the narrow range over which increased $\dot{V}A$ results in improved pAO_2. Note that hypercapnia occurs over a similar range. From the point of view of treatment of hypoxemia, then, increasing $\dot{V}A$ is generally not very useful, but when it is, it coincides with a need to increase it as therapy for hypercapnia. Essentially, improvement in pAO_2 due to increases in $\dot{V}A$ is limited by the concentration of oxygen in the inspired gas (FIO_2) and the practical extent to which $\dot{V}A$ can be increased voluntarily or mechanically. From Figure 13.1b, it is clear that a far more effective way of increasing PAO_2 is to increase FIO_2. With some qualifications, then (vide infra) this is a major therapeutic modality in ARF.

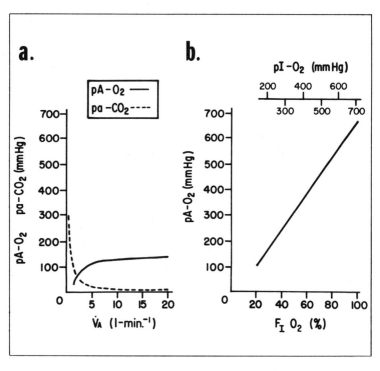

FIG. 13.1:   a) Plot of alveolar ventilation ($\dot{V}A$) vs. alveolar
pO2 (pAO2), (continuous line) based on a modifi-
cation of the alveolar gas equation,

$$pAO2 = pLO2 - K \frac{(\dot{V}O2)}{\dot{V}A},$$

and a superimposed plot of $\dot{V}A$ vs. arterial pCO2
(paCO2) based on the equation $paCO2 = K \frac{(\dot{V}CO2)}{\dot{V}A}$
(discontinuous line)

b) Plot of concentration of inspired oxygen (FIO2)
or partial pressure of inspired oxygen (pIO2) vs.
pAO2.

Assume: (1) barometric pressure = 760
          (2) $\dot{V}O2$ = .250 1-min.$^{-1}$
          (3) $\dot{V}CO2$ = .200 1-min.$^{-1}$
          (4) pACO2 = paCO2
          (5) inspired gas is air in (a)
          (6) $\dot{V}A$ = 4 1-min.$^{-1}$ in (b)

Probably the most important pathophysiologic mechanism of hypo-xemia in ARF is ventilation perfusion ($\dot{V}/\dot{Q}$) imbalance.[4] Much of what is currently done in the management of ARF is directed at improving low or zero (venous to arterial shunt) $\dot{V}/\dot{Q}$ ratios in the lung. Thus the removal of secretions, whether by coughing, chest physiotherapy or tracheal suction, allows ventilation of underven-tilated but perfused regions and hence the transfer of oxygen into and carbon dioxide out of the pulmonary capillaries. The admin-istration of bronchodilators serves a similar purpose. Should hypoxemia resist reversal by the administration of appropriate FIO_2, removal of secretions and bronchodilation, further thera-peutic escalation is necessary, but the goal of improving $\dot{V}/\dot{Q}$ ratios remains the same. It is well known that airway closure may occur in the tidal breathing range in some pathologic states. Because air-way caliber increases with lung volume[5], such airway closure may be reduced by increasing the mean lung volume at which the lungs are functioning. This can be achieved with the aid of a respirator by increasing the tidal volume (VT), or, when necessary, by the application of positive pressure to the airways throughout exhalation (positive end-expiratory pressure - PEEP) thereby increasing end-tidal lung volume.

HYPERCAPNIA: The relationship between $paCO_2$ and $\dot{V}A$ is shown in Figure 13.1b. From this, it can be seen that the treatment of hypercapnia requires an increase in $\dot{V}A$. Fortunately, when $\dot{V}A$ is low (and the $paCO_2$ is high) small increases in $\dot{V}A$ will result in large decreases in $paCO_2$. Improvement in $\dot{V}A$ may be achieved in much the same manner as was discussed above for the treatment of $\dot{V}/\dot{Q}$ abnormalities; that is, by removing secretions, broncho-dilation, and by increasing the mean lung volume during the respira-tory cycle.

DIAGNOSIS OF ACUTE RESPIRATORY FAILURE

We have defined ARF as the abrupt deterioration of pulmonary func-tion resulting in hypercapnia and/or hypoxemia. The history and physical examination are important in determining the presence of ARF, but the clinical assessment is often difficult because many of the predominant features of ARF are non-specific, often do not dis-criminate amongst its various causes and even may occur when ARF is absent.

1. DYSPNEA, TACHYPNEA:
   a) May be absent
   b) May be present without ARF
      (1) Anxiety
      (2) Neurologic disorders
      (3) Metabolic acidosis

2. CYANOSIS:
   a) Detection is often difficult and is dependent on a number of factors.
      (1) Quantity of reduced hemoglobin - requires 5 grams or more.
      (2) Cyanosis generally not detected until arterial oxygen saturation falls to 60 - 70%.
      (3) May be misleading since it can be caused by peripheral blood stasis rather than respiratory failure.
      (4) Skin thickness and quantity of pigment present
      (5) Color perception of observer
      (6) Alterations of hemoglobin or hemoglobin derivatives, e.g. methemoglobinemia, sulfhemoglobinemia.

3. RESPIRATORY DEPRESSION:
   a) Clinical detection of hypercapnia is difficult.
      (1) CO_2 is colorless
      (2) CO_2 is odorless
   b) Respiratory depression may cause or be caused by an elevated $paCO_2$.
   c) Rarely, respiratory depression and CO_2 retention occur as a compensatory mechanism secondary to metabolic alkalosis.

ACUTE RESPIRATORY FAILURE IN CHRONIC OBSTRUCTIVE PULMONARY DISEASE

The importance of exacerbations of chronic obstructive pulmonary disease (COPD) as a cause of ARF is reflected in the fact that 5 to 10 million Americans are partially or totally disabled by COPD. Chronic bronchitis and/or emphysema cause in excess of 25,000 deaths each year in the United States, a figure which at one time appeared to be doubling every 5 years.[6] COPD is the most common cause of chronic cor pulmonale. The latter is estimated to account for 8 - 10% of those patients with heart disease who present to physicians and hospitals for diagnosis and treatment. Advanced COPD is characterized by airway obstruction, chronic hypoxemia, hypercapnia and pulmonary hypertension. In this setting, superimposed ARF is frequently complicated by right and often left ventricular failure. Heart failure worsens lung failure which in turn worsens heart failure in a vicious cycle of deterioration. Thus, effective treatment requires a clear understanding of the pathophysiological events leading to both pulmonary and heart failure.

PATHOPHYSIOLOGY OF HEART FAILURE IN COPD: It is known that lowered alveolar oxygen tension results in pulmonary vasoconstriction. In the presence of alveolar hypoxia, an increase in H+ ion concentration (such as occurs in acute CO_2 retention) results in further vasoconstriction.[7] The pulmonary hypertension which develops represents a significant afterload for the normally thin right ventricle (RV) and, particularly when abrupt and severe, leads to RV failure. In essence,

pulmonary hypoxia ———→ pulmonary vasoconstriction ———→

pulmonary arterial resistance ——→ pulmonary hypertension ——→

right ventricular enlargement ———→ right ventricular failure

Treatment must thus consist of correcting both the hypoxic state and, by improving alveolar ventilation, correcting the H+ ion increase as well.

TREATMENT OF ARF DUE TO COPD: In the presence of COPD, ARF is usually secondary to respiratory tract infection. The latter causes an increase in the volume and tenacity of the sputum and may also be associated with acute bronchoconstriction.

There are six major factors to be considered in the management of ARF due to COPD.

1. Hypoxemia
2. Hypercapnia
3. Indications for endotracheal intubation
4. Airway obstruction
5. Infection
6. Heart failure

1. Hypoxemia: In patients with chronic CO_2 retention, hypoxemia is the major ventilatory stimulus. In this setting, overzealous correction of hypoxemia may suppress ventilatory drive and aggravate hypercapnia. The latter may further suppress the central nervous system and this may continue until respiratory arrest occurs. Yet, hypoxemia is the life-threatening abnormality and immediate measures should be instituted to improve oxygenation. Controlled oxygen administration, introduced by Campbell,[8] allows partial correction of hypoxemia (substantially improving hemoglobin saturation and oxygen content of arterial blood (Figure 13.2), without significantly raising $paCO_2$ levels). Continuous mental status assessment is critical in the management of ARF complicating COPD.

A. Nasal Prongs:
  a) The flow of oxygen should be 2 1/min. or less.
  b) The desired effect is to raise the paO_2 without significantly raising the $paCO_2$. An arterial oxygen tension of about 50 - 60 mm Hg is a reasonable goal in that hemoglobin saturation is usually sufficient and hypoxic ventilatory stimulus is not removed.
  c) The $paCO_2$ should be carefully monitored. If elevation of $paCO_2$ does not produce drowsiness, the oxygen enriched mixture may be continued. In general, the $paCO_2$ should not be permitted to increase more than 10 mm Hg.

B. Venturi-type mask:
  a) This is preferable to nasal prongs.
  b) The lowest oxygen concentration (24%) should be used after obtaining a baseline arterial blood gas sample.
  c) If the desired elevation in paO2 is not attained, the next higher O2 concentration (25, 28, 30, 35%) can be used, but with careful monitoring of mental status and paCO2.

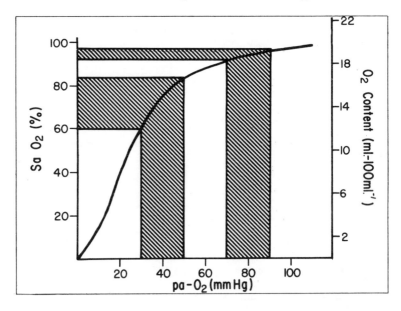

FIG. 13.2:   Oxygen - hemoglobin dissociation curve. A 20 mm Hg change in arterial pO2 (paO2) from 30 to 50 mm Hg results in a much larger increase in hemoglobin saturation (SaO2) or O2 content than does a similar change in paO2 from 70 - 90 mm Hg.

2. Hypercapnia: In the conscious patient who is oriented, measures to correct the hypercapnia should be conservative and secondary to improvement of oxygenation. Improved alveolar ventilation can be achieved by urging the patient to breathe deeper and slower. Intermittent positive pressure breathing, (IPPB), is frequently used but a convenient way to administer aerosolized bronchodilators but is more expensive and no more effective than various hand-held nebulizers.

3. Indications for Endotracheal Intubation: In the recent past, many patients were intubated and maintained on mechanical ventilation. The high incidence of complications and mortality, the magnitude of nursing care involved, coupled with recent knowledge of the benefits of controlled oxygen therapy have led to more stringent criteria for intubation:

a) depressed sensorium is the major indication for intubation in ARF complicating COPD.
b) progressive clinical deterioration in spite of maximal non-invasive therapy, as reflected by decreasing paO_2, increasing $paCO_2$ and acidemia.
c) excessive secretions poorly managed by cough or tracheal suction (usually occurs in association with b.)

Intubation by the nasotracheal (preferable) or oral route should be carried out with a sterile, soft, or floppy-cuffed catheter. Such soft cuffed catheters have reduced the risk of tracheal erosion and, providing optimal catheter care practices have been carried out, can usually be left in place for periods up to a week.

On the basis of chronic CO_2 retention and diuretic therapy for cor pulmonale, many patients with COPD have high bicarbonate and low serum chloride levels. A dangerous tendency in such patients is the overly vigorous correction of hypercapnia to "normal" rather than "baseline" levels. This may produce a pH of greater than 7.55 and the associated risk of severe neurological and cardiac dysfunction. Confusion, tremors, asterixis, myoclonic jerks, seizures and malignant ventricular dysrhythmias may result in death. Furthermore, if a chronically hypercapneic patient is hyperventilated on a respirator for several days, renal bicarbonate loss will occur. Upon extubation, if the $paCO_2$ returns to its baseline hypercapneic state, a dangerous respiratory acidemia could result. Clearly, mechanical ventilation should be controlled so as to approach slowly and maintain a normal pH rather than a normal $paCO_2$.

4. Airway Obstruction:
    a) <u>Retained Secretions</u>: In patients with COPD who present in ARF, reversible components of airway obstruction are due to copious, infected secretions and bronchoconstriction. Cough should be forcefully encouraged as often as every 15 minutes and should be preceded by chest physiotherapy at least once every hour until significant improvement has occurred. If the patient is still unable to raise sputum, tracheal suction should be employed.

    (1) A soft catheter should be passed transnasally or orally
    (2) A sterile catheter and gloves should be used each time
    (3) Suction should not be applied while the catheter is being inserted; once it is in place, intermittent suction should be applied for no longer than 10 - 15 seconds in order to avoid depleting the lungs of gas.

    b) <u>Bronchoconstriction</u>: Bronchodilators such as the sympathomimetic amines and xanthine derivatives are most effective in those patients with a strong component of bronchoconstriction, such as in asthma, but are also useful in COPD. They relax airway smooth muscle and secondarily may facilitate mobilization of secretions.

Isoproterenol is the most commonly used sympathomimetic amine. However, it increases myocardial oxygen demand and thus other agents which are more B2-receptor specific (salbutamol, terbutaline, isoetharene) are preferable in patients with coronary artery disease.

Aminophylline is a xanthine derivative which relaxes bronchial smooth muscle, stimulates heart muscle and acts as a diuretic.

A prototype therapeutic regimen is as follows:

Isuprel:

1. administer by aerosol as often as every 2 hours
2. approximate dose is 2.5 mg (0.5 ml of a 1/200 solution) in about 3 ml. water, introduced into nebulizer
3. monitor carefully for excessive tachycardia, dysrhythmias, hypotension
4. do not use in patients with a history of increasing usage prior to development of ARF in order to avoid "reflex" bronchoconstriction and dysrhythmias.

Aminophylline:

1. Give an initial dose of 6 mg/kg slowly over a period of 10 minutes or so, thus minimizing the risk of nausea, vomiting, hypotension, dysrhythmias.
2. maintain blood levels by administering an IV drip of 1 mg/kg/hour [11]
3. in the very ill or in those patients in whom therapy appears unsuccessful, doses can be adjusted on the basis of blood aminophylline levels. (therapeutic range 10-20 ugm/ml)

The role of corticosteroids in the management of ARF due to COPD is, at best, controversial.[12] They certainly have no primary therapeutic role and, in our opinion, ought only to be used as a last resort.

Sedatives are contra-indicated because too often they aggravate respiratory depression.

5. Infection: The majority of patients with COPD who develop ARF do so on the basis of superimposed acute respiratory tract infections. Clinical deterioration is usually heralded by increased sputum production and color change from frothy white to yellow or green. Although commonly S. pneumonia or H. influenzae are found in sputum isolates, differentiation between colonization and infection is difficult, and whether or not such organisms truly are offending agents is uncertain.[13] Probably the majority of cases are due to viral infections.[13] In spite of these controversies, the recommended practices are:

(1) pre-antibiotic chest x-ray, sputum smear and cultures if acute pneumonia is present.
(2) in the absence of pneumonia (for which specific therapy is indicated), administration of a broad spectrum antibiotic with activity against H. influenzae such as ampicillin 250 - 500 mg PO qid or tetracycline 250 - 500 mg PO qid for 7 to 10 days.

6. <u>Heart Failure:</u> Cardiac failure frequently accompanies severe hypoxemia, hypercapnia and acidemia. In many instances there may be left ventricular as well as right ventricular failure. The use of digitalis remains controversial for the treatment of cor pulmonale. Chronic levels of hypoxemia do not appear to increase digitalis "sensitivity" which appears more to be related to the degree of acute hypoxemia and metabolic acidosis developing with the onset of ARF as well as to the hypokalemia which occurs as a result of diuretic therapy. Also, the risk of developing toxicity is greater in these patients because of the difficulties inherent in assessing "digitalis effect" in the presence of sinus tachycardia and myocardial ischemia. Therefore, digitalis should be used with caution, and then only after appropriate and effective oxygenation and ventilation have been instituted. Supplemental potassium chloride should be administered to replenish losses due to diuretics.

ADULT RESPIRATORY DISTRESS SYNDROME (ARDS)

DEFINITION: ARDS is a syndrome characterized by acute respiratory failure due to abnormalities in the peripheral gas exchange units of the lung (alveoli, capillaries, interstitium)[14] which occurs as a complication of a broad spectrum of medical and surgical conditions. (See Table III)

THE DIAGNOSIS IS MADE BY:

1. Clinical picture of ARF
2. Progressive and severe hypoxia unresponsive to FIO2 = 100% due to intrapulmonary shunting. Hypercapnea may develop late and is an ominous prognostic sign.
3. Increased "stiffness" of the lung (decreased compliance) in association with progressive airspace consolidation on chest x-ray (fluffy infiltrates, acinar shadows).

THE PATHOLOGY OF ARDS IS CHARACTERIZED BY:

1. Interstitial and alveolar edema and hemorrhage due to "leaky pulmonary capillaries. "
2. Pulmonary capillary microthrombi
3. Proliferation of Type II pneumocytes
4. Hyaline membrane formation

292/ Respiratory Emergencies

TREATMENT: The treatment of ARDS is frequently difficult, complex and frustrating because the combination of the severe underlying disease state and ARF results in a very poor prognosis. Therapy involves the maintenance of oxygenation as well as specific and supportive measures related to the underlying disease. The latter is managed according to general principles previously outlined. Hypoxemia unresponsive to non-invasive measures is the major indication for intubation in ARDS. A volume-cycled respirator is recommended.

TABLE III
CAUSES OF ARDS[14]

SHOCK OF ANY ETIOLOGY	INHALED TOXINS
INFECTIOUS CAUSES	oxygen
gram-negative sepsis	smoke
viral pneumonia	corrosive chemicals,
bacterial pneumonia	$(NO_2, Cl_2, NH_3,$
fungal pneumonia (rare)	phosgene, cadmium)
Pneumocystis carinii (rare)	
TRAUMA	HEMATOLOGIC
fat emboli	DISORDERS
lung contusion	intravascular coagu-
nonthoracic trauma	lation
head injury	massive blood trans-
	fusion
	? postcardiopulmonary
	bypass
LIQUID ASPIRATION	METABOLIC DISORDERS
gastric juice	pancreatitis
fresh and salt water	uremia
hydrocarbon fluids	paraquat ingestion
DRUG OVERDOSE	MISCELLANEOUS
heroin	lymphangitic carcino-
methadone	matosis
propoxyphene	increased intracranial
barbiturates	pressure
	eclampsia
	postcardioversion

GUIDE TO RESPIRATOR MANAGEMENT: a rough estimate of
initial tidal volume is 10 cc/kgm.

1. Tidal Volume: As the pO2 falls, the VT should be increased in
   an effort to maintain adequate paO2. Because the lungs are
   stiff, too large a VT will result in high end-inspiratory airway
   pressures and increases the risk of pneumothorax.

2. FIO2: If larger VT does not improve the severe hypoxemia, the
   concentration of oxygen in the inspired air should be increased.
   Optimally the paO2 should be maintained at a level of about 70 -
   80 mm Hg. Above this, large increases in paO2 result in only
   small changes in oxygen content (see Figure 13.2). Needlessly
   high FIO2 increases the risk of "oxygen toxicity" which would
   only further complicate gas exchange problems.

3. PEEP (positive end-expiratory pressure); CPPB (continuous
   positive pressure breathing): PEEP prevents end-expiratory
   collapse of lung segments and improves oxygenation by increasing mean lung volume during the respiratory cycle. The combination of increasing VT and PEEP represents the maximal
   mechanical alteration to increase the space available for gas
   exchange.

4. ECMO: The use of extra-corporeal membrane oxygenation
   (ECMO) is the subject of intense investigation in some centers.
   As yet, indications for its use and its efficacy have not been
   clearly established.

High positive airway pressures (due to large VT, stiff lungs, and
PEEP) are in part transmitted to the pleural space and mediastinal
contents and hence may 1) decrease venous return and cardiac output; 2) squeeze capillaries shunt thereby increasing pulmonary vascular resistance, diverting blood to non-ventilating lung units and
decreasing paO2. It should be appreciated that the goal of therapy
is not merely an increase in paO2 but an increase in oxygen delivery.
Decreases in cardiac output (C.O.) will be counter-productive since:

$$O2 \text{ delivery} = C.O. \times O2 \text{ content of arterial blood}$$

Thus, if the decrease in C.O. is greater than the increase in O2 content, oxygen delivery will have been reduced. If measurement of
C.O. at the bedside is not readily available, it can be assumed on a
clinical basis that it is adequate if the patient is reasonably warm
and has an adequate blood pressure and urine output. If a pulmonary
artery catheter is available, one can follow mixed venous oxygen content ($C\bar{v}_{O2}$) as PEEP is increased. A fall in $C\bar{v}_{O2}$ may be taken to
indicate a reduction in C.O. and oxygen transport.

ANCILLARY MEASURES:

1. Balloon catheter pressure monitoring (SWAN-GANZ): The pulmonary artery balloon catheter is useful to guide fluid and pressure management in ARDS where excessive volume replacement may increase pulmonary capillary pressure and aggravate pulmonary edema due to "leaky" capillaries and yet where insufficient fluid replacement may lead to hypotension, diminished cardiac output and possibly increased lung damage.[15] The catheter permits monitoring of left ventricular end diastolic pressure as reflected by the pulmonary "wedge" pressure or by pulmonary artery diastolic pressure and it therefore also aids in the diagnosis of left ventricular failure, co-existent with ARF in ARDS and COPD.

2. Corticosteroids: Although there are animal data to suggest improved survival in fat embolism and oxygen toxicity [16,17] the use of steroids in ARDS remains controversial. No definite recommendations can be made about indications or dose. Most commonly, they are used in high doses when treating ARDS due to gastric acid aspiration, gram negative sepsis, fat embolism and smoke inhalation.

3. Anticoagulants: Although the use of heparin has been suggested to prevent occurrence and propagation of microthrombi in the pulmonary capillaries, there are as yet insufficient data in the literature on which to base firm recommendations.

4. Antimicrobial therapy: Almost invariably during the course of ARDS, the pulmonary secretions become infected, usually with a mixture of gram negative and gram positive organisms. Whether administration of a broad spectrum antibiotic improves the prognosis by elimination of such infection, or worsens it by predisposing the patient to infection with resistant bacterial strains is not clear. Vigorous removal of secretions by catheter suction through the endotracheal tube should be emphasized.

5. Extubation: Because of the many complications and hazards of respirator therapy (infection, reduction of C.O., pneumothorax, pneumomediastinum, difficulty in communication), early extubation is an important event in the recovery of the patient. Extubation is usually a relatively simple procedure in patients with ARF not due to lung disease (e.g. drug overdose). However, in patients with lung disease, proper timing of extubation may be difficult.

Some of the many guidelines which have been forwarded as indications for extubation as as follows: [18]

1. Respiratory rate < 30/minute
2. Vital capacity > 15 ml/kgm body weight; > 10 ml/kgm body weight

3. Tidal volume > 10 ml/kgm
4. Vital capacity > 1.0 1; vital capacity > 15 ml/kgm body weight
5. Resting minute ventilation < 10 1/min
6. Maximal voluntary ventilation $>$ twice minute ventilation
7. Dead space/tidal volume < 0.6
8. Maximum inspiratory mouth pressure > -20 cm H2O
9. A-aD$_{O2}$ < 350 mm Hg while breathing 100% oxygen
10. Minute ventilation less than 180 ml/kgm/min. for paCO2 of 40 mm Hg

The multiplicity of available criteria underscores the fact that no single one is foolproof or without exception. They are designed, directly or indirectly, to assess roughly the ventilatory and oxygen transfer capability and reserve. No matter what criteria are used for discontinuing mechanically assisted ventilation, maintenance of satisfactory arterial blood gases during a trial of spontaneous ventilation is the most important final denominator in the decision making process. This may be achieved via a T-tube attached to the patient's airway or from the reservoir of the Intermittent Mandatory Ventilation (IMV) apparatus. The latter is a technique devised by Downs et al [19] to allow the patient to breathe spontaneously while still being administered a diminishing number of assisted breaths per minute. Although promising, whether or not IMV is a superior method of weaning from mechanically assisted ventilation, awaits satisfactorily large controlled trials of weaning methods.

ARF DUE TO DRUG OVERDOSE

The ARF of drug overdose is a unique syndrome since the target organ is usually normal. The abnormality is a regulatory one in which the respiratory center is severely depressed by drugs such as heroin, morphine, barbiturates, etc. Because the population of users is generally a young one, the great majority of patients who suffer overdose do not have underlying cardiopulmonary disease.

If no complications such as aspiration or pulmonary edema develop, the treatment consists of supporting respiration by mechanical means until respiratory depression clears. The following guidelines are recommended:

1. Intubation by nasotracheal or orotracheal tube is generally required to protect the airway from aspiration and to provide assisted respiration when alveolar ventilation is inadequate (elevated paCO2).

2. Following intubation, gastric lavage may be carried out. The presence of an endotracheal tube in place prevents aspiration during the lavage process.

3. As the respiratory depression lightens and the patient can initiate respirations spontaneously, the respirator may be placed in the assist mode.

4. Indication for extubation is the presence of a sufficient gag reflex and the ability of the patient to maintain a normal $paCO_2$. Under these circumstances, weaning from the respirator is usually not a problem.

ACKNOWLEDGMENTS

We are grateful to Ms. Betty Gillum for preparation of the manuscript and to Ms. Rosemary Phillips for preparation of the figures and tables.

REFERENCES

1. Bates, D.V., et al.: Respiratory Function in Disease. Second Edition, W.B. Saunders Company, Philadelphia, p. 442, 1971.

2. Austrian, R., et al.: Clinical and physiologic features of some types of pulmonary diseases with impairment of alveolar-capillary diffusion. The syndrome of "alveolar-capillary block". Am J Med 11:667-685, 1951.

3. Finley, T.N., et al.: The cause of arterial hypoxemia at rest in patients with "alveolar capillary block syndrome". J Clin Invest 41:618-622, 1962.

4. West, J.B.: Respiratory Physiology - the essentials. The Williams and Wilkins Company, Baltimore, p. 51, 1974.

5. Briscoe, W.A., and DuBois, A.B.: The relationship between airway resistance, airway conductance and lung volume in subjects of different age and body size. J Clin Invest 37:1279, 1958.

6. Bulletin of National Tuberculosis Association. Report of the Task Force on Chronic Bronchitis and Emphysema. May 1967.

7. von Euler, U.S., and Liljestrand, G.: Observations of the pulmonary arterial pressure in the cat. Acta Physiol Scand 12: 301, 1946.

8. Campbell, E.J.M.: Respiratory Failure: The relation between oxygen concentrations of inspired air and arterial blood. Lancet 1:10, 1960.

9. Murray, J.F.: Review of the state of the art in intermittent positive pressure breathing therapy. Am Rev Respir Dis 110 Supple.), 193, 1974.

10. Cherniak, R.M.: Intermittent positive pressure breathing in management of chronic obstructive pulmonary disease: current state of the art. Am Rev Respir Div 110 (Suppl.), 188, 1974.

11. Mitenko, P., and Orilire, R.I.: Rational intravenous doses of aminophylline. N Engl J Med 289, 6000, 1973.

12. Lertzman, M.M., Cherniack, R.M.: Rehabilitation of patients with chronic obstructive pulmonary disease. Am Rev Respir Dis. 114, 1145, 1976.

13. Tager, I., Speizer, F.E.: Role of infection in chronic bronchitis. New Engl J Med 292, 563, 1975.

14. Hopewell, P.C., Murray, J.F.: The Adult Respiratory Distress Syndrome. Annual Review of Medicine 27, 343, 1976.

15. Shoemaker, W.C.: Pattern of pulmonary hemodynamic and functional changes in shock. Crit Care Med 2:200-210, 1974.

16. Wertzberger, J.J., Peltier, L.F.: Fat embolism: the effect of corticosteroids on experimental fat embolism in the rat. Surgery 64:143, 1968.

17. Sahebjami, H., et al.: Influence of corticosteroid on recovery from oxygen toxicity. Am Rev Respir Dis 110, 566, 1974.

18. Sahn, S.A., et al.: Weaning from mechanical ventilation. JAMA 235, 2208, 1976.

19. Downs, J.B., et al.: Intermittent Mandatory Ventilation: An evaluation. Arch Surg 109:519-523, 1974.

B: STATUS ASTHMATICUS
by Michael S. Goldstein, M. D.

Status asthmaticus is a prolonged severe asthmatic attack not relieved by the usual doses of bronchodilators (ephinephrine, isuprel).

Its prompt recognition is essential to reduce the overall mortality
rate of status asthmaticus of 1 - 2% which rises to 10% in those patients requiring intubation and assisted ventilation. [1]

A careful history and physical examination can identify these patients
who are at higher risk and simple laboratory tests will confirm the
clinical findings. The patient is usually an older, non-atopic asthmatic who has been experiencing increasing symptoms over several
days to weeks. Frequently, the patient's recent course has been
marked by repeated emergency room visits or hospitalizations and/
or the need for several courses of steroids. The precipitating factors may be inapparent but infection (URI, bronchitis, pneumonitis),
drug reaction (ASA) or heavy exposure to the sensitizing agents are
prominent historical findings.

It is important to recognize that the evaluation of the patient's status
cannot be solely based on symptoms of dyspnea and perception of
audible wheezing since McFadden's studies revealed considerable
obstruction may be present in the absence of these symptoms. [2]

The usual course of status asthmaticus is quite insidious as is
suggested by the pathology seen in nearly all fatal cases. There
are grossly overinflated lungs which fail to collapse even when removed from the thoracic cavity. Microscopically there is diffuse
mucous plugging of small and moderate-sized airways, and edema
and eosinophilic infiltration of the bronchial walls with hypertrophy
of the mucous glands.

Rebuck outlined the physical findings and laboratory tests which identify those patients with the most serious asthmatic attacks. [3] These
are listed in Table I.

McFadden emphasized that retraction of the sternocleidomastoid
muscles identified those patients with the most severe obstruction. [2]
The pathophysiological mechanisms which explain these serious findings have been reviewed. [4] In summary, there is both severe small
and medium-sized airway obstruction due to mucous plugging, mucosal edema, and bronchospasm. This results in high airway resistance
and overinflation of the lung. The overinflation of the lung seems to
be related to small airway involvement and both are more slowly reversible than the large airway component. [5] This state of overinflation results in marked increase in dead space ventilation and work

of breathing. Overdistention of the lungs causes profound cardio-vascular disturbance which includes hypotension due to low cardiac output, exaggerated pulsus paradoxus, a direct increase in pulmonary vascular resistance and pulmonary hypertension resulting in acute cor pulmonale. The hypoxemia and hypocapnea can easily be explained by the non uniform distribution of ventilation and perfusion with resulting right to left shunting. Late in the course when the process becomes more generalized there is a gradual rise in $PaCO_2$ related to increased dead space ventilation, muscle fatigue and severe obstruction.

TABLE I

PHYSICAL FINDINGS:
1. Disturbances of consciousness
2. Such dyspnea as to make speech very difficult
3. Central cyanosis
4. Gross thoracic overinflation
5. Exaggerated pulsus paradoxsis ($>$ 12 mm)
 	
LABORATORY FINDINGS:
1. PaO_2 less than 60 mm
2. Elevation of $PaCO_2$ (40 mm or greater)
3. Chest x-ray showing gross pulmonary overinflation
4. Pneumothorax or pneumomediastinum
5. $FEV/_1$ sec less than 1L, vital capacity less than 0.5L
    (both failing to increase after inhalation of bronchodilator)
6. EKG evidence of pulmonary hypertension ("p" pulmonae R
    heart strain pattern)

The management of status asthmaticus can be divided into specific and general measures (See Table II). Most of the general measures are concerned with restoring the normal clearance of sputum while the specific measures deal mainly with bronchodilation.

TABLE II

GENERAL MEASURES:
1. Hydration (IV fluids)
2. Humidified oxygen
3. Physical therapy (percussion, postural
    drainage)
4. Antibiotics
5. Avoidance of sedation and antihistamines
 	
SPECIFIC MEASURES:
1. Inhalation of Beta adrenergic receptor
    stimulators (ephenephrine, isuprel, salbutimol)
2. IV aminophylline administration
3. Steroids (1-2 gm) over 24-48 hours
4. Conservative vs. aggressive therapy

Good hydration (3 to 4L/24 hours) seems to be associated with decreasing the viscosity of the sputum and thus aids in expectoration of the viscous sputum and mucous plugs. Nasal catheter oxygen may be adequate to improve oxygenation but it is extremely drying to the respiratory mucosa and a high humidity mask is preferable. When $PaCO_2$ is elevated, controlled O_2 therapy is necessary. Avoidance of any form of sedation such as tranquilizers and barbituates when treating the patient conservatively is essential to maintain good patient cooperation and to avoid further depression of the medullary center. Antihistamines should also be avoided since they tend to cause an increase in the viscosity of the patient's sputum. Because respiratory infection is such a common precipitating cause, antibiotics should be used even though the infection may be difficult to document.

USES OF BETA ADRENERGIC RECEPTOR STIMULATING AGENTS

Twin jet nebulization of sympathomimetic substances should be done routinely on a 3 - 4 hourly basis. These beta-stimulating substances catalyze the conversion of ATP to cyclic AMP by their action on membrane bound adenylate cyclase. This leads to an increase in intracellular cyclic AMP levels. The accumulation of cyclic AMP leads to bronchial smooth muscle relaxation and interference with generation and/or release of the chemical mediators which induce bronchospasm, increased capillary permeability, etc.

B-stimulators should be continued even if the initial response is poor since it is difficult to predict when the Beta receptors will again be fully responsive and to assess clinically all beneficial effects of thse agents (increased ciliary motility, decreased bronchial mucosal edema, small decreases in the lung volume). In the 1960's with the widespread introduction of Beta adrenergic stimulators with gas filled propellants, there was an upsurge in sudden deaths associated with their use (especially those containing isoproterenol). This was thought to be due to the induction of serious arrhythmias by their excessive usage or the delay in seeking medical attention because of the temporary relief they imparted. Obviously the judicious use of these agents implies using these agents in aerosol, in the correct concentrations and not more often than every three hours to avoid a cumulative effect and induction of serious arrhythmias.

A listing of these agents is seen below along with their comparative receptor activity. The best agent should be a purely Beta 2 stimulator and have a long lasting effect (only salbutamol has both of these properties). (See Table III)

TABLE III			
	RECEPTOR	LENGTH OF ACTIVITY (hours)	SIDE EFFECTS
VAPONEPHRINE (Racemic ephinephrine)	B_1, B_2	2	tachy- arrhythmias
BRONKOSOL (isoetharine)	B_1, B_2	2	"
ISOPROTERENOL	B_1, B_2	2	"
TERBUTALINE	B_1, B_2	2 - 4	"
SALBUTAMOL	B_2	2 - 4	tremors

There is little evidence that there is any advantage to the use of IPPB machines instead of twin jet nebulizers for administering these substances. This evidence suggest patients with the very lowest $FEV/1$ sec may not be able to inhale the medications without the aid of the positive pressure.[6] Much more serious is the recent observation of deterioration and death associated with the use of IPPB.[7] Several of these cases developed subcutaneous emphysema, hypercapnea and pneumothorax or pneumomediastinum. The positive pressure respirator may be forcing air into a limited, still patent part of the bronchial tree (where the alveoli are already at their maximum FRC). This results in disruption of the alveolar walls and the development of interstitial emphysema leading to pneumomediastinum and pneumothorax.

USE OF IV AMINOPHYLLINE

Aminophylline is a salt of theophylline and ethylenediamine. Its therapeutic effectiveness is dependent on the amount of anhydrous theophylline equivalent that it contains. Theophylline inhibits the enzyme phosphodiesterase in its conversion of cyclic 3'5' AMP to 5' AMP and, therefore, results in the accumulation of cyclic AMP. Since it works by a different biochemical pathway then B adrenergic stimulating agents, it is usually effective even when the Beta receptors seem refractory to stimulation.

Recent clinical pharmacological studies have revealed certain important principles for the effective use of aminophylline (See Table IV). The majority of serious side effects are avoidable by adhering to the principles outlined in Table III and are closely related to the plasma levels of the drugs. (See Table V)

TABLE IV

PRINCIPLES FOR THE USE OF INTRAVENOUS AMINOPHYLLINE

1. The decrease in airway obstruction is proportional to the blood levels of theophylline.[8]

2. These blood levels can be achieved by giving a loading dose of 5mgm/Kgm and then 1mgm/Kgm/hr thereafter (in patients whose metabolism of aminophylline is normal).

3. That statement #2 can not be totally relied upon and that plasma theophylline levels must be obtained in all patients receiving significant amounts of IV aminophylline in status. This is because a) there is a large variation in the metabolism of aminophylline in normal individuals, b) aminophylline is primarily metabolized in the liver; therefore, patients with congestive heart failure (ASHD or cor pulmonale) must receive approximately 2/3 of the calculated dose for maintenance and patients in serious liver dysfunction should probably receive only 1/2 the calculated maintenance dose and both groups followed by the theophylline plasma levels.[9,10]

4. The dangerous side effects of aminophylline can largely be avoided by keeping within the therapeutic range 10 to 20 mgm/L of plasma theophylline. (See Table V)

TABLE V
SIDE EFFECTS OF AMINOPHYLLINE [8]

PLASMA CONCENTRATION	THEOPHYLLINE	
mgm/1 liter	Efficacy	Toxicity
5 - 10	minimal	
10 - 20	optimal	Minor GI Nervousness
20 - 40		Major GI Arrhythmias
40 - 60		Seizures

THE USE OF STEROIDS

Recently McFadden et al concluded in a short term clinical study that steroids administered acutely in asthmatic attack had no demonstrable effect given along with frequent inhalation and isoproterenol compared to isoproterenol alone.[11] There are two major objections to this study: 1) this study did not have an experimental group treated with steroids alone and 2) it contradicts a large body of literature which indicates important therapeutic benefits of steroids in status asthmaticus. [12,13]

One of the biochemical effects of steroids may be the enhancement of cell sensitivity to catecholamines; others include the stabilization of lysosomal membranes, interference with the Type III asthmatic reaction (late onset, complement binding reaction). The recommended dosages vary between 1 to 2 gm of hydrocortisone/day starting with an initial dosage of 4 mgm/Kgm followed by 3 mgm/Kgm/24 to 48 hours. The short term use of these high dosages has not been associated with serious side effects and its rationale is: 1) to cover the small group of steroid resistant asthmatics with persistent eosinophilia,[14] 2) to offer any nonspecific anti-inflammatory steroid effect, 3) to cover long term steroid treated patients who are relatively adrenal insufficient.

CONSERVATIVE VS. AGGRESSIVE THERAPY

Initially all patients with status asthmaticus, unless they are moribund or have had a respiratory arrest, deserve a trial of conservative therapy in an intensive care unit with the measures outlined above. If, however, the patient's status further deteriorates as evidenced by rising $PaCO_2$ (> 5 mm) or profound unrelenting hypoxemia or decreasing awareness, than prompt intubation and artificial ventilation should be initiated. There are specifal difficulties encountered when patients in status asthmaticus are placed on respirators which include: 1) the very high inspiratory pressures often required due to high airway resistance and maldistribution of ventilation, the patient breathing out of phase with the respirator. This necessitates the use of a volume limited respirator, at times heavy sedation (IV morphine or valium) and curare-like agents in order to 1) adequately ventilate the patients and 2) minimize the significant incidence of barotrauma (pneumothorax, pneumomediastinum). Other procedures which have been attempted with variable results are the use of therapeutic bronchoscopy and bronchial lavage in order to remove the tenacious mucous plugs. Since the majority of the plugs are in the smaller, peripheral airways, doing bronchoscopy with its risk of producing greater transient hypoxemia must be weighed against its therapeutic advantages. Tracheostomy is not indicated since most patients can be extubated in 24 to 48 hours.

REFERENCES

1. Sheehy, A.F., et al.: Treatment of Status Asthmaticus. Arch Int Med 130:37-42, 1972.

2. McFadden, E.R., et al.: Acute Bronchial Asthma. N Eng J Med 288 (5):221-225, 1973.

3. Rebuck, A.S., Read, J.: Assessment and Management of Severe Asthma. Am J Med 51:788-798, 1971.

4. William, M.H., Jr.: Pathophysiology and Treatment of Severe Asthma. N Y State J of Med 73 (20):244-251, 1973.

5. McFadden, E.R., Lyons, H.A.: Airway Resistance and Uneven Ventilation in Bronchial Asthma. J Appl Physiol (4):365-370, 1968.

6. Choo-Kang, Y.F., Grant, I.W.: Comparison of Two Methods of Administering Bronchodilator Aerosol to Asthmatic Patients. Br Med J 2(5963):119-120, 1975.

7. Karetzky, M.S.: Asthma Mortality: An Analysis of the Years Experience, Review of the Literature and Assessment of Current Modes of Therapy. Medicine 54:471-484, 1975.

8. Piafsky, K.M., O'Gilvie, R.I.: Dosage of Theophylline in Bronchial Asthma. N Eng J Med 292 (23):1218-1222, 1975.

9. Jacobs, M.H., et al.: Clinical Experience with Theophylline Relationships Between Dosage, Serum Concentration and Toxicity. JAMA 235 (18):1983-1986, 1976.

10. Zwillich, C., et al.: Theophylline-Induced Seizures in Adults Correlation with Serum Concentration. Ann Int Med 82:784-787, 1975.

11. McFadden, E.R., et al.: A Controlled Study of the Effects of Single Doses of Hydrocortisone on the Resolution of Acute Attacks of Asthma. Am J Med 60:52-59, 1976.

12. Editorial: Cortico Steroids in Acute Severe Asthma. Lancet 2 (7926):166-167, 1975.

13. Collins, J.V., et al.: The Use of Corticosteroids in the Treatment of Acute Asthma. Q J Med 44 (174): 259-273, 1975.

14. Horn, B.R.: Total Eosinophil Counts in the Management of Bronchial Asthma. N Eng J Med 292 (22):1152-1155, 1975.

C: PULMONARY EMBOLI

by Arthur A. Sasahara, M.D.,
G.V.R.K. Sharma, M.D.,
Donald E. Tow, M.D.,
Kevin M. McIntyre, M.D.,
and Alfred F. Parisi, M.D.

Pulmonary thromboembolism (PE) is a very common disease occurring most often as a complication in hospitalized patients. It is said to occur with equal frequency in medical and surgical patients, but our impression is that it occurs with greater frequency in older medical patients. Although the precise incidence of pulmonary embolism is not known, a two-year Medical-Surgical study in our hospital revealed an incidence of 23/1000 in-patients.[1] Based on this and other studies, it seems reasonable to expect non-fatal pulmonary embolism to occur in 20/1000 in-patients and fatal pulmonary embolism to occur in 5/1000 in-patients.[2] Country-wide, fatal PE can be expected in about 142,000 patients and non-fatal PE in about 568,000 patients (Table 1). The modern paradox is that as advances are made in medical practice, the frequency of PE is increasing.

TABLE 1

MORBIDITY AND MORTALITY: D.V.T. AND PULMONARY THROMBOEMBOLISM

PREVALENCE IN U.S.A. HOSPITALS (ICD 1966)

D.V.T.	182,000 (0.64%)
P.E.D.	106,000 (0.38%)

PREVALENCE BASED ON:

FATAL P.E.	4-5/1000 INPATIENTS
NON-FATAL P.E.	20/1000 INPATIENTS

TOTAL P.E. IN U.S.A.

FATAL P.E.	142,000
NON-FATAL P.E.	568,000

The mortality of untreated PE is high, ranging from 20-35%, but once recognized and treated, it becomes a disease with a low mortality. In the National Heart and Lung Institute (NHLI) Urokinase Pulmonary Embolism Trial (UPET), the overall two week mortality was 8.3%.[3]

Despite great advances in diagnostic procedures, the major problem in PE today is underdiagnosis. In addition, PE is also overdiagnosed, particularly in institutions where housestaff serve as primary physicians. This paradox is explained by the fact that (1) the diagnosis is difficult to make on clinical grounds; (2) there are no specific, dignostic laboratory tests and (3) the disease, on the whole, is self-limited and if unrecognized and no recurrence occurs, the patient will recover and be discharged with the wrong diagnosis.

We will examine in detail, the various facets of the clinical, diagnostic and therapeutic status of pulmonary thromboembolism.

CLINICAL PICTURE

SYMPTOMS: [3,4] When pulmonary embolism (PE) occurs, a number of symptoms may occur (Table 2) which are relatively non-specific:

1. dyspnea:
   a) most common; occurring in 80-100% of patients.
   b) characteristically, the respiratory distress complained of by the patient is out of proportion to the degree and extent of objective abnormal findings.

2. cough:
   a) occurs in 40 - 60% of patients
   b) usually non-productive, unless patient has underlying chronic obstructive pulmonary disease.

3. apprehension:
   a) occurs in 50 - 60% of patients
   b) more frequently in massive PE
   c) patients may seem anxious in smaller or submassive PE

In others, additional symptoms, more related to pulmonary infarction, may occur which raises the level of awareness of PE.

4. pleural pain:
   a) occurs in 50 - 70% of patients
   b) may or may not be associated with hemoptysis
   c) associated more often with submassive PE (less than 40% occlusion of the total pulmonary vascular space) than with massive PE.

5. hemoptysis:
   a) occurs in 30 - 35% of patients
   b) characteristically blood-streaked, in contrast to mitral stenosis in which blood alone is expectorated
   c) infrequently results in significant blood loss, in contrast to mitral stenosis.

6. syncope:
   a) occurs in 15% of patients
   b) difficult clinical differential diagnosis from acute massive myocardial infarction
   c) distention of the neck veins is very helpful if visible. In acute massive PE, the neck veins are distended; in acute myocardial infarction the veins may not be distended.

TABLE 2

UPET: PRESENTING SYMPTOMS

| | ALL | PREVALENCE % | |
		MASSIVE	SUBMASSIVE
DYSPNEA	81	79	83
PLEURAL PAIN	72	62	84*
APPREHENSION	59	61	56
COUGH	54	50	60
HEMOPTYSIS	34	27	44
SWEATS	26	27	24
SYNCOPE	14	22*	4

Some of these symptoms are related to the size of the embolic occlusion and some are not. Pleural pain is more often a symptom of submassive PE while syncope is associated far more often with massive PE. The other symptoms are not related to the massivity of the embolic process and can be considered simply as part of the disease complex.

SIGNS: [3,4] The signs which result from the embolic process are similarly non-specific in the majority of patients. (Table 3)

1. tachypnea: (respiratory rate greater than 20/min):
   a) occurs in 80 - 90% of patients
   b) characterized as "fast and shallow"

2. tachycardia (heart rate greater than 100/min):
   a) occurs in 40 - 50% of patients
   b) generally, the larger the emboli, the greater the tachycardia, although no statistical significance has been found in this relationship from the NHLI Urokinase Pulmonary Embolism Trial.

3. rales:
   a) occurs in 50 - 60% of patients
   b) occurs more frequently in patients with underlying cardiopulmonary disease, as a manifestation of congestive failure.

4. fever:
   a) occurs in 40 - 50% of patients
   b) generally of modest elevation, to 101 - 102 degrees, F., rarely to 103.
   c) shape of fever curve tends to be flat, in contrast to "spiking" shape caused by systemic infections.

5. sweating:
   a) occurs in 30 - 50% of patients
   b) results from the sympathetic discharge occurring in patients with anxiety and cardiopulmonary distress.

6. thrombophlebitis:
   a) occurs in 30 - 35% of patients

Several of the findings noted on physical examination in the acute period of pulmonary embolism are related to the size of the embolic process. These are related to the cardiopulmonary responses to embolic occlusion.

7. loud pulmonary closure sound (S_2P):
   a) occurs in 50 - 60% of patients
   b) often difficult to assess in patients with respiratory distress
   c) if "P_2" (2nd left sternal border) is louder than "A_2" (2nd right sternal border), it can be assumed that pulmonary closure is accentuated
   d) associated much more in patients with massive PE, as a manifestation of the greater pulmonary hypertension which results from massive PE.

8. S_3 and S_4 gallop heart sounds:
   a) occurs in 30 - 35% of patients
   b) probably related to right ventricular hemodynamics which can be inferred if these gallop sounds vary with respiration. (RV gallop)
   c) associated much more frequently in patients with massive PE which disturbs RV function more than does submassive PE

9. cyanosis:
   a) occurs in 15 - 20% of patients
   b) associated much more frequently with massive embolism than with submassive
   c) simply represents a greater degree of hypoxemia which results from a large embolic occlusion.

TABLE 3

UPET: PRESENTING SIGNS

		PREVALENCE %	
	ALL	MASSIVE	SUBMASSIVE
RALES	53	50	57
↑ P_2	53	60*	44
PHLEBITIS	33	42	21
S_3, S_4	34	47*	17
SWEATING	34	41	24
CYANOSIS	18	28*	6
↑ RESP (>16)	87		
↑ PULSE (>100)	44		
FEVER (≥ 37.8)	42		

Hence, the "typical" picture of patients with acute PE is relatively non-specific in nature and could be part of any cardiopulmonary distress syndrome. The "classic" picture of hemoptysis, pleural pain and thrombophlebitis does not occur very often and if the physician requires these findings before making the diagnosis, a large majority of patients with pulmonary embolism will be undiagnosed.

DIAGNOSTIC STUDIES

LABORATORY STUDIES: Although a number of abnormalities may occur, the laboratory tests, similar to the clinical picture, are essentially non-specific. The once promising serum LDH and GOT and bilirubin application to suspected patients with PE has not proved to be helpful.[5] In our own experience, only 20% of patients with proven PE (by angiography) had the triad of elevated LDH and bilirubin, in the presence of a normal GOT. In addition, 20 % of these patients had no alterations of these tests on serial determination. When the bilirubin was elevated, there was good correlation with the presence of right heart failure, suggesting that the source of elevation was related to liver congestion. The liver is very sensitive to hypoxemia which is very common in acute PE. Our belief is that these tests do not have sufficient sensitivity or specificity to play any role in the diagnostic evaluation for PE.

CHEST X-RAY: The chest x-ray continues to be a standard screening test for all patients with cardiopulmonary disorders. From the UPET study, a useful analysis of the plain film findings was recently made.[3] The two most common changes noted were the presence of a consolidation and the elevation of a hemi-diaphragm (41%). The consolidation represents a pulmonary infarct although the majority of these infiltrates were originally considered to represent pneumonia. The elevated hemi-diaphragm on the involved side represents decreased lung volume which results from the frequent atelectasis occurring in PE. Hence, the combination of a pulmonary infiltrate or consolidation and an elevated hemi-diaphragm on the affected side should suggest pulmonary infarction rather than pneumonia. (Table 4)

TABLE 4

UPET: FREQUENCY OF CXR ABNORMALITIES

	% PATIENTS
CONSOLIDATION	41
HIGH DIAPHRAGM	41
PLEURAL EFFUSION	28
PLUMP PUL. ARTERIES	23
ATELECTASIS	20
LV ↑	16
FOCAL OLIGEMIA	15
RV ↑	5

ELECTROCARDIOGRAM: Like the plain chest film, a number of abnormalities on the electrocardiogram have been recorded in patients with acute PE.[6,7] Some of the more common changes are shown in Table 5.

The most common arrhythmias were ectopic beats, both atrial and ventricular, while the most common sustained arrhythmia was paroxysmal atrial fibrillation. Although paroxysmal atrial flutter may occur in acute PE, its frequency is not significant.

TABLE 5

UPET: FREQUENCY OF ECG ABNORMALITIES

	%	PATIENTS
RHYTHM DISTURBANCES		11
APB	3	
VPB	9	
A. FIB	3	
P PULMONALE		4
QRS ABNORMALITIES		65
RAD	5	
LAD	12	
IRBBB	5	
RBBB	11	
S1-Q3-T3	11	
ST-SEGMENT		44
T-WAVE ↓		40

Most commonly, QRS changes were noted, as were ST-T abnormalities. However, most of these changes were considered nonspecific. Only 11% of patients showed the pattern of acute cor pulmonale (S_1-Q_3-T_3 pattern), the only recognizable pattern specific for massive pulmonary embolism.

Our belief is that the ECG is quite sensitive in responding to acute PE, but not very specific. However, it is most useful in excluding acute myocardial infarction which generally is considered in the differential diagnosis. Hence, it remains a valuable ancillary study to be performed in all patients with suspected PE.

ARTERIAL OXYGEN TENSION: One of the most popular tests used in the evaluation of patients with suspected PE is the measurement of arterial oxygen tension.[8] (Fig. 13.3). Its usefulness is derived from the fact that virtually all patients with pulmonary embolism develop some degree of hypoxemia. In fact, there is a significant inverse relationship between the size of the embolic occlusion and the level of arterial oxygen tension.[9] In the UPET study,[3] there was a broad range of oxygen tensions from the low 30's to the mid-90's, with an average oxygen tension of 62 mm Hg, a significant impairment of oxygen transport. (Fig. 13.3). Approximately 12% of patients with proven PE had a level above 80 mm Hg. Few had values in the 90 range. Hence, it can be stated that in patients with suspected PE, if the arterial oxygen tension is 90 or more, the likelihood of PE is not very great. In fact, fewer than 10% of patients with PE have tensions 90 or more.

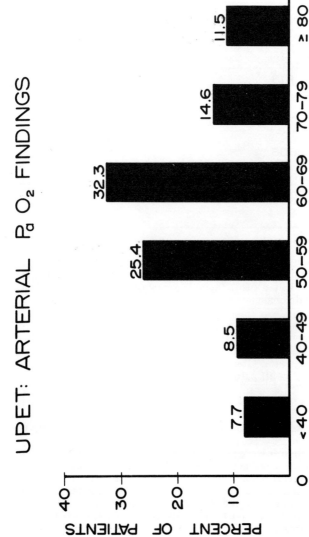

FIG. 13.3: Arterial oxygen tension values in patients with pulmonary embolism from the Urokinase Pulmonary Trial (UPET). Average pO2: 62 mm Hg. Note that 11.5% of patients had pO2 values more than 80 mm Hg.

In order to use the oxygen tension determination in the diagnostic evaluation, it should be noted that the confidence one can place on this test is related directly to the accuracy with which the clinical laboratory performs the test. It is known that the oxygen electrode in commercially available blood gas instruments is quite unstable, requiring frequent recalibration with standard gas. Without recalibration, the variability of the oxygen tension measurement may be as high as $\pm$ 10 mm Hg. Therefore, before one can use this test safely and reliably, the reproducibility and reliability of the determination in the clinical laboratory must be known.

PERFUSION LUNG SCAN: Following the completion of the studies previously discussed, the patient with suspected PE should have perfusion lung scanning to help confirm the clinical impression. If PE has occurred, the multiple-view perfusion scan should show some abnormalities. To date, false negative scans have not been a problem.[10] "False positive" scans have been a major problem in the past, until it was realized that the interpretations expected as "positive or negative" for pulmonary embolism were beyond that available from the scan. Since the perfusion scan is a "map" of the distribution of regional pulmonary blood flow, the only reasonable interpretation would be that confined to the presence or absence and distribution of pulmonary blood flow. Hence, a lung scan should be interpreted as normal or abnormal. If abnormal, the defects should be described regarding extent and shape of the lesions. From extensive experience, scan defects can now be characterized as having low, medium or high probability of having been caused by pulmonary embolism.[11]

1. High Probability Scan:
   a) multiple lesions, one lung or both
   b) occur as concave defects on the lateral edge of lung or wedge-shaped or segmental defects conforming to the vascular pattern.

2. Medium-Low Probability Scan:
   a) may be single or multiple...generally corresponds with some other abnormality on the plain chest film
   b) lesions not clearly identifiable as segmental or vascular in configuration. Tends more to be round or long and crosses lung segments; most common seen in patients with obstructive lung disease.
   c) it should be noted that patients with chronic obstructive pulmonary disease also have segmental or vascular lesions. The difference in pulmonary embolism is that these characteristic lesions occur much more frequently.

Despite these helpful refinements in lung scanning, there are still areas in which the perfusion scan is less helpful, as in patients with underlying heart and lung disease. In these patients, the presence

of symptoms and signs suggesting PE may require pulmonary angiography for confirmation. However, in young patients without underlying heart or lung disease, a compatible history and physical examination, with a high probability perfusion lung scan, may be all
that is required before initiating anticoagulant therapy.

SELECTIVE PULMONARY ANGIOGRAPHY: Since selective catheter
pulmonary angiography was popularized and used routinely in patients with suspected pulmonary embolism in 1964,[12] it has remained
the standard in diagnosing PE during life. Although a number of
findings have been reported, an angiogram can be said to confirm
PE when the following are present.[13,14]

1. an intravascular filling defect
2. an arterial vessel cutoff
3. other findings which have been described in PE, but are not
   diagnostic in themselves, include:
   a) focal flow retardation (asymmetry of flow)
   b) pruning of vessels
   c) non-filling of vessels

Pulmonary angiography is most helpful in patients with underlying
heart and lung disease who are suspected of having PE. These patients may present with non-specific symptoms and signs and may
have an abnormal scan with medium to low probability lesions. A
ventilation scan may or may not be helpful. The arterial oxygen
tension is lowered, but could be the result of the underlying disease
or the pulmonary embolism or both. In such a clinical dilemma, an
angiogram may be definitive.

Selective pulmonary angiography may also be very useful in patients
without prior heart and lung disease. Pressures in the right side of
the heart and the pulmonary circulation can be measured, in addition
to demonstrating the emboli. Since there is a relationship between
size of the embolic occlusion and the severity of the hemodynamic
responses to PE, measurement of pressures yield valuable diagnostic and therapeutic information.

Since many institutions do not have adequate angiographic facilities
or a trained team to perform studies of good quality with safety,
other, less invasive means are now being investigated as an aid to
diagnosis.

ELECTRICAL IMPEDANCE PLETHYSMOGRAPHY (IPG): Some
years ago, Sevitt and Gallagher noted a strong correlation between
massive pulmonary embolism and deep vein thrombosis at the
autopsy table.[15] Recently, Kakkar and his group, utilizing the
radioactive fibrinogen test, noted the same relationship between
deep vein thrombosis and pulmonary embolism.[16] We chose to
investigate the usefulness of electrical impedance plethysmography

in detecting deep vein thrombosis in patients with pulmonary embolism, with the hope that if a similar strong relationship could be demonstrated, the IPG might be used diagnostically in patients with suspected PE. Since IPG detects deep vein involvement and can be performed simply and rapidly, it appeared to be a very promising diagnostic aid to pulmonary embolism.[17]

In our study of patients with angiographically confirmed pulmonary embolism, 95% had an abnormal IPG indicative of deep vein thrombosis.[18] The correlation between abnormal IPG findings indicative of deep vein thrombosis and contrast ascending venography has been in the range of 90-93%. None of these patients had history or evidence of major pelvic disease, pelvic surgery or pelvic manipulation. In addition, analysis of our data showed that in patients suspected of having PE, if the IPG showed abnormalities indicative of deep vein thrombosis, pulmonary angiography would be positive in 90% of these patients. On the other hand, if the IPG were normal, indicating a patent deep venous system, angiography would be negative in 90% of the patients.[18]

The results of these studies are very promising for they make the same strong relationship between pulmonary embolism and deep vein thrombosis. Its usefulness is shown in Figure 13.4 which outlines one approach to diagnosis:

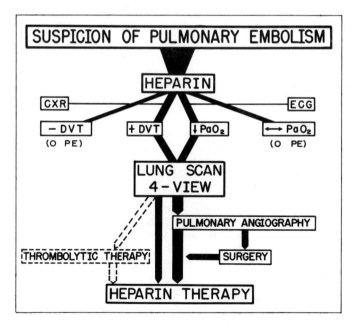

FIG. 13.4: Diagnostic schema explained in test.

1. suspicion of PE should be broadened if underdiagnosis is to be corrected.

2. a heparin "cover" of 7500 - 10,000 units should be administered while the diagnostic studies are being obtained. Immediate heparinization should decrease the probability of recurrences in patients with PE.

3. the chest x-ray and ECG should be obtained in all suspected patients.

4. if a well-performed arterial oxygen tension is 90 mm Hg or more, the likelihood of PE is remote. If the paO2 is less than 90, lung scanning should be performed.

5. if the IPG assessment of the leg veins is normal, the likelihood of PE is remote. The diagnostic workup may be terminated here if scanning is not readily available. (Correct in about 90% of patients). If the IPG is abnormal, perfusion lung scanning should be performed.

6. lung scanning assessment of the perfusion pattern is central in this diagnostic schema.
   a) if the perfusion scan shows multiple, high probability lesions, and the patient has no prior heart or lung disease, heparin treatment may be started immediately without angiography.
   b) if the perfusion scan shows low to medium probability lesions, pulmonary angiography is recommended.

7. pulmonary angiography is recommended especially when some form of surgical intervention is contemplated, e.g., inferior vena cava interruption or pulmonary embolectomy. (It is axiomatic that such procedures entail unnecessary risks without benefit in the absence of PE).
   a) experience dictates that no pulmonary embolectomy be performed without prior pulmonary angiography to confirm PE and identify the magnitude and location of the lesions.
   b) experience also dictates that some objective means to assess the deep veins be performed prior to caval interruption.

Further experience with the non-invasive techniques such as the IPG or the ultrasound Doppler method may provide further data which may minimize the need for pulmonary angiography.

TREATMENT

MEDICAL THERAPY: There is little disagreement now that the primary treatment of acute pulmonary embolism is medical, whether standard anticoagulant or thrombolytic therapy is employed. Currently, the cornerstone of medical therapy is heparin.

Heparin may be administered by a number of routes, as it has been for many years. However, recent clinical data indicate that the continuous, intravenous method may be the most effective.

1. Subcutaneous route:
   a) administered every 4 - 6 hours
   b) absorption not always predictable, making control difficult
   c) local bleeding may occur if small vessel nicked

2. Intramuscular route:
   a) unsafe method resulting frequently in muscle hematoma. Not recommended.

3. Intravenous route:
   a) predictable absorption - control easier
   b) intermittent injections:
      1) usually every 4 - 6 hours
      2) dose generally 5000 - 7500 units every 4 hours or 7500 - 10,000 units every 6 hours
      3) monitor dose by obtaining clotting test just prior to next dose. Maintain clotting test 2 - $2\frac{1}{2}$ times control level. If Lee-White clotting time: 20 - 30 minutes; if partial thromboplastin time; 60 - 80 seconds
   c) continuous pump infusion
      1) loading dose of 3000 - 5000 units, depending upon size.
      2) start pump infusion to delivery 1000 units/hour.
      3) wait several hours for stabilization and then obtain clotting test.
      4) depending upon level of clotting achieved, make pump adjustments and wait several hours for stabilization before obtaining another clotting test. Once the proper dosage established, check test daily.
      5) majority of patients require daily maintenance dosage between 1000 - 1800 units/hour.

Recent information suggests that the continuous infusion of heparin by pump is the safest method to administer the drug. Salzman and his co-workers showed a 1% incidence of major bleeding in patients receiving heparin by pump infusion, monitored by the partial thromboplastin time.[19] In contrast, when patients received heparin by the intermittent intravenous route, whether monitored or not by clotting tests, the incidence of bleeding was 8 - 10 times greater. Our experience, as well as others, confirms these findings.

In the UPET study, observations were made of the relationship between clotting times and bleeding in patients who were receiving a continuous infusion of heparin. When the clotting times were above 60 minutes (control = 10 minutes), 20% of these patients bled, while 5% of the patients whose clotting time were between 30 - 60 minutes bled. No patient whose clotting times were within the therapeutic range of 30 minutes or less bled.[3] If one applies these observations to the 6-hour intermittent method as shown in Figure 13.5, it can be demonstrated that the first several hours after a bolus of heparin (about 10,000 units), the blood is rendered incoagulable or out of "therapeutic range" and that the patient is at "high risk" of bleeding. On a 24 hour basis, the patient is at "high risk" for about 12 hours. This demonstration of the kinetics of heparin therapy may account for the irreducible number of patients who bleed on intermittent, intravenous heparin administration. (Table 6)

TABLE 6

BLEEDING COMPLICATIONS (SALZMAN et al. NEJM 292: 1046-1050, 1975)			
	Q4-PTT	Q4-BW	PUMP
MAJOR BLEED	6(8%)	7(10%)	1(1%)
MINOR BLEED	16(22%)	11(16%)	18(26%)
HEPARIN DOSE			
ALL PATIENTS	31,740	35,560	24,480
MAJOR BLEED	32,200	43,280	22,400
MINOR BLEED	31,690	34,730	24,510

Therefore, it appears that the most effective and safe method of heparin administration is by continuous pump infusion, with monitoring of clotting tests to ensure effective anticoagulation.

Duration of Heparin Therapy: The duration of heparin therapy depends upon subsidence of the acute process, which is best reflected by clinical improvement. However, it has been shown that 7 - 10 days are required for the thrombi in the deep veins to become firmly adherent to the vein wall (preventing reembolization) or to undergo lysis.[20] For the same reasons, we believe it important that these patients be hospitalized and kept at bedrest until the risk of recurrence becomes less. Several days prior to anticipated ambulation on the 7th to 10th day, heparin doses may be reduced and orally administered anticoagulant therapy begun. Equally acceptable in the uncomplicated patient is the institution of orally administered drugs simultaneously with heparin, providing a longer time in which to achieve the desired therapeutic range for the oral drugs.

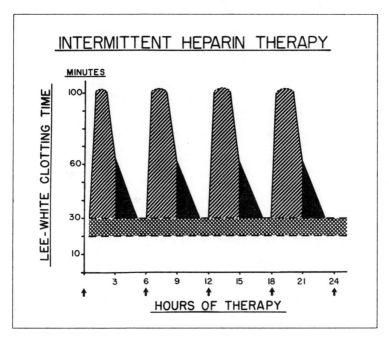

FIG. 13.5: Kinetics of heparin therapy when administered intravenously or an intermittent basis every 6 hours. See text.

ORAL ANTICOAGULATION: As mentioned previously, there are
several methods to administer oral anticoagulants, depending upon
the clinical state of the patient. In the patient who is very ill from
the disease, with complicating factors such as severe heart failure,
we believe that heparin alone simplifies one aspect of a very complex therapeutic problem. Heparin should be maintained as long as
the patient is at bedrest. Oral drugs may be started at a subsequent
time when the patient improves and ambulation can be projected.

The oral drugs are maintained for such periods of time that the patient is at high risk of re-thrombosing and re-embolizing. When
the risk diminishes, the drugs may be terminated. How does one
determine when the "high risk" period is over? We believe that the
high risk period is over when the deep vein thrombosis clears and
emboli in the lungs have lysed or have stabilized. In practice, patients return to our clinic on a monthly basis. During each visit,
an IPG and a perfusion lung scan are performed. When the IPG converts to normal, indicating patency of the deep venous system, and
the lung scan normalizes or stabilizes on two successive monthly
visits, we discontinue oral anticoagulants. This assumes that the
patient has returned to full activity. Our experience has been that the
IPG converts to normal and the scan normalizes or stabilizes in the
majority of patients within 2 - 4 months following hospital discharge.

If the IPG persists in its abnormality, contrast venography is recommended to assess the anatomic problem. If extensive disease is present in the venous system, long-term anticoagulation may be considered if the patient is reliable.

SURGICAL THERAPY: With the exception of pulmonary embolectomy, the surgical techniques employed in pulmonary embolism are for the purpose of preventing recurrent episodes. Since more than 90% of thromboemboli originate in the lower extremities, surgical maneuvers have been directed toward interruption of the venous system. The inferior vena cava is the most effective site for interruption. The indications for surgical interruption (Table 7) are as follows:

1. contraindication to anticoagulation
2. recurrence during adequate intravenous heparin therapy
3. recurrent PE during adequate chronic anticoagulation
4. as part of the package of pulmonary embolectomy

Other indications which were recommended in the past and which are now debated include:

5. septic pelvic thrombophlebitis with pulmonary emboli
6. near-fatal pulmonary emboli

TABLE 7

INDICATIONS FOR INFERIOR VENA CAVA PROCEDURES
1. CONTRAINDICATIONS TO ANTICOAGULATION
2. RECURRENCE DURING *ADEQUATE* ANTICOAGULATION
3. SEPTIC PELVIC THROMBOPHLEBITIS WITH EMBOLI
4. RECURRENT PULMONARY EMBOLI
5. NEAR-FATAL PULMONARY EMBOLI
6. PULMONARY EMBOLECTOMY

Effective antimicrobial therapy now appears to make possible a total medical approach to the problem of septic thrombophlebitis with emboli which occurs most commonly in patients who suffer septic abortion. In patients with massive, near-fatal emboli, effective heparin therapy with vigorous medical cardiopulmonary support has resulted in a mortality rate of about 18%, which is less than many reported series of pulmonary embolectomy. The anticipated fatal recurrences while on heparin therapy in these patients have been rare.

The majority of patients requiring surgical venous interruption are those in whom some contraindication to anticoagulation exists. The recognition and proof of recurrence during the acute phase of PE is a difficult clinical problem which cannot be resolved without the aid of perfusion lung scanning or pulmonary angiography.[3] Only by employing these tests, particularly angiography, can the distinction between recurrent PE and fragmentation and distal migration of the original clot be made with any assurance. The importance of this distinction lies in the therapy. If true recurrence occurs, the patient may be considered a heparin failure and caval interruption performed. The process of fragmentation and distal migration of the original clot simply requires continuation of the heparinization.

Recurrence During Oral Anticoagulation: If recurrence develops during well-controlled oral anticoagulation during the recovery period or during chronic anticoagulation at home, and this is the first recurrence, reanticoagulation with heparin is recommended. Subsequently, several courses are available, depending upon a number of factors:
1. cardiopulmonary status of the patient
2. magnitude of re-embolization
3. assessment of the deep venous system
4. nature of the predisposing event

If the underlying cardiopulmonary status is stable and satisfactory:
1. if the re-embolic episode is submassive
2. if the deep veins are minimally abnormal
3. if the predisposing event to the re-embolic episode is temporary (e.g., leg fracture)
4. Recommendation: treat again with intravenous heparin, following the same time course sequence as in the original episode.

If the underlying cardiopulmonary status is unstable with the recurrence:
1. if the re-embolic episode is massive
2. if the deep veins are grossly abnormal
3. if the predisposing event is chronic, e.g., chronic heart failure
4. Recommendation: caval interruption.

Although interrupting the cava will prevent further embolization in the acute period of PE, recurrences may occur at a subsequent time. In addition, the morbidity and mortality of such procedures under general anesthesia have kept their use limited to the stated indications. Recently, the introduction of the inferior vena cava umbrella filter which can be positioned under fluoroscopy with local anesthesia has minimized the hazards of cava interruption[21] (Figure 13.6). To date, over 10,000 filters have been implanted with a complication rate of approximately 2-3% and a recurrence rate also of approximately 2-3%.

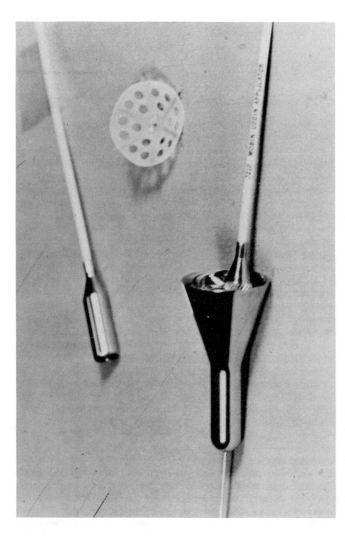

FIG. 13.6: Inferior vena cava umbrella filter (Mobin-Uddin filter). Inserting catheter on top; umbrella filter with perforations (middle) and (below) the retracting cone to close umbrella and attach catheter.

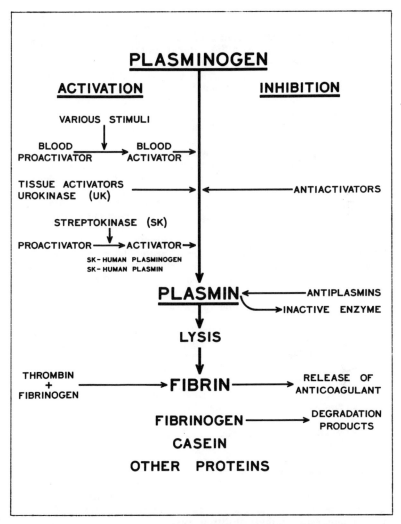

FIG. 13.7: Schema of mechanism of thrombolytic action. Streptokinase and urokinase are activators which maximally
activate the natural fibrinolytic mechanism.

PULMONARY EMBOLECTOMY: Pulmonary embolectomy, the oldest and most heroic of surgical procedures designed to treat pulmonary embolism is being performed in fewer patients with massive pulmonary embolism.[22] The reasons for this decrease are probably related to a better understanding of the pathophysiology of PE, as well as more information on the natural history of the disease. Currently, the indications for embolectomy are:

1. massive PE with shock, not corrected and stabilized by vigorous medical means
   a) poor urine production
   b) systolic pressure less than 90
   c) cold, clammy skin
2. confirmed by pulmonary angiography
3. would probably die without mechanical removal of emboli
4. availability of a trained surgical team experienced in open-heart surgery. The mortality of pulmonary embolectomy ranges between 40 - 100% in different series. The procedure, however, may be life-saving in the infrequent but appropriate clinical situation.

THROMBOLYTIC THERAPY: Although thrombolytic agents have had extensive clinical use, it was not until the National Heart and Lung Institute sponsored the Urokinase Pulmonary Embolism Trial (UPET), that large series of patients were studied in a randomized, modified double-blind trial to determine comparative drug efficacy (Fig. 13.7).

In Phase I, a trial was carried out to compare therapeutic efficacy between heparin and urokinase. This was an acute phase study in which it was determined that patients treated with urokinase resolved their pulmonary thromboemboli more rapidly than did patients treated with heparin alone (Figs. 13.8a, 8b). In the Phase II, Urokinase-Streptokinase Pulmonary Embolism Trial (USPET), the trial was carried out to compare drug efficacy amongst three regimens:

1. Urokinase administered for 12 hours (as in Phase I, UPET)
2. Urokinase for 24 hours
3. Streptokinase for 24 hours

All patients received heparin and subsequently oral drugs in the recovery period. It was shown that in general, all three regimens were comparable in their ability to resolve pulmonary emboli as assessed by pulmonary angiography. However, when perfusion lung scanning and cardiac hemodynamics were used to assess drug efficacy in patients with massive PE, 24 hours of Urokinase appeared to be the best regimen. Greater reperfusion on the lung scan and a greater fall in pulmonary artery pressure resulted in those patients treated with 24 hours of Urokinase, as compared with 24 hours of Streptokinase. There was greater improvement also when compared with 12 hours of Urokinase, but this difference was not statistically significant.

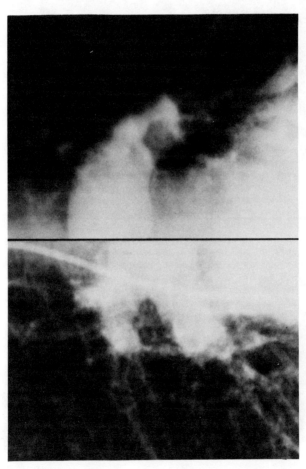

FIG. 13.8a: Closeup of pulmonary angiogram showing vessel cutoffs in vessels supplying the right upper and right lower lobes (left) and a large filling defect in the lobar artery supplying the left lower lobe (right).

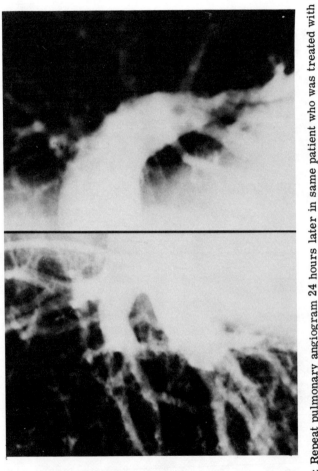

FIG. 13.8b: Repeat pulmonary angiogram 24 hours later in same patient who was treated with 12 hours of urokinase, followed by intravenous heparin. Note the marked improvement compared with Fig. 13.8a. This degree of clot resolution is common in patients with thrombolytic therapy, but very uncommon in patients treated with heparin.

There was more rapid clearing of the deep vein thrombosis and seemingly, a more rapid clinical improvement. Although not yet available in this country, the rapid advances made by the pharmaceutical industry in producing a lower cost urokinase and streptokinase should spur on the necessary investigations before being approved for release to the general professional community. The use of such agents will represent the first medical application of a drug to treat the thromboembolic event itself.

ACKNOWLEDGMENTS

We are grateful to Ms. Betty Gillum for preparation of the manuscript and to Ms. Rosemary Phillips for preparation of the figures and tables.

REFERENCES

1. Sasahara, A.A.: Unpublished data.

2. Sasahara, A.A.: Current problems in pulmonary embolism: Introduction. In Sasahara, A.A., et al.: Pulmonary Emboli. New York, Grune & Stratton, p. 1, 1975.

3. The Urokinase Pulmonary Embolism Trial: A National Cooperative Study. Circulation 47 (Suppl 2), 1973.

4. Sharma, G.V.R.K., et al.: Pulmonary embolism: The great imitator. Dis Month 22:(#7) 4-38, 1976.

5. Wacker, W.E.C., et al.: Diagnosis of pulmonary embolism and infarction. JAMA 178:8, 1961.

6. Littmann, D.: Observations on the electrocardiographic changes in pulmonary embolism. In Sasahara, A.A. and Stein, M.(eds). Pulmonary Embolic Disease. New York, Grune & Stratton, pp. 206-213, 1965.

7. Stein, P.D., et al.: The electrocardiogram in acute pulmonary embolism. In Sasahara, A.A., et al.: Pulmonary Emboli. New York, Grune & Stratton, pp. 65-76, 1975.

8. Szucs, M.M., et al.: Diagnostic sensitivity of laboratory findings in acute pulmonary embolism. Ann Int Med 74:161, 1971.

9. McIntyre, K.M., and Sasahara, A.A.: Hemodynamic response to pulmonary embolism in patients free of prior cardiopulmonary disease. Amer J Cardiol 28:288, 1971.

10. Tow, D.E., and Simon, A.L.: Comparison of lung scanning and pulmonary angiography in the detection and follow-up of pulmonary embolism: The urokinase pulmonary embolism trial experience. In Sasahara, A.A., et al.: Pulmonary Emboli. New York, Grune & Stratton, pp. 57-64, 1975.

11. Poulose, K., et al.: Characteristics of the shape and location of perfusion defects in certain pulmonary diseases. New Engl J Med 279:1020, 1968.

12. Sasahara, A.A., et al.: Pulmonary angiography in the diagnosis of pulmonary thromboembolic disease. New Engl J Med 270: 1075, 1964.

13. Simon, M., and Sasahara, A.A.: Observations on the angiographic changes in pulmonary thromboembolism. In Sasahara, A.A., and Stein, M. (eds) Pulmonary Embolic Disease. New York, Grune & Stratton, pp. 214-224, 1965.

14. Dalen, J.E., et al.: Pulmonary angiography in experimental pulmonary embolism. Amer Heart J 72:509, 1966.

15. Sevitt, S., and Gallagher, N.G.: Venous thrombosis and pulmonary embolism: a clinicopathologic study in injured and burned patients. Br J Surg 48:475, 1961.

16. Kakkar, V.V., et al.: Natural History of postoperative deep vein thrombosis. Lancet 2:230, 1969.

17. Wheeler, H.B., et al.: Diagnosis of occult deep vein thrombosis by a non-invasive bedside technic. Surgery 70:20, 1971.

18. Sasahara, A.A., et al.: Pulmonary embolism: the target organ. In Madden, J.L. and Hume, M.(eds). New York, Appleton-Century Crofts, pp. 91-102, 1976.

19. Salzman, E.W., et al.: Management of heparin therapy. Controlled clinical trial. New Engl J Med 292:1046, 1975.

20. Wessler, S., Freiman, D., et al.: Experimental pulmonary embolism with serum-induced thrombi. Amer J Path 38:89, 1961.

21. Mobin-Uddin, K., Utley, J.R., et al.: The Inferior vena cava umbrella filter. In Sasahara, A.A., et al.: Pulmonary Emboli. New York, Grune & Stratton, pp. 163-171, 1975.

22. Sautter, R.D., et al.: Pulmonary embolectomy: review and current status. In Sasahara, A.A., et al.: Pulmonary Emboli. New York, Grune & Stratton, pp. 143-161.

D: ACUTE PULMONARY EDEMA
by Marvin A. Sackner, M.D.

Acute pulmonary edema will be discussed in two contexts, that
which relates to cardiogenic and that to non-cardiogenic causes.
Its definition is common to both circumstances, i.e., a pathologic
state in which there is abnormal extravascular water storage in the
lung. In its earliest stages, pulmonary edema is difficult to diagnose. Fine rales related to pulmonary congestion may not be heard
even when lung water is doubled as estimated by indicator dilution
methods. The chest roentgenogram may also be normal under these
circumstances. Furthermore, fine rales are more often heard as
a result of the sudden opening of small airways which were closed
at dependent portions of the lungs because of aging, obesity, and
chronic bronchitis. Unfortunately, present day pulmonary function
tests are not sufficiently sensitive to be reliable in the detection of
early pulmonary edema.

CLINICAL SETTING

To establish a diagnosis of whether pulmonary edema is on a cardiac
or non-cardiac basis (Adult Respiratory Distress Syndrome), the
clinical setting is quite important. (Tables I and II) If the patient
has previously had left sided heart failure, then the diagnosis is
more likely that pulmonary edema is of cardiac origin as a result of
leaking of fluid from the capillaries into the airspaces due to elevated left atrial pressure. On the other hand, non-cardiogenic pulmonary edema is more often seen in younger patients who have an
antecedent episode of trauma, fluid overload, acute pancreatitis,
shock, etc. Peripheral signs of congestive heart failure such as
venous distention, hepatomegaly, peripheral edema and decreased
urinary output are common in cardiogenic but not in non-cardiogenic
pulmonary edema.

TABLE I		
PULMONARY EDEMA - CLINICAL SETTING		
	Cardiac	Non-Cardiac
(L)-sided heart failure	Common	Uncommon
History of trauma, shock pancreatitis	-	+
Signs of CHF	+	-
↑(L)Ventricle by x-ray	+	-
Arterial PO$_2$	↓	↓

TABLE II		
PULMONARY EDEMA - CLINICAL SETTING		
	Cardiac	Non-Cardiac
Arterial PCO_2	↓ early ↑ late	↓
Arterial PO_2 < 60mm with 100% O_2 breathing	Uncommon	Common
Metabolic acidosis	Common	Uncommon
Pulmonary Arterial Pressure	↑	Normal or slightly ↑
Wedge Pressure	↑	Normal
Cardiac output	↓	↑ or normal

The chest roentgenogram is helpful in the differential diagnosis of cardiogenic versus non-cardiogenic pulmonary edema. An enlarged cardiac silhouette is most likely related to a cardiogenic cause, although a patient with an acute M.I. with LV failure and pulmonary edema may have a normal silhouette. Arterial blood gases show a diminished oxygen tension in both conditions. In non-cardiogenic pulmonary edema, carbon dioxide tension is normal or reduced; in cardiogenic pulmonary edema, carbon dioxide is reduced in the very early stages but later on is normal or elevated. One of the features of non-cardiogenic pulmonary edema (Adult Respiratory Distress Syndrome) is the problem in establishing normoxia even when 100% oxygen is breathed. Arterial oxygen tensions less than 60 mm Hg with 100% oxygen breathing are common. In severe cardiogenic pulmonary edema, the same finding may occur because hypoxemia is caused by the interference with gas exchange due to the liquid leaked into the alveoli from the capillaries. However, with diuretics in cardiogenic pulmonary edema, usually there is prompt relief of hypoxemia.

Patients with cardiogenic pulmonary edema generally have metabolic acidosis if the edema is of a moderately severe to severe nature. It was formerly thought that the commonest arterial blood gas abnormality in acute cardiogenic pulmonary edema was acute respiratory alkalosis, and while this probably occurs very early in the condition, most patients admitted to emergency rooms will have mixed features of metabolic and respiratory acidosis along with hypoxemia. The metabolic acidosis is related to poor tissue perfusion due to diminished cardiac output resulting in lactic acid accumulation from anaerobic tissue metabolism. In contrast, non-cardiogenic pulmonary edema is rarely associated with metabolic acidosis because cardiac output is usually normal or elevated.

The Swan Ganz catheter aids in the differentiation of cardiogenic from non-cardiogenic pulmonary edema. It also serves to guide fluid and electrolyte therapy. Pulmonary arterial pressure is either normal or slightly elevated in non-cardiogenic pulmonary edema; the pulmonary wedge pressure (an index of left atrial pressure) is almost always normal. In cardiogenic pulmonary edema, the pulmonary arterial and wedge pressures are elevated due to left ventricular failure. The measurements of vascular pressures are mandatory in patients who have clinical features of both cardiogenic and non-cardiogenic pulmonary edema. Such an example might be a patient with pulmonary edema with hypertensive or arteriosclerotic heart disease who has abdominal sepsis secondary to a perforated diverticula. If there is access to measurement of cardiac output either with thermal indicator dilution curves directly with the Swan Ganz catheter or indirectly with pulmonary arteriovenous oxygen differences (a normal arteriovenous O_2 difference is 4.5 vol%; an increased arteriovenous O_2 difference reflects reduced and a decreased arteriovenous O_2 difference an increased cardiac output), then the cardiac output is found to be reduced in cardiogenic and increased or normal in non-cardiogenic pulmonary edema.

There have been a myriad of conditions and terms reported in association with the Adult Respiratory Distress Syndrome which most authors use to designate non-cardiogenic pulmonary edema. These include the "traumatic wet lung", the picture that develops with either chest wall or abdominal trauma after an automobile accident, with blunt trauma, etc.; "shock lung" occurring after acute blood loss as first described in the Vietnam war, and non-cardiogenic pulmonary edema after fat emboli, amniotic fluid emboli, following prolonged cardiac bypass, and disseminated intravascular coagulation. The latter is of interest because about 20 to 25% of patients with non-cardiogenic pulmonary edema display the laboratory features of a coagulopathy with diminished platelets, elevation of fibrin split products, and a prolonged prothrombin time, but only about 5% have overt bleeding. Aspiration pneumonitis and nonbacterial pneumonias are the commonest precipitating medical causes of Adult Respiratory Distress Syndrome. Septicemia, acute renal failure, burns, fluid overload, smoke inhalation, drug overdose, kerosene inhalation, irradiation, and cerebrovascular accidents have also been described as precipitating non-cardiogenic pulmonary edema. The pathogenesis of excessive capillary leakage of fluids is not understood but it has been found that edema protein is similar in composition to plasma protein.

The onset of pulmonary edema of cardiac origin often occurs an hour and one half to two hours after the patient has gone to bed. It is believed that this time delay is related to fluid mobilization from the extremities in the supine position creating an increased venous return which cannot be adequately dealt with by a compromised heart. However, increase of cardiac output and pulmonary capillary blood volume on changing from the erect to supine position takes place within minutes. Approximately ninety minutes after onset of sleep, the first period of rapid eye movements (REM sleep) occurs. In this period of sleep, pulse rate and respiratory frequency show an increase compared to other stages of sleep. Perhaps the attendant increased work of breathing and the cardioacceleration together with the increased venous return precipitate the clinical picture of acute pulmonary edema since this is often the time relationship for paroxysmal nocturnal dyspnea. In addition, history of excessive salt intake after eating salty foods prior to retiring is often obtained from the patient with acute pulmonary edema.

THERAPY

In acute pulmonary edema of cardiogenic cause, the first line of treatment is administration of morphine, oxygen, rotating tourniquets and furosemide, whereas in non-cardiogenic pulmonary edema the first line of treatment is to provide adequate oxygenation. Morphine is not recommended for Adult Respiratory Distress Syndrome but generally will not be deleterious to those patients with the associated causes listed above. Both patients with cardiogenic pulmonary edema and Adult Respiratory Distress Syndrome require oxygen therapy. The problem is how to effectively administer it. In cardiogenic pulmonary edema, oxygen is given by mask or nasal cannula and can be employed similarly in non-cardiogenic pulmonary edema, but there is a tendency to intubate patients with non-cardiogenic pulmonary edema relatively early in the course of the disease because of more profound hypoxemia. If arterial oxygen tension fails to rise above 60 to 70 mm Hg with 100% O_2, intubation and mechanical ventilation with positive end expiratory pressure should be employed to help elevate arterial oxygen tension. With cardiogenic pulmonary edema, since cardiac output is reduced, venous return might be further compromised by mechanical ventilation but since positive airway pressure might not be transmitted through the fluid filled lungs to the great veins, one cannot predict that this will occur. Intravenous theophylline infusion may be utilized in those patients in whom a strong element of bronchospasm is present. Theophylline is also helpful in reducing venous pressure but has the hazard of inducing cardiac arrhythmias in some patients.

Confronted with an elderly breathless patient whose lungs show both wheezes and rales, the differential diagnosis between obstructive lung disease and acute pulmonary edema is difficult by physical diagnosis. It is mandatory to obtain a chest roentgenogram in a patient with suspected pulmonary edema. With early pulmonary edema, the upper lung veins appear distended. There may be enlargement and loss of definition of hilar structures. Septal lines in the lower lung fields may be observed. Peribronchial and perivascular cuffing and pleural effusion also may be found in acute pulmonary edema. Later on, diffuse alveolar infiltrates develop. Although the roentgenographic pattern of the lungs is similar for both cardiogenic and non-cardiogenic pulmonary edema, the occurrence of this pattern in a young patient with a normal size heart should lead one to suspect Adult Respiratory Distress Syndrome. The elderly patient with cardiac enlargement will most likely have cardiogenic pulmonary edema.

Morphine: Morphine is the time honored drug for treatment of pulmonary edema of cardiac origin. To this day, the reason for its effectiveness is not clear. Morphine produces peripheral venous pooling in the limbs to the extent that a normal individual will pool about 70 ml while a patient with acute pulmonary edema will pool approximately 120 ml of blood. This quantity of blood pooling does not explain the dramatic improvement in symptoms that patients with pulmonary edema experience after morphine administration. Possibly, blood also pools in the splanchnic bed because if morphine acts to decrease the quantity of blood presented to the lungs, there must be a larger extrapulmonary site for blood storage. Splanchnic pooling has not been measured but there is suggestive evidence that this may occur. Another site for pooling which has been measured qualitatively is the systemic resistance vessels. Dilatation of these vessels would lead to a reduction in ventricular afterload. Finally, morphine produces euphoria which may in itself reduce dyspnea and by a calming effect diminish work of breathing which would relieve a portion of the demands on the heart. However, it should be cautioned that morphine can worsen the situation because of its depressant action on the respiratory center. Morphine should be cautiously administered to patients in whom an antecedent pulmonary history cannot be obtained. It is relatively contraindicated if co-existing CO_2 retention is present. In a large series of elderly patients we investigated several years ago, combined respiratory and metabolic acidosis, with a pH less than 7.30 occurred in about one quarter of the patients. The average blood pH in these patients was 7.10 with a range from 6.75 to 7.30, indicating that the acidosis was severe. Metabolic acidosis by itself was the second most common occurrence in 10% of cases followed by respiratory acidosis. The point here is that in patients with respiratory acidosis, morphine tends to worsen the situation and one cannot make a clinical distinction among the various acid-base abnormalities without obtaining an arterial blood gas analysis. There are two options when confronted with acute pulmonary edema as a medical emergency. If arterial blood gases cannot be obtained immediately, a small dose of morphine, e.g., 5 mg subcutaneously, can be administered and the patient carefully observed or morphine can be withheld since patients with pulmonary edema often improve with other modalities of therapy.

Diuretic Agents: Diuretic agents take hours to achieve peak renal effect yet they should be included in the initial approach to the patient with acute pulmonary edema. Furosemide given intravenously exerts a beneficial effect which appears to be related to an immediate decrease in peripheral venous tone which presumably causes pooling of blood. Furosemide is indicated whether the pulmonary edema is cardiogenic or non-cardiogenic. It will be effective in the former and partially effective in selected cases of the latter as in those with non-cardiogenic pulmonary edema precipitated by fluid overload. The failure to improve after diuresis can serve as a therapeutic-diagnostic test.

Oxygen: Hypoxemia is corrected by oxygen administered by nasal cannula or face mask. If this is ineffective, then positive pressure breathing should be considered. Patients with acute pulmonary edema of cardiogenic origin often have severe metabolic and respiratory acidosis. The following description serves as such an example: a 75-year-old woman with acute pulmonary edema and hypotension associated with myocardial infarction, had a blood pH of 6.94, base excess -17 mEq, carbon dioxide tension 91 mm Hg and oxygen tension 60 mm Hg while receiving mechanical ventilation with 100% oxygen. Marked sinus bradycardia developed and five ampules of sodium bicarbonate, each containing 44.5 mEq sodium bicarbonate were given intravenously in rapid succession. Arterial blood gases showed marked improvement with return to normal blood pH since the base deficit was corrected by sodium bicarbonate and the increased carbon dioxide tension by mechanical ventilation. Diuresis ensued and blood pressure and pulse returned to normal within 20 minutes.

Sodium Bicarbonate: There has been controversy in the literature as to whether sodium bicarbonate should be given to patients with acute pulmonary edema who have metabolic acidosis. The arguments against administration include aggravation of pulmonary edema because sodium bicarbonate adds a load of sodium to the extracellular fluid as a hyperosmolar solution, and correction of pulmonary edema with morphine, oxygen and furosemide promotes metabolism of lactic acid to endogenous bicarbonate within an hour. I agree that the latter might occur but I have not seen worsening of pulmonary edema when sodium bicarbonate has been administered. On the contrary, the patient's complexion, anxiety and urinary output usually improve almost immediately after correction of metabolic acidosis. Furthermore, with severe metabolic acidosis in the elderly patient, one might not be able to wait for self-correction of the acidosis because of its deleterious effects. These include a synergistic effect with hypoxemia in elevating pulmonary arterial pressure leading to right ventricular systolic overloading, diminution of cardiac pacemaker activity, loss of arterial vasomotor tone, and reduction in cardiac output and renal blood flow. Therefore, I believe that sodium bicarbonate should be given to correct the metabolic acidosis associated with cardiogenic pulmonary edema. (Please refer to the chapter on "Severe Acid-Base Abnormalities" for the details of administration)

Mechanical Ventilation: Treatment with intermittent positive pressure breathing was advocated for pulmonary edema for many years. It was thought that this modality would force fluid filling the alveoli back into the capillaries. But there is no evidence whatsoever that positive pressure breathing forces fluid back into the pulmonary capillaries. With IPPB, there is a positive pressure wave generated during inspiration; expiration is passive at atmospheric pressure. This was the conventional way of treating patients with IPPB up through the late nineteen sixties. It generally involved placing a mask over the face of an anxious patient with pulmonary edema and administering IPPB when he entered the emergency room. He became more frightened, anxious, apprehensive and fought the respirator and his attendants. Frequently when tidal volume was measured, the ventilation was less while the patient was breathing on the pressure limited respirator than during spontaneous breathing. This was a major reason that provoked us to initiate arterial blood gas monitoring of such patients. We concluded that intermittent positive pressure breathing was useful only for those patients who had CO_2 retention and that those patients were better handled with volume limited respirators. Another aspect of IPPB therapy deals with its effect on flattening liquid in the alveoli against the alveolar wall to produce less distance for oxygen to diffuse from the alveoli into the pulmonary capillaries. This circumstance occurs during inspiration but during expiration, the liquid refills the alveoli so that the diffusion distance lengthens. This contrasts with continuous positive pressure breathing which may consist of intermittent positive pressure breathing (IPPB) plus positive and expiratory pressure (PEEP) or IPPB plus PEEP with intermittent mandatory ventilation (IMV). In the latter, spontaneous breathing is permitted along with a fixed number of breaths per minute delivered by the respirator. Positive pressure in the airways is maintained throughout both inspiration and expiration and the liquid film in the alveoli is thinned so that the diffusion distance for gas exchange is markedly shortened, thereby helping to improve arterial oxygenation. Provided venous return is not impaired, it can be employed in selected cases of cardiogenic as well as in most patients with non-cardiogenic pulmonary edema.

Another benefit of continuous positive pressure breathing is the relief of small airway obstruction. Patients with pulmonary edema of cardiogenic or non-cardiogenic causes appear to breathe in a manner similar to a normal person who is breathing close to residual volume (volume of air left in the lung after a maximal expiration). If the patient is breathing close to residual volume prior to institution of treatment, pulmonary blood flow, which is gravity dependent, perfuses the dependent zones, but the airways are closed in this zone. These regions are perfused but not ventilated resulting in right to left shunting. This occurs in both cardiogenic and non-cardiogenic pulmonary edema and contributes greatly to the observed hypoxemia. When functional residual capacity is restored toward normal by continuous positive pressure breathing, previously closed airways become patent and ventilated. This factor plus thinning of edema fluid in the alveoli facilitates oxygenation of the pulmonary capillary blood.

Lower values of arterial oxygen tension usually are found in Adult Respiratory Distress Syndrome than cardiogenic pulmonary edema. Values ranging from 20 to 35 mm Hg are not uncommon on room air breathing. The vast majority of patients with this syndrome can be oxygenated with IPPB coupled with positive end expiratory pressure (PEEP) but the response is variable and depends upon the optimal level of PEEP. Most patients will be adequately oxygenated (pO_2 > 70 mm Hg on FIO_2 of .6) with PEEP ranging from 5 to 20 cmH_2O. However, a 15 to 20% pneumothorax rate is associated with PEEP if administered over a period of several days or more. The cardiac output in Adult Respiratory Distress Syndrome is usually unaffected by PEEP because the pressure is poorly transmitted to the great veins and cardiac output is normal or high prior to its application.

After achieving success with PEEP in Adult Respiratory Distress Syndrome, we employed this modality in cases of cardiogenic pulmonary edema who had severe coexisting hypoxemia not responsive to oxygen administration. Initially, we were apprehensive about using positive end expiratory pressure breathing along with IPPB because of the potential of decreasing the venous return with subsequent deterioration in cardiac output, but this has not happened. In those patients with cardiogenic pulmonary edema and severe hypoxemia that require intubation, the respiratory management is the same as in Adult Respiratory Distress Syndrome. If they cannot be oxygenated satisfactorily, i.e., arterial oxygen tension greater than 70 mm Hg, on 60% inspired oxygen with the respirator, with normal pCO_2, 5 cmH_2O PEEP will be applied and systemic blood pressure and urinary output carefully monitored. If the blood pressure or urinary output falls, PEEP is removed. The latter rarely occurs. It should be cautioned that not every patient with either cardiogenic or non-cardiogenic pulmonary edema is a candidate for continuous mechanical ventilatory support. The majority of the cardiac patients can be handled with furosemide, oxygen, correction of acid-base disturbance, and occasionally morphine and theophyllin, whereas Adult Respiratory Distress Syndrome can be occasionally treated by breathing high concentrations of oxygen by face mask. If fluid overload is present in the latter, then diuretics may be helpful. In contrast to chronic obstructive pulmonary disease and asthma, the sensorium is of much less importance in deciding upon when to intubate in Adult Respiratory Distress Syndrome than the values of arterial blood gases. Intubation and continuous positive pressure breathing is recommended on the basis of the finding of an arterial oxygen tension less than 60 mm Hg on breathing 60% or greater oxygen. The hospital mortality rate for patients with severe Adult Respiratory Distress Syndrome requiring mechanical assistance approaches 75%.

REFERENCES

1. Sackner, M.A.: Arterial blood gas analysis. Med Times 95: 79-97, 1967.

2. Avery, W.G., et al.: The acidosis of pulmonary edema. Am J Med 48:320-324, 1970.

3. Fishman, A.P.: Pulmonary edema; the water-exchanging function of the lung. Circulation 46:390-408, 1972.

4. Staub, N.C.: Pulmonary edema. Physiol Rev 54:678-811, 1974.

5. Cutchavaree, A. and Sackner, M.A.: Adult respiratory distress syndrome. J Florida Med Assn 61:429-436, 1974.

E: SPONTANEOUS PNEUMOTHORAX
by Morgan Delaney, M.D.

Pneumothorax refers to the escape of air into the pleural space, generally resulting from the rupture of a subpleural bleb or cyst. The leakage of air causes the lung to collapse, and impairs the normal functioning of the chest bellows. As the lung collapses, the site of rupture tends to seal, limiting the degree of collapse. However, if the site of air leakage remains open, or if a valve-like mechanism allows air to enter but not leave the pleural space, the intrapleural pressure may rise to dangerously high positive levels. This situation, known as a tension pneumothorax, usually leads to impaired venous return to the heart and markedly abnormal gas exchange--a life-threatening occurrence. The recognition and treatment of these events is not difficult, and should be mastered by every physician.

Spontaneous pneumothorax occurs in two settings. The first of these is in the young adult male between the ages of twenty and forty years, in otherwise good health, with no notable past history of lung disease. Furthermore, affected men tend to be tall and thin, as well as athletic. Most of these individuals can be demonstrated to have thin-walled bullae or cysts located at the apices of their lungs (if the lungs are ultimately examined at thoracotomy.) These lesions are usually not visualized on a routine chest film. An occasional individual demonstrates no pulmonary or pleural abnormality at surgical exploration.

The characteristic profile of the affected individual, as well as the presence of blebs or cysts with no previous history of lung disease, had lead to several interesting theories concerning the pathogenesis of these lesions. Some authors have considered them to be congenital in origin; others have called attention to the stresses applied to the upper lobe structures by the forces of gravity, noting that they would be more pronounced in the taller individual. It has also been considered that the upper lobes are normally less well perfused and ventilated in the upright individual; a rapid growth rate relative to pulmonary vasculature may serve to compound the relative ischemia leading to bleb formation. A role of subclinical bronchial infection has also been proposed.

Spontaneous pneumothorax also occurs secondary to clinically manifest disease of the lung or pleura. The majority of cases in this setting occur in individuals with generalized emphysema and/or chronic bronchitis. Other less frequent causes are asthma, pulmonary tuberculosis, necrotizing pneumonia, lung abscess, and bronchogenic carcinoma. Pneumothorax occurs with great frequency in the patient requiring positive pressure mechanical ventilation, especially if positive end-expiratory pressure (PEEP) is utilized.

The occurrence of pneumothorax is usually heralded by the sudden onset of symptoms. Chest pain is invariably described, usually accompanied by dyspnea. The pain may be constant or pleuritic in character. It is frequently localized anteriorly with occasional radiation into the neck, back, or abdomen. The severity of dyspnea has been related to the degree of collapse and to the presence and severity of underlying lung disease. In less than 10% of cases a non-productive cough will be described. The onset of symptoms is not usually related to vigorous physical exertion; and may, indeed, awaken the patient from sleep.

The physical findings depend on the degree of collapse that has occurred as well as the presence of underlying pulmonary or systemic disease. The detection of a small amount of free air in the pleural space is difficult. In general, the most notable signs consist of hyperresonance to percussion on the involved side, accompanied by diminished or absent breath sounds. Subcutaneous emphysema may be seen or felt as crepitations under the palpating fingertips, if air has dissected, either through the interstitial connective tissue of the lung back towards the mediastinum and subsequently along soft tissue planes into the subcutaneous tissues of the neck and chest wall, or through a rent in the mediastinal pleura directly into the mediastinum. Mediastinal emphysema often produces a peculiar "crunching" sound during ventricular systole.

Because a tension pneumothorax is a life-threatening emergency, its clinical manifestations deserve special emphasis. The signs of lung collapse and hyperexpansion of the affected hemithorax are usually marked. There is evidence of mediastinal displacement with tracheal shift toward the unaffected side and movement of the area of cardiac dullness. The patient becomes hypotensive and cyanotic. Cardiac arrhythmias are common. Immediate relief of the pressure within the hemithorax must be achieved to save the patient's life.

A small gauge needle or a small plastic catheter can be inserted into the hemithorax through the second anterior intercostal space to relieve the pressure and decompress the mediastinal contents, before a more definitive decompression procedure is undertaken.

The ultimate method of diagnosis is the demonstration on chest x-ray of free air within the pleural space, with separation of the lung parenchyma from the chest wall. It is difficult to accurately quantitate the degree of pulmonary collapse from the chest film, but many observers will estimate the size of the pneumothorax as a percentage of lung pneumothorax, greater than fifty percent, a marked pneumothorax. If a tension pneumothorax is suspected, there is usually not time to confirm the diagnosis by radiographic means.

The diagnosis of spontaneous pneumothorax should be suspected in any young male who experiences the sudden onset of chest pain and dyspnea, as well as in any individual with underlying lung disease who develops similar symptomatology. Pneumothorax may cause the stable patient with chronic obstructive airways disease to develop respiratory failure. The symptomatology is not pathognomonic, but chest x-rays should allow differentiation from other clinical entities such as coronary artery disease, congestive heart failure, pneumonia, and pulmonary thromboembolism.

The therapy of spontaneous pneumothorax depends upon the degree of lung collapse, upon whether there is progression of collapse and whether respiratory insufficiency is present. A small pneumothorax, causing minimal respiratory distress to the patient, and which does not show evidence of progression by chest film, may be treated conservatively, by means of bedrest and close observation. Intrapleural air is absorbed at a rate of approximately one to two percent of the hemithorax volume per day. Thus, a ten percent pneumothorax would require about eight days to re-expand. An ancillary measure that may be beneficial is the breathing of high concentrations of oxygen. This maneuver lowers the blood nitrogen tension and favors the diffusion of nitrogen out of the pleural space into the capillary blood.

Any pneumothorax larger than 20-30%, that shows evidence of progression, that causes the patient to become very symptomatic, or that leads to the development of frank respiratory failure must be treated more aggressively by tube thoracostomy with water-seal drainage to evacuate the air and re-expand the collapsed lung. A trocar may be used to facilitate tube placement, or a small incision may be made. The site of insertion varies with the location of the pneumothorax, but in general the second or third anterior intercostal space in the mid-clavicular line should be utilized. In women, for cosmetic purposes, the preferred site is the anterior axillary line in the third intercostal space.

After appropriate anesthesia, the trocar is inserted through the chest wall until the pleural space is entered. A soft number catheter (18-28 F or 18-26 Foley) is then threaded through the trocar into the pleural cavity and the trocar is withdrawn. The catheter is secured to the chest wall with suture material and connected to a water-seal system. An occlusive dressing is applied to the entrance site to prevent any air leaks. All connections between the catheter and the water-seal-system should be taped to prevent the connections from becoming dislodged. Negative pressure suction is usually not required to effect re-expansion of the lung unless there is an ongoing air leak.

Re-expansion should be complete in several hours. Generally the tube can be removed after 48-72 hours, provided the lung remains expanded when the tube is clamped. If the lung fails to re-expand within 48-72 hours, bronchoscopy should be performed to examine the patency of the airways. Lack of re-expansion after seven days, or continued air-leak through the tube indicative of an open rent in the lung are indications for thoracotomy to surgically oversew the tear in the lung or to resect the implicated blebs or bullae.

The recurrence rate of spontaneous pneumothorax is high, especially in the younger age group. The recurrence may be on the same side or involve the opposite lung. The incidence of recurrence is much higher in that group of patients treated conservatively than in that which initially is treated by tube thoracostomy. Recurrence is generally an indication for surgical intervention with resection of the blebs or bullae and obliteration of the pleural space. The most popular procedure to obliterate the pleural space, and that associated with the lowest incidence of further recurrences, is parietal pleurectomy. Other less efficacious procedures include scarification of the pleural surface, using a gauze sponge to effect the abrasion, or the instillation of irritating substances, such as talc, into the pleural space to produce pleurodesis.

REFERENCES

1. Killen, D.A., and Gobbel, W.G.: Spontaneous Pneumothorax. Boston, Little, Brown and Co., 1968.

2. Lichter, I., and Gwynne, J.F.: Spontaneous pneumothorax in young subjects. Thorax 26:409, 1971.

3. Horne, N.W.: Spontaneous Pneumothorax: Diagnosis and Management. British Medical Journal 1:281, January, 29, 1966.

4. Editorial: Spontaneous Pneumothorax and apical lung disease. British Medical Journal, December 4, 1971.

CHAPTER 14: MISCELLANEOUS EMERGENCIES

A: HEAT ILLNESS
by Bernard Elser, M.D.

Three main syndromes associated with elevated environmental
temperatures have been described:

A. Muscle Cramps
B. Heat Exhaustion
C. Heat Stroke

Whereas muscle cramps affect predominately a young, healthy,
well-trained group of individuals, the latter two syndromes are
generally seen in individuals who are subjected to prolonged heat
and or physical stress without prior conditioning or acclimatization.
The mortality rate may be as high as 75% in acute heat stroke with
significant residual deficits in those who survive.

The elevated body temperatures which are seen in environmental
heat illness are the result of several factors:

A. Increased heat production from:
    1. exogenous sources - environmental heat
    2. endogenous sources - metabolic processes

B. Diminished ability to dissipate heat by:
    1. Radiation
    2. Conduction
    3. Convection
    4. Vaporization of sweat

Heat produced in the body as a result of accelerated metabolic processes is usually far greater than that generated as a result of increased environmental heat. Whereas an individual who is directly
exposed to bright sunlight may gain an average of 150 K. calories
per hour, the heat derived from endogenous sources, mostly metabolic processes, varies with physical activities; endogenous heat
production in the basal state averages about 75 K calories per hour
while that produced under maximal physical exertion can be as high
as 900 K calories per hour.

The maintenance of normal body temperature and function requires that this thermal load be dissipated, and this must occur under varying environmental conditions. When the environment is cool, a heat gradient exists and heat can be dissipated from the body by radiation, convection, and conduction. If environmental temperatures become equal to or exceed body temperature however, heat can be lost only by vaporization of sweat. Each 1.7 ml. of sweat vaporized relieves the body of one K calorie of heat. The maximum rate of sweat production in an unacclimatized individual is approximately 1.5 liters per hour. Assuming complete vaporization of sweat (which is related to the dryness of the ambient air and air movements) with only minimal losses of sweat due to dripping, etc., the total amount of heat which can be dissapated by this means is approximately 750 K calories per hour. Therefore, a progressive rise in body temperature is almost inevitable under conditions of near maximum heat production with elevated ambient temperature and humidity. Rectal temperatures, however, may not reflect this marked elevation; during maximum physical stress rectal temperatures may reach 104 degrees F., while simultaneous measurements of muscle or hepatic venous blood may indicate temperatures approaching 107 degrees Farenheit. Individuals who are well-trained and acclimatized to the heat have improved heat dissipation and increased metabolic efficiency, demonstrating a smaller rise in body temperature with a given amount of physical stress.

The major physiological effect of the increased body heat is on the cardiovascular system. There is a loss of effective circulating blood volume as a result of sweating, a hypothalamically mediated dilatation of skin vessels (to further aid in the dissipation of heat), a loss of plasma volume into exercising muscle cells, and, during physical exertion, a shunting of blood flow to muscle itself. These effects are partially counteracted by splanchnic vasoconstriction and a hyperkinetic cardiac response.

There is also an endocrinological response to heat stress. There is increased secretion of growth hormone and activation of the renin-angiotensin system with increased production of aldosterone. The effect of the latter on sweat glands is to promote sodium reabsorption, but as it requires several days to reach peak effect its importance may reside in the production of the acclimatized state. Under conditions of maximal physical stress and maximal sweat production, flow rates may be too high to achieve significant sodium reabsorption and its effect may be negated.

MUSCLE CRAMPS

Muscle cramps are the most benign of the heat related illnesses. It is an acute disorder of skeletal muscle, characteristically occurring in well-trained, heat acclimatized individuals following an episode of intensive muscular exercise. It is characterized by brief, intermittent, spontaneously resolving, severe muscle cramps in those muscles which have been subjected to intense activity. The exact mechanism of its production is not known although it is believed to result from an acute deficiency of sodium in the muscle. Treatment consists of oral sodium replacement and is usually rapidly effective.

HEAT EXHAUSTION

The most common of the disorders resulting from heat illness is called heat exhaustion. It results from a loss of salt and water and its signs and symptoms include thirst, weakness, fever, encephalopathy, aprasthesia, and tetany. Terminally, it may develop into acute heat stroke. The clinical picture may be somewhat different where there has been inappropriate replacement of water without salt. Under these circumstances dehydration and weight loss may not occur, the volume of urine and sweat may remain normal, and there frequently is no complaint of thirst. However, symptoms including nausea, vomiting, weakness, frontal headache and muscle cramps may develop and may indicate a state of hyponatremia and water intoxication.

HEAT STROKE

The most severe but least common of the heat related illnesses is heat stroke. It is a syndrome consisting of:

A. Delirium
B. Coma
C. Anhidrosis
D. Hyperpyrexia

It has classically occurred in epidemic form during heat waves affecting predominately the elderly. More recently, however, it has also been seen under other circumstances, affecting, for example, young healthy military recruits and athletes, both of whom are known to be subjected to intense physical stress in hot environments without adequate acclimatization.

There are many factors which favor the development of heat stroke. These include accompanying cardiovascular disease, diabetes mellitus, malnutrition, and alcoholism. Ethyl alcohol is a potent, cutaneous vasodilator, and may promote the uptake of heat from the environment. Other risk factors include barbiturate poisoning (sweat gland necrosis), scleroderma (sweat gland entrapment), history of skin burns, previous heat stroke (sweat gland necrosis, and any accompanying acute infectious febrile illness. It may also be seen with various drugs, for example, cogentin, anticholinergics, antihistamines, phenothiazines, L.S.D., and amphetamines. Any condition associated with increased muscular activity may also enhance its appearance (seizures, delirium, trauma, and extremely agitated psychotic individuals.) In addition to its cardiovascular effects, other structural and metabolic effects may be seen. Lactic acidosis as a consequence of increased lactate production by muscle and liver, rhabdomyolysis, with resulting hyperkalemia, and acute renal insufficiency may be seen in severe cases. Paradoxically, hypokalemia may also be noted and is a consequence of the effects of aldosterone with increased losses of potassium in sweat and in the urine. If severe, this may result in kaliopenic nephropathy with its resultant vasopressin resistant polyuria and increased susceptibility to even further water and salt losses.

In the heart subendocardial hemorrhage, fragmentation and rupture of muscle fibers, and patchy myocardial necrosis have been noted. Jaundice as a result of hepatic cellular damage is common but residual deficits are rare. Disseminated intravascular coagulation (DIC) with hypofibrinogenemia and activation of the fibrinolytic system has also been reported. Other effects include hypocalcemia and elevated serum enzymes (SGOT, SGPT, LDH, CPK). An SGOT level of less than one thousand has been reported to be associated with a good prognosis in patients with acute heat stroke.

THERAPY

The mainstay of treatment includes recognition and rapid lowering of the body temperature. This may be accomplished by submersion in an ice bath or by vigorous massage with ice in the wake of a high powered fan to promote vaporization. Massaging of the skin is important to promote cutaneous blood flow and block the vasoconstrictive effect of the water. Although parenteral fluids must also be given to counteract the inevitable intravascular volume depletion which has occurred, care must be taken not to infuse too much fluid too rapidly, as the peripheal vasoconstriction following reduction in body temperature may lead to centralization of the fluid and result in acute pulmonary edema. If these measures are not successful in elevating blood pressure, a beta-adrenergic stimulator such as isoproterenol may be more efficacious than a vasoconstricting alpha-adrenergic stimulator which would diminish further heat dissipation. In cases of impending pigment nephropathy, mannitol, furosemide, and alkalinization of the urine are necessary. If present, disseminated intravascular coagulopathy (DIC) should also be treated.

During the cooling phase, shivering, (which leads to increased heat production) and generalized convulsions may be seen. Cholorpromazine (50 mg. I. V.) to block the shivering, as well as anti-convulsant medication should be administered.

Occasionally, the etiology of the hyperthermia is not immediately obvious. Although environmental causes are common, other etiologies must also be considered. The differential diagnosis of heat stroke includes acute infectious febrile illnesses such as falciparum malaria, acute meningococcemia, and Rocky Mountain spotted fever to mention a few. Malignant hyperthermia (following general anesthesia) and CNS lesions (hypothalamus) are both associated with hyperthermia but are readily recognized by the setting in which they occur or the accompanying signs. Under any circumstances, however, hyperthermia of any cause should be vigorously treated.

REFERENCES

1. Knochel, J.P.: Environmental heat illness. Arch Int Med 133:841-864, 1974.

2. Gottschalk, P.G., Thomas, J.E.: Heat Stroke. Mayo Clin Proc 41:470-482, 1966.

3. O'Donnell, T.F., Clowes, H.A.: The circulatory abnormalities of heat stroke. N Engl J Med 287:734-737, 1972.

4. Romeo, J.A.: Heatstroke. Md Med 131:669-677, 1966.

4. Clowes GHA Jr., O'Donnel, T.F. Jr.: Current Concepts: Heat stroke. NEJM 291:564, 1974.

B: HYPOTHERMIA
by Bernard Elser, M. D.

Lowering of the body temperature below the normal range may be seen under a variety of circumstances. Although mild reductions in temperature may frequently accompany various systemic disorders, clinically significant hypothermia, defined as a rectal temperature below 95 degrees F., is most commonly accidental and related to exposure to cold. (Table 1) The actual incidence depends upon many factors including season, location and population. The elderly are particularly at risk when exposed.

Determining the presence and severity of hypothermia requires the availability of a thermometer capable of registering low body temperatures, and has clinical therapeutic, and prognostic significance.

PATHOPHYSIOLOGY: Hypothermia may be viewed as an imbalance between heat production and heat conservation. It may result from the decreased production of heat secondary to a decreased metabolic rate as seen, for example, in classical myxedema, or from excessive losses of heat as seen in immersion or exposure in cold environments. The normal physiological response to hypothermia is mediated by humoral and neurological responses through the temperature control center in the anterior and posterior hypothalamus. It produces shivering, which can triple the metabolic rate and thus increase the production of heat as well as a variably intense peripheral vasoconstriction to decrease the loss of heat. In severe cases, these responses may be absent. As body temperature falls below 90 degrees F, shivering stops and an extrapyramidal type of diffuse muscle rigidity and fine tremor appear. In the elderly, there is an age-related decline in autonomic nervous system function leading to an impairment of thermoregulatory capabilities. This may explain the high incidence of hypothermia in this population.

With the exception of accidental exposure and some of the iatrogenic causes, most of the other disorders rarely present with rectal temperatures less than 95 degrees F. The mechanism by which they produce hypothermia is variable. The hypothermia associated with hypoglycemia is directly related to intracellular glucopenia and cannot be correlated with the concentration of extracellular glucose, insulin, or free fatty acids. The antipyretics, especially acetylsalicylic acid, do not generally lower body temperature below normal. In the occasional patient with leukemia or a lymphoma, they may cause hypothermia. Ethanol is commonly associated with hypothermia because its vasodilating and anesthetic properties interfere with the normal physiological response to cold with resulting increased heat loss. On the other hand, ethanol potentiates the effect of hypothermia in decreasing cerebral metabolism and thus can be considered protective during periods of anoxia in hypothermic patients. In addition, it decreases the critical temperature at which ventricular fibrillation occurs, which is probably the most common mechanism of death in hypothermia. Barbiturates prevent shivering and thereby block an important defense mechanism against hypothermia. Hypothalamic lesions of different etiologies may present with hypothermia. Interestingly, the hypothermia is also protective by decreasing central nervous system metabolism. Gram positive as well as gram negative bacteremia may present as hypothermia, as can hepatic coma and uremia.

TABLE 1
ETIOLOGY OF HYPOTHERMIA

A. Accidental Exposure
 	
B. Iatrogenic
  1) Hypothermic blankets
  2) Cold blood or IV solutions
  3) Gastric lavage with iced solutions
  4) Peritoneal lavage
  5) Antipyretics
  6) Surgically induced
 	
C. Drug Related
  1) Ethanol
  2) Barbiturates
  3) Opiates
  4) Phenothiazines
  5) Imipramine
 	
D. Endocrinological
  1) Hypoglycemia
  2) Myxedema
  3) Hypopituitarism
  4) Adrenal insufficiency
  5) Diabetic ketoacidosis
 	
E. Neurological
  1) Hypothalamic lesions
    a) tumors
    b) strokes
    c) trauma
  2) Wernicke's Encephalopathy
 	
F. Infectious
  1) Bacterial sepsis
 	
G. Hepatic Coma
 	
H. Uremia

CLINICAL MANIFESTATIONS: Hypothermia usually presents as an acute disorder with diffuse systemic manifestations. The clinical signs may change as the temperature continues to fall.

CENTRAL NERVOUS SYSTEM

With decreasing body temperature, cerebral metabolic needs, cerebral blood flow, and oxygen consumption fall. There is a rough correlation between body temperature and state of consciousness. Patients with body temperature above 90 degrees F are usually fully conscious except where there is another coexisting disorder which accounts for the altered mental status. As the temperature falls below 90 degrees F, shivering ceases and a generalized muscular rigidity with occasional fascicular twitching appears. With decreasing temperatures, there is progressive paralysis of the central nervous system, coma, appearance of involuntary movements, and finally decreased activity of vital medullary centers with alterations in pulse, blood pressure, and respiratory rate. Pupillary light reflexes, deep tendon reflexes, and voluntary motion are lost at 80 degrees F, spontaneous respirations cease at 68 - 77 degrees F and the EEG becomes flat at 68 degrees F.

Interestingly, there have been reports of resuscitation and return to normal function of patients with hypothermia and flat EEG's. This has led to the specific exclusion of hypothermia-associated flat EEG from criteria for brain death.

CARDIOVASCULAR SYSTEM

As the body temperature falls, sinus tachycardia, one of the earliest normal physiological responses to cold exposure, is soon replaced by sinus bradycardia, and then at 85 degrees F, by atrial fibrillation with a slow ventricular response. Despite the slow heart rate, cardiac output is initially adequate because of increased myocardial efficiency and decreased metabolic oxygen requirements.

Many changes may be seen on the ECG as the body temperature falls. In addition to sinus bradycardia and atrial fibrillation with a slow ventricular response, one may see relatively specific "J" waves, usually on the lateral chest leads, which are elevations at the junction of the QRS and ST segments. One may also see flat or inverted T waves and prolongation of the QRS duration and the QT intervals. Finally, as cooling continues, there is loss of atrial activity, the appearance of idioventricular activity, and as the usual terminal event, ventricular fibrillation. Cardiac action ceases at approximately 70-75 degrees F.

Where patients have been resuscitated from severe hypothermia, myocardial infarctions have been noted. This may have been the initiating event or may be the result of decreases in coronary blood

flow during hypothermia. Alternatively, it may have been precipitated by therapy: external rewarming may cause peripheral vasodilatation and hypotension. Also, the cold heart may not be able to
keep up with the increased peripheral metabolic requirements.

RESPIRATORY SYSTEM

The respiratory system is also affected by hypothermia. Slow and
sighing respirations are common and occasionally Cheyne-Stokes
resporations are seen. Where pneumonia is present breathing may
become rapid and stertorous.

Hypoxemia and hypocarbia are frequently noted. The blood gas
analyzer must be corrected for body temperature to prevent spur-
iously high pO_2 and pCO_2 values. The cold induced shift of the oxygen dissociation curve to the left makes less oxygen available to the
tissues at a given pO_2, although metabolic requirements for oxygen
are also less. Spontaneous respirations cease at 68 degrees - 76
degrees F body temperature.

RENAL

Although Renal Blood Flow and glomerular filtration rates are decreased during hypothermia, the effect on tubular function is quantitatively greater. There is a decreased tubular reabsorption of
water - a cold diuresis - leading to volume depletion and azotemia.
At a body temperature of 86 degrees F, urine flow rates may be
three times normal. Shifts in body fluids, from the intravascular
space to the intracellular space of up to 20 - 30% may also be seen
and contribute to the volume depletion and azotemia. There are,
however, no consistent or specific changes in serum electrolytes.
Total cessation of urine production, anuria, is seen at 68 degrees F
body temperature.

OTHER: Many of the other organs are also affected to a greater or
lesser extent.

The skin is cold and frequently cyanotic, owing to intense peripheral
vasoconstriction. The coldness of the skin is also noted in covered
areas, for example the axilla and groin, giving away the true nature
of the core hypothermia. Edema of the skin, especially about the
face, with a pliable consistency, may give the appearance of myxedema. As this may be the initiating event rather a secondary manifestation of hypothermia, it must be investigated.

Hypothyroidism, adrenal insufficiency, and hypopituitarism may present as hypothermia. Decreased function of these organs is also
seen as a manifestation of hypothermia of other causes, and is pro-
portionate to the fall in body temperature below 90 degrees F. Nevertheless, the utilization and detoxification of the hormones is also

diminished which explains the lack of clinically obvious endocrine deficits. The basal metabolic rate is increased 3-6 fold during the early compensatory phase of hypothermia, but below 95 degrees F, there is a roughly linear fall with decreasing body temperature.

The hematological system is also affected. Leukopenia and thrombocytopenia are frequently noted, possibly secondary to sequestration in the liver, spleen, and splanchnic bed. A hemorrhagic diathesis, secondary to decreased circulating platelets with capillary oozing is important in iatrogenically induced surgical hypothermia. Blood viscosity is increased approximately 5% for each degree centigrade fall in body temperature and is compounded by the rising hematocrit seen as a consequence of intravascular fluid shifts.

Pancreatitis may be seen in more than 30% of cases, although the classical physical signs may not be present. Gastrointestinal bleeding may also occur. With the decreased liver function seen in severe hypothermia, altered drug detoxification and drug poisoning is a definite risk.

THERAPY:

    I.   Passive Rewarming
          a) warm room
          b) blanket

    II.   Active Rewarming
          a) surface rewarming
             1. electric blankets
             2. warm baths
          b) "Core" rewarming
             1. peritoneal dialysis
             2. extracorporeal blood rewarming - hemodialysis

Controversy still exists about the various methods used in the treatment of hypothermia.

With mild degrees of hypothermia (> 95 degrees F) and in those where the hypothermia is solely a manifestation of an underlying systemic disorder, treatment involves passive rewarming and therapy of the primary disorder.

With more profound degrees of hypothermia, more intensive methods are needed. External surface rewarming is dangerous as it causes peripheral vasodilatation with rapid diversion of blood from critical visceral organs. The cold heart is unable to maintain an adequate cardiac output to meet the increased peripheral vascular space and metabolic requirements. Infarctions, especially of the heart, occur.

With the almost universal availability of warm water and the technical difficulties inherent in setting up core rewarming devices, warm baths, using water temperatures of 105-115 degrees F, have been recommended and successfully used. However, difficulties in literally handling a comatose patient in a bath while monitoring vital signs and cardiovascular status, as well as the adverse effects noted above, make this a dangerous procedure.

Far safer and effective are core rewarming methods. Restoration of normal core temperature by hemodialysis, using externally warmed blood, or by peritoneal dialysis, using externally warmed dialysate (to 98.6 degrees F) is beneficial and safe. Large volumes of fluid are frequently necessary, but corticosteroids, vasopressors, and prophylactic antibiotics are usually not helpful. Other modalities which may be useful include warmed low molecular weight dextran to block the sludging and hyperviscosity, and succinylcholine to control the shivering. Anti-arrhythymic agents (i.e. lidocaine) are needed to decrease myocardial irritability and diminish the risk of ventricular fibrillation during rewarming through the critical temperatures (70 - 75 degrees F). Routine diagnostic and supportive methods, i.e., endotracheal intubation, monitoring urine flow, blood gases and pH, electrolytes, and the various hematological parameters are necessary. Active rewarming should cease at a body temperature of 95 degrees F to prevent hyperthermic overshoot.

REFERENCES

1. Duquid, H. and Simpson, R.G.: Accidental Hypothermia, Lancet 2: 1213, 1961.

2. Lash, R.F., et al.: Accidental profound hypothermia and barbiturate intoxication: a report of rapid "core" rewarming by peritoneal dialysis. JAMA 201: 123, 1967.

3. David, D.M., et al.: Accidental hypothermia treated by extracorporeal blood warming. Lancet 1: 1036, 1967.

4. Tolman, K.G. and Cohen, A.: Accidental hypothermia. Can Med Assoc J 103: 1357, 1970.

5. Freinkel, N., et al.: The hypothermia of hypoglycemia. New Eng J Med: 287, 841, 1972.

6. Trevino, A., et al.: The characteristic electrocardiogram of accidental hypothermia. Arch Int Med 127: 470-472, 1971.

7. Collins, K.J., et al.: Accidental Hypothermia and Impaired Temperature Homeostasis in the elderly. British Medical Journal 1: (6057): 353-6, 1977.

8. A definition of irreversible coma. Report of the ad hoc committee of the Harvard Medical School to examine the definition of brain death. JAMA 205: 337-340, August 5, 1968.

C: NEAR-DROWNING
by Robert R. Kirby, M. D.

INTRODUCTION: Approximately 8000 people die from drowning each year in the United States. Thousands of others sustain episodes of near-drowning. Over half the victims are under 30 years of age and the highest incidence occurs in the 10 to 19 year age group. These figures indicate that a knowledge of the pathophysiologic aspects of drowning is of considerable importance to any physician who has occasion to treat victims of near-drowning in either a primary or consultative role.

Much useful knowledge has been derived from animal experimentation, autopsies, and clinical studies in the past decade. Prior to this period, information on drowning was based on animal data from the 1940's in which total immersion was employed. These studies indicated that death usually resulted from significant electrolyte abnormalities, fluid shifts, and ventricular fibrillation. However, they involved the aspiration of massive quantities of water, and thus their applicability to the majority of human cases of drowning and near-drowning in which lesser quantities are aspirated was suspect. More precise recent work has resolved many of the questions which were previously not answered.

PATHOPHYSIOLOGY: Approximately 10 to 12 percent of drowning victims do not aspirate water. This observation may in part be related to the occurrence of acute laryngospasm, or reflex breath holding and such "drowning" represents acute asphyxia only. If the victim is rescued before significant cerebral anoxia supervenes the prognosis for full recovery is excellent.

In 80 to 90 percent of cases water is aspirated, and asphyxia is complicated to varying degrees by direct pulmonary damage, fluid and electrolyte changes, and infection. If the individual survives the acute episode and has not sustained central nervous system dysfunction, the most important problem is that of pulmonary damage and respiratory insufficiency.

Here it becomes necessary to ascertain whether the episode occurred in fresh or salt water, because the pathophysiologic changes differ and the implications for therapy vary accordingly. In the case of salt water aspiration, the hypertonic fluid draws large quantities of additional fluid into the lungs from the circulating plasma. Significant pulmonary edema results, and hypoxemia is often profound owing to perfusion of fluid-filled alveoli (shunt). In some cases the fluid transfer from the circulation to the lungs is so great that hypovolemia and cardiovascular instability may occur.

With fresh water aspiration the hypotonic fluid passes rapidly into the circulation, and within two to three minutes little or no water can be removed from the lungs. Fresh water, however, destroys or inactivates pulmonary surfactant. Alveolar collapse may then occur, and subsequently pulmonary edema is seen as a result of direct damage to the alveolar-capillary membrane.

A summary of the changes occurring in fresh and salt water near-drowning is shown in Table 1.

TABLE 1	
NEAR-DROWNING	
FRESH WATER	SALT WATER
-hypoxemia -metabolic acidosis -minimal changes in electrolytes -initially increased blood volume -pulmonary edema (destruction of surfactant and damage to alveolar-capillary membrane)	-hypoxemia; right-to-left shunting -pulmonary edema-often massive -metabolic acidosis -minimal changes in serum electrolytes and hemoglobin -decreased blood volume

Data from clinical and laboratory studies suggest that death from drowning is associated with water aspiration of less than 22 ml/kg in 85 percent of cases. Experimentally, aspiration of 44 ml/kg of fresh water is required to produce ventricular fibrillation and significant electrolyte and blood compositional changes. Therefore, it appears that a maximum of 15 percent of victims of fresh water drowning may sustain ventricular fibrillation. In the majority of cases (85 percent) death results from hypoxemia and metabolic acidosis.

The serum electrolyte and hemoglobin values which have been recorded for patients who have near-drowned are shown in Table 2.

TABLE 2	
NEAR-DROWNING Electrolyte values (mEq/liter) and hemoglobin (grams/100 ml)	
SALT WATER	FRESH WATER
Na+ 152.3 ± 6.2	137.3 ± 3.7
Cl- 113.5 ± 7.1	87.2 ± 3.3
K+ 4.0 ± 0.5	4.0 ± 1.0
Hgb 13.5 ± 2.3	13.0 ± 0.9

These values again emphasize that in most cases changes are not great and are certainly not life-threatening. Therefore the administration of distilled water in salt water near-drowning and hypertonic saline in fresh water near-drowning is not indicated and is potentially more dangerous than the effects of the near-drowning episode itself insofar as electrolyte changes are concerned.

TREATMENT: Treatment of victims of near-drowning may be divided conveniently into first-aid, on-the-scene measures, and subsequent in-hospital therapy. Immediate resuscitation measures include clearing of the mouth and pharynx of any foreign matter including vomitus. In salt water near-drowning postural drainage may be of considerable benefit in ridding the lungs of excessive fluid and pulmonary edema. Postural drainage should not be employed in fresh water near-drowning since absorption of the water into the circulation occurs so rapidly. If the victim is apneic, mouth-to-mouth resuscitation should be administered together with closed chest cardiac massage if the circulatory status is in doubt. The administration of oxygen is advisable if it is available. One should resist the impulse to allow a victim of near-drowning who appears to be fully recovered at the scene to return home prior to observation in a hospital. The phenomenon of "secondary drowning" or post-immersion syndrome may occur up to 24 hours following successful resuscitation.

In the hospital, observation in an intensive care setting should be maintained for a minimum of 24 hours following the incident. Chest roentgenograms and serial arterial blood gas and pH measurements at known FIO_2's are mandatory. Hypoxemia ($PaO_2 < 60$ torr at $FIO_2 = 0.21$) should be treated by oxygen administration and PEEP or CPAP by mask or following tracheal intubation. In salt water near-drowning PEEP or CPAP alone in the spontaneously breathing patient is usually sufficient. In cases of fresh water near-drowning supplemental mechanical ventilatory support (IPPY or IMV) is often required owing to the destruction or inactivation of pulmonary surfactant.

Significant metabolic (non-respiratory) acidosis (B.E. > -5 mEq/l) should be treated by appropriate bicarbonate administration. There is no good evidence to suggest that either synthetic glucocorticoids or prophylactic antibiotics are of any value in near-drowning. However, if the patient has aspirated water which is known to be contaminated with coliform organisms, there may be some advantage to early treatment with broad-spectrum antibiotics pending culture confirmation.

The clinician must not lose sight of the fact that severe salt water near-drowning pulmonary edema may be associated with significant hypovolemia. In such instances mechanical ventilation and PEEP may exacerbate the condition. Careful cardiovascular monitoring, including insertion of a pulmonary artery catheter, is indicated. Such monitoring also allows direct calculation of the degree of venous admixture and intrapulmonic shunt.

Finally, post-immersion syndrome may occur after apparently successful resuscitation and recovery. It is usually seen within 14 hours of the near-drowning episode and is characterized by recurrence of respiratory distress, hypoxemia, pulmonary edema, pneumonitis, fever, and leukocytosis. The possibility of this syndrome occurring again emphasizes the necessity of close patient observation for at least 24 and preferably 48 hours.

REFERENCES

1. Swann, H.G., Brucer, M., Moore, C., et al.: Fresh water and sea water drowning: a study of the terminal cardiac and biochemical events. Tex Rep Biol Med 5:423, 1947.

2. Modell, J.H.: The pathophysiology of drowning and near-drowning. Springfield, Thomas, 1971.

3. Modell, J.H., Moya, F.: Effects of volume of aspirated fluid during chlorinated fresh water drowning. Anesthesiology 27: 662, 1966.

4. Modell, J.H., Moya, F., Newby, E.J., et al.: The effects of fluid volume in sea water drowning. Ann Intern Med 67:68, 1967.

5. Modell, J.H., Davis, J.: Electrolyte changes in human drowning victims. Anesthesiology 30:414, 1969.

6. Ruiz, B.C., Calderwood, H.W., Modell, J.H., et al.: Effects of ventilatory patterns on arterial oxygenation after near-drowning with fresh water. Anesth Analg 52:570, 1973.

7. Modell, J.H., Calderwood, H.W., Ruiz, B.C., et al.: Effects of ventilatory patterns on arterial oxygenation after near-drowning in sea water. Anesthesiology 40:376, 1974.

8. Hasan, S., Avery, W.F., Fabian, C., et al.: Near-drowning in humans: a report of 32 patients. Chest 59:191, 1971.

9. Clarke, E.B., Niggemann, E.H.: Near-drowning. Heart and lung 4:946, 1975.

10. Modell, J.H., Graves, S.A., Ketover, A.: Clinical Course of 91 Consecutive Near-Drowning Victims. Chest 70:231-238, 1976.